TRIBUTES TO IOWA TEACHERS

People nurture the soil to bring forth its greatest abundance as teachers and schools nurture students to bring forth their greatest potential.

Tree Planting Group,
by Grant Wood, 1937.

Tributes to

IOWA STATE UNIVERSITY PRESS *and the*

Iowa Teachers

Edited by William L. Sherman

IOWA STATE EDUCATION ASSOCIATION

WILLIAM L. SHERMAN, APR, is the Public Relations Specialist for the Iowa State Education Association.

FRONT COVER: *Arbor Day.* Grant Wood, 1932. Oil on masonite panel, 24" × 30". Commissioned by the Cedar Rapids Community School District as a memorial to Catherine Motejl and Rose L. Waterstradt, teachers at William McKinley Junior High School, where Grant Wood also taught. Reproduced by permission of the Cedar Rapids Community School District.

BACK COVER: *Young Corn.* Grant Wood, 1931. Oil on masonite panel, 24" × 29⅞". Commissioned by the Cedar Rapids Community School District as a memorial to Linnie Schloeman, a teacher at Woodrow Wilson Junior High School. Reproduced by permission of the Cedar Rapids Community School District.

FRONTISPIECE: *Tree Planting Group.* Grant Wood, 1937. Charcoal, pencil and chalk on paper, 24¾" × 28". Developed from a preparatory drawing for *Arbor Day.* Reproduced by permission of the Cedar Rapids Community School District.

QUOTE ON PAGE ii: John C. Fitzpatrick, Cedar Rapids Community School District.

Designed by Bob Campbell

BK
$15.00

♾ Printed on acid-free paper in the United States of America

First edition, 1996

Library of Congress Cataloging-in-Publication Data

Tributes to Iowa teachers / edited by William L. Sherman.—
 1st ed.
  p.   cm.
  Includes indexes.
  ISBN 0-8138-0908-8 (alk. paper)
   1. Teachers—Iowa—Biography. 2. Eulogies—Iowa. 3. Teacher—student relationships—Iowa. I. Sherman, William L., APR.
  LA2315.I8T75   1996
  371.1′0092′2—dc20
  [B]   96-34674

Last digit is the print number: 9 8 7 6 5 4 3 2

Contents

Preface

Many who read this book will recall the scene from *Mr. Holland's Opus* where he helps a young girl learn to play the clarinet. As the girl struggles, Mr. Holland asks: "What do you like best about yourself?" The girl says it is her red hair. Her father has told her it reminds him of the sunset, she explains. "Then play the sunset," Mr. Holland admonishes.

In this book of teacher tributes, Iowans and former Iowans of all ages with a wide range of ages, occupations, backgrounds, and experiences share how their teachers motivated them by encouraging them to "play the sunset." Reading these expressions of gratitude helps one better appreciate the influence our teachers have had on us and on our society at large. For example, a former Bedford student recounts how lessons learned in elementary school have influenced the teaching methods he uses at the Yale University Medical School.

It is important to note that most of these testimonials were solicited. We asked presidents of our local affiliates to suggest individuals ISEA could contact. ISEA also developed a contact list. Some contributors appeared on both lists. One writer, who learned about this project from a friend who had been asked to write a testimonial, requested and was granted the opportunity to write a testimonial.

ISEA decided to produce this book of tributes and a companion student video to help support and contribute to Iowa's sesquicentennial observance. In a proposal submitted to the Iowa Sesquicentennial Commission we suggested that "through these testimonials Iowans should have a greater understanding and appreciation of the role teachers and schooling played in the development of our state." The Commission agreed and endorsed the Teacher Testimonial project.

Arbor Day, the painting featured on the front cover, was produced by Grant Wood, Iowa's best-known artist and a former Cedar Rapids teacher and University of Iowa faculty member. Wood painted his famous Arbor Day scene for the Cedar Rapids Community School District as a tribute to two Cedar Rapids teachers concerned about environmental issues. They were Catherine Motejl and Rose Waterstradt. They both taught with Wood at William McKinley School. Wood took the *Arbor Day* painting with him and displayed it in an exhibit in Chicago, where it was sold. He agreed to paint another Arbor Day scene for the school district. *Tree Planting Group,* the refined charcoal and chalk study print displayed on the frontispiece, was as far as he got with the "second" Arbor Day scene.

Another Grant Wood painting, *Young Corn,* ap-

Catherine Motejl, Rose Waterstradt, and Grant Wood (*arrows, left to right*) at a McKinley School faculty breakfast in 1923. *Courtesy of Cedar Rapids Community School District Archives, William McKinley School.*

ix

pears on the back cover of the book. *Young Corn* was commissioned by the Cedar Rapids Community School District in 1931 when students at Woodrow Wilson School mounted an extensive penny campaign to help pay for a painting to memorialize teacher Linnie Schloeman, whom they felt embodied the ideal of rural Iowa as depicted in Wood's work. A rendering of *Young Corn* was used as the official Iowa Sesquicentennial commemorative stamp, which the U.S. Postal Service issued August 1, 1996, in Dubuque.

The other drawings used to illustrate this book (the first one is reproduced on the next page) were created by Iowa students for the annual "Design A Decal" competition sponsored by the ISEA and Art Educators of Iowa. This program was organized to give recognition to young artists and to support art education. Winning designs are printed in sheets of 48 by ISEA and are provided to teachers to use to provide positive feedback to students and parents. Somehow it seems appropriate to give students a chance to provide an expression of appreciation to Iowa teachers. Student artists and their teachers are identified in an index at the back of this book.

Originally, ISEA had planned a limited, self-publication of this collection. A reading of the first tributes to arrive at ISEA seemed to indicate that they might be of interest to a broader audience. The early manuscripts and publication ideas were shared with the representatives from Iowa State University Press. They also felt a broader audience would find this collection appealing. For this we are grateful. It will allow us to help more people better understand and appreciate contributions made by Iowa teachers.

As we near the end of Iowa's sesquicentennial observance and approach the beginning of a new century, it seems right to honor teachers with this publication and to see that it is shared as widely as possible. ISEA views this book as a tribute to all Iowa teachers, who have helped make our system of public education the best in the world.

William L. Sherman, APR
PUBLIC RELATIONS SPECIALIST
IOWA STATE EDUCATION ASSOCIATION

A Tribute to Teachers Everywhere

I had a hard time learning how to read, but my first-grade teacher, Estelle Shaver, was very much a genius. She was a stout woman, who favored navy-blue dresses. Sleeveless. She stood at the blackboard and wrote vigorously with large, loopy handwriting. Parts of her upper arms seemed almost alive. Auxillary arms. We gave them names.

It was a classroom like thousands of other classrooms. Lincoln and Washington looked down from high above the blackboard at us. On the bulletin board, there were cheerful displays of fall leaves and spatter-paintings.

Miss Shaver taught me to read by the simple expedience of asking me if I would be so good as to stay after school and read aloud as she corrected worksheets. She told me that I had such a lovely voice, and she loved to hear me read more than she had a chance to in the classroom.

She managed to save my life. I had a problem, and she managed to solve it with-

From a speech presented to the Minnesota Education Association in October 1995.

by Garrison Keillor

out ever making me think I was in trouble. I did her a great favor of entertaining her, and in this way I got educated. It was for Estelle Shaver that all the children of Lake Woebegon are above average.

There were many teachers. Helen Story and Lois Melby and Helen Fleishman, who made us memorize poems. There was Miss Moehlenbrock, who taught us, in the fourth grade, about Frankie and Johnny, who were lovers, and Lord how they could love. He was her man, but he was doing her wrong. We loved to say those lines in the fourth grade, but we hardly understood what "doing her wrong" meant.

He was her man, but he was doing her wrong. That's why she pulled that 44 out. ... It was exciting stuff. Sex and violence, and we loved to hear about it. It was Miss Moehlenbrock who taught us meter—and the poetry of Emily Dickinson—by showing us what I've never forgotten: that most of Emily's poems can be sung to the tune of "The Yellow Rose of Texas."

These people gave me my life. Since I left school, I have been pursuing the life of writing and books, and so it is my pleasure and my duty to stand up for public education when it comes under attack.

Iowa Teachers

I have been fortunate. Many teachers have influenced my life, both personally and professionally. As a student, I was positively impacted by many teachers from kindergarten through high school. It would be too hard to single out just one.

However, from a professional standpoint, several outstanding teachers have shaped me as a teacher, as a school administrator, and today as an education administrator in state government. This may be a different way of looking at teacher influence, but for me the personal impact of these individuals has been substantial indeed.

Most of us have mixed feelings about our first year of teaching. My first year was also the first year of an "open concept" elementary school, and about half of the staff were first- or second-year teachers. Those of us in the intermediate unit (grades four through six) were forever thankful for Vickie Bastron (later Vickie Richards). Physically diminutive, Vickie was our mentor, our cheerleader, and our drill sergeant. She was intense. Intense in the way she organized all aspects of complicated team-teaching environments. Intense in her dislike for winter playground supervision. But most of all, intense in her commitment to the learning needs of kids and setting expectations for "difficult" kids that no one but Vickie could have helped them to achieve.

It took several teachers to help me to understand that education is a truly developmental process. They showed me that teaching needs to flex to meet the needs of kids and not the other way around. Marie Scott was a special education teacher who could work with a child for a day or two and then describe with great clarity and simplicity how the physical, social, cognitive, and emotional development of that child had interacted to bring him to his present educational circumstance. Peg Shea understood early adolescent kids so well that she could always find ways to help them succeed. As a ninth grade English teacher, Linda Gardner knew that a highly structured environment was exactly what some kids needed—especially those that, just a few years later, would have been considered behaviorally disabled.

If you've never worked in a team-teaching situation, you can't imagine the professional learning and support that can take place when you share a group of students and their instruction program with one or more colleagues. You learn that another team member may have the "key" to a student that you just couldn't reach. If you team with really great teachers, then a little of that technique has a chance to rub off. You can get instant feedback and very meaningful support. It's the most professional experience possible. I was fortunate to work with Jean Blumgren (later Jean Ives) and Judy Jeffrey in a very positive team-teaching relationship.

It is difficult to maintain strong relationships with practicing teachers when you work in state government. But for several years I was able to work closely with the individual who was selected as Iowa Teacher of the Year and served as Ambassador for Education the following year. Pam Johnson, a former sixth grade teacher who is now director of educational television for Iowa Public Television, was the first Ambassador and helped to get the program organized. She is still teaching when she presents to legislative committees and others about the Iowa Communications Network. Nancy Mounts has transferred her commitment to her classes of family living students to a regional commitment, helping students succeed through Tech Prep and School-to-Work. If there is a way to get support for a program that kids need, Nancy will find it. Pam, Nancy, and other great teachers in the Ambassador program have helped to keep me involved with teaching through their own teaching experiences and through all they learned traveling and meeting with teachers across the state.

There is much risk in only listing a few of the teachers who have been a great and positive personal influence for me. There are certainly many more. I will continue to be influenced by these professionals and other great educators who are the heart of Iowa's educational system.

Ted Stilwill
DIRECTOR, IOWA DEPARTMENT OF EDUCATION

THINK BACK to when you were in school.

Maybe it was that first grade teacher who made you feel excited about coming to school. Maybe it was a third grade teacher who helped you conquer cursive writing. Or maybe it was the junior high teacher who gave you an "A" on that special speech, even though your voice was changing. Perhaps it was that high school teacher who helped you decide on a career or a college.

Everyone can think of at least one special teacher who made school important: A person who gave you that little extra push and that little extra confidence. Someone who cared about you and made a difference in your life.

2

3

4

TRIBUTES TO IOWA TEACHERS

5

6

7

Bob Gress

ADAIR–CASEY JUNIOR–SENIOR HIGH SCHOOL

It was not the scheduled lesson plan, but the eighth-grade girls' request was an earnest one.

The class was physical education, and the instructor was Bob Gress, who was also a science and driver's education teacher and girls' basketball and track coach. Those girls who were eighth graders in the late 1960s were begging him to break tradition and teach females the mysterious concepts of football.

Probably, Gress was unable to mask his amusement.

Anyway, he scrapped his prepared lesson plans, and we played football. That particular day, Gress taught us about first downs and punts and quarterback sneaks. But through the rest of my junior high and high school years at Adair-Casey Community Schools, Gress taught my classmates and me a great deal more.

Somehow, through the emotional challenges of both dealing with teenagers and coaching sports, Gress continually maintained a calm, patient demeanor. When students disobeyed instructions, he taught that discussion was a more effective remedy than shouted reprimands. When the score was tied with 10 seconds left on the clock, he taught that clear, methodical planning was a more effective tactic than panic.

If a request was reasonable, Gress considered it. If an argument was valid, he acknowledged it. If a rule was rational, he respected it—but if it called for an exception, he allowed it.

Take, for example, the case of the freshman girl who was never an outstanding runner, but who worked hard right along side the rest of the track team. All spring she stumbled through courses of wooden hurdles, suffering banged-up ankles and cinder-scraped knees, but sometimes earning a third- or fourth-place ribbon in a race. Still, she finished the season shy of the number of points required to earn a school letter.

Then, on the day the awards were given, Coach Gress announced a new clause in his rules allowing a runner who had placed in a conference meet (or something of that nature) to be awarded a letter. Suddenly, the less-than-glorious runner had qualified.

Through his integrity, fairness, patience, and caring in dealing with young people, Bob Gress represented standards that today I, as a parent, strive to model.

I wonder if he ever realized how much that track letter meant to me.

Jane Schorer Meisner

FREE-LANCE WRITER AND FORMER PULITZER PRIZE–WINNING WRITER
FOR *THE DES MOINES REGISTER*
URBANDALE, IOWA

Rosemary Weld

BALLARD COMMUNITY HIGH SCHOOL

I'll never forget the day Miss Rosemary Weld's car showed up in the driveway of our Story County farm. My emotions were a mix of terror and dread.

Miss Weld was my tenth grade Spanish teacher. I'd been out of school for a couple of weeks because of a serious health problem, and she was at the house to provide me with some one-on-one tutoring so I could catch up while I was on the mend.

I was tired and apprehensive. I still have trouble trilling my Rs and, for other reasons, wasn't the best of Spanish students. At the time, all I could think was that Miss Weld was showing up at the door to add to my misery.

Was I ever wrong. She showed up—I'm sure on her own time and initiative—not because she wanted to torment me in any way, but because she had faith in me, because she wanted me to learn, and because she wanted me to return to class in shape so I wouldn't be too far behind my peers.

I've never forgotten that special lesson from a special teacher.

As an editor, part of my job is to raise expectations—expectations my colleagues have for our newspaper, and expectations Iowans have of themselves. As a teacher, Rosemary Weld's job was to raise my own expectations of myself—as a student and a citizen.

I was fortunate to have had a long list of teachers who were so very wise, who took such great care in their work, and who put in so much extra effort in behalf of their students. They were the kind of teachers who would call me in to ask if anything was upsetting me after I did more poorly than they thought I should have done on a test. They were the kind of teachers who challenged conventional wisdom. They were the kind of teachers who were role models in terms of how they respected others.

They were the kind of teachers who, like Miss Weld, were demanding and hardworking yet full of love and respect for their students and for their profession.

I think now about the successes I've had and the wonderful things others in my class have done with their lives. It's a credit to our families, of course. But it's also a credit to those teachers who gave us so very, very much.

Dennis R. Ryerson

EDITOR, *THE DES MOINES REGISTER*
DES MOINES, IOWA

7

10

Ron Hackbarth

BAXTER COMMUNITY SCHOOL

I am writing this testimonial about a person who was a very big influence in my life. His name is Ron Hackbarth. Ron grew up in Dows, Iowa. He attended William Penn College, later transferring to Iowa Wesleyan, where he graduated. He then became a teacher and coach at Baxter Community School during my junior high and high school career.

He was very well liked and respected by his students. He instilled a very strong work ethic in his students and gave them a special sense of pride in what they did. He became somewhat of a hero to the students when his reserve unit was called to active duty during the Cuban Missile Crisis. I also remember being in his biology class when the superintendent brought the sad news of President Kennedy's assassination. As tragic as the news seemed to us, Coach reassured us that everything would be okay.

He was very instrumental in my decision to become a teacher and coach. He helped me make my decision on what college to attend. He remained supportive during my college career and was the person who was most responsible for my first teaching and coaching position at Davis County Schools in Bloomfield, Iowa. During that first year of teaching, I spent many evenings at the Hackbarths' discussing the happenings of the day and getting as much advice as I could on solving problems that had arisen.

After one year of working in the same district with him, he left the coaching profession and became a successful school administrator in Washington, Iowa. Because of health reasons, he was forced into an early retirement. He now resides in Texas. He and his wife still correspond with many people in our community and almost always stop by when they visit Iowa.

Stanley J. Allspach
JSA INSURANCE SERVICES
BAXTER, IOWA

12

13

Irene Fosness

CONRAD CONSOLIDATED HIGH SCHOOL

Irene Fosness was the most influential teacher in my high school life–hands down! She taught English, drama, and speech. She and her husband, Paul, had no children. I think we high schoolers were her children.

I have never encountered a person so ambitious for the success of students.

We drove her little Studebaker car through ice and snow and fog to high school speech contests. We usually won. She entered me in a Methodist Church speech contest. She coached me through the state finals to finally place third in a multi-state contest.

She staged a serious high school class play, *Smilin' Through*. It wasn't the normal comedy fluff. It was the first and last time I pulled the trigger on a hand revolver, loaded with blanks. That was probably the most effective part of the play, but she chose productions to make high school students stretch.

She read "Mary White" in that English classroom, in the southeast corner on the top floor of the high school. It's the story an Emporia, Kansas, newspaper man wrote about the death of his daughter who hit her head on a tree branch while horseback riding.

10

Irene's voice broke and tears ran down her cheeks as she finished the story. I had never seen a grown person cry in public. It made an impression. The image is still there, vivid after 50 years.

I suppose there were times when we felt Irene was too controlling. She did her job with such intensity, like Bobby Knight and basketball. But she achieved results.

She wanted me to go to Northwestern in Chicago and major in journalism. My dad said we could afford Iowa State. I majored in agricultural journalism and continued to get involved in state productions and anything related to English, drama, and speech.

There's no question in my mind that she was the prime motivator that allowed me to work a lifetime in radio. In broadcasting, you write, you speak, and you put in a little drama. All these things we learned with Irene Fosness at Conrad Consolidated High School.

Lee Kline

FARM BROADCASTER (RETIRED), WHO RADIO
DES MOINES, IOWA

14

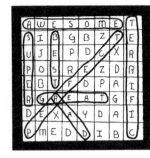

Mary Helen Wainwright

BANNER SCHOOL, ROSS TOWNSHIP

The elementary educational experience of most of my present peers consisted of either a private school or selected public school where they were surrounded by many other children their own age and such a number and array of teachers that my colleagues cannot recall individual teachers with ease. They primarily remember the building, some of their friends, and the relationship of the school to home and parents, which were more consistent elements of their lives.

That was not my experience. I was a member of the last eighth-grade class to graduate from the Iowa rural country school system, the year before reorganization and bussing country kids to local towns. In fact, I have a rather sharp image of my little white one-room schoolhouse with the pony barn behind, where I installed my horse during the warm spring and fall breezes–when the best time of the day was heading home on the dead run, mud flying and saddle bags flapping. I can picture that schoolhouse inside and out. I can remember the texture of the various desks, and how I graduated to the elite left front corner of the seating arrangement. However, what I remember in sharpest relief against the old blackboards was the young country schoolteacher with whom I spent the majority of my daylight hours between fall and spring, from fourth to eighth grade, from 1954 to 1959.

My tribute is to that teacher, Mary Helen Wainwright, and also to the institution of Iowa's one-room country schoolhouses and the generic country schoolteacher who represented all of the educational resources for rural children from kindergarten through eighth grade. She was to their education what the country doctor was to medicine. She was the science, math, and social studies teacher; the nurse and substitute mother when flesh and egos were bruised on the playground. She was the disciplinarian, and a particularly effective one. She was the psychologist and counselor for the little ones who were beginning to learn in the sandbox what socialization was all about, and for the eighth graders who looked upon adolescence and the inevitable move to Bedford High School with an apprehension that was communicated primarily by behavior.

I continue frequent visits to my home in Bedford and have watched Mary Helen age, but more slowly than the rest of us. She has, in fact, to this day, continued to teach in the Bedford public school system. When I think of her, however, it is that young woman sitting at the front table of the school calling the nine classes, usually only with one or two students in each grade, to recite before her, and those flashing dark brown eyes spoke their message clearly. She expected only the very best from you. She was the personification of continuous challenge.

She pulled her own son of my age from the local town school because she felt that she could provide a better education for him and, simultaneously, competition for me, who apparently was turning into a bored bully. And compete we did. With those penetrating eyes, a quick smile, or a well-timed frown, she pitted us against ourselves and each other and did so without favoritism.

If I wanted to put a cat's brain in formaldehyde or bring a microscope to school because I discovered the wonders of hatching shrimp and new-formed crystals, she encouraged me. Should we build a huge Grecian temple out of Ivory soap? Of course! Could we possibly construct a detailed replica of the Golden Gate Bridge from Styrofoam and toothpicks? Why not? Could we read more books than had ever been consumed in a country school? Of course! When the books ran out, there were more to come.

I am sure there were moments when I must have questioned the sensibility of my growing need to absorb and achieve and her encouragement of that, but I do not remember them. I am sure I was sometimes bewildered by her intolerance of behavior I thought was the natural product of a 10-year-old boy's mission—to torture younger children—but I do not remember those times, either.

I remind my own students and neurosurgical residents that their educational experience is one punctuated by steep inclines of frenzied learning and plateaus of consolidation. The "Wainwright" years were the first and, perhaps, most important of these learning curves for me. I also reflect that the country school system not only challenged me but challenged teachers like Mary Helen Wainwright to be the very best they could be. Perhaps without knowing what was meant by the Eastern academic institutions' new drive to provide a "liberal education," she, in fact, was providing that through common sense.

As I watch my own children, who can write better than I could in college, speak foreign tongues, and visualize mathematics as a comfortable language, I sense that they are learning more at a younger age than I did. I only hope, however, that they will be able to reflect upon an individual or two, like Mary Helen, who made a difference not so much in what they learned, but who instilled within them, as she did within me, the love to learn.

Dennis D. Spencer, MD

HARVEY AND KATE CUSHING PROFESSOR AND CHIEF OF NEUROSURGERY,
YALE UNIVERSITY SCHOOL OF MEDICINE
WOODBRIDGE, CONNECTICUT

16

Esther Palmer

IOWA #8 COUNTRY SCHOOL, NEAR BELLE PLAINE

I was extremely fortunate in having Esther Palmer as my very first teacher. She taught in a one-room, one-teacher country school known as Iowa #8, which was located near Belle Plaine in Benton County in the late 1920s and early 1930s. I had her as a teacher for grades one, two, and three, which was for the years ending May 1933, 1934, and 1935, and at the conclusion of which she ended her teaching at the Iowa #8 school.

She had a great interest in each student. I always felt that all of the students enjoyed going to school with Mrs. Palmer as their teacher. She was even involved during our recess periods, making sure that there was always fair play between all the children, irrespective of their grade level in the school, which ranged from grades one through eight.

Many of her students became achievers later in life. Her style of teaching had a lot of one-on-one as well as a personal interest in each individual student.

I have always felt that an individual's initial school experience has a lot to do with what happens in their future school interests as well as their achievements. We would all be better off if there were more Mrs. Palmers, not only in the teaching profession but, also, in this world. As a matter of interest, Mrs. Palmer, who is now in her 90s, still enjoys good health and lives in Belle Plaine, Iowa. (Note: I was very sorry to see the demise of country schools. I happen to feel that something was lost when they were ended.)

Henry B. Tippie

CORPORATE EXECUTIVE AND RANCHER
AUSTIN, TEXAS

18

Viva Parker

BELMOND ELEMENTARY SCHOOL

Forty years ago, I couldn't wait to get to school each morning, mainly because of a fun and creative fourth grade teacher by the name of Viva Parker.

Mrs. Parker was small in stature, very strict, and very demanding, yet she was a grandmotherly figure, full of love and concern for all of her students. She demanded respect from each of us. Respect for our peers, respect for private and school property, and respect for her and our elders. She reminded us over and over again, "Remember the 'Golden Rule'—do unto others as you would have them do unto you."

Personal hygiene was important to her. Daily we had clean fingernail checks, clean handkerchief checks, and teeth checks. Remember the yearly dental cards that would line our classroom?

Good penmanship was a must in her room. She refused papers that were sloppy and difficult to read and papers that had been ripped or heavily erased. She taught us the Palmer Penmanship Method and expected us to do our best.

Every Friday we looked forward to spell downs. Occasionally we competed against the other fourth grade section. We always learned so much more than just spelling words. One day in particular, we were spelling so well and she was having trouble retiring us—she walked over to a large map, pointed to Mexico, and our next two words that sat down several of us were Ixtacihuatl and Popocatepetl. Believe it or not, I had a boy in my section correctly spell Popocatepetl and my section won bragging rites for the day. I have always remembered they were volcanoes in Mexico, but I do have to confess to checking the spelling before writing this paper today.

I have so many wonderful memories of my fourth grade year and it has been fun writing this testimonial. Mrs. Parker touched the lives of hundreds of impressionable 10-year-olds as she taught for 40 years. How fortunate I feel to have had this delightful woman as a teacher and role model. I think of her often with much admiration. I hope everyone has experienced a "Mrs. Parker" at some time in their life.

Vicki Quigly

GROCER AND HOMEMAKER

BELMOND, IOWA

20

Tambi Heiter

BONDURANT–FARRAR HIGH SCHOOL

I took three years of Spanish with Mrs. Tambi Heiter, who, in addition to using conventional Spanish instruction, is a great believer in games and other challenging applications in which to enhance students' knowledge. We would frequently play Trivial Pursuit—in Spanish. She and I developed a "Spanish Jeopardy!" tournament, complete with a broad base of categories including Mexican history and verb usage. She commissioned students to make cartoon flash cards to help beginning-level classes with vocabulary.

Perhaps the most creative and ambitious project with which she challenged us was to write and produce a short video production. We wrote "San Antonio," a Spanish-language parody of nighttime soaps that explored the brutally competitive lives of rival picante sauce manufacturers, with scenes of betrayal and greed, and an assassination plot involving a trio of Mexican Ninjas. Mrs. Heiter supervised the script, helping us with complex verb tenses and conversational Spanish dialogue, and oversaw our production.

Mrs. Heiter has been instrumental in promoting an atmosphere of creativity at

Bondurant-Farrar and in encouraging the school to invest in students' creative endeavors. My junior year she volunteered to direct the spring play but was unable to find a light comedy with a substantially large cast (she wanted to involve as many students as possible). I told her I had an idea for a one-act murder mystery comedy and would appreciate the opportunity to have it produced. She recommended to the administration that I write the play that year. When the production received the go-ahead, Mrs. Heiter worked in the capacity of producer, acquiring all the necessary elements, as well as skillfully directing the production.

Mrs. Heiter has always put students first. She masterfully walks the line of being both a teacher and a friend—encouraging, challenging, supporting. She has made education her priority and has regularly found effective, original methods to accomplish this goal.

When a student looks forward to class and enjoys the process of learning, education works best. This has always been true with Mrs. Heiter.

Sean Gannon

WRITER AND VIDEO EDITOR
BONDURANT, IOWA

Dennis & Pat Wright

BOYDEN–HULL HIGH SCHOOL

Two of the many fine teachers that have had a positive influence on our lives are known simply as "The Wrights." Dennis and Pat Wright began teaching at Boyden-Hull Community School in 1968 when we were in junior high. They were fresh out of college, newly married, and ready to conquer the world. They both displayed a refreshing enthusiasm that was welcomed by their students.

Dennis taught in the junior high and Pat was at the high school. Everyone they came in contact with enjoyed their efforts and caring attitude toward kids. They made their classes interesting, fun, and educational, and they were both involved in extra-curricular activities.

An example of their caring attitude was demonstrated a couple of years later. Dennis had been drafted into the service during our freshman year. He was home on leave and attended a freshman basketball game one evening. After the game, several of us decided to go to the Wrights' house to welcome him home. Even though it was probably the last thing they wanted, Dennis and Pat invited us in, served pop and snacks, and visited for a couple of hours. We, the students, thought we were doing them a great service by giving of our free time. However, as we grew older, we all came to realize that, once again, the Wrights were on the giving end.

Dennis and Pat have continued to teach in our district. Two of our three children have had the pleasure of having them for teachers. They continue to give of themselves and their time. In addition to teaching, Dennis is the athletic director and coaches and sponsors the Quiz Bowl team. Pat sponsors the annual school yearbook in addition to directing the libraries in both of our buildings. She also has videotaped hundreds of athletic contests as an aid to our coaches. Even though their two sons are now in college, they continue to support all school activities.

We are very fortunate to again live in the same school district we both graduated from. It definitely was one of the drawing cards to get us to relocate here. The Wrights have had a very positive influence on us as well as many students that followed after us. We are sure that they both had an influence on our daughter, as she is now in college studying to be a teacher.

The Wrights don't know what it is to sit back and take it easy. They continue to be involved in our district at several levels, and they continue to influence students. They have helped develop many students who are leaders in our society today. The Wrights rank at the top of numerous past students' lists of favorite teachers.

Doug and Janelle Beukelman

DEMCO MANUFACTURING
BOYDEN, IOWA

James Arneson

CEDAR FALLS HIGH SCHOOL

23

As a junior in high school, I took my first course in psychology. The class was Intro to Psychology and the instructor was James Arneson. I remember Mr. Arneson as a caring, effective, and good-natured teacher.

I became fascinated learning about human behavior and would later take more classes and do reading on my own to understand what drives us all to be who and what we are. Because of Mr. Arneson's introduction of this topic in my life and his enthusiasm for his subject, I am still driven to understand myself and those around me better.

My career combines a financial background with the human resource area, so I am able to apply some of my educational background in my dealings with a diverse group of employees on a daily basis.

On a personal and social level, I seem to have become known as a good listener and someone to talk over problems and concerns with, which I get great fulfillment from. I believe my contentment and enjoyment of life have to do, in part, with my

24

positive experience in Mr. Arneson's class. I lost track of him after high school, but I wish him well and thank him for influencing my life.

Karen S. Page

TREASURER, PORTER'S CAMERA STORE
CEDAR FALLS, IOWA

24

Walter Gohman

MALCOLM PRICE LABORATORY SCHOOL

Walter Gohman, a teacher of chemistry and general science at the Malcolm Price Laboratory School in Cedar Falls, taught me both science and self-confidence. For a young girl in the 1950s, a woman scientist meant Madame Curie—but who could imagine her as an eighth grader? Science was something for very bright boys who knew exactly what they were doing. But in *our* science class, Mr. Gohman expected as much of the girls as the boys.

At the beginning of the year, I was more interested in the school chorus than in science. But Mr. Gohman sensed a dawning curiosity and steered me toward the part of science that is experimental. He suggested that I do a project for a science fair. The investigation was pretty simple—having to do with the effect of mouthwashes on bacteria—but he let me know that he considered it important. He set up space in a back room where I could store equipment, grow bacteria, and conduct my experiment. I remember becoming so absorbed that at the end of the day he would rattle his key in the door and say, "I'm locking up—which side do you want to be on?" He was interested in everything I did and he helped me every single day. With such positive encouragement I gained confidence right away. From that first project grew many more, of increasing sophistication, leading to trips to national science fairs and, ultimately, to my becoming a finalist in the Westinghouse Science Talent Search.

As much as Mr. Gohman encouraged us as scientists, though, he also understood that we were teenagers. Once I traveled with him, another student, and another teacher to a national science fair in Indianapolis. When we stopped to eat dinner, I left my retainer on the table in a napkin and didn't remember it until we were back on the road. I panicked because I knew how much that retainer had cost my parents! Mr. Gohman calmly turned the car around, drove back to the restaurant, and found the precious retainer in a trash bin. I was so embarrassed at my absentmindedness that I couldn't believe anyone could still have faith in my intellectual potential. But Walt Gohman looked beyond my imperfections and immaturity, and made me feel important and valued as a scientist. Throughout my years at Price Lab School, he and my other teachers made it seem completely natural that a young girl should be interested in science and able to compete successfully with other young scientists.

The self-confidence that Walter Gohman taught me in that eighth-grade class has never deserted me. I will always be grateful to him for challenging me, encouraging me, and—most of all—believing in me.

Mary Sue Coleman

PRESIDENT, UNIVERSITY OF IOWA
IOWA CITY, IOWA

E.W. Fannon
Bill Jerome

CENTERVILLE HIGH SCHOOL

When I was a student at Centerville High School many years ago, there were two individuals who were very meaningful in my educational career. E.W. Fannon was the superintendent of schools. He told me "Simon, you have the ability to achieve anything you want to achieve in life. You simply need to work hard. Education is something no one can take from you." And he was a man of discipline, a man of vision, a man of encouragement, and in spite of my skin color he said, "You can achieve. You will have obstacles always in life, but you can overcome those."

Another individual who helped me a great deal was my high school coach, Bill Jerome. He is a dear friend of mine who lives, I think, in the Fort Madison area. Bill Jerome taught me a lot about anticipation in life. That came from basketball practice. He would tell us to try and anticipate another person's moves, so we could intercept the ball.

I have also used that in my personal life—to be prepared and to anticipate all sorts of obstacles that might be out there in the world today. Bill Jerome said, "Simon, always have courage. Keep your head high when you walk." My mother also told me that.

So, the two individuals who influenced me very much in my education were E.W. Fannon and Bill Jerome. They taught me to be prepared and keep your guard up at all times. They said, "Work hard and you will succeed." I thank them for the lessons they taught.

Simon Estes

RECIPIENT OF IOWA AWARD, 1996
INTERNATIONAL BARITONE OPERA SINGER
ZURICH, SWITZERLAND

27

Carolyn Eggleston

CENTRAL HIGH SCHOOL

Carolyn Eggleston, our high school music teacher, allowed anyone who participated in choir the opportunity to cultivate a skill that could be used for the rest of their life. She always demanded 100 percent effort from her students, and yet she created a fun atmosphere to sing in.

When competing in solo or choral contests, her attention to detail and striving towards perfection always left you with a feeling of pride for the school you represented. Those qualities can be carried through to the work we perform today. She always expected your best effort and you could feel accomplishment when you were finished.

I have a great respect for all teachers who taught me in school and also those who are now teaching our children.

The skills Carolyn Eggleston imprinted into her students–to give an honest effort, expect success, strive for perfection, and make it enjoyable work—are with me today. These are qualities I hope can be passed on to our children.

Murl McCulloch

FARMER
CAMANCHE, IOWA

29

Phyllis Anderson

VAN ALLEN ELEMENTARY SCHOOL

Miss Anderson, my first grade teacher, opened the world of reading and science to generations of Iowa students by using innovation and creativity.

As we progressed toward literacy, she provided patient guidance and gentle correction. She also gave us an inviting, seemingly endless, library—which she tailored, both literally and figuratively. She literally sewed colorful books for us to carry everywhere. Using wallpaper samples, she bound chapters of old readers into indestructible, appealing books we could call our own. She was our Gutenberg.

Figuratively, she guided us to the works that best stimulated our appetites. One day, she even handed me a scientific research manuscript by the man for whom our school was named—James Van Allen—which sent me looking into the heavens for years.

Before we were introduced to any formalized science curriculum, Miss Anderson also exposed us to the beauty and wonder of biology. A farmer as well as a teacher, she annually brought into her classroom chicken, duck, and goose eggs. Our desks encircled a huge transparent incubator containing warmers and a sitting, clucking hen. We, in turn, were surrounded by Miss Anderson's large hand-drawn illustrations of daily stages of embryonic development, which hung laminated around our room.

We watched life grow and then peck its way out of eggs and into our hands. These lessons in embryology were almost at a level I only re-encountered in medical school, and they may very well have subconsciously guided me there.

Jeff McKinney, MD

RESIDENT PHYSICIAN,
YALE–NEW HAVEN CHILDREN'S HOSPITAL
HAMDEN, CONNECTICUT

31

Richard Simpson

CLARION HIGH SCHOOL

Many teachers have had a significant impact on my life, but one comes first and quickly to mind. Richard Simpson, a teacher of business courses and journalism at Clarion High School, was certainly among the few most influential educators of my elementary and secondary school years.

Now some will express surprise that a president of a liberal arts college would point to a teacher in vocational courses as among the most influential. However, Richard Simpson's teaching demanded that we use the skills and reasoning developed in other college preparatory courses. His teaching supported the work of those who taught English, for example, and his encouragement extended well beyond his own classroom.

Simpson was one of those teachers totally committed to the educational program of the school and the work of its students. He was for many years the adviser to the weekly school newspaper, the yearbook, and the Future Business Leaders of America chapter. He was always the adviser to the junior class, which meant he was adviser for the prom every year and responsible for the concession stand at all athletic events. In all these endeavors he sought excellence from his students, inspired creativity and leadership and responsibility. He encouraged and cajoled, befriended, and modeled with tireless efforts. He knew virtually every student, took an interest in each student's endeavors (whether or not he had them in class), and attended school events with a loyalty surpassed by none other.

Underlying Richard Simpson's educational endeavors was a genuine affection for students. His disappointment in our failings was short-lived, but his enthusiasm for our achievements never waned. He always had a warm welcome, a broad smile and a hearty laugh to share, and his classroom was a gathering place for students during lunch period and after school. Students participated in his programs because of appreciation for him and because whatever he touched was well done. We were drawn to excellence. He helped build a firm foundation for effective citizenship and future learning.

As Iowa celebrates its sesquicentennial, it is appropriate to honor those who have always been among our communities' most important citizens—our teachers. To achieve excellence in education we need great teachers, and attracting persons to the teaching profession who have the potential for greatness depends partially on the honor those who choose this noble profession are afforded by their fellow citizens. Thus, in writing this, I salute not only Richard Simpson but numerous others of his colleagues who contribute so much to the education and lives of young people growing up in Clarion. When we "cut the cake" during this sesquicentennial year, our teachers should get the first slice!

William E. Hamm

PRESIDENT, WALDORF COLLEGE
FOREST CITY, IOWA

35

Ralph Currie

CORNING HIGH SCHOOL

33

First to set the stage: as a young teenager, I had a lot of self-confidence as a gifted athlete, a good rapport with my peers, and a determination not to be included as a "pond" of the establishment.

Mr. Currie played several roles that influenced my life—first, as a teacher who taught science, chemistry, physics, and a World War II course called "Preflight." Through his excitement about the forces at hand that created flight for man and how through "dead reckoning" (flight navigation) man could arrive at his planned destination, he opened up a whole new horizon for me. I became a private pilot as soon as finances permitted. Today, each flight is truly made enjoyable by the basic aeronautical understanding of the forces at work.

Mr. Currie also was the principal of Corning High School. One of his responsibilities was being the disciplinarian. Since I had the opportunity to appear before him many times, I always felt his punishment quite severe to the act committed. However, he always made sure that you understood the reasons for their selection.

In raising my own children, I have often reflected on how Mr. Currie would ap-

36

ply the punishment for the infraction committed. It was important to me for our children to understand the rules with which to live by and the consequences suffered if violated.

Mr. Currie was also my counselor. He always said that nothing was easy but if you strive to accomplish a goal and discipline yourself to attain it, success would be forthcoming. From this, I believe nothing is impossible if you have the will and determination to stay the course.

Ralph Currie believed in people and he even believed in me. I am eternally grateful.

Austin B. Turner

PILOT AND PAST OWNER OF A.B. TURNER AND SONS DEPARTMENT STORE
CORNING, IOWA

34

Dick Stahl

CENTRAL HIGH SCHOOL

Dick Stahl was never really my teacher, but I remember him as one of the best that I had. Growing up in Iowa, I had many good teachers, and it's hard to narrow the list. But Dick Stahl stands out in my mind for two reasons. One: he gave me a break, and two: many years later, I became his teacher.

1967, sophomore year at Central High School in Davenport, Iowa. I had gone to Catholic schools for my grade school and junior high education, then found myself in the public system, in a very large school with many different activities and social groups. I liked the variety offered at Central, but having always been a shy person, there were days when I literally found myself "going up the down staircase."

Then I saw a notice go up for tryouts for a play, a melodrama, to be performed in the spring of the year. As a kind of therapy to overcome my shyness, I had been in theater all my life and often had been cast in the sweet little princess roles. I hated those parts. What I always wanted to be was the mean old witch.

"Ha, ha, Hansel, you're just about plump enough to make a tasty dinner. Gretel, hurry with those sticks. We'll make a nice, big fire."

Those were the lines I wanted but never got.

The melodrama had two female roles, one for a sweet young thing, and another for a middle-aged, eccentric woman who dropped dead in the final moments of the play. I walked into the theater room and there was a young teacher, one who was also new to the school. Dick Stahl's eyes met mine and I thought, that's it, he's pegged me for the ingenue. I wanted to throw up.

He asked me to read for the part, and I did. Then he had various boys read the male parts. After that, he scanned the room and I sensed a certain nervousness. He thought he didn't have anyone to read for the older woman's part.

"I want to try that," I said.

"You?" he asked, hearing my soft voice, glancing at my blond hair, my thin frame.

"Yes," I said. I took the stage, book in my hands, knees shaking. I opened my mouth and out came a loud, commanding voice, one that rose from somewhere deep inside myself that I had been trying to tap for years, one that needed to be let out, to allow myself to grow in my own self-determined direction.

Dick Stahl gave me the part. Now, years later, when I have become a middle-aged, eccentric woman, I no longer remember the name of that character, or even the name of the play, but I do remember the thrill of blasting out my lines throughout the CHS auditorium and the fun I had dropping dead at the curtain. I carried the self-confidence that role gave me throughout the rest of my career.

Fifteen years after that production, I almost dropped dead again one morning when I was conducting a weekend poetry-writing workshop for the University of Iowa. There, seated at the seminar table, was Dick Stahl. After all those years, though in a different guise, he was the same person. Focused, intelligent, knowledgeable, able to take risks and work with surprises. The poetry that he wrote and has now published reflected these same qualities.

In that workshop, our lives came full circle. As a teacher, I was able to give back something of what a fine teacher had given to me. And isn't that what education is all about?

Mary Swander

RECIPIENT OF THE 1996 RUTH SUCKOW AWARD
AUTHOR AND PROFESSOR OF ENGLISH, IOWA STATE UNIVERSITY
AMES, IOWA

36

40

C.W. Hach

DAVENPORT HIGH SCHOOL

37

How will I ever forget the first day I entered the journalism classroom of C.W. Hach in the old sandstone building, Davenport High School? He was so incongruously young (a mere 22) in a building that will be a century old in a few years. Certainly, Mr. Hach was no Mr. Chips. In fact, it was his choice that his students (migosh, what a switch in academia) call him C.W.

"Learn to love words, to cherish them, to wallow them around in your mouth like a piece of hard candy" were his first words to the class. He then said to take a few sheets of paper and write about a recent experience "just so I could see what you have going as a writer." I recall the piece I did, with a lead:

"She looked up at me with big brown eyes, and I knew she was mine. I wrapped my arms around her. It was instant love."

Well, I was not writing about a Lana Turner or other heartbeats of the time, but was describing how I had just picked out a cocker spaniel puppy from a litter of six.

C.W. said to me the next day: "That was a grabber. You can write. I'm going to put this piece in the *Black Hawk,* the school newspaper."

41

This was my introduction to a land of wonder—my land of words. Lo, in a young lifetime of schooling, C.W. Hach was the first to firmly encourage me. "You've got the stuff," he repeatedly said. "You have a way of writing the way people talk."

I was hired after high school graduation by a Davenport newspaper, and spent stints with the United Press and International News Service (even as a publicist with Ringling Bros. and Barnum and Bailey Circus) but am "here to stay" at the *Quad City Times.* Whatever I have accomplished, I owe to the encouragement of C.W. Hach. In my most recent book, I signed it: "C.W.—My thanks for opening the door for me to the wonderful world of words." In a current issue of *Reader's Digest,* I have a piece and scribbled on the margin: "Thanks again, C.W."

I often find myself quoting C.W. Hach:

"Words: They sing. They hurt. They sanctify. They were our first immeasurable feat of magic. They liberated us from ignorance and our barbarous past. For without those marvelous scribbles which build letters into words, words into sentences, into systems and sciences and creeds, man would be forever confined to the self-isolated prison of the cuttlefish or the chimpanzee."

Bill Wundram

COLUMNIST, *DAVENPORT–QUAD CITY TIMES*
DAVENPORT, IOWA

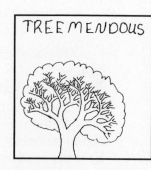

Marie Cronk

DAVIS COUNTY MIDDLE SCHOOL

When I started school, I lived in a rural school district which did not have a school. Students in that district were tuitioned to "town" school in Bloomfield. There, I was an ordinary student with no particular feelings that I was, or would be, anything other than average.

In my fifth-grade year, our family moved and I had to attend a one-room country school for the first time ever. The school had eight students in kindergarten through eighth grade—a far cry from the classrooms of about 25 students to which I had become accustomed. There was also, as was normal for country schools, one teacher.

This particular teacher was not destined to be one of my favorites. She, in fact, did little for my educational ego and I viewed my intellectual faculties as just average or maybe less. I didn't do badly in school, but I did not excel.

By the time I reached eighth grade, the country school closed and I returned to "town" school. That may have been the happiest day of my life. During one of those first, few happy days I was stopped after math class by Marie Cronk, who had encountered me in my earlier years.

43

"You are much smarter than I remember you being," she said in a forthright manner.

I have pondered that moment many times, even wondering if she was using a psychological approach on me or if she was just stating fact. Whatever, it worked. My confidence in the classroom immediately rose. I began thinking of myself as a "good student." I received better grades and I believe I learned more than I would have otherwise. I went on to high school, where I was on the honor roll; on to the University of Iowa, where my grades weren't bad and where I graduated with a bachelor's degree.

I've often wondered if I would have been able to attain what I have without Marie's one, simple sentence.

Gary Spurgeon

PUBLISHER/EDITOR, *BLOOMFIELD DEMOCRAT*
BLOOMFIELD, IOWA

Dorothy Hall

CALLANAN AND MERRILL MIDDLE SCHOOLS

40

Sometimes, when she wakes up early, Miss Hall recites the 23 helping verbs just for fun.

"Oh, me," she thinks. *"Is, are, was, were, be, being, been, am, may, can, must, might, would."* Miss Hall sort of sings them, there in her bed, and repeats the last few to jog her memory if she gets stuck.

"Must, might, would.

"Must, might, would. Could, should, have, has, had, do, did, done, shall, will."

Some things in life are so certain. For 40 years, Dorothy Hall taught ninth-grade English in Des Moines. She taught the certainties, the basics, the building blocks for sentences, for paragraphs, for stories and for lives. For 40 years, her life followed a lesson plan. Semester after semester. Year after year, until Miss Hall became a legend.

Ben Harrison needs only to hear the name and he can picture Miss Hall at the front of the classroom. "Well, bear in mind that I was smaller at the time," says Harrison, 72, "but I think of a large woman, maybe close to 6 foot, I don't know, and towering over most junior high boys and girls, and she was what my mother would have called 'big-boned.'"

45

She spoke in a staccato, straight-at-you voice, Harrison says. Not one of those that trailed off and let you stare out the windows. Miss Hall used direct sentences. "And there wasn't any nonsense."

She must have been 7 feet tall.

"She was sort of the George Patton of the junior high school," Alan Cubbage says.

"Just towering," Andy Lyons says. He and Cubbage were classmates, the second generation in their families to have Miss Hall.

"I don't think I would use the word 'like,'" says Cubbage.

"I respected her, admired her," says Harrison, Hall's student in the 1938–39 school year. "I think I began to like her maybe sometime after World War II, honestly."

Miss Hall taught English with a vengeance. "And you know why?" she once said. "It was because I had so little."

Miss Hall, who taught 30 years at Callanan Middle School and 10 years at Merrill Middle School, made kids memorize the 23 helping verbs, the 54 prepositions (in alphabetical order), the eight parts of speech (and their definitions) and exceptions to the rule, "i before e except after c." Warnings about her class circulated as fast as school lunch menus.

Miss Hall makes you give oral presentations using five note cards that fit in the palm of your hand. Miss Hall makes you copy all kinds of grammar, punctuation and spelling rules in ink. And if you start with black ink and finish with blue—or the other way around—Miss Hall makes you start over.

Miss Hall is a terror. That was the word passed from class to class. "She kept very iron discipline," Bruce Kelley says.

46

She must have been 9 feet tall.

Kelley had her in 1968–69, her final year of teaching.

"Nobody talked in her class. Nobody passed notes. Nobody even looked behind them because," Kelley says, "you just didn't."

You didn't chew gum. You didn't slouch. You didn't fidget. You didn't sass.

"I got in trouble once, and it was just devastating," says Kelley, now 42 and the president and chief executive officer of EMC Insurance Cos. in Des Moines. Miss Hall made him stay after class, he says. "She caught me yawning."

Dan Hunter remembers how Miss Hall talked about the fate of recalcitrant boys: "He'd have been a millionaire if he'd have learned his prepositions."

Miss Hall is old now. How old, she won't say. "It frightens me to think about it, let alone to say it out loud," she says. But a newspaper article published in March 1979 gave her age as 74, which makes her 91.

"Smarty," she says when you do the math. Miss Hall can't add two and two, she says, and that's one reason she chose to teach English.

But the woman who required memorization now jokes that forgetting is the thing she does best. She lives in a nursing home, the health center at Calvin Community in Des Moines.

Fresh flowers arrive monthly from former students, but she can't remember who sends them. "It's so maddening to keep forgetting all the time," she says.

The flowers are from the Roosevelt High School Class of 1945. Members chipped in to buy them after Bud Green stood up and made an announcement at the 50-year reunion last summer. "I just said, 'Miss Hall is still living,'" he says. "And everybody gasped."

He asked his classmates to contribute if she influenced their lives. "Now, that's not to degrade other teachers," he says. "She's on a plateau above them, that's all."

She must have been 11 feet tall.

She taught approximately 8,000 students, including former Gov. Robert Ray. Her spelling rules have been published around the country in Michael Gartner's column about words.

She didn't expect to get old. Her parents, Frank and Jessie Hall, died young, and Miss Hall, their only child, thought she would, too. But she has outlived friends, cousins and students. She lives with a roommate who gets confused and asks if it's dinnertime in the middle of the day.

"It's the middle of the afternoon," Miss Hall tells her.

"Huh?" her roommate asks.

"Two o'clock in the afternoon," Miss Hall says loudly. She doesn't tower anymore. Miss Hall, 5 feet 7 inches, sits in a wheelchair. She doesn't walk or leave Calvin Community, but she entertains many guests.

And she teaches. Calvin Community's Deb Bodson says she used to ask Miss Hall if she wanted to "lay" on the bed. The correct word is "lie." But Bodson couldn't keep lie and lay straight, she says. "I just finally got to the point. I said, 'Dorothy, do you want to stretch out on the bed?'"

Miss Hall is thankful that she gets along as well as she does, thankful for kind things that people do for her. And when she hears that former students say she did lots for them, she says, "Well, I hope I did."

Worn copies of "Miss Hall's Ink Section," the rules she distributed to students, are in several files. Cubbage, Drake University's marketing director, keeps his on a shelf in his office next to Strunk and White's *The Elements of Style*. He consulted it a few weeks ago.

When he and other former students write words and try to remember whether they are spelled "i before e" or "e before i," they recite, "Neither leisured foreign neighbor seized the weird heights during the reign of their sovereign king. ..."

Thousands of people have some pretty obscure party tricks.

Marjorie Spevak can still recite the prepositions. She's 74. She visits her former teacher twice a year, and she still calls her Miss Hall.

Ray says he still feels a little awkward saying, "This is I," but he knows that it is correct. Miss Hall taught him. She attended his speeches, he says, "and I always asked her if I did OK."

Once, legend has it, she sent him a good-luck note: "Dear Robert, I hope you do well on your oral report. Remember not to use too many 'ands.' If you make a mistake in grammar, don't go back and correct it. Ninety percent of your listeners won't know the difference."

A Des Moines doctor tells of the time Miss Hall had surgery years ago. He stopped to visit her in the recovery room. She was just coming to when he leaned over his former teacher and said, "Aboard, above, about, across..."

As Miss Hall began to wake up, she heard someone else in the room ask, "Where am I *at*?" And she thought hazily, "I'll have to do something about that."

Gartner, editor of *The Daily Tribune* in Ames, regularly mentions Miss Hall in his words column and quoted from her Ink Section. He met her 17 years ago after he read about her. He called her and asked for a copy of the Ink Section. "And she said, 'Listen, honey.' She says, 'You've got more money than I do. I'll give you a copy of the Ink Section if you'll Xerox it and give me back 10 of them.'"

And he did.

In his column, Gartner, former president of NBC News, calls Miss Hall his favorite teacher, though she didn't teach him. "I don't know whom I had for English, to tell you the truth," he says. Many people assume he had Miss Hall, and she has stopped explaining.

When people ask her what Gartner was like in ninth grade, she says, "Just like he is now. Kind of a smart ass."

It's easier that way, she says.

Gartner's column, now published in a handful of newspapers, used to run in 100 newspapers. People around the country have read about Miss Hall. Some ask Gartner whether she truly exists.

"She's real," he tells them. "It's too bad you never had her."

This article, "Miss Hall Lessons, Both Unforgettable," by Mary Ann Lickteig appeared in the *Des Moines Sunday Register* on March 24, 1996. Reprinted with permission by *The Des Moines Register,* 1996.

50

David Linder

HOOVER HIGH SCHOOL

41

Most of the defections, I think, were plotted during the two-a-day workouts, when we were swimming something like six miles daily, although some of us rehearsed our speeches before the new season began. The excuses varied, of course— too much homework, the part-time job was too demanding, maybe an illness in the family. One of us even insisted that he preferred to join the debate team rather than endure another season of grueling workouts and that awful gnawing in the stomach during the minutes and hours before stepping onto the starting block for the 200-yard individual medley.

Very few of us succeeded in persuading Coach David Linder that we should quit the swimming team. He was always ready with a response to even the best arguments, perhaps because he had heard them all before. No, he wanted us on the team, he insisted to even the most marginal athletes. I knew even then that, try as I might, I would never win a championship for Coach Linder (the best I managed was to qualify for the state meet), but he wanted me to remain with the team. He wouldn't let me quit.

51

I can think of many teachers who have had a profound influence on my life—an eighth-grade English teacher who drilled us on the rudiments of grammar, a high school government teacher who instructed us about the vagaries of the Iowa precinct caucuses—but Coach Linder taught me the virtues of discipline, fortitude, and persistence. In the years since my final sprint toward the finish line, I have been tempted many times to throw in the towel, to surrender in the face of professional or personal adversity. Quitting has rarely been an option, however, in large part because of Coach Linder. He wouldn't let me quit.

Randall Balmer

PROFESSOR OF RELIGION, BARNARD COLLEGE
NEW YORK, NEW YORK

42

Donald Murphy

HOOVER HIGH SCHOOL

43

The education that I received as a student in the Des Moines Public Schools was terrific. It prepared me to succeed in a career in medical research. A sincere interest in science developed during my junior year at Hoover High School when I learned chemistry from Mr. Donald Murphy. He provided me with a challenging hands-on curriculum taught with enthusiasm. This experience did not point me directly toward a career in science but rather fostered an understanding that science can provide the keys to solving problems. In addition, his teaching style gave me one of the greatest assets, a self-confidence that I was capable of succeeding in science.

Once at Drake University, I tried several majors but found none to my liking until I returned to science. I subsequently obtained a bachelor's degree in biology and decided to apply that knowledge toward the service of caring for others as a physician.

But it wasn't until I began to take care of children with fatal diseases that I became determined to integrate my love of science with medicine. Watching children die from genetic diseases despite a barrage of modern medicines was very painful. I

53

wanted so badly to save their lives, but we didn't have the answers. As a result, I stopped focusing on what we couldn't do and began to ask the critical question, "Could we change the underlying cause of the disorder as a new way to treat these diseases?" This led me into a research career that combines scientific research and clinical medicine.

Over the past 10 years, I have had the opportunity to work with two other physician-scientists in developing and applying gene therapy for the treatment of children with a form of the "bubble boy disease." As a result of these efforts, we were the first to demonstrate that gene transfer has the potential to improve the health of children with devastating diseases.

The insight, knowledge, and self-confidence that I acquired at Hoover was a critical component in preparing me to participate in the first human gene therapy experiment. The implications of this event are unfolding as more than 1,000 patients have now been treated with gene therapy.

I sincerely thank Mr. Murphy for recognizing the potential in his students and insisting that I take the time to appreciate not only what is known but what can be learned through asking the tough questions. Through his efforts, I have had the privilege to directly participate in scientific discoveries that may have changed the history of medicine.

Kenneth W. Culver, MD

DIRECTOR OF GENE RESEARCH AND CLINICAL AFFAIRS, ONCOR PHARM, INC.

GAITHERSBURG, MARYLAND

Mike Wilson

GREENWOOD ELEMENTARY SCHOOL

44

Those of you who remember P.E. classes as merely playing games have obviously not had Mr. Wilson as your instructor. He was not your typical whistle-blowing, refereeing, making-sure-you-showered type of teacher. He focused on teaching skills that would keep many of us health conscious for the rest of our lives. He had a knack for inspiring and encouraging kids. No matter if you were athletically inclined or not, he made you believe that you could do anything.

I met Mr. Wilson when I attended Greenwood Elementary School. Being an extremely shy individual, it was difficult for me to express myself. At all costs, I would avoid answering questions, reading aloud, or a fate worse than death—going to the chalkboard to solve a math problem! Mr. Wilson was a person with a great sense of humor (world-famous impersonation of Kermit the Frog) who would instill within me the confidence I needed to be successful.

Mr. Wilson taught us a variety of things from soccer to bowling to my all-time favorite, square dancing! It was here that I got to hold hands with Joey DeMarco, the shy but most-liked boy in the third grade. I still know bits and pieces of "Sweet Geor-

55

gia Brown," one of the songs from which we learned to dance.

When I think back to Mr. Wilson, I have nothing but fond memories. I know many people think of their favorite teachers as those that taught history, math, sciences, etc. These classes were crucial elements in furthering my education. I would not be where I am today without the wonderful teachers in the Des Moines Public School system (Mrs. Lauer and Mr. Cummings–math; Mrs. Maloney–chemistry; Mr. Van Dyke–science; Mr. Holcomb–English; Mrs. Robinson–ACT preparation; and, of course, Mr. Hewins, my high school coach).

However, I owe a special thanks to Mr. Mike Wilson. He was not "just doing his job" when he convinced me to run against a sixth grader while I was in the fourth grade. I came from behind to pass the girl, only to fumble the baton and lose the race. It was from this challenge that my athletic career had its beginning. My running paid for college and later gave me the opportunity to participate in the 1992 Olympics.

Thanks, Mr. Wilson. You are awesome!

Natasha Kaiser-Brown

OLYMPIC SILVER MEDALIST
ASSISTANT TRACK AND FIELD COACH, UNIVERSITY OF MISSOURI–COLUMBIA
COLUMBIA, MISSOURI

Jacqueline Burnett

PRESCOTT ELEMENTARY SCHOOL

45

S ome of the lyrics, she admits, are about her student days. And some are about her students.

Jacqueline Burnett, who teaches special education at Dubuque's Prescott School, stood before about 1,000 of her district colleagues this week and sang a song about teaching.

But it wasn't just any song.

It was her very own song. Burnett, who's been teaching at Prescott for nine years and in Dubuque for another eight years, wrote the lyrics and the melody. She asked Nancy Woodin, of Dubuque, to help with the piano accompaniment.

It was also a song about teaching character. Teachers, says the song, can teach their subjects and they can teach things like compassion, confidence, and acceptance.

It was a popular song, too. It sparked a standing ovation from the employees of the Dubuque Community School District. And it made Burnett the star of the district's annual assembly to kick off the new school year.

Superintendent Marvin O'Hare said the song was just what he was trying to say

57

when he told district staffers he wants them to think about teaching character this school year. That's why, after hearing her sing at First Congregational United Church of Christ one Sunday, he asked her to sing at the assembly.

And Burnett? What did she think about the idea?

Well, she went home and wrote about 20 versions of the lyrics before she had what she wanted. And, "It was a little frightening to stand up in front of 1,000 of your peers."

But she sang out. And as she did, more than a few eyes moistened. And then everybody stood to applaud.

"I was surprised and very touched by that," she said. "I was overwhelmed."

She's also convinced that the values in her song do belong in public school classrooms.

"There are so many different things that teachers have to impart to students in today's culture," she said. "It goes beyond basic education. There are people who don't think school should instill values, but I don't know how teachers could do otherwise."

This article by Mike Krapfl appeared in the Dubuque *Telegraph-Herald* on August 25, 1995. © 1995, Telegraph-Herald. Reprinted with permission.

"Lessons for Life" reprinted by permission of Jacqueline Burnett.

LESSONS FOR LIFE

Jacqueline Burnett

In my memory there is a teacher
who found a way to touch my life.
Compassion I could see
as he bandaged my scraped knee.
Compassion I have learned in my life.

In my memory there is a teacher
who found a way to reach my soul.
And confidence was born
as I learned to play my horn.
Confidence I've learned in my life.

As children we receive
the legacy we'll leave.
When you look into their eyes,
your own reflection will arise.

In my memory there is a teacher
who found a way to heal my pain.
Accepted I would be
as she helped and guided me.
Acceptance I have learned in my life.

Touch a heart, shape a soul,
change a life.

Ardis Bergfald

EAGLE GROVE COMMUNITY HIGH SCHOOL

46

The most notable teacher having a positive influence in my life was Ardis Bergfald. She was my tenth grade English teacher during the 1952–53 academic year at the Eagle Grove Community High School.

There were no prerequisites with Mrs. Bergfald. One need not be the best student or the most popular nor a star athlete to command her attention. Instead she took interest in all of her students and treated each one with dignity and uniqueness. Her genuine concern gained the respect of the student and allowed her to expand the teaching of grammar to that of life itself.

Mrs. Bergfald enabled me to place the problems and insecurities (so overwhelming in the mind of a 15-year-old student) into a broader and more proper perspective. She nurtured my self-esteem and confidence through gentle encouragement and understanding. Her goodness lit up my darkness and paved for me an easier journey in my further endeavors.

To my knowledge, she never received any awards or recognition, but in the hearts and minds of her many students she was, indeed, most notable.

Gary J. Groves

ATTORNEY
WEBSTER CITY, IOWA

47

Carson Griffith

GRAND JUNCTION HIGH SCHOOL

48

Although I can name several candidates for this honor, one in particular stands out among the rest. His name is Carson Griffith and he teaches music in Grand Junction.

Carson helped me to develop skills in vocal music so that I am able to enjoy a more fulfilling life in music. His patience and instruction helped me achieve All-State status as a vocal musician. More importantly, his influence helped me to appreciate music in all of its many forms. In so doing, it has provided an outlet for the expression of the joy of life through worship and song.

Carson had an innate ability to attract all the students to his room. Many young men who couldn't carry a tune in a bucket took a chance to participate in boys' chorus. Carson made them feel welcome and gave them a chance to learn the same appreciation I have come to know.

Carson Griffith's unending devotion to his students and his avocation makes him a perfect choice for this recognition.

Craig Rowles, DVM

CARROLL VETERINARY CLINIC
CARROLL, IOWA

49

Edith Larsen

ELK HORN–KIMBALLTON ELEMENTARY SCHOOL

Hey, Mrs. Larsen! Look what I drew last night!"

"Wow, Jan! Those football helmets are sure neat. You colored them so nicely. How many different helmets did you draw?"

"Twenty-six! There are 26 NFL teams, but the Minnesota Vikings are my favorite. That's why that helmet is a little bigger than the rest."

"Well, I'll have to start cheering for your Vikings then. All of the helmets are neat."

With that compliment, I was running out the door for recess, anxiously awaiting the beginning of another playground football game. I could not wait to make a diving catch for the game-winning touchdown–just like my beloved Minnesota Vikings. This was not an unusual dream for a second grader, but the thing that made this particular dream a bit unique was the fact that I was a girl! Twenty years ago, there were often many people, including some teachers, that felt compelled to inform children as to what dreams were appropriate for girls and what type of dreams were appropriate for boys. But not Mrs. Edith Larsen! She had no rules for dreaming. She saw the good in every child's dream and did everything possible to support those dreams. I began dreaming in the second grade and I have never stopped.

Mrs. Edith Larsen was always a favorite of elementary students. She was the type of person that seemed to be your mother and grandmother marvelously wrapped into one person. Her smile was always inviting, and her eyes intently met yours—even if she had heard the same "show-and-tell" story 20 times in a row! Compassion could be felt by her every touch and action. Mrs. Larsen had that sensational ability to make every student feel special. I wanted to stay in second grade forever!

But, time has a way of marching on. Eventually, the second grade came to a close and the years seemed to pass so quickly. Although I have attained high school and college diplomas and a masters degree, a part of me has always remained in second grade. The "dreamer" in me continues to flourish because of the confidence that Mrs. Larsen instilled in me. I am so thankful that Mrs. Larsen encouraged my drawings of football helmets and allowed me to have fun playing football—even though I was a girl. She gave me the freedom to "tackle" the world and become everything I dared to be. I learned then that believing in yourself and in your dreams was the fun and exciting part of life.

Today, I am still dreaming, and I am still having fun. Regardless of how long I am blessed to live, a part of my heart will always be in second grade with Mrs. Larsen. Every now and then I think of those football helmets and I smile; I always hope that Mrs. Larsen is still smiling too. I hope she realizes that I am only one of her many students, still dreaming because she taught us how.

Jan Jensen

ASSISTANT WOMEN'S BASKETBALL COACH, DRAKE UNIVERSITY

DES MOINES, IOWA

Kristy Hibbs-Burr

ESTHERVILLE HIGH SCHOOL

I knew I would like Mrs. Burr the first time I met her. She branded me "the lone frosh" in January of 1990 when I was the only freshman to try out for her mock trial team. But she didn't hold my inexperience against me, placing me on the varsity squad that year. She seemed to enjoy my overly aggressive, TV-lawyer cross-examination style. Every time I forced a witness into an unavoidable trap, her face lit up and a sly chuckle could be heard coming from her direction. It was the start of four great years of time invested in her literature and composition classes and her mock trial team.

To Mrs. Burr, students came first. Whether you had attained only three credits in two years of high school or had scored a 36 on your ACT exam—it didn't matter to her. She treated all students with respect and had the ability to communicate with both underachievers and overachievers alike, something many teachers are unable to do. In addition, Mrs. Burr always found time to chat with students. I once saw her converse for 10 minutes with a student about motorcycle parts—definitely not her area of expertise—and she did it with such ease that she might have been discussing the poetry of Walt Whitman.

Humor and Mrs. Burr went hand in hand. I never dreaded a Mrs. Burr class because I knew she would keep things lively. Whatever the situation, she was never without an anecdote about her family, a teacher with whom she had once taught, or her dog and cat. She always was able to find humor in the idiosyncrasies of human behavior.

I doubt that Mrs. Burr ever wanted to do anything but teach, and I must conclude that the hundreds, probably thousands, of students who have had a seat in her classrooms are thankful for that.

Travis Ridout

STUDENT, CENTRAL COLLEGE
PELLA, IOWA

52

Marvin Septer

FAIRFIELD HIGH SCHOOL

Any testimonial about Marvin Septer and his positive influence on my life must be more than a teacher testimonial. Yes, Mr. Septer was my ninth-grade physical science instructor and he was a tremendous teacher. I certainly don't want to minimize that, but he was so much more than just a teacher.

Marvin Septer is the kind of teacher who believes his responsibility to young people does not end when the school bell rings. He was my Sunday School teacher. He was my eighth-grade football coach. When I began working for the Fairfield Community School District summer maintenance crew while in high school, Marv took me under his wing on the paint crew. He not only taught me the finer points of plastering, puttying, and painting but also the value of hard work and responsibility to one's employer.

Later, he and a junior high school counselor, Dan Buttery, asked me to join them in a partnership—MDM Contracting (which stood for Marv, Dan, and Myron)—to do painting and light construction in the summer. Although I was only 18 years old, they treated me as an equal partner and included me in all decisions, including our initial meeting with a local attorney to draft the partnership documents. I spent many hot summer days with Marv—painting, pounding nails, glazing windows, pouring concrete, and talking about life in general. He was always positive, energetic, and willing to share his infectious laugh, sometimes to the point of tears.

Marv was also the Fellowship of Christian Athletes (FCA) sponsor at Fairfield High School. It had always been a tradition at Fairfield High School that a half-dozen or so athletes would go to FCA camp in the summer before their senior year. I was one of the half-dozen slated to go the summer of 1975. A couple of weeks before we were to leave, one of our friends and fellow FCA campers, Brad Wickliff, an outstanding student and athlete, was killed in a motorcycle accident. We were shaken to the core. Marv took us to FCA camp, anyway.

At FCA camp, we found that our Christian faith provided answers to many of the questions that had arisen in our hearts and minds since Brad's death. We told Marv on the way home that we wanted to start an active FCA chapter at Fairfield High School and share what we had found. He was behind us 100 percent. That year, our FCA meetings grew to more than 100 young people in attendance. Lives were changed. Marv was there the whole time, quietly supporting us, helping us to make good decisions for our lives, helping us search for the answers to difficult questions about life, helping us to lead lives of honesty, integrity, and service to others.

I am only one of the young people that Marv has influenced over the years. Others could tell similar stories of his selfless desire to support and help young people as they struggle through their difficult teenage years.

Marv Septer was more than just a tremendous teacher. He was, and is, a tremendous friend.

Myron L. Gookin

ATTORNEY
FAIRFIELD, IOWA

Leon Plummer

FARRAGUT HIGH SCHOOL

54

They buried Leon Plummer here 20 years ago, after a funeral that packed the gymnasium that now bears his name.

Still, the smiling, rotund Plummer—forever "Mr. Plummer" or "Coach Plummer" to the Farragut girls who played basketball for him—guides them daily, as if he were still on the bench to provide a disapproving glare or a reassuring nod.

He travels the Midlands with Janice Pierce Anderzhon as she sells nursery stock.

He helped keep Terri Brannen's eyes on her goal as she pursued a degree in veterinary medicine.

He works the fertile soil of southwest Iowa with Becky Albright Head.

And he prowls courtside still at girls basketball games with Janelle Gruber Bryte, whose first coaching job set her behind Plummer's old desk.

Plummer, who died of a heart attack at age 41 in 1976, took 10 teams to the state tournament in 19 years of coaching girls basketball at Farragut. His Admiralettes won the state title in 1971.

To his former players, though, the Farragut trophy case is not the best measure of a man who spent his life leading young people. Coach Plummer's real legacy, they say, is his enduring influence in the lives of others.

"He really molded young women," said Bonnie Bickett MacKenzie. "The patience, the discipline, the teamwork, the hard work, the fun, the respect. I'm who I am partially because of him."

Ms. Anderzhon, a starter who watched most of the '71 championship game from the bench, remembers Plummer with the same fondness as the reserve guard involved in the game's key play.

Tanya Bopp Bland, the spunky guard who drew a charging foul on a girl nearly a foot taller than she was, called her coach "the greatest influence on me, other than my faith."

Ms. Anderzhon, a regional sales representative for a nursery wholesale company, likewise credited the coach with shaping the woman she has become.

"I'd be lying if I said it didn't hurt," she said of Plummer's decision to replace her for most of the title game. But she admired him too much to object. "I didn't ever say a word. I was happy for the team. I felt that I would be very selfish if I was to pout around."

The team, and obeying the coach, mattered most to Plummer's girls. In interviews a quarter-century later, Adettes—starters, subs and benchwarmers alike—used the word "respect" immediately when asked about the coach. "Team" followed quickly.

"We all respected him," Dr. Brannen said, "and would have done anything the way he wanted us to do it."

Dr. Brannen by any measure was a star in Iowa girls' basketball. She was the only

Adette named to the '71 all-tournament team and was named first-team all-state twice. She is the only Adette in the Iowa Girls' Basketball Hall of Fame.

But she wasn't a star in Farragut girls' basketball, because Plummer had no stars, only the team. The accolades made Dr. Brannen uncomfortable as a youth and drew little notice from the coach.

"I'm glad he didn't make an issue of it," said Dr. Brannen, now working at a veterinary clinic in Calgary, Alberta. "I just was much happier to be recognized as a team."

Her humility was typical of the Adettes. Plummer wouldn't show players their personal statistics after games.

A visit by *The World-Herald* last month to the Waterloo, Iowa, school where Mrs. MacKenzie teaches prompted colleagues to recognize her basketball achievements at a school assembly. She was a starting forward on the '71 championship team.

As students applauded and Mrs. MacKenzie blushed, a teacher called out, "How many points did you make?"

"I don't know," she answered with a smile and a shrug, "but we won." (She scored 17 points.)

Plummer grew up in Burlington Junction, Missouri. His only sibling was a younger sister. He was a pretty good basketball player but especially enjoyed baseball, said his widow, Sally Ashler, now remarried and living in Hamburg, Iowa.

He began coaching at Farragut in 1957, his second year out of college. He assisted the football coach and coached younger boys in summer baseball. But Plummer made his mark coaching the girls' sports, building a dynasty that dominated southwest Iowa softball, track and especially basketball for nearly two decades.

"I think he always preferred girls," Mrs. Ashler said. "He thought they worked harder for him. The male ego gets in the way with boys."

And he understood the girls. His daughter, Laura Krein, now of Underwood, Iowa, said, "He knew the symptoms of PMS before they ever identified it as PMS."

Plummer and his assistant coach, Max Livingston, who died last summer, taught the fundamentals of basketball to Farragut girls from the time they entered fourth grade. They were paid to coach junior high and high school, but Plummer and Livingston started the elementary program on their own time on Saturdays so the girls would know the game by the time they were ready to compete.

There would be plenty of time for scrimmaging and playing later. In drills they would continue into high school, the young girls practiced dribbling, passing, rebounding, learning how to cut off a girl who was driving into the lane.

Failing to learn a skill was not an option. "You redid it and redid it and redid it until it was right," recalled Mrs. Head, who farms with her husband, Jim, about nine miles north of Farragut.

Mistakes carried penalties. "I did a lot of pushups. Oh boy, did I do a lot of pushups!" said Penny Phillips.

But his practices were fun, too. Though always demanding, he'd joke sometimes when the girls would least expect it. He'd play the Harlem Globetrotters' "Sweet Georgia Brown" theme music.

Barb Young Lundgren, who was a sophomore guard on the championship team, still has a copy of the mimeographed training code that spelled out Plummer's expectations: no smoking or drinking, of course. Junk food was discouraged, and girls had to follow a strict curfew.

"We heard, or thought, he would go out and drive around to see if any of us were out late," Dr. Brannen recalled.

Plummer always insisted, Mrs. Bryte said, that "we should behave like young ladies off the court, but on the court we should play like boys."

Ms. Anderzhon said she once started getting in trouble and running around with some wild kids. Plummer called her to his office and expressed his concern.

"I went out of there angry," she recalled. But she stopped hanging out with those kids. "I was headed in the wrong direction," Ms. Anderzhon said.

The Sunday morning after winning the state championship, Plummer still expected the girls to attend church, even though they had been up all night celebrating.

Even in the off-season, Plummer would lay down specific goals for each girl, spelling them out in notes to take home over the summer: work on dribbling, cut down on traveling, practice your free throws.

"He probably instilled in all of us the idea of having a goal and working toward it," Dr. Brannen said.

Plummer expected his players to execute what they had learned in practice and concentrate on the game. "When you had a timeout and he was talking to you, you wouldn't dare look up in the crowd," said Ms. Anderzhon.

The concentration Plummer demanded made it easier for the girls to play under the pressure and emotion of the tournament. Dr. Brannen said, "We played almost like robots."

When youthful emotions surfaced, Plummer knew whether to respond sternly or calmly.

Janelle Gruber Bryte remembers her anxiety upon being fouled repeatedly late in the championship game as Mediapolis was trying to come back.

As the youngest forward, she knew the opponents were hoping she would be too nervous to make her free throws. After missing a couple, she looked over to the bench. "Coach Plummer just goes like this," Mrs. Bryte said, making an exaggerated upward shooting motion. "He didn't say anything. He just motioned that I should put more arch on the shot. He was so calm, and he got me concentrating on my shot instead of my nervousness."

Her free throws sealed the victory.

Of the '71 Adettes, Mrs. Bryte followed most closely in Plummer's footsteps, becoming the coach of Farragut's junior high girls a couple of years after Plummer's death. She remembers the feeling of awe as she sat at his old desk and found his old practice notes.

"The first couple years I coached, I was going to be just like him," she said. "I was going to be the woman counterpart to Coach Plummer.

"But my personality is so much different. It didn't take me long to learn I could be a very good coach, but I was going to have to do it with my personality."

Mrs. Bryte does, though, find herself using his very words when coaching, telling her team to "go meet the pass" or "take care of the ball." When one of her players is being guarded too roughly, she needles the referee with a phrase Plummer favored: "Get her a saddle."

She moved in 1993 to Pomeroy-Palmer in northwest Iowa, where she still teaches and coaches.

Plummer's lessons extended beyond the basketball court. He taught junior high science and high school biology. And he taught compassion and acceptance of other people.

"He was always helping the underprivileged," Mrs. Bryte said. When some children in Riverton, where he lived, needed help to pay for a summer camp, he raised the money, "and I know part of it came from his pocket," she said.

His daughter, Julie Plummer, who teaches children with learning problems in Shelby, Iowa, said, "Dad always had a way of taking in kids and adults who were different from the mold."

Plummer returned from coaching after the 1976 state tournament, where the Adettes lost in the first round. He was going to be high school principal and spend more time with his children, three teenagers, a 4-year-old and a 2-year-old.

But he died of a heart attack less than two months after he quit coaching. He was somewhat overweight and smoked unfiltered Camels, but his death, at age 41, came as a shock.

Friends, fans, family, Adettes past and present and coaches from across Iowa came to Farragut's gym, which has a capacity of about 2,500, for the funeral. They filled the bleachers and the folding chairs set up on the court where Plummer's girls played.

His widow spent the summer writing more than 2,000 thank-you notes.

The Adettes mourned as though they had lost a father. "I never told him how much he meant to me in my life," lamented Ms. Anderzhon.

Mrs. Head draws great solace from the fact that she had told him. She was the oldest of three Albright sisters—Becky, Pam and Teresa—who started at forward for Farragut from 1968 to 1976. When Teresa was a senior, the sisters decided to write letters to Plummer the week of state tournament, thanking him for his years of guidance.

"I feel good because I know before he died, he knew exactly what I thought of him," Mrs. Head said.

After the service, Plummer was buried in the cemetery north of Farragut, where his gravestone reads, "Every kid's friend."

When Mrs. Ashler visits the grave, she usually finds flowers, though she doesn't know who puts them there. "There's somebody he touched that's still remembering."

This story by Steve Buttry originally appeared in the March 5, 1996, issue of *The Omaha World-Herald*. Reprinted with permission by *The Omaha World-Herald*.

55

Lura Sewick

FOREST CITY MIDDLE SCHOOL

56

A teacher who really made a difference in my life was my eighth-grade U.S. history teacher at Forest City, Lura Sewick.

Lura Sewick taught for many, many years in Forest City, and she was really a dynamic teacher. She was kind of an unforgettable person because she had one blue eye and one brown eye and she always wore purple. So, that was certainly something that would get the students' attention.

She also had a tremendous love of America and American history, and I remember she was a very demanding teacher. We had to do a lot of time lines and we learned a tremendous amount about history. It was during that year that I had her in eighth grade that I decided I wanted to go into a career of public service and run for political office some day.

One of the things that I remember she taught were what she called "the three Rs of good government." And, of course, everybody's familiar with the first R, which stands for rights. The first 10 amendments to the Constitution of the United States are called the Bill of Rights. As American citizens, we're very jealously protecting those rights we have and recognize that's one of the great things about this country—

because people's rights are protected by the Constitution.

She also taught us that with rights must also go respect—respect for other people's rights. That means respect for your parents, respect for your teachers, respect for other people. As part of that respect, she would make us say something good about every other person in the class. So, you had to find something positive or some compliment to make to every other student in the classroom.

She also taught us responsibility. An important responsibility of being a citizen was to register and to vote. I know that long after she retired—she's still living and I think she's 91 now—she still sees to it that everyone in the little town of Burt, Iowa, where she lives, becomes registered to vote as soon as they're old enough. She's also been a stickler about getting absentee ballots to people that are away in the service or in the hospital or something like that.

She was a teacher who really brought American history to life and motivated a lot of students. At the same time, she taught us by example to be good citizens. I had a lot of good teachers growing up that had a very important influence on my life, but I think more than anyone else, I would credit Lura Sewick for my serving as Governor of Iowa today.

Terry E. Branstad

GOVERNOR OF IOWA
DES MOINES, IOWA

William Hueser

GEORGE COMMUNITY HIGH SCHOOL

57

William Hueser was my teacher all four years of my high school education at George Community High School. Mr. Hueser not only taught me typing skills, shorthand, bookkeeping, and secretarial training, he also taught us about everyday life and what it would be like in the so-called "real world" after high school. He gave us valuable advice on getting along in the work field after high school in a way that I and none of my classmates ever forgot.

At the time, he was teaching us (without any of us realizing it) by telling us of his past experiences and past experiences of his peers. He was a great teacher and is a good friend.

I have been out of school for almost 34 years, and in those 34 years I have lived in my hometown working as a bookkeeper. The last six and one-half years my husband and I have owned and operated the bowling alley in George.

There is hardly a day that goes by that there isn't something or some saying that goes through my mind that reminds me of the days in high school and Mr. Hueser. I still enjoy bookkeeping or any kind of secretarial duties and this is because Mr.

Hueser taught us how to enjoy what we had to learn in his class.

I have one son who attended George Community High School. He also had Mr. Hueser as a teacher and enjoyed his classes. As a matter of fact, I think if my son was writing this testimonial he would be saying the same things I am.

Again, William (Bill) Hueser was a wonderful teacher and is still a very good friend, and I thank him for his influence in my life. Thanks, Bill!

Janice Martens Koerselman

OWNER AND MANAGER, MUSTANG LANES BOWLING ALLEY

GEORGE, IOWA

Steven Young

GLADBROOK HIGH SCHOOL

58

I first met Mr. Young when I was only in fourth grade at Gladbrook Elementary School. He was the high school drama teacher and had a group of his drama students performing for the elementary students in a series of one-act plays. This was new for many of us, as Mr. Young brought his students to the classrooms to perform these plays. It was unheard of for high school students to "come back down" once they left the halls of elementary school, unless it was to terrorize some unsuspecting fool who wandered into high school "no man's land."

As I reached junior high and high school, I was a student in several of Mr. Young's classes, as he taught English, Spanish, and advanced English composition classes. I saw firsthand that he was not an ordinary teacher. He would teach his lessons, then start a group discussion on the importance of the lessons or how we need to prepare for life after high school. There were times when I did not appreciate these group discussions or everything he was trying to teach me as I tried to understand exactly what an indirect object was, when to use a semicolon, what the dif-

82

ference was between "further" and "farther," and that "quicklyer" was not found in any English dictionary.

On several occasions, he exposed me to some of the great literature classics and forced me to read such books as *To Kill a Mockingbird, A Day No Pigs Would Die, The Scarlet Letter, Tom Sawyer, Huckleberry Finn,* and several others. In today's age of videos and book cassettes, I could have rented a copy or listened to the author read the book to me. I have a greater appreciation for actually reading the book and letting my imagination run wild with images of what was taking place within the book.

As my senior year began, topics of earlier group discussions came back to haunt me as the biggest question that I had was, "What am I going to do after I graduate?" I had a few options but chose to try and gain a nomination to the United States Military Academy at West Point.

Again, Mr. Young helped me by writing a letter of recommendation and getting more from my other teachers and school officials. Mr. Young, along with my mother, used his personal time to help me prepare for, including how to conduct myself during, the interview. (I was going to have several before I could receive a nomination to West Point.) All of my preparation eventually paid off, as I did receive a nomination from the Honorable Cooper Evans, then gained admission to, and eventually graduated from, West Point as a member of the Class of 1988.

I visited Mr. Young whenever I was home on leave from school and discussed how things were going in my studies. Years later, while I was stationed in Germany, my mother told me that Mr. Young transferred to another school and was a high school guidance counselor. I was sad that he was not in Gladbrook anymore, but happy for him because he was doing what he always had been doing throughout his life—helping other students prepare themselves for the future.

I never had another chance to see or talk to Mr. Young again, as he passed away two years ago. I look back on my junior high, high school, and college days and feel very fortunate to have known Mr. Young—the teacher, the guidance counselor, and, most importantly, my friend.

Capt. Marc R. McCreery
7TH SPECIAL FORCES GROUP (AIRBORNE)
FORT BRAGG, NORTH CAROLINA

59

Willa Nolin

GLIDDEN–RALSTON COMMUNITY SCHOOL

60

I have always considered the years that I spent at Glidden-Ralston Community School to be a positive learning experience. The education which I received was of the highest quality and helped to set the foundation for the success that I would later achieve. The standard of excellence established at the Glidden-Ralston Community School is a tribute to all past and present teachers, as well as the Glidden community, school board, and school administration. The standard of excellence continues to this day, with measures taken to assure that it will continue far into the future.

Although many teachers had a positive influence on my life, Mrs. Willa Nolin had the most notable and lasting influence.

I feel that academic success and the influence that a teacher has on students is best measured by the positive role model they are in both their personal and professional lives. I have known Willa nearly all of my life, both in and out of the classroom. I had many occasions to see firsthand how Willa conducted her personal life, with her family and within the community. The dedication and caring which Willa displayed continued into the classroom.

85

Willa demonstrated the practicality of the theory of advanced mathematics and the technical sciences through meaningful and understandable examples and demonstrations which were not above the student's level of understanding. This approach to teaching created a stimulating and fun environment in which to learn subjects of a highly technical nature and to see how they applied to real life. Willa always encouraged students to excel and do the best that they could, while at the same time being patient and helpful if students didn't grasp concepts the first time they were presented. Willa was respectful and considerate toward students and was always willing to give of her time, during and after school, to help students. Willa was a constant and consistent positive role model, both as a teacher and a person.

Willa practiced and instilled in her students, by her example, a standard of excellence that made Glidden-Ralston Community School an environment that fostered learning, while providing a quality education and a positive life experience.

Steve Zimmerman
CERTIFIED VALUE ENGINEERING SPECIALIST
SCRANTON, IOWA

61

Annette V. Shultz

GREENE ELEMENTARY SCHOOL

62

The most important educator in my life is a third-grade teacher in Greene, Iowa.

The community in which she lives is a typical Iowa farm town. While rural, Greene has always prided itself on the quality of its school system and placed high expectations on its educators.

Three keys to this teacher's success are her dedication to students, her creative approach to the learning process, and her personal fortitude.

When I was in kindergarten, we had a classmate who could not communicate verbally. This teacher was the special education teacher at that time and was challenged with helping this student learn to communicate. She spent many hours working with this student and the student's family. Upon high school graduation, the student went on to college and has since married and started a family. The one-time special education teacher was a very proud guest at the wedding of this student.

The following year, she became a third-grade teacher—the position which she still holds.

In the classroom she has always found new and creative ways for teaching her

87

students. Often times these methods incorporate one of her personal interests. An example of this would be her approach to teaching beginning multiplication and division. Incorporating her passion for geology, she provides each students with a cup full of fossilized shellfish (found in local quarries). Using these three-dimensional prehistoric objects, the students are able to grasp these intangible math concepts and learn some geological history of their surroundings.

Foremost in my mind, I feel that this teacher's personal fortitude is a quality that has most impressed me.

Newly married to a local man, she moved to Greene in 1963 and began teaching. Five years later, her husband was severely injured in an automobile accident. This left him in need of nursing home care, and she with two preschool-aged children to raise.

The teacher I am speaking of is Mrs. Annette V. Shultz. She has been able to rise above this personal tragedy and remain dedicated to her husband and children, teaching, and the community. She has provided me with a model to refer to throughout my life. Thanks, Mom!

Craig S. Shultz
INTERIOR DESIGNER
CHICAGO, ILLINOIS

63

Edna Lee Houston
George Westby
Ruth Barnes
Avilda Buck
Wilson Goodwin
Leroy Smay

GREENFIELD ELEMENTARY AND HIGH SCHOOLS

Teachers in Greenfield when I was a boy in the 1930s were the most special group in town. Perhaps pastors were on their level, though there were not that many of them and their doctrine had none of the frightening certainty of English grammar and arithmetic. There were doctors and lawyers, but only a couple or three of each and, with luck, the exposure to them was minimal.

89

And, as I recall, there were only one or two families judged to be rich in my community, which meant that intellectual capital was more important than money and that led to solid respect for educators.

George Westby, the high school principal who lived two doors down from me, was a god in my young eyes. I saw him stride to school in the early morning in a three-piece suit, gold watch chain glinting in the sun, fedora squarely on his head. "There goes Mr. Westby," my mother would say as we watched out the kitchen window.

There was reverence in her voice, a hint of the hope that all Depression-ridden families had vested in the schools, the only sure way to better lives. Mr. Westby was soon gone. But others like him followed, good and devoted people, always held in awe.

I see that parade of administrators and teachers and coaches now in my mind, all worthy in some way of our esteem. Today I understand why. Back then I was part of a society that required unquestioning discipline and hard work. Teachers as much as anyone outside our families made us worthy citizens, if that was to be.

Edna Lee Houston taught my father in kindergarten, and me too. She was forever soft-voiced and tender-handed, knowing and caring from whence we came. She set the standard of our high expectations that followed.

Ruth Barnes lived with her sister on the north side of town and for nearly a half-century she taught high school Latin, which seemed so strange in that land of corn and hogs. Yet, when I looked back from my writing career I could see that while I never learned much Latin, I did learn grammar from Miss Barnes. And I did learn to finish what I started.

There was Avilda Buck, too, who taught us algebra and trigonometry and during World War II took us into her home summers and nights for advanced tutoring so we would be a jump ahead of others when we went into service.

And Wilson Goodwin taught us basketball and science and was such a genial and respected figure that at least one of my classmates became an Air Force meteorologist, as Mr. Goodwin had been during the war.

Leroy Smay, with the patience of Job, built a band out of a lot of tin ears and forever the strains of Bach and John Philip Sousa have lived side by side in most of our minds. Enduring treasure.

No wonder the teachers in our tiny culture were revered. They imparted the exhilaration of learning, the worth of thought. For that they received enduring honor and affection. It was a splendid partnership.

Hugh Sidey

CONTRIBUTING EDITOR, *TIME* MAGAZINE
POTOMAC, MARYLAND

64

Mildred Kellam

GREENFIELD HIGH SCHOOL

I was fortunate to have grown up in a small Iowa town. There are a number of benefits. One is the sense of community, of being part of a group of people that know you and care about you. At times it seemed to me as if the entire town was keeping an eye on me and participating in guiding my development. Although I did not always enjoy this supervision as a youth, I have now come to value it and to appreciate the role that my hometown and its citizens played in my growth to adulthood. One of the most prominent figures in these memories was a neighbor, a friend and a teacher, Mildred Kellam.

Mrs. Kellam lived up the block from my family. For most of my life I didn't realize she had a first name. She was always Mrs. Kellam. (As a child it apparently didn't occur to me that she would have a first name and as an adult I still couldn't seem to bring myself to address her in any way but as "Mrs. Kellam.") She was a very neat and orderly woman with a natural dignity that didn't demand respect as much as just drew it out as if there were no alternatives that were possible. She presented a very severe and intimidating image to me, but that feeling always seemed to dissolve with her ready smile and a kind voice that conveyed her genuine happiness to see me or any other young person.

My first memorable interactions with Mrs. Kellam occurred when I was a neighbor kid trying to earn some money by mowing lawns during the summer when I was 12 or 13 years old. She had high expectations of the quality of work I would do in mowing her lawn, higher expectations than I had. She always demanded more effort, more attention to detail and better work than I planned to deliver. She let me know in no uncertain terms that I could do better than I started out to do and that she expected me to do my best. (I didn't always provide the best lawn care service, either in terms of promptness or quality.) Mrs. Kellam was understanding the first time and patient in explaining her expectations, but was always unrelenting in her demand that I do my best. These were the same qualities that she brought to her teaching.

Mrs. Kellam taught high school mathematics. She taught with patience, understanding, and a determination to help us discover our own capabilities. She always expected us to work up to those capabilities. She understood the difficulties many of us faced as her students in algebra and calculus. She worked with us patiently as long as we applied ourselves to our task, and, in the end, she accomplished her goal—although most of us didn't have any idea what it was.

Now, upon reflection, I realize she invested most of her time and effort not so much in showing us how to solve the immediate math problem we were dealing with, but rather she was teaching us how to teach ourselves, how to figure things out for ourselves so that we would always be able to find ways to solve our own problems. In the classroom, this woman helped her students find abilities in ourselves we didn't know we had, gave us the desire to find and develop other abilities and, most of all, instilled an expectation of excellence in the application of those abilities. Mrs. Kellam accomplished the formidable task of raising her students' expectations of themselves and providing them with the ability to develop their own tools to achieve those expectations.

She did not seem to regard her profession as a job that began and ended with the school bells. Her students were not tasks to be accomplished. She was a part of our lives and we were a part of hers. Teaching was only a facet of her involvement in the whole of our growth and life in the community. When I saw her outside of class, she would inquire about how and what I was doing and demonstrate her genuine concern for my well-being and growth as a person. At times, when it seemed necessary, she would offer advice or guidance. This continued to be true long after I had moved on from her classes and the Greenfield school system. This genuine compassion and continuing concern for the overall development and progress of their students was characteristic of many of the teachers I was fortunate to have in that school system.

Mrs. Kellam was a remarkable part of growing up in Greenfield. This was true not only for the traditional virtues of a teacher, which she possessed in abundance, but also because she was part of our lives in the community and helped to instill the values that guide us today. Personally, she helped me to find more within myself than I knew was there and she helped give me the confidence and independence to develop it and use it myself. She believed in me and invested a part of herself in me. I'll always be grateful, appreciative, and, of course, respectful.

Doug Armstrong, DVM

HENRY DOORLY ZOO
OMAHA, NEBRASKA

94

Richard Peebler

GRINNELL HIGH SCHOOL

L ooking back on my high school days, I remember that when I entered Grinnell High School in 1952, everything was old. The building was old (a new one was completed in 1960); the faculty and administration were old. But while I was a student at GHS, gradual changes began to take place. A new principal was hired in the fall of 1953, replacing an icon who had been in that position for what must have been 40 years. The faculty also began to change.

In 1954, at the start of my junior year, Richard Peebler was hired to teach math. He was like a breath of fresh air. Mr. Peebler had taught for three years prior to coming to Grinnell and was probably only 25 or 26 when he first taught in our system. He was enthusiastic about his subject. His energy was boundless.

I always looked forward to attending his math classes because I knew we were going to be challenged and that we would learn. He was firm but not dictatorial, and we could laugh and learn at the same time. A true testament to his abilities is the fact that several of my colleagues went on to be high school math teachers, and a couple even earned Ph.D.s in math-related fields. In short, we were ready for the type of instruction that he brought to us, and we prospered under his tutelage.

Mr. Peebler also took an interest in his students outside of the classroom. He followed our extra-curricular activities and took a real interest in all phases of our development. He was drafted as our class advisor and enthusiastically assisted in all of our projects.

In my senior year, I was chosen to be Master Counselor of our local DeMolay chapter. When it was time for me to step down, Dick Peebler appeared at the ceremony and presented me with a past Master Counselor's pin which had been given to him when he relinquished the same office several years earlier. I still have the pin. I cherish it—not because it has great value—but because of the thoughtfulness with which it was given.

Dick Peebler left Grinnell High School with our class, and in the fall of 1957 began a career that has spanned 40 years at Drake University. During that time, he has been a professor of accounting and for 20 years was the dean of the College of Business. I know that through the years he has continued to encourage young men and women as they pursue their academic goals and also as they grow and mature in all facets of life.

Richard K. Ramsey

PRESIDENT, RAMSEY-WEEKS, INC.
GRINNELL, IOWA

Robert "Bob" Pryor

CENTRAL SCHOOL

67

In 1932–33, one of my junior high years at Central School in Iowa Falls, my math teacher was Robert "Bob" Pryor. Mr. Pryor also was my junior high basketball coach.

In class, he ruled with authority, keeping order by rifling erasers and hitting those of us who might not be as attentive as he wished. He was remarkably accurate and could "pick off" an unruly boy at the back of the room. Under Mr. Pryor, discipline was learned.

On the basketball court he was equally demanding and we gave him 100 percent each game. Although stern of exterior, he was considerate and understanding, and he made the game fun.

One afternoon—either by request or by order—I was helping Mr. Pryor clean blackboards. He suddenly said, "Billy, sit down. I have something important to tell you." To this day, I can still feel the surge of fear welling up in my stomach. I didn't know what I had done to bring down his wrath.

Mr. Pryor looked intently at me, moved quite close and said, "Billy, remember what I am going to tell you today. You are an excellent basketball player. You have

97

great competitive desires. But, you are going to be small physically. All your team-mates are going to be much taller than you. Therefore, you must do these things to keep up with them. 1. Always give everything you have. Never let up—outfight them. 2. Don't drink coffee. It's not good for you. 3. Never, never smoke a cigarette, as it cuts your wind. All of your friends will be smoking and you will be in better shape than they."

With that, Mr. Pryor said, "See you tomorrow, Billy. You are a good boy."

At age 75, I can attest that I have never had a cigarette in my mouth—not one puff. Coffee? Still only a cup when driving home from a talent show or late night event.

I feel that Mr. Pryor, on that afternoon, epitomized what teaching is all about—impressing the impressionable at precisely the right moment. Mr. Pryor also was a short man with a lot of "fight" and he could sure "peg" an eraser when needed.

Bill Riley

BROADCASTER AND STATE FAIR PROMOTER
CLEAR LAKE, IOWA

68

Mary Egan
CASS COUNTY RURAL SCHOOL

Dorothy Bowley
Ray Dillard
Gustava Price
JEFFERSON–SCRANTON HIGH SCHOOL

Donald B. Johnson
Russell Ross
George Chambers
Willard Boyd
UNIVERSITY OF IOWA, IOWA CITY

A number of teachers have had a significant impact on my life, so it's impossible to single out just one.

The list begins with my grandmother. Mary Egan taught school in a one-room schoolhouse in Cass County before she met my grandfather and she had to quit teaching. That didn't stop her love of reading and learning. Their home was always full of good books and there was always a warm lap where you could go to read them.

As a boy, one of life's pleasures was time at Grandpa and Grandma's house,

99

where an old set of the *World Book Encyclopedia* was as much fun as licking the mixing bowl at cookie baking time.

She helped teach a love of learning and reading early on. From her came the ethic which my parents passed on to me: Get a good education because they can never take that away from you. That is an ethic taught to many in Iowa over the years and it has paid off handsomely for our state.

A second teacher who has played a large role was Dorothy Bowley, the school librarian who coached my high school debate team. My parents had started me to school a year early, so I was always behind the older boys in competitive athletics. But in the library, I didn't get shoved around. Mrs. Bowley taught me how to look up books and articles. She also taught speech and debate, where she helped teach the power ideas and words can have when they are effectively used in tandem.

Other teachers were Ray Dillard, who taught a love of literature, and Gustava Price, who taught a love of history.

In college, several teachers drilled a simple ethic—how to ask questions and think critically. Donald B. Johnson, Russell Ross, and George Chambers exemplified what college is really all about—teaching you how to think and to appreciate the work of those who did.

One great teacher was Willard Boyd. He taught courage. It wasn't in a classroom. As president of the University of Iowa in the early 1970s, he had the unwelcome task of trying to preserve a great university in the face of the student unrest of the Vietnam era.

As a student activist, I got a chance to watch him up close. He saw the university as a place that should not be torn apart by those with other agendas. I remember long, late-night talks with him. He taught that a college education can't teach you everything there is to learn, it can only teach you what you don't know and, maybe, the right questions to ask.

That made the place worth preserving to him. He faced down radicals who believed in violence. He faced down alumni threatening to withhold money. He faced down legislators threatening to impose laws. And he did it all with great civility at a time when that was a rare commodity.

We all owe a lot to the great teachers we have known. Most of us will spend our lives trying to live up to what they really taught us.

Their values—teaching with love, asking questions, keeping perspective, appreciating beauty, knowing how to find what you don't know, civility and courage—are traits that have marked the great teachers I have known.

David Yepsen

POLITICAL EDITOR, *THE DES MOINES REGISTER*
DES MOINES, IOWA

69

Gary Busby

JOHNSTON HIGH SCHOOL

70

I have known Gary Busby in various ways during my life—as my teacher/coach, as an opposing coach, and as a comrade in education. I have always found Gary to be a positive, hardworking, and enthusiastic person.

Teachers influence students in many ways—some by how they teach, others by the person they exhibit to students over a long period of time. Gary Busby was the type of teacher who influenced students by displaying a keen sense of propriety and helping students achieve success in many ways, both in and out of the classroom.

Gary taught science and coached wrestling at Johnston High School and served as co-leader of the Fellowship of Christian Athletes organization while I attended school. Today, Gary is the assistant middle school principal at Johnston Middle School.

Gary's positive role model taught me values that I wanted to exhibit and live my life by. I enjoyed being around Gary, both in and out of school, at different activities. Good role models are very important to students who are trying to discover who and what they want to be as they grow and become adults.

Many of my former classmates have commented on how they enjoyed Gary's classes. Gary was ahead of the current trend in science education. Students were doing lots of hands-on experiments as well as self-exploration-type projects in his classes during the early 1970s.

Little did I know at that time that Gary's influence would also affect how I would deal with people in my current professional occupation. I, too, am a science teacher—thanks to Gary's influence! Gary has made a great impact on how I teach science to my students today. I still seek Gary's advice and insights as I continue to grow and serve the community of public education.

I am thankful to have had a good role model who lived his life by displaying values and ideals that I found beneficial while learning about the type of person I wanted to be! Hopefully there are more Gary Busbys out there helping to bring our youth into our communities as productive citizens.

Kelly E. Rohlf
PRINCIPAL, STEWART ELEMENTARY SCHOOL
WASHINGTON, IOWA

71

Darwin DeVries

KINGSLEY HIGH SCHOOL

72

He strides into the classroom with a grin and a sparkle in his eye, then barks, "Take everything off of your desk except a pencil and a piece of paper!" The thought of a pop quiz in his class still strikes a chord of fear in me.

Although it has been nearly 10 years since I graduated from high school, there is one teacher who stands above the others—literally as well as figuratively—that has had an extremely positive influence on my life. A tall, athletic, and at times intimidating teacher and coach, Mr. Darwin DeVries can best be described as an educator and motivator. A man of strong convictions, Mr. DeVries practiced what he preached. Dedication, honesty, integrity, and motivation were virtues he radiated each time he stepped into a classroom. He would not favor mediocrity; rather, he challenged every student to achieve his or her best, whether it was in the classroom or on the court.

His classes were known for their toughness—pop quizzes, long and challenging homework assignments, and the dreaded problems on the board. "Forgetting" homework at home or unfinished assignments were not tolerated. At the time, his classes seemed like boot camp compared to some other courses. But in the process, Mr. De-

104

Vries taught responsibility and time management as well as the core fundamentals of algebra, trigonometry, and calculus.

Mr. DeVries, being a teacher of mathematics and a coach for basketball and baseball, was an extremely busy man. But that did not stop him from making himself available before school, during lunch and study halls, and after school for assistance on homework or other projects. It was obvious by the cluster of students following him from class to lunchroom to gym that his efforts weren't unnoticed or unappreciated.

It wasn't until I went to college that I received a deeper appreciation of his influence. It seemed that other students in my college classes had never had to derive their own mathematical formulas, complete their homework, or feel the pressure of a pop quiz. In a roundabout way, Mr. DeVries had prepared me for college (and life) more than any textbook could have. I hope that all students who pass through his class will realize that the tough teachers are usually the BEST teachers.

Laura L. Phelps, CPA

CURRENTLY STAY-AT-HOME MOTHER
KINGSLEY, IOWA

73   105

Donnabelle Oliver

LAWTON JUNIOR–SENIOR HIGH SCHOOL

74

I had more than one teacher who influenced my life in a positive manner. However, the one I wish to comment on is Donnabelle Oliver, one of my high school math teachers.

From the very beginning of my high school days, Mrs. Oliver made me want to think, reason, and find answers to all problems relating to math and science.

The techniques she used made our assignments fun. She taught us shortcuts in problem solving (that I still use today). Using her shortcuts, we would race to see who could finish first. We learned efficiency while we explored many math concepts.

The more problems I solved, the easier it got and the more fun it became. My math skills improved enough to allow me to exempt a college math class and make other college math and science courses fun and interesting.

My major area of study in college (Mechanized Agriculture) is heavily dependent on math. I was able to do an independent study on how diesel engine efficiency is affected by various add-on components. This procedure was both fun and interesting.

Had I not had this math interest instilled in me by Mrs. Oliver, I probably would not have done this independent study.

I also like to weld and manufacture or improve various tools and farm equipment that I use in my occupation. If I weren't interested in math, these skills perhaps would not even be possible. The success and efficiency of my operation is highly dependent on my math and science skills. Because of her positive influence on my life, I believe Donnabelle Oliver has truly made a difference.

Kirk Flammang

GRAIN AND LIVESTOCK FARMER
LAWTON, IOWA

75

107

Casey Foster
MAPLETON VALLEY ELEMENTARY SCHOOL

William Christensen
MAPLE VALLEY HIGH SCHOOL

Many teachers have had a positive influence on my life. The first teacher to change my life was my third-grade teacher, Casey Foster, who taught me to apply myself and to work up to my abilities. She turned my life around at that time, but the teacher who had an influence that continues to this day is my high school government and physics teacher, William Christensen.

Mr. Christensen was the first teacher to really prepare students for college. He taught us to organize our work and to think for ourselves. However, his example of community involvement made the biggest impression on my life. Many teachers teach community involvement, but Mr. Christensen still practices what he teaches. He has been active in church, political affairs, and community activities the entire period I have known him.

William Christensen moved out of the classroom and into administration shortly after I graduated from Maple Valley High School, but his example continued working for over 25 years as high school principal. He remains an active Rotarian, church man, and community leader. Today he is retired, but I am proud to call him a personal friend who continues the example of "Service above Self."

Edward L. Maier

PHARMACIST AND PRESIDENT, MAIER FAMILY PHARMACY, P.C.
MAPLETON, IOWA

77

Robert J. Majerus

MAQUOKETA HIGH SCHOOL

78

With the many questions surrounding the direction of American education at the present time, I can say with certainty that recognition opportunities such as these for truly exceptional teachers in the state of Iowa are of great importance and richly deserved.

During my formative high school years, I was fortunate to have as a teacher an individual who was more than just an educator—he was my father. This combination awarded me the greatest opportunity to have a parental figure genuinely interested in my academic achievements and my educational experience as a whole. It is because of this that I am pleased and take great honor in being able to speak for Robert J. Majerus.

Mr. Majerus had dedicated his life to promoting excellence in education. For the past 29 years, he has been a high school English instructor. Since 1968, he has instructed eastern Iowa students at the Maquoketa High School as a member and chairman of the English department, providing guidance and stability to the community's educational system.

Highly respected in his field of expertise, Mr. Majerus is an inspirational, energetic, and responsible teacher. He possesses the undefinable "with-it-ness" which allows him to carry on a positive and highly productive rapport with his students. He demands quality and effort from those he instructs while guiding them through their language arts course work—all the while emphasizing its importance no matter what path they choose later in life. His students, in turn, give him the respect he commands and are able to take with them the skills needed to be successful in life.

In addition to his classroom contributions, Mr. Majerus promotes the well-roundedness of Maquoketa students outside the academic school day. He is a positive supporter of the extra-curricular programs at MCHS, provides tutorial assistance throughout the year, and is a regular speaker at school functions and community-sponsored banquets. His genuine care and concern for young people is admirable.

The formal training I received from my father and many caring and knowledgeable teachers in the Maquoketa school system challenged, shaped, and readied me for "the real world" awaiting. A combination of Frank Strathman's sense of humor in delivering his biology lessons—Dennis Street's bottomless pool of patience with his geometry students—Karen Tilton's drive to make us better speakers—Mark Hillebrand's sound advice on what to expect in college—Chuck Wolf's unique delivery and enthusiasm—Holly Parmer's opening the door to diversity and other cultures in our daily French class—Claire Hoye's ability to positively connect with his students—Kent Crawford's zest for the fine arts—Sherm Burns' professional demeanor and mastery of his mathematical material—along with a host of other special people boasting special gifts, helped lead me down the bountiful path of education while building in me the confidence to use the knowledge gained in any way I desired. I feel fortunate to have received my strong education in the state of Iowa—and as a Cardinal at Maquoketa High School.

Robert C. Majerus

ENGLISH INSTRUCTOR AND FOOTBALL COACH, SYCAMORE HIGH SCHOOL

SYCAMORE, ILLINOIS

79

112

Gary Foster

MAQUOKETA VALLEY SENIOR HIGH SCHOOL

80

When I was asked to write a statement about a teacher who has contributed to my well-being, there was not doubt in my mind who I would write about. Mr. Gary Foster was my biology teacher as a sophomore and my psychology teacher as a senior in high school. Mr. Foster was the best teacher I'll ever have. He taught not only from the textbooks, but taught many life lessons as well. Mr. Foster leaves a positive lasting impression on most of his high school students.

One of the things that makes Mr. Foster such a great teacher is his ability to relate well with his students. He presents the material in such a way that students can easily learn and understand it. He also strives to help his students remember the material, not only for the test, but beyond it. He does this by giving examples that the students can understand and relate to. He takes many difficult subjects and simplifies them so his students can understand them.

Mr. Foster also cares a lot about his students. You can tell he cares because he is always interested in what you have to say. Whenever his students come back to visit him after graduation, he is always eager to talk. He is interested in how college is go-

113

ing or just life in general. He shows a genuine interest in all of his students, current or former.

There are so many things that make Mr. Gary Foster a wonderful teacher and person. His ability to relate to his students and his obvious interest in all of his students' lives are just two of the best. Mr. Foster teaches more than just science, he teaches his students about life. Mr. Foster has contributed to my well-being as a person, and most of his students, no doubt, would say the same.

Stephanie K. Zumbach

STUDENT, IOWA STATE UNIVERSITY
AMES, IOWA

81

William H. Emanuel

MARTENSDALE–ST. MARY'S JUNIOR–SENIOR HIGH SCHOOL

82

While many educators are quality members of their profession and are positive influences to the children they teach, I am certain that few have exhibited the dedication to their careers and the personal interest in their students' futures as William H. Emanuel has in his career. Now retired, Mr. Emanuel was my former instructor in junior high physical science and high school earth science, chemistry, and physics from 1982 to 1987.

His teaching of science went beyond the textbook and class syllabus. In fact, Mr. Emanuel took the extra effort to generate interest and enthusiasm for science in each of his students through out-of-the-classroom activities—from recycling drives and field trips to sponsoring a special commemoration and viewing of Halley's Comet. The costs and time for these activities came from his own personal sacrifice.

Many were the Saturdays when he was to be found in his classroom, available for "weekend" help sessions, to aid students in their science homework and studies. He encouraged and helped students with special science projects, science fairs, and other related studies, but I particularly noticed that his interest in students didn't apply to just those who did well in science courses. In fact, he took a special effort to

115

assist those who needed the extra help in their studies.

Often times if a student did poorly in class, Mr. Emanuel knew that the problem might not just be the subject at hand, but larger problems or concerns with the student's personal or home life. On many afternoons, he would allow students to stay after school to help them with their homework for an hour or two, and he would then chauffeur two to three of them home, since they would otherwise not have had anyone to provide them transportation.

But the one thing that stands out most to me about Mr. Emanuel, was the fact that after you completed his courses, his concern was still there. When I left for college after my senior year Mr. Emanuel said to me, "Write to me while you are in school and let me know how you are doing. When you're back on a weekend or for vacation, drop by and visit!" Many of my former classmates, including me, were always happy to write to and receive letters from Mr. Emanuel while they were in college. It was an extra boost to know that someone was still rooting for you in your pursuits!

In 1991, I completed my studies at Iowa State University, receiving a Bachelor of Science degree. I have spent the last five years working in the scientific community as an environmental consultant. I owe Mr. Emanuel a great amount of credit for providing me the encouragement and support that has allowed me to succeed as I have. As an educator, he has truly passed the "torch" from one generation to the next.

Mel E. Pins

ENVIRONMENTAL CONSULTANT

NORWALK, IOWA

Orville A. George

MASON CITY HIGH SCHOOL

83

Orville A. George was born in Hopkins, Minnesota, and attended the local schools. He then enrolled at the University of Minnesota from which he received the BA as well as the MA degrees.

He served his country during World War I, and began his career in the Mason City school system in 1919. The Mason City Junior College had begun in the fall of 1918 and was part of the Mason City Independent School District. The college was under the direction of a faculty committee on which Mr. George served.

While his principal responsibilities were teaching math at the college level, he also taught junior and senior math in the high school. He not only fostered behavioral discipline, but his teaching methods developed a mental discipline that his students found helpful throughout their lives.

For several years after reaching the age of retirement he was asked to continue teaching, which he did, finally retiring in 1963 with more years as a junior college instructor than any person in the state.

He was a life member of ISEA and an active member of the Iowa Association of

117

Mathematics Teachers, American Legion, Voiture 66 of the Forty and Eight, National Retired Teachers Association, Senior Chamber of Commerce, and life member of the Pioneer Museum Society.

During his long and successful teaching career, he was well-known by fellow teachers throughout the state of Iowa as an outstanding teacher of mathematics and was highly respected as such by all of his co-workers as well as by his students and the entire Mason City community.

Arthur M. Fischbeck

RETIRED PARTNER IN FISCHBECK PRICE INSURANCE
MASON CITY, IOWA

84

Alice L. Riter

MASON CITY HIGH SCHOOL

Many young teachers have had a profound influence on my life, from Miss Young (my kindergarten teacher who told me not to be a bully) to Neil Puhl (my journalism instructor who showed me how to make a simple sentence sound good). But the one who opened my mind the most, and probably prepared me to live abroad, was a teacher during my junior year at Mason City High School, Alice Riter.

For 33 years I have resided abroad. Why? Looking back, I feel it was inevitable that I would find and experience the places Miss Riter discussed in class: London, Paris, Madrid, Munich, Prague, and Rome. I was born with an adventurous spirit and she, I believe, knew how to mold it for the better.

I didn't get off to a good start in Miss Riter's "advanced placement" U.S. history class. Miss Riter required that we all buy, each week, the Sunday edition of the *New York Times* as our textbook. I complained to my football coach that I didn't have the money or the interest to buy an east coast newspaper that reported more rowing results than Big Ten scores. I really fought hard to get transferred out of her class, until she introduced me to Arthur Daley's column. I had never read a sportswriter who quoted Shakespeare. Suddenly I had a new outlook, not only on athletics but on politics, the arts, and humanity.

Everyone that year had to read a minor masterpiece of world literature and report on it to the class. I had to study John Jay's *Letters From Abroad*. I envied a friend's assignment (Machiavelli's *The Prince*) but stuck with my ambassador's accounts of life in Paris and London—and was soon hooked on Europe and life there in the 18th century.

Alice Riter never married. Every summer she took an exciting trip somewhere. After I graduated in 1960, she concentrated her passions south of the border. I had known her as a short, thin woman with straight gray hair and functional lace-up shoes. But my younger sister remembers her coming back from South America wearing bright clothes, loop belts, silver bangles, and necklaces from Peru. But both of us agree, she was a teacher from the old school mode who loved her job and loved to learn. She had a grasp on what the world really was and maintained a firsthand knowledge of life through her travels.

You didn't have to be the most intelligent student to get a good grade from Miss Riter; you just had to be the most interested. She gave me my first "A."

Paul J. Polansky

DIRECTOR, CZECH HISTORICAL RESEARCH CENTER, AND
WRITER/HISTORICAL RESEARCHER
SPILLVILLE, IOWA

Alice Thie

MEDIAPOLIS HIGH SCHOOL

86

The teacher who I feel had the most positive influence in my life is my high school business teacher, Mrs. Alice Thie. It seems to me that I had quite a few good teachers through the years, but Mrs. Thie is definitely a standout. She not only knew the subjects she taught—and taught them well—but she also cared about her students as people.

I took more than one class with Mrs. Thie. She taught typing, shorthand, bookkeeping, and an all-encompassing business class in which we simulated an office and each had a job within that office. I learned so much in those classes, including how I felt about working under someone else's authority or as the office manager. Mrs. Thie asked questions and listened to the answers we gave her about those feelings.

Mrs. Thie was instrumental in me getting my first job. She told us that a local office was looking for a couple of part-time employees and helped us prepare for the interview.

Mrs. Thie was more than a teacher to us. She was the junior class sponsor and, in that capacity, helped us plan the junior–senior prom. She was the leader of our Fu-

121

ture Secretaries' Club and she was our friend. She shared personal anecdotes with us about her life and we shared ours.

She was not only close to the business students but she was (and still is) great with all students. My boyfriend—who is now my husband of 18 years—took beginning typing with Mrs. Thie. He has very large hands and had a lot of trouble hitting one key at a time. Mrs. Thie was very patient with him and took him under her wing. She knew he wasn't going to type for a living, but she encouraged him to do his best. She graded him more on how much effort he was putting into the class and how hard he was trying than how many words per minute he typed or how many errors he had.

Mrs. Thie is still teaching at Mediapolis High School. She teaches computers instead of mimeographing but her interest in her students is still genuine. I have children at the Mediapolis Elementary School and I sure wish they could have Mrs. Alice Thie when they get in high school. She's the best!

Cindy Orth

HOMEMAKER
BURLINGTON, IOWA

87

Mr. Cottrell
MOUNT PLEASANT HIGH SCHOOL

Raymond Crilley
Delbert Wobbe
Thomas Poulter
IOWA WESLEYAN COLLEGE, MOUNT PLEASANT

E.P.T. Tyndall
Alexander Ellett
UNIVERSITY OF IOWA, IOWA CITY

My life is a kaleidoscope of memorable teachers.

First and foremost were my parents, who by precept and example imbued me with the basics of personal conduct—the pleasures and satisfactions of study and hard work, strict moral standards, and high aspirations.

In the public schools of Mount Pleasant, I recall many fine teachers who insisted on rigorous learning and a no-nonsense approach to understanding what one knows and what one does not know. My favorite subjects were arithmetic, grammar, algebra, geometry, Latin, physics, and manual training. Among high school teachers, I was most indebted to Mr. Cottrell, who taught a senior course in physics with an accompanying laboratory.

Later at Iowa Wesleyan College, I again had outstanding teachers, among whom were Dr. Raymond Crilley in mathematics, Dr. Delbert Wobbe in chemistry and geology, and especially Dr. Thomas Poulter in physics. The latter was an individual of extraordinary competence and insight; and it was he who was the most influential in guiding me into research and toward graduate work in physics at the University of Iowa. There, Professors E.P.T. Tyndall and Alexander Ellett were my mentors. Their instruction and guidance prepared me for an independent career as a research physicist and university teacher. As such, I have been able to pass on what I have learned to hundreds of young students. And thus the process repeats itself!

I am forever grateful to the many teachers that I had during my formal education. But that was only the beginning of my good fortune. In subsequent years, I have benefited immeasurably by informal teaching by colleagues all along the way and, most importantly, by my wife of 50 years. Even at age 81, these pleasures continue.

Indeed, I am overwhelmed by the fundamental role of the student-teacher relationship in any significant career.

James A. Van Allen

PROFESSOR EMERITUS OF PHYSICS, UNIVERSITY OF IOWA
IOWA CITY, IOWA

Olga Piersall

MUSCATINE JUNIOR HIGH SCHOOL

89

Olga Piersall has a special place in the heart of many. At her funeral last winter, witnesses were given about her caring and understanding nature. They told of her compassion and determination. She was the rock, the steady force, the one who followed through and got things done. Indeed, she has made an impact on many lives.

Miss Piersall was a single woman with no children of her own, and yet she had thousands of children whom she nurtured. I was one of those.

My family and I had moved to Muscatine. I had left a class of eight and was now beginning junior high with 270 other students. I knew one person in the entire school. Miss Piersall, counselor, arranged for me to be in the same classes and home-room with my friend. Also in my classes, there was another girl who had been afflicted with polio. As I look back, that was probably well-planned. It was those little things she would do that made a big difference in the lives of junior high students.

Although I was physically handicapped, Miss Piersall recognized my need to be "normal." She encouraged me to participate and never made an issue of my handi-

125

cap. If you had a problem, she was there to help. Miss Piersall related well to kids and was not afraid to have fun. During the sock-hops she was known to be the leader of the bunny-hop line.

Her advice, support, and encouragement did not stop when you left the halls of junior high. She was always there. A friend of mine tells this story:

She had gone to the beauty shop to get her hair styled for graduation pictures and left with a not-so-good look. She was devastated. She saw Miss Piersall, who came to the rescue. Miss Piersall restyled her hair and the pictures came out great. What a lifesaver! It was those little things she did that sent a powerful message.

I guess you never left her care. She had a way of keeping track of you. If you did something good, she would acknowledge the accomplishment. If you needed help, she offered.

When I came back to Muscatine as a teacher, as Muscatine Education Association President, and then as Muscatine School Board member, Miss Piersall was one of my cheerleaders. Because I held her in such high regard, her vote of confidence meant a great deal to me. She made me feel special. Isn't that what we should all do?

Nancy Panther

SCHOOL BOARD MEMBER AND FORMER TEACHER
MUSCATINE, IOWA

Catherine R. Miller

MUSCATINE HIGH SCHOOL

90

C atherine R. Miller ranks just below our parents as the person who most profoundly influenced our worldview during our formative years.

Catherine was a global educator before the term was coined. Long before such things were commonly done, she brought the wider world into her high school Spanish classrooms through recordings of Spanish opera, visits from Latin American students from various colleges, requiring us to keep current notebooks of news articles from Spanish-speaking countries, and putting on fiestas for the public, including appropriate food, dress, dances, and the learning of Spanish songs.

Threaded throughout this was her constant push to make us see the complexities of political situations there and here ("There are at least three sides to every issue."), and to help us understand and value the backgrounds (social and political), differences and similarities, and the importance of other cultures. In short, she introduced, or strengthened our awareness of, the Family of Humankind.

Through all of her years, Catherine's private life has matched her frequent pub-

127

lic utterances. Indeed, it is a seamless whole. Predating any organized "migrant council," she was teaching English to local Puerto Rican workers, helping families who worked in the tomato fields to improve their living conditions, serving as translator and advocate—and mobilizing others, including past and present students, to help.

Again and again, her voice has been heard in meetings, in letters to the editor and to legislators and others, in personal telephone calls, and in notes or packets of information dropped off at the front door. She has promoted justice and equity through her words, as well as her continuing actions on behalf of all disenfranchised people of whatever background.

Catherine's other great cause is world peace and related global issues. She has devoted her time, skills, tireless energy, and resources to that end.

Now in her 80s, Catherine remains an inspiration and a model for what one committed and determined person can do. Her still-blazing passion and her tenacity and accomplishments both prick the conscience and encourage all who are working to make the world a better place—to keep on trying!

Mary Jo Stanley

HOMEMAKER AND COMMUNITY VOLUNTEER

Dick Stanley

CHAIRMAN, STANLEY CONSULTANTS, INC.
MUSCATINE, IOWA

128

91

Areta Schmidt

SHILOH SCHOOL, AREA VI SCHOOL IN MUSCATINE COUNTY

92

Have I had a teacher who influenced me and could I write a short statement about him or her? Sure, no problem. I can do that. Now the deadline has arrived and what I said I could do now must be done. But, can I choose only one?

Should it be the high school teacher who, by his own enthusiasm, made U.S. history one of my favorite subjects? And even though it wasn't really part of the class, interjected the American government angle that may be responsible for me being a school board member today. Certainly a worthy candidate.

Or maybe the junior high teacher/coach who I had so much respect for that I admitted to him that I had been chewing gum when he told me that another teacher thought that I had been. By the way, gum chewing was a grievous offense that carried a 10-day detention penalty back in the mid-sixties. Obviously a person who influenced me.

While I admire and respect both of these teachers, I choose instead to write about the person who, in my mind, embodies what a teacher is.

I was fortunate enough to experience the one-room schoolhouse through the

129

first half of the seventh grade. Even more fortunate, I believe, was that the building was still K–8. It was here that I had the teacher that I believe was a most positive influence on me. She was my teacher for kindergarten and grades five and six, as well as a neighbor and family friend.

When I come home for a school board meeting in 1996, I think of all the things that have been discussed. They more than likely include racial and gender equity, inclusion, activities, building maintenance, art, food service, planning periods, student contacts, administrative duties, and the list goes on and on. More often that not, I end up thinking back to those one-room schools and the the individual teachers who staffed them. What I end up thinking is that these were people who could, with great pride and accuracy, use one of today's popular slang sayings, "Been there, done that."

So, to teachers across the state of Iowa, congratulations and thanks from all of us. And a special thanks and salute to my teacher, Areta Schmidt of Shiloh School, a part of what was known then as Area VI Schools in Muscatine County. I couldn't have asked for a better teacher or a better place to start.

Tom Welk

MUSCATINE SCHOOL BOARD MEMBER
MUSCATINE, IOWA

Marilyn Woodruff

NEW HAMPTON HIGH SCHOOL

93

"N ever! Never will I be glad that Miss Woodruff was my English teacher!" I spoke these words so passionately to my parents that they ring clearly in my memory more than 30 years later. Antle, Brunsvald, Dierks, Harmon, Hutloff, Kaiser, Krumm, Maupin, Nehring, Throndson, Woodruff, and others dance through my mind when I think about my 13 years in the New Hampton schools. All shared in shaping our values, defining our culture, and furnishing our minds. All deserve our thanks. But Miss Woodruff was perhaps most noteworthy because she was so difficult for us to appreciate while we were her students.

We thought of her as a tyrant, forcing us to memorize line after useless line from Macbeth; to master long lists of vocabulary words; to write and rewrite sonnets, essays, and biographies which she would correct and criticize "unmercifully." Few students would say that they liked her or her class.

Ironically, years later, as I reflect on my own 18 years as an English teacher, I realize that by the time I left the classroom, I was trying to teach more as Miss Woodruff did than as did any of my other teachers. I was demanding memorization

131

of Shakespeare and others, demanding mastery of long lists of difficult spelling and vocabulary, demanding rewrites of papers, and not accepting faulty grammar or mechanics.

I had come to value the emphasis that Miss Woodruff had put on vocabulary and correct usage of the English language, and I wanted my students to have similar skills. I had come to realize that her criticism of our careless writings had not stifled our creativity, but it had given us the confidence to believe that through effort we could produce work that even she would accept. I wanted my students to have the same confidence. I had come to realize the worth of the poetry which was carved into my memory, and I wanted to furnish my students with similar gifts.

While I was in her classroom, I was too young and too inexperienced to appreciate what she was forcing us to realize in ourselves, but now I am able to say sincerely, thank you Miss Woodruff.

Gary Borlaug

EDUCATIONAL PROGRAM CONSULTANT,
BUREAU OF PRACTITIONER PREPARATION AND LICENSURE,
IOWA DEPARTMENT OF EDUCATION
DES MOINES, IOWA

94

Vida Nelson

NEW MARKET COMMUNITY HIGH SCHOOL

One of my many teachers who left a lasting impression was Miss Vida Nelson. She was "old" from our (now admittedly narrow) point of view. We figured (rightly or wrongly) that she was a teenager during World War I. To teenagers in the 1970s, that made her ancient. Why was she memorable?

Miss Nelson ran a tight ship. Ironically, she probably couldn't or wouldn't hurt a fly, but she sure didn't give you that impression when you were in her gaze. She meant business and other teachers and all the students took her at her word. If she said to do it, you did it. So, as is perhaps always the case with the best teachers, she maintained discipline.

Miss Nelson made you learn in more of the classic mode—read the assignment and be able to articulate the answers in the test. No multimedia show or entertainment in the name of education. Having said that, she allowed and encouraged knowing about the world around you rather than just what was in the book.

For example, in her American government class, she often gave extra credit for correct answers to current event questions. The incentive was not just to memorize the book, but to read, watch, or listen to the news. It meant we students discussed current events with each other before a test so we would have a chance at the extra points. Whether we correctly anticipated or not, the exercise effectively made us more aware of the world around us.

At our 20-year high school reunion we were still fondly telling "Miss Nelson" stories—a fitting tribute to a fine and memorable teacher.

Terry Tobin

LEGAL COUNSEL, THE PRINCIPAL FINANCIAL GROUP
DES MOINES, IOWA

Terry Brown

NORTH CENTRAL JUNIOR–SENIOR HIGH SCHOOL

96

Teachers influence tomorrow's leaders every day in the classroom, through coaching and other extra curricular activities. The lessons that are taught help prepare students to succeed in society.

I was fortunate during high school to be influenced by a teacher that went the extra mile on every occasion. Although not a student in his classroom, I was team manager for the girls' basketball team he coached. He taught me the importance of hard work and dedication, the very skills I needed to accomplish my career goals after high school.

Terry Brown was the industrial tech teacher and girls' basketball coach while I attended North Central Community Schools in Manly. I worked with Mr. Brown for four years as manager of the high school basketball team, and the first thing I learned from him was to *never* quit. He taught me that perfection is attainable and I should strive for it. I knew he expected us to give 100 percent—anything less was unacceptable. He also demanded that we have proper respect for people and their property. His example of work ethic was reinforced by his expectations of us.

135

When I first started working with Mr. Brown, I was timid, shy, and unsure of myself. He made me believe I was competent and that anything was within my reach.

I knew that becoming a registered nurse would take dedication and hard work, and I was prepared for the commitment after the lessons in accomplishments Mr. Brown taught.

Growing up in the Midwest was a privilege I am grateful for. I have wonderfully supportive parents who taught me a strong value system. Having a teacher like Mr. Brown gave me the confidence to accomplish my career goals.

I am currently a registered nurse working in cardiac surgery. Part of my career satisfaction is knowing I'm impacting patients' lives by assisting the physicians to heal them as well as giving direction in finding total well-being.

Jean Woodiwiss Torgeson, RN

CARDIAC SURGERY NURSE
MANLY, IOWA

97

Harry Gamble

NORTH KOSSUTH SENIOR HIGH SCHOOL

98

When reflecting upon my high school years at North Kossuth, it is not difficult for me to name Harry Gamble as a teacher who has had a positive impact on my life. As my grammar and composition teacher for four years, Mr. Gamble not only taught me the fundamentals of English, but he taught me fundamentals of life as well.

In the classroom, Mr. Gamble instructed in explicit detail the English language and its usage. I, along with my classmates, spent many hours writing and rewriting until the work met his standards. Papers and speeches had to fall within the length or time requirements, or your grade would suffer. This process not only taught excellent grammar skills, but it taught discipline and precision as well. Mr. Gamble enjoyed keeping his students alert by encouraging them to be aware of what was going on around them. His bonus questions for quizzes often concerned current events or quiz directions contained loopholes simply to see how observant students were. I failed a quiz once by placing all the correct answers in all the wrong answer spaces, simply because I didn't look to see how the answer sheet was numbered. To this day,

137

I read instructions word-for-word and am often commended for my attention to detail—all a result of Mr. Gamble's quiz.

I chose to pursue an education in the field of public relations after high school, a decision I relate directly with my experiences in Mr. Gamble's classroom. He taught me to enjoy writing and speaking and to appreciate the talents I have. His words of approval were present, but he was careful not to overdo it, for he didn't want me to think that I had ever reached perfection. There was always something I could be doing better.

Mr. Gamble has influenced the lives of many students throughout his career at North Kossuth, and he continues to do so with each day he teaches. I can honestly say that if I didn't have Mr. Gamble as a teacher, I probably wouldn't have been as successful in college as I have been. In my opinion, Mr. Gamble is by far one of the finest teachers I have ever had the pleasure of meeting.

Kathryn R. Heldorfer

SENIOR HONORS STUDENT, UNIVERSITY OF SOUTH DAKOTA
VERMILLION, SOUTH DAKOTA

99

Marilyn Aden

NORTH LINN SENIOR HIGH SCHOOL

100

My high school teacher, Marilyn Aden, coached a team of "winners." Just ask her. As the leader of my high school speech team, she guided me through four years of competition and taught me many valuable lessons.

Through her persuasive skills, Mrs. Aden brought a young guy on board the competitive speech team. I still reflect and ask myself what potential Mrs. Aden saw in me as a freshman. After all, I was the standard 13-year-old kid. Regardless, my participation on the team is one of my most rewarding experiences. It developed self-confidence, a feeling of competence, and increased my abilities to express thoughts verbally. In total, she taught me to be a more effective communicator.

Although Mrs. Aden viewed speech competitions as important events, her priorities remained in the welfare of her students. My most memorable occasions are of Mrs. Aden's predictable pep talks. A competition never passed without her standing at the front of the bus, looking back at her students, growing a huge and sincere grin, and reminding us of her priority. She always proudly and with heart proclaimed, "Your are all winners. You have made it this far."

139

Beyond high school, Mrs. Aden's influence continues to affect my life. My high school competitive speech experience fueled a collegiate major in communication, developed my skills needed to intern as a television news reporter, and motivated me to attain my Iowa High School Speech Association judging certificate. Now, when judging speech contests or living my daily life, I remember the advice of Mrs. Aden. "You are all winners. You have made it this far."

So, as I prepare to graduate from college with degrees in public communications and political science, Mrs. Aden needs to know that she is a winner and has helped me make it this far.

Jason Zabokrtsky

STUDENT, LUTHER COLLEGE
DECORAH, IOWA

101

Miss Kuhn
WALKER ELEMENTARY SCHOOL, WALKER

Rita Houlihan
Leigh Fleming
NORTH LINN SENIOR HIGH SCHOOL

102

L ike many others, I would have difficulty identifying only one teacher who had a significant influence in my life. Three teachers contributed important aspects to my life and my work in education.

The first was Miss Kuhn, sixth-grade teacher at Walker School. She taught me the value of work—hard work. Miss Kuhn seemed to be, in my eyes, the hardest teacher; she required the most work of anyone I had ever experienced. She had spelling tests constantly. She also made us stand up and recite Presidents of the United States, the Gettysburg Address, and the Preamble to the Constitution. All of those activities and the homework that she kept giving us taught me the value of work. I learned that whatever I did the rest of my life was going to require work.

How could Miss Kuhn give all that work and get away with it? Well, first of all you had to understand that Miss Kuhn had been at Walker probably since the exis-

141

tence of Walker. She also had my father in sixth grade. The whole community knew that Miss Kuhn was going to make you work. Not until the end of the year, when she took the whole class out to Betty's Grove where we had a picnic, did we find out that she smiled and she was "kind of nice." But there was no question in her mind or her students' minds that success in life would involve work, hard work.

The second teacher that had an important impact on my life was my high school mathematics instructor. Miss Rita Houlihan helped me decide to become a math teacher. Miss Houlihan taught me patience and to go back and try again. She motivated me to rework problems until I came up with the correct answers. "Look at your problems carefully, find out where the mistakes are, and always review your work," she stressed. These two important lessons built my knowledge base in mathematics and helped me succeed later in life. Miss Rita Houlihan, who I had for four years, taught me that "stick-to-itiveness" was important to future success.

The third teacher who had a significant impact on me was a teacher fresh out of college. His name was Leigh Fleming. He was a music teacher, filled with excitement and enthusiasm, who would have a significant influence on students. Leigh Fleming instilled in me an appreciation of the classics. This was a valuable lesson that I have carried with me all my life. Mr. Fleming taught us the importance of experiencing new and different challenges. He used classical music and drama events to expand our horizons. Those are experiences I never would have gotten if it hadn't been for Mr. Fleming.

These three teachers taught me not only subject matter, not only facts and figures and textbook content, but they taught me valuable lessons of life. They taught and modeled hard work. They taught me patience and perseverance. They taught me to always expand my horizons. These things are valuable lessons of life.

I have spent my life trying to instill these concepts into my students. Miss Kuhn, Miss Houlihan, and Mr. Fleming have not only influenced my life, but they've influenced thousands of my students as well. What more valuable lessons could we provide for the next generation?

Robert J. Gilchrist

PRESIDENT, IOWA STATE EDUCATION ASSOCIATION, AND
TEACHER AND COACH, LINN–MAR COMMUNITY SCHOOL DISTRICT
MARION, IOWA

103

Ogden Faculty

OGDEN SCHOOLS

104

Rather than think back to my school days, I would like to comment, if I may, about our current teachers in Ogden.

Since my retirement in 1986, I have tried to relay to my community some of the many benefits that come from living in a caring environment.

Certainly high on my list has been my association with the faculty in Ogden. I have served on several citizen committees and have been so impressed with the caring attitude of the staff. Their concern is certainly of the students and not of the paycheck. Curriculum is of constant concern.

In my assignments on church boards and with civic outreach programs I am always sitting beside many of the faculty who are there to volunteer to make Ogden a step ahead with local concern.

Finally, I am so impressed with the continued effort of the faculty to communicate with the school district families and to foster an understanding of school policy and direction.

Dean M. Ohlson

RETIRED PHARMACIST
OGDEN, IOWA

Ralph Dillon
Randy Wright
OSKALOOSA HIGH SCHOOL

105

A native Iowan who has had a major influence in the field of movie animation and special effects credits two high school teachers for helping him get where he is.

Scott "Zax" Dow graduated from Oskaloosa Senior High School in 1978. He participated in the marching band and took part in musicals and plays. Now he works in Los Angeles, producing computerized special effects, industrial videos, and regional television commercials. And he teaches others how to do animations at the American Film Institute in Hollywood.

Dow's story was distributed to newspapers nationwide by the Associated Press (AP) after first appearing in his hometown paper, the *Oskaloosa Herald*. The AP reported that Dow has created his special effects and digital visuals in a home-based animation studio.

Dow was born in Ottumwa. In 1975, his parents bought the Chief Mahaska Restaurant in Oskaloosa and operated it for 20 years. Dow says his attraction to animation and the world of visual display resulted from the wit and wisdom of two Oskaloosa teachers.

145

"Ralph Dillon was not one of my teachers, but he was very much a part of my life," Dow explained. "He taught my dad science when he was in high school and was a substitute teacher in my day. He invoked the spirit of play. He said science was nothing to be afraid of, that science should be respected, yes, but should be fun."

"And Randy Wright, my theater teacher in high school, gave me the chance on stage to find out what I could do," Dow told the AP.

For the movie *Precious Find*, Dow designed a 20-story, pentagon-shaped space station and the lighting for it. He also used his computer to create digital "extras"—animated characters that replace live extras.

Dow has also done interactive demos for Microsoft, Intel, Lexmark, Quantum, and others plus many industrial videos. Perhaps his most widely viewed productions are the animated football game plays for weekly NFL broadcasts on the Fox television network.

Rewritten by William L. Sherman from an AP news story that appeared in the *Omaha World-Herald*, March 6, 1996.

106

146

Bob Witzenburg

PEKIN COMMUNITY HIGH SCHOOL

107

The teachers I had when I was young were so important in shaping my educational and career success. It is a very difficult task to select one teacher who has excited a positive influence in my life. I have been fortunate to have had many terrific teachers who have made it possible for me to be where I am now. To all of them, I would like to say thank you.

The teacher I have chosen to talk about is Mr. Bob Witzenburg. Mr. Witzenburg played a very important role in my high school education. He taught chemistry, advanced chemistry, and physics. I am now an optometrist and these particular subjects have been a fundamental part of my undergraduate and graduate education. He made these difficult subjects more interesting and learnable. He was very knowledgeable in these areas and, more importantly, he was very good at explaining it to his students. He provided me with a very solid background in these subjects, which made the college-level courses much easier to handle. He also taught me how to study. Learning these study skills really prepared me for college and, later, optometry school.

147

In addition to his excellent teaching abilities, Mr. Witzenburg was also a very nice person. He was easy to talk to, eager to answer questions, and always willing to help his students learn. He was also encouraging and supportive to me when I expressed interest in becoming a doctor.

I haven't seen or spoken with Mr. Witzenburg for a long time, but I hope he knows how important he was to me.

Laurie Collett, OD

OPTOMETRIST
CHICAGO, ILLINOIS

108

Ray Doorenbos

PELLA HIGH SCHOOL

109

Throughout my years in the Pella Community Schools, mathematics was always my favorite area of study. Starting in elementary school, where some of my teachers encouraged individualized programs to allow students to learn at their own pace, I gained confidence in my academic potential. In middle school, my teachers' unique styles of teaching showed all students that math could be interesting and fun. Talented teachers made math that was becoming intangible more concrete and easier to understand.

It was through high school math, though, that I became especially confident and prepared for the academic challenges of my premedical courses in college. I was fortunate to have Ray Doorenbos for four years of high school classes of math and computer science, shortly before his retirement in 1984.

The atmosphere of Mr. Doorenbos's classroom was unique compared to the average high school classroom. There was a level of intensity present that did not allow for discipline problems. Mr. Doorenbos's personal style of perfection and diligence transferred to each of us when we were under his direction. He challenged us to

149

perform at our greatest potential, which was now necessary to master the more difficult material of the college preparatory classes he was teaching. Because of his expertise in communicating difficult concepts, we were able to excel in these classes. The confidence and self-satisfaction we gained propelled a majority of my classmates and me to excel at the next level of our education.

Despite the respect that he received, Mr. Doorenbos was also very kind-hearted, patient, and approachable. He was available to us outside of class and even the school day for extra help. He was very devoted to us, his students. He cared about each of us as individuals and encouraged us, whether male or female, to set our goals high. Then, years later, he was genuinely interested in hearing how we had reached those goals.

Mr. Doorenbos was also a leader in initiating computer education at Pella High School. At a time in his life when nearing retirement could have consumed his mind, he became the first teacher of computer programming. Computers became his passion personally and this was shared with us in the classroom.

Although Mr. Doorenbos never had children of his own, he certainly left a legacy in the lives of hundreds of Pella students.

Lori Vander Leest Wenzel, MD

OBGYN ASSOCIATES
IOWA CITY, IOWA

Roxine Hild

GLADBROOK–REINBECK HIGH SCHOOL

110

I don't know many people my age that make it a point to stop by and visit a former teacher whenever they can. I guess that says a lot about Mrs. Roxine Hild, my high school math teacher.

When I was asked to participate in this book, there was no doubt who I would be writing about. Mrs. Hild's name jumped in there right away. But just like back in high school, I have waited until the last minute to complete this chore. I only hope it does her justice.

Her true strength lies not with her ability to instruct children on how to crunch numbers and balance equations, but to learn about themselves. At a time in your life when you have a lot of doubts, Mrs. Hild was always there to guide you along. Mostly through her "no nonsense" attitude and way of doing things. She gave each student the latitude to be a strong individual while at the same time making sure that he or she was a focused part of the group.

The teenager's creed in high school is "I'll never use this stuff, so why do I have to learn it?" In some aspects it's true. To date, I don't think I have ever used the Pythagorean theorem or bisected angles since leaving her class, but I can now tell

151

you that there is something I picked up in her classroom that I use every day—a better sense of myself.

She would always give me this look if I acted up or became frustrated with the problem in front of me. The glance let me know that she wasn't buying it—that she knew I was just testing her—and, more importantly, she wasn't going to let me. If I honestly didn't understand, she was more than ready to come to my desk and help me out as an individual or put it on the overhead to help me work it through with the group. I guess that says it all right there. She taught me how to solve problems and how to come at a problem from a variety of directions—and that's something I use every single day.

More importantly, I consider her my friend. Her support and friendship mean a great deal to me even though we only speak a handful of times each year. But each time, the friendship and relationship grows a little more.

Thanks, Mrs. Hild.

Craig Rickert

SPORTS ANCHOR/REPORTER, KWWL-TV
WATERLOO, IOWA

Lewis Bredeson

RICEVILLE HIGH SCHOOL

112

I am honored to write about Mr. Lewis Bredeson, my high school history teacher and principal. Without his guidance, I doubt if I would be where I am today.

When I was in grade school and high school, I knew I wanted to teach more than anything else. At that time, one could prepare to be a one-room school teacher by taking certain courses in high school. I began this program my junior year.

One noon hour, just prior to 1 p.m. classes, Mr. Bredeson walked up to my desk and said, "Weston, don't you want to go on to college?" I answered immediately in the affirmative. "Why are you taking normal training courses? Would you not rather like to teach at the high school level?"

In five minutes, I knew my answer. I walked up to his desk and informed him I was dropping my normal training curriculum and would have as my goal to be a high school music teacher!

I would have been happy as a one-room school teacher, I know. But where would that have led me? Mr. Bredeson was a graduate of Luther College. The infer-

153

ence is obvious. Forty-seven years later as a member of the faculty of Luther, I still re-member that 12:50 p.m. encounter with a man who changed the direction of my life!

Weston H. Noble

DIRECTOR OF MUSIC, LUTHER COLLEGE
DECORAH, IOWA

113

154

Paul Filter

ROCKFORD HIGH SCHOOL

114

The best testimonial to a teacher I ever wrote is in my book *Just Beyond the Firelight.* The piece is called "Leonard." It's about one of my instructors at Northern Iowa who encouraged me to pursue a doctorate at the University of Indiana and then return to teach at UNI.

In addition, my high school coach, Paul Filter, was not only a fine coach, he also was a serious classroom teacher. In my senior year, when it became clear to him that I was going to become an all-state basketball player and receive college scholarship offers, he took me aside and had this to say (I'm paraphrasing, of course, since the event happened 40 years ago):

In the long run, basketball is not important, and you must begin preparing yourself for a life beyond basketball. I repeat: It's not important. You don't think so now, but it's true.

It only took me another two years to figure out he was correct. He's one of a

155

handful of people who changed my life, and I still keep in touch with him. His words got me out of short pants and into life.

Robert Waller

AUTHOR AND FORMER TEACHER AND DEAN,
COLLEGE OF BUSINESS, UNIVERSITY OF NORTHERN IOWA
LIVING ON A RANCH IN WEST TEXAS

115

Frances "Fannie" Vacha

ST. ANSGAR MIDDLE SCHOOL

116

My life has been blessed by good schools and great teachers. My start came at St. Ansgar Community School, where from 1947 to 1959 some of Iowa's most dedicated public school teachers nurtured my classmates and me along—Mae Chancellor, Joe and Margaret Jordahl, and Frances "Fannie" Vacha.

Along the way I've been lucky enough to study under the best of the best: At the University of Iowa, physicist James Van Allen and poet Paul Engle; at Columbia University in New York City, philosopher Jacques Barzun; and at Harvard Law School in Cambridge, Massachusetts, constitutional scholar Archibald Cox. I even married a teacher, Professor Karen A. Conner of Drake University in Des Moines.

But the very best of the best was Fannie Vacha (rhymes with ha ha), my sixth-grade teacher at St. Ansgar Middle School.

Fannie was the arch-typical Iowa schoolteacher of her generation.

Born in 1881 of Bohemian emigrants to Iowa, Fannie was a beloved pioneer teacher who taught for 51 years in the St. Ansgar Community Schools, from 1904 to 1955. She was a legend in my hometown. A natural teacher known for her strict dis-

157

cipline and perfect penmanship, Fannie taught three generations of many families in our community. My mother, Norma, had Fannie in the sixth grade in the 1920s; I had Fannie for my sixth grade in the 1950s. So did hundreds of youngsters in between.

When Fannie died in 1963 at age 81 she left a treasured legacy aptly characterized in her obituary published by the weekly *St. Ansgar Enterprise:* Fannie's "outstanding quality was her ability to make her pupils feel they were worthwhile and although prospects looked very unpromising at times, she never seemed to lose faith in them. She placed that importance on the worth of the individual. Her untiring efforts to assist and advance the pupils who were slightly backward in grades, will long be remembered."

A spinster and avid gardener, who never drove a car or enjoyed indoor plumbing, Fannie made the ultimate pronouncement on her faith in education after her death in 1963. In her will, Fannie left her entire estate–$121,500–to help complete construction of a new high school in my hometown. The grateful citizens of St. Ansgar remembered her with an honorary plaque placed in the new school.

Fannie's remarkable faith in education and love of and dedication to her pupils is the very stuff that has made Iowa's public schools the envy of the nation.

Gary G. Gerlach

PUBLISHER, *THE* (AMES) *DAILY TRIBUNE*
AMES, IOWA

Henry Geery

SAYDEL HIGH SCHOOL

It is difficult for me to identify a teacher who has had a positive influence in my life because there have been several. From the Roberta Menoughs and Charles Nagles of elementary school to the Dave Hansens and Pete Cramers of junior high, numerous teachers have served as role models and inspirations for me. Doug Larche, a drama instructor and football coach (how's that for a combination?) taught me that it was okay to enjoy athletics and drama. Gene McCurdy (math) and Mildred Cox (English) expected more of me than I expected of myself. Gail Wiederholt nurtured my creativity during her writing class. Believe me, there were many others and I hesitate to name the aforementioned for fear of leaving some out. But the schoolteacher that impacted my life the most was Henry Geery.

Mr. Geery was a government and economics teacher at Saydel High School. I remember taking a nine-week course in the social studies curriculum during the third quarter of my senior year. I had at least five or six credits beyond what was necessary for graduation, but this course was required for graduation under school policies. I went to class every day, but I did none of the daily assignments. When the final exam was given, I scored the highest in the class with a perfect paper. Assuming that my grade would be less because I hadn't done the required daily work, I was stunned and outraged that he had the nerve to **fail** me for the entire course. This meant that I would have to repeat the course during the fourth quarter, thereby removing that "free period" from my final quarter schedule. I schmoozed, argued, pleaded, and begged, but Mr. Geery would not give in.

As one might guess, I repeated the course and did the daily work. As Mr. Geery called me to his desk to review my grade just prior to the final exam, he asked me what I had learned from the experience. I told him that each of us is responsible for his/her own choices and the resulting consequences of those choices. With that he smiled, gave me an "A" and excused me from the final exam.

To this day I don't remember the exact content of that course, but the lesson(s) that Henry Geery taught during that class remain with me.

I attended Henry Geery's funeral on the 4th of July about three years ago. As I listened to the various eulogies, it was obvious that Mr. Geery influenced many lives, much the same as he had mine.

Timothy Pratt, CFP

AMERICAN EXPRESS FINANCIAL ADVISORS
WEST DES MOINES, IOWA

Velma Ady

SHENANDOAH HIGH SCHOOL

118

Mrs. Ady was a real lady. She taught sophomore English and American literature. She was also assistant principal in charge of the junior high school. Everyone learned in her class and, at the same time, enjoyed it. She was a woman of small stature, yet commanded respect and could discipline easily. She was well liked by students and yet she wasn't "one of the kids," as some tried to be.

Betty Jane Rankin Shaw

PRESIDENT, EARL MAY SEED AND NURSERY
SHENANDOAH, IOWA

George Haws

SHENANDOAH HIGH SCHOOL

119

My father, Herman Offenburger, died of a heart attack while shoveling snow on Christmas Eve in 1961. I was 14 and a freshman in high school in Shenandoah in southwest Iowa, and it had never even occurred to me that I might lose Dad so early.

My mother, Anna Offenburger, did an amazing job of seeing me and my younger sister on through our high school and college years.

But I'm pretty sure now that if a very special teacher hadn't taken a special interest in me soon after Dad died, I might well have strayed during high school. I probably would not have been as attentive to my studies, as responsible and enthusiastic on my job as a sportswriter for the *Shenandoah Evening Sentinel,* or as loyal and respectful to Mom as I was.

That teacher is George Haws, although 35 years later I can still barely call him "George." He'll be forever "Coach Haws" in my mind and heart. Coach Haws taught us history in eighth grade, he coached us in football, basketball, and track and he served as Shenandoah High athletic director. So I had regular contact with him, not only in the classroom, but also as I covered the school sports scene.

I spent most of that Christmas vacation after Dad's death at home, grieving. I dreaded going back to school when classes resumed, not knowing what to say to my friends and teachers. But I did go back that first morning.

In my first-hour English class, suddenly the classroom door opened and in walked Coach Haws. "Mr. Hufford," he asked, "can I have Chuck Offenburger for a few minutes?" He motioned me to follow him out of the classroom. "Let's go," he said, once we were in the hallway. "We need to talk."

He led me down the stairs, through the ground-floor restroom, on down the steps to the school basement, where the old gym, coaches' office, and boiler room were located. That boiler room was a place where students dared not go, uninvited. He led me in there and closed the door. He pulled out a cigar—first time I'd ever seen him smoke one—lit it and finally said, "Sorry about your Dad."

"Thanks," I said, looking away, trying to stop the tears I was afraid were coming.

"You know, I lost my Dad when I was a freshman in college," Coach Haws said. "He had a heart attack, too. It was sure hard without him, just like it's going to be hard for you without your Dad."

"Uh-huh," I said.

There was a long pause. "I want to tell you something," he said. "I'm going to be watching you. If you need help, tell me—understand?"

"I will, Coach," I said. "Thanks."

"And one more thing," he said.

"Yeah?" I said.

"If you get out of line, it'll be my boot and your butt, you got that?"

163

"Yes," I said, and my tears began giving away to a grin, which I tried like heck to hide.

"Now get on back up to class," he growled.

And that's how it was the rest of my way through high school. I'd talk to him two, three, maybe four times a week. He'd stop me in the hallways to see how I was getting along. He often talked to my mom, making sure I was helping at home.

That's how a friendship was born that continues yet today, years after we both left Shenandoah. George Haws went on to teach and coach at Lewis Central in Council Bluffs and then at Marshalltown, where he retired five years ago. I considered it one of the nicest honors I've ever received when I was asked to speak at his retirement party.

A lot of time has passed since that morning in the boiler room in the basement of Shenandoah High School in early 1962.

I don't know how many times through the years when I've been facing some big problem or decision, I have called Coach Haws or dropped in on him at Marshalltown. "A coach's work is never done," I always tell him on those occasions. "Okay," he'll say. "Sit down and tell me about it." And whatever it is that's been bugging me is always better when I leave him.

Chuck Offenburger

"IOWA BOY" COLUMNIST, *THE DES MOINES REGISTER*
DES MOINES, IOWA

Chleo Weins

SIOUX CITY CENTRAL HIGH SCHOOL

120

Old Sioux City Central High had some inspirational teachers during my three years there (1955–58). But the one who impressed me most was a teacher whose class I never took–Chleo Weins.

I don't even recall meeting him until three years after I graduated. It was the summer of 1961 and Chleo, then 36, was standing in a freight car adjacent a downtown Sioux City warehouse. Shirtless and dripping with sweat, he sure didn't look like a schoolteacher. And the only teaching he did that day was showing the new guy–me–how to move 100-pound bags of sugar and powdered milk from the freight car into the warehouse.

I didn't even know he was a teacher until he mentioned warehouse duty was only a summer job.

"What do you do the rest of the year?"

"I teach math, Central High," he grunted as we lifted a bag.

For a few seconds, I was speechless. I knew what I was doing in the hot, humid warehouse and hotter freight cars: earning some money between semesters at the

165

University of Iowa. But what in the world was a schoolteacher doing there?

"Economic necessity," Chleo said. He explained that satisfying as classroom work was, it just didn't pay enough for him to take the summer off. He had a wife and two sons to support. So he sweated out his "summer vacations" at Bekins Warehouse.

I never saw Chleo Weins again after that warehouse stint. But I thought about him every time the question of teachers' pay came up. To me, he symbolized every underpaid educator who ever toiled during the summer to make ends meet. (Journalists, incidentally, feel they are first cousins to communicators such as teachers and librarians.)

Twenty-nine years ago, when I wanted to write on changes in the teaching profession, I called Chleo for an interview. He brought me up to date. He stayed at Central three more years before moving into administration. He was junior high principal, assistant principal at Sioux City North, and then, until his retirement in 1986, principal at the Career Education Center housed in the old Central Annex.

His summer work experience reads like something out of Jack London: three summers at fill-in duty at Swift and Co., two at Wonder Bread as a bread slicer, two on night security patrol, and six summers at the warehouse.

"On those summer jobs, I never mentioned that I taught," he said. "But the word always seemed to get out. At those places—especially Swift and Co., where I cleaned cut guts and stomachs and carried brains around—it gave people a different concept about teachers. They found out we are human, just like everybody else."

Although Chleo Weins never instructed me in the classroom, he taught me a lot about the teaching profession in the pre–collective bargaining era. It made me appreciate all the talented educators who kept persevering year after year. Those who did, touched thousands of lives.

Jerry Elsea

OPINION PAGE EDITOR, *THE CEDAR RAPIDS GAZETTE*
CEDAR RAPIDS, IOWA

121

122

Loren Straube

SOUTH WINNESHIEK HIGH SCHOOL

Although I encountered very good teachers at South Winneshiek High School, undoubtedly I would not be where I am today had it not been for the support and encouragement of my chemistry/physics teacher, Loren Straube. Mr. Straube was especially good at convincing me that, yes, I could go on and succeed in the field of chemistry. This sort of confidence was extremely important as I got to college and to graduate school, where the level of the people around me got higher. Still, I never felt inferior. Of course, this had a lot to do with the people with whom I was interacting at the time, who were not concerned with *where* I was from, but interested in *what* I could do. However, that I could do it was largely dependent on Mr. Straube's influence.

I think the most convincing aspect of Mr. Straube's teaching comes from the fact that many former South Winneshiek students have gone on to receive advanced degrees in science and medicine. While this is a reflection of the entire math/science department at South Winn, it is largely due to Mr. Straube's influence and his involvement in the UNI Math/Science Symposium. His enthusiasm for this program is obvious and is appreciated by both students and by the UNI faculty.

Although I may be in the minority, I always thought Mr. Straube had a very effective teaching style. Chemistry and physics are difficult subjects, and students' problems are often blamed on poor teaching. However, I always thought Mr. Straube did a very fine job. He always tried to use common, everyday examples to explain complex, microscopic phenomena. In other words, he explained things in words and concepts that we could comprehend. Of course, this would sometimes get him into trouble, as the students would try to carry the analogy too far, but he was always careful to not overstep. I try to use this approach when I teach.

Paul G. Wenthold

RESEARCH ASSOCIATE, UNIVERSITY OF COLORADO
BOULDER, COLORADO

123

Ron Ambroson

TITONKA CONSOLIDATED HIGH SCHOOL

124

I n recalling my days at Titonka Consolidated High School, I can remember several teachers that influenced my views on society and my career choices. In particular, Mr. Ron Ambroson had a great influence in shaping my personality and my career successes.

In the mid-1980s, Mr. Ambroson was teaching government and economics and coaching football at Tyke High School. In the classroom, Mr. Ambroson was an extremely effective teacher who motivated his students through positive comments and actions. He showed a genuine interest in the material he presented and he challenged his classes to appreciate and fully comprehend the subject's value. This devotion to education was clearly evident to his students and it encouraged them to step up their scholastic performances. Although the subject matter was often difficult, I remember that my class always looked forward to attending Mr. Ambroson's classes.

After completing the day's classes, Mr. Ambroson carried his teaching skills to the football field. He excelled at coaxing each athlete to perform at their highest level and he praised each and every player for their efforts. No member of his squad—starter or third-stringer—lacked for attention and words of encouragement. He placed strong emphasis on teamwork and taught us how to work together to achieve a common goal.

The devotion that Mr. Ambroson has for teaching young minds is to be admired. It is critical that high school students interact with positive role models, such as Mr. Ambroson, during a time of development that often sets the tone for the rest of their lives. His examples of leadership and positive teaching techniques have been very influential in my own day-to-day management and guidance of research teams. In summary, the devotion to one's career and motivation to succeed that has been passed on by Mr. Ambroson are universal in nature—and can be applied to life—long after we have completed our high school education.

Charles L. Leeck

POSTDOCTORAL FELLOW/BIOTECHNOLOGY RESEARCH,
UNIVERSITY OF WISCONSIN–MADISON
MADISON, WISCONSIN

125

171

Ken Wulf

TRI-COUNTY COMMUNITY HIGH SCHOOL

I am honored to have the opportunity to help recognize Mr. Ken Wulf as an outstanding Iowa teacher. During my four years (1966–1970) at Tri-County Community High School, I took several of his math courses. Up to this point in my elementary and junior high education, mathematics was not a subject that I enjoyed and found that I struggled through each semester. However, the learning environment changed as a result of Mr. Wulf's dedication and effective teaching skills in the classroom. He would willingly give his free time to help me and other students better understand problem areas. He required his students to be attentive and yet made the lessons interesting so that I wanted to increase my knowledge of mathematics. As a result of his thorough teaching and sincere interest in me, I found his classes my favorite courses and achieved high marks.

His personal interest in his students did not stop in the classroom. His enthusiasm for sports was tremendous, especially girls' basketball. As a player, I can remember him giving us pep talks and being very supportive, whether we won or lost the game. It meant a lot to me and the rest of the team to know he would voluntarily come to our games and keep the statistical records for the coaches. It was quite obvious caring for his students didn't stop in the classroom.

As I look back on those four years of high school, Mr. Wulf did have an impact on my life. Why? Because he believed in me. He provided the learning environment for my self-confidence to grow and not be afraid to tackle new experiences in life. This attitude has served me well over my 22-year career with DuPont Ag Products.

I believe Mr. Wulf is very deserving of this recognition and appreciate being able to give my testimony.

Barb Hervey
U.S. DISTRIBUTION MANAGER, DUPONT AGRICULTURAL PRODUCTS
CHADD'S FORD, PENNSYLVANIA

127

Martin Lundvall

WEST JUNIOR HIGH SCHOOL

128

Throughout grades K–6, academics just didn't seem that high on my list of priorities. Fishing, hunting, sports, and getting into some kind of trouble were higher on my list of things to do. I had a good environment during these years between my parents' guidance and the local YMCA. And yes, the elementary school provided great teachers, but something was lacking to put me in the best direction. My grades and the learning I could have had didn't reflect my ability or what I should have been working for. Maybe it was trust or simply never letting anyone get very close to me during these years.

Once junior high came, organized sports were offered. Looking back on my old report cards, elementary arithmetic didn't go too well. In fact, none of my grades here are worthy of bragging rights, yet one of my teachers in junior high, my math teacher, also coached wrestling. Something clicked here—for not only was I able to excel in wrestling, but I also had that someone who now inspired me in the classroom. I guess it took an outside activity that I wanted to participate in to make me wake up in the classroom.

My positive rapport with Mr. Martin Lundvall away from the classroom gave me a new feeling about teachers in the classroom. I believed in what he said in sports and how he went about it. So in math class, I paid attention as well. I had already known the feeling of being a successful athlete through the YMCA and early years of summer baseball, but listening to teachers somehow didn't seem the same. But now, since one of my coaches also taught me in the classroom, it seemed different. I now started listening, believing, and doing my work in his class as well. I received an above-average grade in math at this time and finally realized that winning in the classroom had similar feelings that winning and participating in sports had been giving me.

This spread to other class work and now all my teachers seemed more like coaches instead of just teachers. I tried harder now because the relationship was different from this point on. It came at a great time because now, sports and class work and coaches and teachers seemed more alike. All of my grades and learning from this point forward were very respectable (well above the average)—in fact with honors—often through junior high, high school, college, and graduate school. As well, my relationship with my future coaches and success in my sport stayed at the highest.

Even more importantly—in my profession of coaching and, as well, in raising my family—the same lessons learned in early junior high in math class from Martin Lundvall, my junior high wrestling coach, have given me the opportunity to believe, listen, and achieve for those influenced by me.

Dan Gable

WRESTLING COACH, UNIVERSITY OF IOWA
IOWA CITY, IOWA

Robert "Bob" Siddens

WEST HIGH SCHOOL

129

Mr. Bob Siddens is a teacher who I have never forgotten. He had a major impact in my life, instilling basic moral and personal characteristics that I have utilized time and time again.

It is trivial to say that he was just a strong motivator at a very influential time in young people's lives—he was so much more.

He stressed to always believe in yourself and set no limitations. You and only you could limit the vast future which lay ahead. "Dedicate yourself to a cause" still rings in my ears as I look back on words of wisdom from Mr. Siddens.

But, more importantly, he taught me that perseverance is the majority of the battle—in life, in school, and in sports. To persevere through all adversity is the key to obtaining success. I found this to be so true in both my professional and personal life.

Words that had impact and meaning shaping the lives of thousands of young people is what Bob Siddens did best.

Thank you, Bob Siddens!

John R. Rooff III

MAYOR, CITY OF WATERLOO
WATERLOO, IOWA

130

Carl Dillon

WAVERLY-SHELL ROCK SENIOR HIGH SCHOOL

Carl Dillon's enthusiasm for literature was infectious. That, along with his winning personality, helped him reach a wide diversity of students.

He certainly influenced me. He encouraged me to write! Little did I know that writing would become a basic tool of my daily work as a broadcast journalist. Or that I would one day author a book!

I met Carl Dillon when I moved to Waverly from New York City. I was a junior in high school. I had attended a private prep school, which prided itself as one of the finest such schools in America. Its teachers were mostly Ivy League–educated. So, when I arrived in Waverly, I was a typically provincial New Yorker–apprehensive about the quality of teaching I'd encounter in small-town Iowa.

My first class with Carl Dillon dispelled those fears. But even more important than his teaching skills were the intangibles he brought to the classroom. He cared for his students. They sensed that, so discipline was never a problem. And he managed to cultivate the unique abilities of each student. To my mind, that's the highest testimonial a teacher can receive.

    I'm honored to have this opportunity to publicly thank Carl Dillon for his positive influence on my life and my career.

John Bachman

NEWSCENTER 13 REPORTER/ANCHOR, WHO–TV
DES MOINES, IOWA

132

133

Alice Armbruster
Geneva Gorsuch
Mary Hubbard
Ardeth Jameson

WEBSTER CITY JUNIOR AND SENIOR HIGH SCHOOLS

It is not easy to limit a statement of the numerous fine teachers I had while going through the Webster City public schools. I will, but not without acknowledging the contributions several made to my upbringing. This was a serious task for them given my proclivities that did not lead entirely to academic stardom.

As I think about these people, they all helped me be successful, not because of their insistence on doing my assignments or working harder on my lessons, but because they obviously cared about me, about my doing well, and pressing me to expand my views and experiences.

The junior–senior high school music teacher, Miss Alice Armbruster (she was quietly known as Trixie), introduced me to vocal chamber music in a madrigal ensemble and choral music, which is still with me today. I completed a BA in music at Grinnell College.

Mrs. Geneva Gorsuch, my high school English teacher in grammar—the real kind with diagraming and all—pushed me to enter extemporaneous speaking in the state contests. She coached me after school and I received a superior rating as a sophomore.

A high school speech teacher, Mary Hubbard, coached our debate team entirely after hours to insure our preparation for successful state contests.

And finally, Mrs. Ardeth Jameson, speech and drama, allowed me to attend a performance of Charles Laughton's production of *John Brown's Body* by Steven Vincent Benet. It opened the world of serious drama to me, although my subsequent work dealt mostly with musical theater and opera.

They were significant to me then and now because they gave me some of themselves—they cared enough to help me be successful.

Robert G. Crumpton

EXECUTIVE SECRETARY, OREGON EDUCATION ASSOCIATION

TIGARD, OREGON

134   181

Mrs. Stevens
Mr. Wedeking

A s I think back to my school years, I believe that each of my teachers had a positive influence in my life.

In 1948, when I was just three years old, I was paralyzed on one side from polio. I spent nine months at St. Vincent's Hospital in Sioux City. I was released when our hospital building was condemned, but I still needed a lot of physical therapy. Consequently, when I started kindergarten, I wore special shoes and was not able to keep up physically with all of my classmates.

The fourth grade was one of my most difficult years. My parents had to drive me to school many days as I always found an excuse to miss the bus. Mrs. Stevens was very kind and understanding to a shy, handicapped little girl and helped me overcome my many social obstacles and, once again, be able to enjoy my classmates.

Mr. Wedeking, my business and accounting teacher, made my business courses a real challenge. I soon realized my desire was to work with figures and people. When I enrolled at Mankato Business School in Mankato, Minnesota, the courses were easy for me since I had an excellent high school teacher. Only when I observed the many other students really struggling did I fully appreciate Mr. Wedeking's driving efforts and ability to instill in us a desire to do work well and understand what we are learning. A job worth doing is worth doing well! He demanded perfection in such a way that we strived to fulfill his expectations.

During my high school years, I had to struggle to learn to be quiet and listen during class. One of my teachers moved me to the back of the room so I wouldn't disturb the whole class, and one even dismissed me from his class for a day. Mr. Wedeking informed me that of the eight Gerber girls he had already taught, I was the worst when it came to talking. However, I believe I should have been graded on my talking as I now get paid well to communicate with my customers. I am now the vice president of our country bank. Being able to communicate with my customers is as important as understanding their numbers that help them make their business decisions.

Delores Gerber

VICE PRESIDENT, IOWA STATE BANK
WEST BEND, IOWA

Bob Reed

WEST DELAWARE MIDDLE SCHOOL

For me, I think 1964 was probably the year several things started to take on a new look. Although I was a good student, decent athlete, and a truly nice guy, it took an eye test during Mr. Reed's eighth-grade civics class to find out I couldn't see. After getting my first pair of "cheaters," two things immediately happened—I could sit in the back of the class instead of having to sit in the front, and I sported the "Buddy Holly" look with those classy, new black frames. However, the reason I'm writing this is because Bob Reed was (and remains to this day) the teacher who has had the greatest positive influence on my life.

It is a very hard task to pick my "favorite" teacher because I really liked school—mainly due to the fact that West Delaware has always employed great teachers. There are lots of my teachers who could be my favorite—some because they were funny, others because they were interesting, and maybe some who were really pretty. It's amazing how much I liked English during my senior year, due to the "youth" of Miss Kerr! However, eighth grade was that transition year between being a junior high

"Mohawk" and a senior high "Manhawk." Junior high was a time when we boys started noticing the girls a little differently, and when we were able to impress them (or so we thought) with our newfound athletic prowess.

I think that's probably why Bob Reed comes to my mind first for this article, since in addition to being my civics teacher, he was also my first real coach. Although probably a guy thing, looking back 30 years I find all of my coaches hold fond memories with me. This may be due to the fact that, back then, all of the coaches were teachers, which put us into daily contact with them.

Even though Mr. Reed was not a large man in size, he was the biggest man I knew, next to my dad. Mr. Reed had my respect from the first day we met. He was firm and tough, but fair. He expected discipline to be maintained—but that was easy since he never expected us to know or do anything that he didn't. He took my little eighth-grade brain—void of any knowledge of what civics even was—and made it hungry to know more. In fact, the only nonsports scrapbook that I ever kept was my eighth-grade civics scrapbook. It has since been misplaced through moving, but by accident and not by design!

I chuckle every once in awhile when I think of the only bad advice Mr. Reed ever gave me. He said, "Max, if you ever have a problem, just write your congressman and he will help you out." I have forgiven him for that one!

I am a salesman by trade, and provide an important service for the community. But my job doesn't hold a candle to the important needs a teacher fills—teachers (right or wrong) are held to a higher standard than most other people. Teachers are role models that have to exude positive influences over their students. When they accomplish that feat, the student will be like me when they grow up—they will be able to remember all of the teachers they had. If I was not engaged in a family business, I would like to be a teacher—just like Mr. Reed.

Max Boren

SALESMAN
MANCHESTER, IOWA

138

Jerry Kinney

VALLEY HIGH SCHOOL

139

Jerry Kinney was my elementary and high school band leader and teacher. In elementary school, he came to our class and demonstrated a few instruments and, from that point on, my life was changed. I do not consider myself a musician anymore, but I will always be a proud member of Jerry Kinney's marching band. Mr. Kinney taught us to play and appreciate music. He also taught us how to be a part of a team.

Mr. Kinney's greatest gift wasn't only that he taught us to work hard. He held high expectations for each of us. He taught commitment to practicing and to making the band the best it could be.

What I remember the most about band was that he made practice a fun time. When it was time to be serious, we were serious and we did well. However, during the down time, you would see Mr. Kinney talking, joking, teasing students, or being teased himself.

He seemed to know what everyone was capable of accomplishing and how to help them reach their potential. He treated each student with respect and he always expressed a genuine interest in each of us as a person.

187

I can think of several teachers who had an impact on my public school career. I was very fortunate to be a student in the West Des Moines Community School District. For me, the world became a much brighter, more interesting place when Jerry Kinney became an integral part of my education.

To this day, I am always excited to see him and I have always wanted to find the right moment to thank him for helping me to become the person I am today.

Thank you for giving me the opportunity to say publicly, "Mr. Kinney, you were a very special person in my life and I just want to say thanks for being my teacher!"

Gerald D. Page

PRINCIPAL, WESTRIDGE ELEMENTARY SCHOOL
WEST DES MOINES, IOWA

140

188

Dorothy Holmberg

BRITT HIGH SCHOOL

Several teachers (and professors) stick out in my mind as "favorites"—those who you felt really cared about you and learning and what might happen to your life. To them, teaching was more than a job—much more. And it showed.

One very special teacher was Dorothy Holmberg, who came from Decorah during World War II to teach at Britt in northern Iowa. A Luther College grad, as I recall.

At the time, I was a farm boy with a most uncertain future. I knew I loved to read and write, and received good grades in English, but I didn't know where such things might take me. Somehow, in her classes, writing as a career became a distant hope. Miss Holmberg's unbridled enthusiasm (in the classroom or directing the junior and senior class plays) sort of rubbed off on some of us.

In the end, I was to spend my career putting words together, for nearly 40 years, on daily newspapers in Marshalltown, Omaha, and Des Moines.

Her influence came during a critical growing-up time in my life. And, I never forgot her.

P.S. Nearly half a century later, I still remember the name of our senior class play, for which she picked me for the lead role. It was *Grandad Steps Out.*

Don Muhm

FARM EDITOR (RETIRED), *THE DES MOINES REGISTER*
DES MOINES, IOWA

142

Vicki Kingsbury

WEST MONONA JUNIOR–SENIOR HIGH SCHOOL

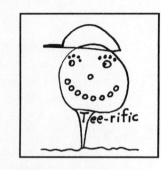

143

When I think back to high school I remember life being so incredibly easy and stress-free, except for one little glitch–tenth grade speech class. I had never experienced so much work and stress in a classroom as I did that year in Vicki Kingsbury's speech class. Mrs. Kingsbury's well-known phrase was, "It's here, it's now, it's real, people!"

I used to think that phrase was a little over-dramatic, but once the real world slapped me in the face, I soon realized it wasn't dramatic enough. Vicki Kingsbury was teaching us how to survive in a demanding society. She forced us to go beyond the assignment, to strive for excellence and not settle for mediocrity. Vicki Kingsbury taught me how to be an individual. Thinking for myself and being confident enough to express those thoughts are traits that I learned in tenth grade speech class.

I recently graduated from college and, as I was looking for a job, my first thought was, IT'S HERE, IT'S NOW, IT'S REAL! Even though finding that first job is a stressful venture, I felt prepared to do so, because of the confidence that Vicki had

191

instilled within me. I finally hooked that "first job" and find that I am constantly pushing myself to do better. Mediocrity is just not acceptable. If Vicki Kingsbury had not motivated me at a young age to go beyond my own expectations, I would probably be wearing a paper hat right now and asking if you wanted fries with that order. Thanks to Vicki, my boss is not Ronald McDonald, and I'm confident that he never will be.

I had several great teachers while attending grade and high school, but no one held a candle to Vicki Kingsbury. She forced me to find myself and to mold that person into an ambitious, confident individual. I used to think that she was too demanding and expected too much of her students, but she was preparing us for life beyond high school—and for that, I thank her.

Jennifer Samson
MONONA COUNTY ZONING AND
ENVIRONMENTAL HEALTH ADMINISTRATOR
ONAWA, IOWA

144

192

Margaret Koob

HAWARDEN RURAL SCHOOL

145

Miss Margaret Koob really influenced the future of this teacher-to-be with her capable handling of children and the deep concern she had for each child. She was totally dedicated to her job and devoted herself entirely to the education and development of each individual.

There were 17 children in this one-room rural school in all eight grades. In the short time that I spent in that environment, I was totally impressed with how she imparted to each of their young minds the importance of their learning and how she instilled in their young hearts the ways of kindness, sympathy, and compassion for others.

Throughout my 50 years of educating young children, I can honestly say that until my retirement in June 1992, hardly a day went by that I didn't think of Miss Koob and the extraordinary impact she made in my meager training to go out into the world and mold young lives and minds.

Kathleen Ronan Tomjack

TEACHER (RETIRED)
ROCK RAPIDS, IOWA

193

Evelyn Wood

146

Arriving at college was, at once, exhilarating, intimidating, and suspenseful for me, having come from a rural southwestern Iowa town. I graduated from a class of seven. My only brush with academic science was a test tube displayed in the hallway trophy case. Any potential for success in arithmetic had been forever vanquished by an elementary teacher convinced that such skills were the inherent domain of boys and men.

Nevertheless, I wanted to be a teacher, and I wanted to taste life outside my sheltered, small-town existence.

It was my freshman advisor at the University of Northern Iowa, Evelyn Wood, who sensed both my fears and my wish to burst forth with confidence.

She checked my first quarter grades. Then, by assuring me that I could have reasonable expectations for being a good student, she provided the spark for confidence-building and dream-shaping. The boost she gave with that initial assessment was followed by more. She instilled a feeling that I could always take problems to her. She provided the personal interest I needed upon entering that huge, unknown

194

college world. She expanded my view of the possibilities for women every time she shared her experiences as a WAVE, and before I graduated, she encouraged me to stay connected to a support system.

Her involvement in the WAVEs was almost mind-boggling to me. Here was a woman (and women were "supposed" to be farm wives, secretaries, nurses, or teachers!) doing highly responsible work in far-off places in wartime—the height of an intimidating situation!

Conversations with Evelyn Wood helped me set new sights. The support system she suggested was the American Association of University Women, a membership which later ushered in my lifelong and enthusiastic commitment to community involvement, leadership, and concern for issues beyond my own private world.

Joy Corning
LIEUTENANT GOVERNOR OF IOWA
DES MOINES, IOWA

TEACHERS

Carolyn Warner

FORMER ARIZONA SUPERINTENDENT
OF PUBLIC INSTRUCTION

Give me your hungry children, your sick children, your homeless and abused children.

Give me your children who need love as badly as they need learning.

Give me your children who have talents and gifts and skills.

Give me your children who have none.

Give them all to me, in whatever form they come, and the people within these walls will help

give you the doctors and the engineers and the scientists and the lawyers and the ministers and the teachers of tomorrow.

We will give you the mothers and the fathers, the thinkers and the builders, the artists and the dreamers.

We will give you the nation of tomorrow.

We will give you the future of Iowa.

We will give you the American Dream.

This poem was presented by the author at the ISEA Summer Leadership Workshop in August 1995.

School Districts

Iowa Teachers

Contributors

Student Artists and Their Teachers

1. **KINGPHET LOVAN**
   Grade 5, Granger Elementary School
   Des Moines
   Teacher: Mary Beth Shambaugh

2. **MARY WALZ**
   Grade 12, Burlington Community High School
   Burlington
   Teacher: Richard Anderson

3. **BRENDA HEYER**
   Grade 12, Benton Community High School
   Van Horne
   Teacher: Jill Olson

4. **HERB HOOVER**
   Grade 8, Brody Middle School
   Des Moines
   Teacher: Catherine R. Chiodo

5. **JENNIFER SINKLER**
   Grade 6, Montezuma Elementary School
   Montezuma
   Teacher: Mrs. Cox

6. **DAMON FINKEN**
   Grade 11, Central Campus
   Sioux City
   Teacher: Mrs. Feltz

7. **NICOLE REAMS**
   Grade 9, Charles City Junior High
   Charles City
   Teacher: Dennis Petersen

8. **KIM MAXWELL**
   Grade 6, Lucas Elementary School
   Chariton
   Teacher: Miss Bierl

9. **SARAH ORD**
   Grade 6, Tri-Center Elementary School
   Neola
   Teacher: Linda England

10. **GREG LONGORIA**
    Grade 9, Sudlow Junior High School
    Davenport
    Teacher: R. Schantz

11. **HEATHER JESSEN**
Grade 8, Brody Middle School
Des Moines
Teacher: Catherine R. Chiodo

12. **ALLISON NASSIF**
Grade 6, Callanan Middle School
Des Moines
Teacher: Karla Fisher

13. **HOLLY WESSELS**
Grade 4, Mar-Mac Elementary School
McGregor
Teacher: Swenette Ogle

14. **CARRIE CUNNINGHAM**
Grade 9, Shenandoah High School
Shenandoah
Teacher: Julia Gee

15. **LUKE HIRSCHY**
Grade 4, Williamson Elementary
Chariton
Teacher: Dianne Richardson

16. **JUDY WILLEMSSEN**
Grade 9, Charles City Junior High School
Charles City
Teacher: Dennis Petersen

17. **JOSH BATTERSON**
Grade 10, Red Oak High School
Red Oak
Teacher: Dan Martinez

18. **PERRY CASAZZA**
Grade 11, Burlington Community High School
Burlington
Teacher: Richard Anderson

19. **LYNDA SCHAU**
Grade 10, Charter Oak-Ute Community School
Charter Oak
Teacher: Sharon Schau

20. **LULU KEDOUTHAI**
Grade 6, Callanan Middle School
Des Moines
Teacher: Karla Fisher

21. **CHRISTOPHER PARKER**
Grade 12, East High School
Des Moines
Teacher: Steve Sams

22. **MICHAEL NICHOLSON**
Grade 10, East High School
Des Moines
Teacher: Steve Sams

23. **SUSAN ELLER**
Grade 10, Denison High School
Denison
Teacher: Joel Franken

24. **DAVE PETTIT**
Grade 9, Benton Community High School
Van Horne
Teacher: Jill Olson

25. **MOLLIE GROSS**
Grade 2, Lark Elementary School
West Monona (Onawa)
Teacher: Mr. Kingsbury

26. **ALEX JURRENS**
Grade 1, Lark Elementary School
West Monona (Onawa)
Teacher: Mr. Kingsbury

27. **RYAN EISELE**
Grade 4, Central Elementary School
West Monona (Onawa)
Teacher: Mr. Kingsbury

28. **MICHELLE MURPHY**
Meredith Middle School
Des Moines
Teacher: McKenzie

29. **DONNY PERRY**
Grade 8, Callanan Middle School
Des Moines
Teacher: Karla Fisher

30. **BECCA EDISON**
Grade 7, Callanan Middle School
Des Moines
Teacher: Karla Fisher

31. **SHANA OSBORNE**
Grade 7, Callanan Middle School
Des Moines
Teacher: Karla Fisher

32. **TRACY FELLMET**
Grade 12, Benton Community High School
Van Horne
Teacher: Jill Olson

33. **PERRY CASAZZA**
Grade 12, Burlington Community High School
Burlington
Teacher: Richard Anderson

34. **AARON RILEY**
Burlington High School
Burlington
Teacher: Richard Anderson

35. **SUSAN ELLER**
Grade 11, Denison High School
Denison
Teacher: Joel Franken

36. **AMY MAURER**
Grade 5, Clay Central Elementary School
Royal
Teacher: Mrs. Jeppeson

37. **SARAH KOONTZ**
Grade 4, IKM Elementary School
Irwin
Teacher: Jean Ferneding

38. **MELISSA UNRUH**
Grade 4, Logan-Magnolia Elementary School
Logan
Teacher: Mrs. Hanigan

39. **BRYAN STREICH**
Grade 10, Denver Senior High School
Denver
Teacher: Diane Johnson

40. **JAMES SCHMITT**
Grade 1, Lark Elementary School
West Monona (Onawa)
Teacher: Mr. Kingsbury

41. **AMY DEMEY**
Grade 11, Denison High School
Denison
Teacher: Joel Franken

42. **HEATH DEWAELE**
Grade 10, Denison High School
Denison
Teacher: Joel Franken

43. **JON BOLDT**
Grade 11, Muscatine High School
Muscatine
Teacher: Dan Kitchen

44. **KRISTINE BARRETT**
Grade 7, Anson Middle School
Marshalltown
Teacher: Mary Lou Thompson

45. **PAOLA MENDOZA BOTELHO**
Grade 12, Dallas Center-Grimes High School
Dallas Center
Teacher: Mary Zirkelback

46. **NICK KANSELAAR**
Grade 8, Howar Junior High School
Centerville
Teacher: Donna Ursta

47. **MATT J. DEWALL**
Grade 11, Pocahontas Area High School
Pocahontas
Teacher: Bill Strack

48. **MIKE ELLIFRITT**
Grade 4, Howe Elementary School
Des Moines
Teachers: Susan Imhoff & Kris Morine

49. **ADAM NOEL**
Grade 7, North Scott Junior High School
Eldridge
Teacher: Mrs. Sharp

50. **TRACY APPENZELLER**
Grade 12, Indianola High School
Indianola
Teacher: Bob Kling

51. **JENNIFER AGAN**
Grade 8, Brody Middle School
Des Moines
Teacher: Catherine R. Chiodo

52. **LINDY KROMMINGA**
Grade 11, Benton Community High School
Van Horne
Teacher: Jill Olson

53. **TORI ALBERT**
Grade 12, Benton Community High School
Van Horne
Teacher: Jill Olson

54. **MATT SAUNDERS**
Grade 4, IKM Elementary School
Manilla
Teacher: Jean Ferneding

55. **RACHEL SANDLER**
Grade 5, Rolling Green Elementary School
Urbandale
Teacher: Joyce Evans

56. **LINDSEY CROWLEY**
Grade 5, Rolling Green Elementary School
Urbandale
Teacher: Joyce Evans

57. **JULIE NELSON**
Grade 11, Burlington Community High School
Burlington
Teacher: Richard Anderson

58. **JUSTIN CARLSON**
Grade 9, Orient-Macksburg Senior High School
Orient
Teacher: Mrs. Leonard

59. **AMIE SNELL**
Grade 8, Eastern Allamakee Middle School
Lansing
Teacher: Laura Aldrich

60. **ABBY WEBSTER**
Grade 4, Manning Elementary School
Manning
Teacher: Jean Ferneding

61. **JESSE DORN**
Grade 1, Lawton–Bronson Elementary School
Bronson
Teacher: Mary Siepker

62. **JIM BENEDICT**
Grade 7, Interstate 35 Junior High School
New Virginia
Teacher: Christine Benedict

63. **ALICIA SEGRERA**
Grade 1, Greenfield Elementary School
Greenfield
Teacher: Darlys Crees

64. **BECKY MENSEN**
Grade 8, Benton Community Middle School
Van Horne
Teacher: K. Loftus

65. **AARON BONNES**
Grade 6, East Middle School
Sioux City
Teacher: Mrs. Karol Holton

66. **MELISSA WITCOMBE**
Grade 7, New Hartford–Dike Junior High School
New Hartford
Teacher: Mrs. Smith

67. **BILL SHEHAN**
Grade 8, Lincoln Middle School
Albia
Teacher: Kim Miller

68. **OLIVER SPARKS**
Grade 6, Winterset Middle School
Winterset
Teacher: Sherrie Silber

69. **JACK MILLER**
Grade 12, East Waterloo High School
Waterloo
Teacher: Larry Cardamon

70. **BRUCE BROWN**
Grade 11, East Waterloo High School
Waterloo
Teacher: Larry Cardamon

71. **RYAN DILLON**
Grade 11, Burlington High School
Burlington
Teacher: Richard Anderson

72. **APRIL SCHUMACHER**
Grade 2, Hudson Elementary School
Hudson
Teacher: Ronda Sternhagen

73. **ROBERT HAUSMAN**
Grade 5, Central Elementary School
West Monona (Onawa)
Teacher: Mr. Kingsbury

74. **ADAM WEILER**
Grade 6, Winterset Middle School
Winterset
Teacher: Sherrie Silber

75. **JESSICA BRIDGE**
Grade 8, Benton Community Middle School
Van Horne
Teacher: K. Loftus

76. **LINDY KROMMINGA**
Grade 12, Benton Community High School
Van Horne
Teacher: Jill Olson

77. **NATHAN LESLIE**
Grade 8, Sac Community Junior-Senior High
Sac City
Teacher: Roger Ring

78. **STEPHANIE FRIEDRICH**
Grade 8, Laing Middle School
Algona
Teacher: Bev Thies

79. **RANDI STAFNE**
Grade 6, Westwood Elementary School
Ankeny
Teacher: Lois Lamansky

80. **SARA STEFFEN**
Grade 4, Crestwood Elementary School
Cresco
Teacher: Stephanie Diederichs

81. **LARRY FRANCK**
Grade 8, Benton Community Middle School
Van Horne
Teacher: K. Loftus

82. **CORD OVERTON**
Grade 1, Hudson Elementary School
Hudson
Teacher: Ronda Sternhagen

83. JASON GARTON
Grade 3, Laurens–Marathon Elementary School
Laurens
Teacher: Mrs. Behrens

84. NICOLE PELICAN
Grade 4, Manning Elementary School
Manning
Teacher: Jean Ferneding

85. TERESA GRONWOLDT
Grade 11, Odebolt–Arthur High School
Odebolt
Teacher: Twyla Godbersen

86. JIM BENEDICT
Grade 8, Interstate 35 Junior High School
New Virginia
Teacher: Mary Roberts

87. MARK MILLER
Grade 5, Elk Run Elementary School
Waterloo
Teacher: Karen Lippe

88. SUZZANNE HORTON
Grade 2, Washington Elementary School
Muscatine
Teacher: Mrs. Lawhead

89. LANCE JENKINS
Grade 8, Sac Community Junior–Senior High School
Sac City
Teacher: Roger Ring

90. LAURA CAMERON
Grade 10, Central Campus
Sioux City
Teacher: Janet E. Siegfried

91. JILL DUFF
Grade 11, Denison High School
Denison
Teacher: Joel Franken

92. DARRIN HEARN
Grade 11, East High School
Waterloo
Teacher: Larry Cardamon

93. JEREMY SUMMERFIELD
Denison High School
Denison
Teacher: Joel Franken

94. KRISTI CHESTER
Grade 4, Maquoketa Valley–Delhi Elementary School
Delhi
Teacher: Mrs. Morrison

95. **BRODIE TIERNEY**
Grade 8, Charles City Middle School
Charles City
Teacher: Dennis Petersen

96. **DANNY BROWN**
Grade 2, Columbus Elementary School
Chariton
Teacher: Dianne Richardson

97. **ANDREA NICCOLAI**
Grade 11, Benton Community High School
Van Horne
Teacher: Jill Olson

98. **RICHARD BUNN**
Grade 9, Nashua–Plainfield High School
Nashua
Teacher: Corwin Dunlap

99. **BRANDON TEACHOUT**
Grade 6, Shenandoah Middle School
Shenandoah
Teacher: Jan Stevenson

100. **BETHANY KINSETH**
Grade 8, Laing Middle School
Algona
Teacher: Bev Thies

101. **LINDSEY DELAVAN**
Grade 3, Fremont-Mills Elementary School
Tabor
Teacher: Janiece Kinzle

102. **LUCAS WOODLAND**
Grade 8, Benton Community Middle School
Van Horne
Teacher: Jill Olson

103. **JIM HARKEN**
Grade 12, East High School
Waterloo
Teacher: Larry Cardamon

104. **KRISTIN KUNZMANN**
Grade 5, Clay Central North Elementary School
Everly
Teacher: Janna Dirks

105. **ASHLEY TROYER**
Grade 5, Kingsley Elementary School
Waterloo
Teacher: Karen Lippe

106. **RANDI CRAIN**
Grade 4, United Community Elementary School
Boone
Teacher: Jean Saveraid

107. CURTIS BERNAND
Grade 12, Burlington High School
Burlington
Teacher: Richard Anderson

108. MISSY BISHOP
Grade 6, Benton Community Middle School
Van Horne
Teacher: K. Loftus

109. JONAH ARNOT
Grade 6, Winterset Middle School
Winterset
Teacher: Sherrie Silber

110. TYLER CARLSON
Grade 12, Burlington High School
Burlington
Teacher: Richard Anderson

111. EMILY HACHMEISTER
Grade 4, Bayard Middle School
Coon Rapids
Teacher: Jean Ferneding

112. JULIE AHERN
Grade 8, James Madison Middle School
Burlington
Teacher: L. J. Oliver

113. JASON SILBER
Grade 6, Winterset Middle School
Winterset
Teacher: Sherrie Silber

114. ERIC KIRKLAND
Grade 4, Pleasant View Elementary School
Pleasant Valley
Teacher: Jane Beckman

115. BRANDON SHARP
Grade 11, East High School
Des Moines
Teacher: Shirley Gooch

116. COLLEEN SCHMITT
Grade 8, Central Middle School
Muscatine
Teacher: Mrs. Frost

117. MELANIE WYATT
Grade 12, Grundy Center High School
Grundy Center
Teacher: Bruce Gordon

118. ZACH HENNINGER
Grade 4, Jewett Elementary School
Waterloo
Teacher: Mary Wikert

119. ELIZABETH BREED
Grade 3, Hudson Elementary School
Hudson
Teacher: Mrs. Sternhagen

120. JEREMY SKEENS
Grade 10, Burlington High School
Burlington
Teacher: Richard Anderson

121. KELLI BECKEL
Grade 6, Winterset Middle School
Winterset
Teacher: Sherrie Silber

122. HILARY WAMBOLD
Grade 1, Greenfield Elementary School
Greenfield
Teacher: Darlys Crees

123. JESS IMES
Grade 6, Winterset Middle School
Winterset
Teacher: Sherrie Silber

124. JESSE KOHL
Grade 1, Lisbon Elementary School
Lisbon
Teacher: Reta Westercamp

125. ZACH HACHMEISTER
Grade 8, James Madison Middle School
Burlington
Teacher: L. J. Oliver

126. ALEX FINK
Grade 11, East High School
Waterloo
Teacher: Larry Cardamon

127. BRANDON PARRISH
Grade 8, James Madison Middle School
Burlington
Teacher: L. J. Oliver

128. TONI HILL
Grade 8, Brody Middle School
Des Moines
Teacher: Catherine R. Chiodo

129. TRACY GOODRICH
Grade 8, Laing Middle School
Algona
Teacher: Bev Thies

130. CURTIS RAY
Grade 4, Jewett Elementary School
Waterloo
Teacher: Mary Wikert

131. KRIS HACK
Grade 11, East High School
Waterloo
Teacher: Larry Cardamon

132. KRISTIN FOGLE
Grade 11, Carlisle High School
Carlisle
Teacher: Tom Allen

133. PETER MOMMER
Grade 7, New Hartford-Dike Junior High School
New Hartford
Teacher: Lin Smith

134. RACHAEL EGGERS
Grade 12, Denison High School
Denison
Teacher: Joel Franken

135. JUSTIN COATS
Grade 7, Sac Community Junior-Senior High School
Sac City
Teacher: Roger Ring

136. SEAN GRIST
Grade 4, Smith Elementary School
Sioux City
Teacher: Kim Vermilyea

137. CANDICE SORENSEN
Grade 6, Shenandoah Middle School
Shenandoah
Teacher: Jan Stevenson

138. DANIELLE NOURSE
Grade 11, Carlisle High School
Carlisle
Teacher: Tom Allen

139. STACY CRECELIUS
Grade 12, Denison High School
Denison
Teacher: Joel Franken

140. CHRISTY PETERSON
Grade 7, Melcher-Dallas Junior High
Melcher
Teacher: Kathy I. King

141. MATT DURHAM
Grade 6, West Middle School
Muscatine
Teacher: Mrs. Kelty

142. RACHAEL MORKEL
Grade 5, Kingsley Elementary School
Waterloo
Teacher: Karen Lippe

215

143. EVAN D. ANDERSON
Grade 5, Arthur Elementary School
Cedar Rapids
Teacher: Ricky Mabry

144. EMILY MINDER
Grade 6, West Middle School
Muscatine
Teacher: Mrs. Kelty

145. CHRISTOPHER JOHNSON
Grade 5, West Burlington Elementary School
West Burlington
Teacher: Mrs. Kurimski

146. ANGIE KAJEWSKI
Grade 8, Laing Middle School
Algona
Teacher: Bev Thies

For more information on
Iowa State University Press books
call or fax:
ORDERS: 1-800-862-6657
OFFICE: 1-515-292-0140
FAX: 1-515-292-3348

Making Sense of Human Rights

Making Sense of Human Rights

Second Edition

James W. Nickel

Blackwell
Publishing

BLACKWELL PUBLISHING
350 Main Street, Malden, MA 02148-5020, USA
9600 Garsington Road, Oxford OX4 2DQ, UK
550 Swanston Street, Carlton, Victoria 3053, Australia

First edition published 1987 by University of California Press.
Second edition published 2007 by Blackwell Publishing Ltd

6   2010

Library of Congress Cataloging-in-Publication Data

Nickel, James W.
Making sense of human rights / James W. Nickel. – 2nd ed.
p. cm.
Includes bibliographical references and index.
ISBN: 978-1-4051-4534-3 (hardcover : alk. paper)
ISBN: 978-1-4051-4535-0 (pbk. : alk. paper)
1. Civil rights.   2. Human rights.   3. United Nations. General Assembly. Universal
Declaration of Human Rights.   I. Title.
JC571.N49 2007
341.4′8–dc22
2006016596

A catalogue record for this title is available from the British Library.

Set in 10/12.5pt Galliard
by SNP Best-set Typesetter Ltd, Hong Kong
Printed and bound in Singapore
by COS Printers Pte Ltd

For further information on
Blackwell Publishing, visit our website:
www.blackwellpublishing.com

Contents

Introduction

When governments do cruel and unjust things to their citizens we are now likely to describe those actions as violations of human rights – instead of simply saying that they are unjust, immoral, tyrannical, or barbaric. Appealing to human rights in order to describe and criticize the actions of repressive governments became common as a popular phenomenon in the second half of the twentieth century. Talk of natural rights and of constitutional rights has long been common among philosophers and lawyers, but since 1948, the idea of human rights has gradually been adopted by journalists, politicians, and the public in many parts of the world. Violations of human rights are now frequently recognized and reported as such by journalists, and many people around the world have adopted "human rights violations" as a category of political thought and appraisal.

The creation of the Universal Declaration of Human Rights (United Nations 1948b) made possible the subsequent flourishing of the idea of international human rights. The Declaration's list of human rights is, broadly speaking, the list that is still in use today. And the international human rights treaties that followed in its wake refined the formulations of these rights and gave them the status of international law.

This book tries to show that the idea of human rights makes good sense and that people should be comfortable, but not unreflective, in appealing to human rights. It does this by examining and evaluating the general idea of human rights, by considering and responding to objections to it, and by offering justifications for particular families of rights.

Many philosophers have constructed theories of rights without reference to the international human rights movement and its documents (for example, Thomson 1990; Veach 1985). Perhaps they proceeded in this way because they were interested in interpersonal morality rather than international political morality, or simply because they wished to construct a moral vision unencumbered by the sometimes dubious normative decisions of politicians and diplomats. My approach here is different. It focuses on the contemporary political project of creating an international law of human rights that promotes decent treatment of people by their governments. I focus on the Universal Declaration and the human rights treaties that followed, not because I think they are without flaws, but because they have given the idea of human rights a determinate meaning that has gained widespread international acceptance.

For human rights norms to succeed in practice they need to be supported both by strong reasons and by effective implementation. Since the end of World War II, a system of international implementation for human rights has been developed and refined, despite many obstacles and setbacks, in the United Nations and other international organizations. This system is described in Chapter 1. But the question of the availability of strong and universally applicable supporting reasons remains. Chapters 4 and 5 offer a sketch of what those reasons are.

In spite of the progress that has been made in listing and protecting international human rights, many people still find the idea of international human rights perplexing and raise questions about what human rights are, what their content is or should be, and whether they can be justified in our messy and diverse world. Conceptual questions pertain to the nature or status of human rights; here one might ask whether human rights are really rights (rather than, say, political goals) or question whether international law is a suitable home for real and robust rights. Questions about the content of human rights pertain to which families of rights can plausibly be taken to be the rights of all people, and about which parties bear duties in connection with these rights. Questions of justification ask whether there are good grounds for believing in universal human rights, whether these grounds transcend cultural and religious differences, and what steps are involved in justifying a right.

This book addresses a number of these sorts of questions, moving from historical and analytical topics to issues of justification and affordability and then on to the discussion of some particular families of rights. Overall, the book sketches a defense of the contemporary idea of human rights against a variety of philosophical and practical objections.

At the conceptual or analytical level my intention is to explain the concept of rights and to show that it is an attractive vehicle for expressing the norms of the international human rights movement. I also offer a general account of what human rights are (a definition, that is, rather than a list) and of what characteristics they can plausibly be said to have. The account given here of the nature and justification of specific human rights, such as the right to a fair trial or the right to freedom of movement, does not take such specific rights to be ultimate moral standards that are unchanging. Instead, it sees the several dozen norms that we now call human rights as attempts to identify the implications for political morality and for national and international law of deeper and more abstract values and norms. Specific human rights respond to familiar and recurrent threats to fundamental human interests and important moral norms. To reflect on human rights requires reflection both on those interests and norms *and* on which political, social, and legal abuses are most dangerous to them.

Human rights are minimal standards. They focus on areas of great injustice. As minimal standards they can hope to be supported by very strong reasons of universal appeal, to be of high priority, and to resist claims of national and cultural autonomy. Even when this view of human rights is accepted, however, it remains difficult to know where lists of human rights should end. There are many serious problems in all human societies, and it is tempting to extend the reach of human rights norms to address all of them. Further, the advocates of many causes would like to get their agendas incorporated in the norms, institutions, and activities of the human rights movement. The question of which families of rights should be included in the documents and treaties of the human rights movement is important and is discussed in Chapters 5 and 6.

The justification of human rights has several stages. The most basic stage involves trying to identify and justify the abstract values or norms that underlie human rights. The second stage involves trying to show that some specific norms follow from these abstract considerations, and that these norms are plausibly conceived as universal rights. Using an analogy to chess, I will often refer to this second stage as the "middle game." A third stage of justification involves defending the measures that will be necessary to protect and promote human rights internationally. To extend the analogy, this might be thought of as the "end game."

This book gives considerable attention to the middle game. Philosophers typically focus on ultimate justification, and political scientists and lawyers usually focus on the end game, with the result that the middle level is largely ignored. I try to remedy this lack of attention by developing an account of the kind of case that needs to be made for a specific right at the middle level of justification. The result may seem insufficiently theoretical to philosophers and insufficiently practical to political scientists and lawyers, but this is a risk I willingly take. I hope to make it obvious that the middle level of justification is a significant area in which the concerns of philosophers, anthropologists, political scientists, economists, and lawyers come together.

There are a number of philosophical topics relevant to human rights that this book does not address. One is metaethics – the epistemology, metaphysics, and psychology of normative discourse. No broad philosophical account of human moral and practical knowledge is offered. I do, however, presuppose that normal humans are capable of acquiring, with luck and effort, moral and practical knowledge. I also presuppose that most people are capable – much of the time – of guiding their behavior by the values and norms they accept (see Rawls 1993). Fortunately, lots of good philosophical work on metaethics is now available (see, for example, Darwall 1998 and Huemer 2005). Other relevant subjects that deserve much greater attention than they receive here include distributive justice, globalization, the law of war, international criminal law, sovereignty, and when coercive and military intervention to protect human rights is justified (see Teson 2005).

This book was first published in 1987 as *Making Sense of Human Rights: Philosophical Reflections on the Universal Declaration of Human Rights* (University of California Press). This revised and enlarged edition brings the book up to date and makes many changes and additions. More than half of its material is new. The subtitle has been dropped because the revised version focuses as much on human rights treaties as on the Universal Declaration. All the chapters have been substantially rewritten. Three old chapters were cut, and new chapters added on lists of human rights (6), due process rights and terrorism (7), economic liberties (8), and minority rights (10).

This is a short book, with chapters that can be read in a single sitting. Extensive bibliographic references are provided. When I first began working on human rights in the 1970s, the human rights literature in philosophy, law, and political science was very limited. I am pleased to be able to say that there is now an abundance of good books and articles on human rights.

I have been extremely fortunate to have many friends who have provided encouragement and assistance during more than 30 years of thinking, teaching, and writing about the philosophy and law of human rights. I am particularly grateful to Louis Henkin for the pivotal role that he played by introducing me to international human rights law at Columbia Law School in 1973. Rex Martin, David Reidy, and Eduardo Viola deserve special gratitude for co-authoring with me papers in the area of human rights. Others who have provided much appreciated discussion, help, and encouragement include Charles Beitz, Nick Bellorini, Richard E. Brown, Allen Buchanan, Joseph Chan, Deen Chatterjee, Beth Difelice, David Duquette, James Griffin, Aaron James, Ranjana Kumar, Betsy Lamm, Tore Lindholm, Peter de Marneffe, Gail Merten, David Miller, Stephen R. Munzer (who wrote comments on many chapters), Thomas Pogge, M. B. E. Smith (who wrote comments on the entire manuscript in 2004), John Tasioulas, Rebecca Tsosie, Johannes A. van der Ven, James

Weinstein, Leif Wenar (who as the reader for Blackwell Publishing wrote very helpful comments and suggestions), and Patricia Denise White. I would also like to thank the Philosophy Department at the University of Colorado, Boulder, and the College of Law at Arizona State University for providing me with sabbatical leaves, summer support, and opportunities to teach this material. Corpus Christi College, Oxford, provided a very enjoyable academic home away from home in the fall of 2004.

Readers who wish to contact me may do so by e-mail at james.nickel@asu.edu. I intend to maintain current bibliographies and accounts of the international law of human rights in my "human rights" entry in the online Stanford Encyclopedia of Philosophy (<http://plato.stanford.edu/entries/rights-human/>).

Chapter 1

The Contemporary Idea
of Human Rights

Human rights, as we know them today, are the rights of the lawyers, not the rights of the philosophers. "Human rights" is not just another label for historic ideas of natural rights. Instead, the term is typically used to describe the specific norms that emerged from a political project initially undertaken after World War I in the minority rights treaties and then continued on a larger scale after World War II. This political project, embodied in the contemporary human rights movement, aspires to formulate and enforce international norms that will prevent governments from doing horrible things to their people and thereby promote international peace and security.

Although today's conception of human rights was surely influenced by ideas of natural rights, there are substantial differences. First, human rights are specific and numerous, not broad and abstract like "life, liberty, and property." The Universal Declaration and the subsequent human rights treaties are lists of specific rights that address particular problems such as imprisonment without trial and suppression of political dissent. The Universal Declaration asserts that "All human beings are born free and equal in dignity and rights." But it is not mainly a declaration of abstract political principles. It declares the specific and numerous rights of lawyers, not the abstract rights of philosophers. Historic bills of rights were the main inspiration.

Second, today's human rights are not part of a political philosophy with an accompanying epistemology. They may make philosophical assumptions, but they do not require acceptance of a particular philosophy or ideology. Because the human rights movement was an international political movement with aspirations to create international law, it did not place great emphasis on identifying the normative foundations of human rights. Postwar efforts to formulate international human rights norms have gone forward despite obvious and persistent philosophical and ideological divisions. To gather as much support for the movement as possible, the philosophical underpinnings of human rights were sketched broadly but vaguely in the Universal Declaration by saying that people are "born free and equal in dignity and rights," and have "equal and inalienable rights."

A dangerous aspect of Hitler's rule, clearly demonstrated during World War II, was its lack of concern for people's lives and liberties. The war against the Axis powers was often defended in terms of preserving human rights and fundamental freedoms. The carnage and destruction of World War II led to a determination to do something to prevent war, to build an international organization to address severe international problems and to impose standards of decency on the world's governments. The United Nations Organization, created in 1945, has played a key role in the development of the contemporary idea of human rights.

The creators of the UN believed that reducing the likelihood of war required preventing severe and large-scale oppression within countries. Because of this belief, even the earliest conceptions of the UN gave the organization a role in promoting rights and liberties. Some early conceptions of the UN Charter suggested that it contain an international bill of rights to which any member nation would have to subscribe, but the idea did not succeed. Instead, the Charter simply committed the UN to promoting human rights. The Charter expressed "faith in fundamental human rights, in the dignity and worth of the human person, in the equal rights of men and women and of nations large and small" (United Nations 1945: preamble). Its signatories pledged themselves to "take joint and separate action in cooperation with the organization" to promote "universal respect for, and observance of, human rights and fundamental freedoms for all without distinction as to race, sex, language or religion" (United Nations 1945, article 1.3).

Shortly after the approval of the Charter, a UN committee was charged with writing an international bill of rights. It was to be similar in content to bills of rights already existing in some countries, but applying to all people in all countries. The UN took a familiar genre, a national bill of rights, and adapted it for use at the international level. An international bill of rights emerged in December 1948 as the Universal Declaration of Human Rights. The Universal Declaration was a set of proposed standards, rather than a treaty. It recommended promotion of human rights through "teaching and education" and "measures, national and international, to secure their universal and effective recognition and observance" (United Nations 1948b; for histories of the Universal Declaration see Glendon 2001; Lauren 1998; and Morsink 1999).

The first 21 articles of the Universal Declaration present rights similar to those found in historic bills of rights. These civil and political rights include rights to equal protection and nondiscrimination, due process in legal proceedings, privacy and personal integrity, and political participation. But articles 22 through 27 make a new departure, incorporating economic and social standards. They declare rights to benefits such as social security, an adequate standard of living, and education.

The Universal Declaration has been amazingly successful in establishing a fixed worldwide meaning for the idea of human rights. Broadly speaking, the list of human rights that it proposed still sets the pattern for the numerous human rights treaties that have gone into operation since 1948. Those treaties include the European Convention on Human Rights (Council of Europe 1950), the International Covenant on Civil and Political Rights ("Civil and Political Covenant," United Nations 1966a), the International Covenant on Economic, Social and Cultural Rights ("Social Covenant," United Nations 1966b), the American Convention on Human Rights (Organization of American States 1969), and nearly a dozen others.

Defining Features of Human Rights

Human rights, as conceived in the Universal Declaration and subsequent human rights treaties, have a number of general characteristics. Eight important features are described briefly in this section. A fuller treatment of the defining features of human rights is provided in Chapter 3.

First, lest we miss the obvious, human rights are rights. But the exact import of this status is unclear and will be one of my subjects of inquiry. I will suggest that at a minimum it means that human rights have *rightholders* (the people who have them); *addressees* (parties assigned duties or responsibilities); and *scopes* that focus on a freedom, protection, or benefit. Further, rights are mandatory in the sense that some behaviors of the addressees are required or forbidden.

Second, human rights are universal in the sense that they extend to every person living today. Characteristics such as race, sex, religion, social position, and nationality are irrelevant to whether one has human rights.

Third, human rights are high priority norms. They are not absolute but are strong enough to win most of the time when they compete with other considerations. As such, they must have strong justifications that apply all over the world and support the independence and high priority of human rights. The Universal Declaration states that human rights are rooted in the dignity and worth of human beings and in the requirements of domestic and international peace and security.

Fourth, human rights are not dependent for their existence on recognition or enactment by particular governments. They exist as legal norms at the national and international levels, and as norms of justified or enlightened political morality. In promulgating the Universal Declaration as a "common standard of achievement," the UN did not purport to describe rights already recognized everywhere. Instead, it attempted to set forth an enlightened international political morality that addresses familiar abuses of contemporary political institutions. Subsequently, however, international treaties were used to make human rights norms part of international law. Their proponents would like to see them embedded in all people's beliefs and actions and effectively recognized and implemented in law, government, and international organizations.

Fifth, human rights are international standards of evaluation and criticism unrestricted by political boundaries. They provide standards for criticism by "outsiders" such as international organizations, people and groups in other countries, and foreign governments.

Sixth, human rights are primarily political norms rather than interpersonal standards. They are standards of decent governmental conduct and mainly speak to social and political leaders and institutions. Governments are their primary addressees. We must be careful here, however, since rights against racial and gender discrimination, for example, are concerned to regulate behavior that is more often private than governmental (Cook 1994; Okin 1998). Still, governmental action is directed in two ways by rights against discrimination. First, the rights forbid governments to discriminate in their actions and policies. Second, they impose duties on governments to prohibit both private and public forms of discrimination.

Seventh, human rights are numerous and specific rather than few and general. Like other bills of rights, the Universal Declaration is a list of specific rights that addresses severe but familiar problems of governments. Accordingly, the Universal Declaration is not a restatement of Locke's rights to life, liberty, and property (Locke 1986, originally published 1689), although some abstract values are identified in the preamble. Instead, it is a list of roughly two dozen specific rights (see Table 1.1).

Finally, human rights set minimum standards; they do not attempt to describe an ideal social and political world. They leave most political decisions in the hands of national leaders and electorates. Still, they are demanding standards that impose significant constraints on legislation, policy-making, and official behavior.

Table 1.1 The Universal Declaration's Rights

Security Rights
- Life, liberty, and security of person (article 3)
- No torture or cruel punishments (article 5)

Due Process Rights
- Right to an effective remedy for violations of rights (article 8) and to a social and international order in which human rights can be enjoyed (article 28)
- No arbitrary arrest, detention, or exile (article 9)
- Right to a trial in criminal cases (article 10)
- Presumption of innocence in criminal cases (article 11)
- No retroactive criminal laws or penalties (article 11)
- No arbitrary deprivation of nationality (article 15)
- No arbitrary deprivation of property (article 17.2)
- Protection of moral and material interests resulting from any scientific, literary, or artistic production of which one is the author (article 27.2)

Basic Liberties
- No slavery or servitude (article 4)
- No arbitrary interference with one's privacy, family, home, or correspondence (article 12)
- Freedom of movement and residence (article 13)
- Freedom to leave and return to one's country (article 13)
- Freedom to seek and enjoy in other countries asylum from persecution (article 14)
- No marriage without full and free consent of the intending spouses (article 16.2)
- Freedom to own property individually and collectively (article 17.1)
- Freedom of thought, conscience, and religion (article 18)
- Freedom of opinion and expression (article 19)
- Freedom of peaceful assembly and association (article 20)
- Freedom to form and join trade unions (article 23.4)
- Freedom of parents to choose the kind of education that shall be given to their children (article 26)
- Freedom to participate in cultural life (article 27)

Rights of Political Participation
- Freedom to participate in government, directly or through freely chosen representatives (article 21.1)
- Equal access to public service (article 21.2)
- Opportunities to vote in periodic and genuine elections (article 21.3)

Equality Rights
- Equality of fundamental rights and freedoms (article 2)
- Legal personality (article 6) and equality before the law (article 7)
- Freedom from discrimination (articles 2, 7)
- Equal rights in marriage and family (article 16)
- Equal pay for equal work (article 22)
- Equal social protection for children born out of wedlock (article 25.2)

Economic and Social Rights
- Social security (article 22)
- Just and favorable remuneration for workers (article 23.3)
- Rest and leisure (article 24)
- Adequate standard of living for health and well-being (article 25)
- Health care (article 25)
- Special care during motherhood and childhood (article 25.1)
- The right to educational opportunities (article 26)

───────────── **Old and New Rights** ─────────────

The authors of today's conception of human rights used familiar ideas about freedom, justice, and individual rights. It is not a distortion to view human rights as the recycling and updating of old ideas within a new, transnational context. The notion of a natural or divine law requiring decent treatment of everyone is ancient. It was wedded to the idea of rights by theorists such as Locke and Jefferson as well as in declarations of rights such as the French Declaration of the Rights of Man and the Citizen (1789, in Ishay 1997) and the US Bill of Rights (1783, in Urofsky and Finkelman 2002). The idea of normative protections of people against their governments is far from new.

The contemporary view of human rights, embodied in the Universal Declaration and the subsequent human rights treaties, differs from earlier – particularly eighteenth-century – conceptions in three ways. Human rights today are more egalitarian, less individualistic, and more internationally oriented. The egalitarianism of recent human rights documents is evident, first, in the great emphasis they place on equality before the law and protections against discrimination. Although eighteenth-century rights manifestos sometimes declared equality before the law, the reality in that era was that basic rights were denied to whole classes of people based on their race, nationality, and gender. Legal protections against discrimination are nineteenth- and twentieth-century developments. Victory over chattel slavery in the Americas came in the nineteenth century, but racist attitudes and practices remain a central problem of our time. The demand for equality for women in all areas of life has also become part of the human rights agenda. The Convention on the Elimination of All Forms of Discrimination against Women (United Nations 1979) condemns discrimination against women and advocates equal rights. Article 11, for example, commits the participating countries to taking "all appropriate measures to eliminate discrimination against women in the field of employment in order to ensure, on a basis of equality of men and women, the same rights."

The egalitarianism of contemporary human rights documents can also be seen in the inclusion of social rights. Earlier lists of political rights were mainly concerned with governments doing things they should not, rather than failing to do things they should. The duties generated by these rights were mainly negative – duties of restraint. Positive duties were found mainly in the duty of governments to protect people's rights against internal and external invasions. Due process rights such as rights to a fair trial, and freedoms from arbitrary arrest, torture, and cruel punishments, were seen as remedies for abuses of the legal system. These abuses included manipulating the legal system to favor the friends and disadvantage the enemies of those in power, jailing political opponents, and ruling through terror. Rights of privacy and autonomy such as rights to freedom from warrantless invasion of home and correspondence, freedom of movement, free choice of residence and occupation, and freedom of association were seen as remedies for invasions of the private sphere, which included governmental prying into the most intimate areas of life and attempts to control people by limiting where they are able to live, work, and travel.

Rights of political participation such as rights to freedom of expression, to petition government, to vote, and to run for public office were seen as remedies for such abuses as refusing to consider complaints by citizens, suppressing dissent and opposition, crippling the development of an informed electorate, and manipulating the electoral system to stay in power.

Even if governments were restrained from the various abuses just listed, however, social and economic problems such as poverty, disproportionate illiteracy among women and girls, disease, and lack of economic opportunities would be undisturbed. Many contemporary political movements have mainly focused on these social and economic problems. One result has been to broaden the scope of the rights vocabulary to include these problems within the human rights agenda. The vehicle for delivering the services demanded by rights to social security, education, and basic health care is the modern welfare state, a political system that uses its taxation powers to collect the resources required to supply essential welfare services. Contemporary notions of human rights are not only more egalitarian than earlier conceptions in the sense that they extend the guarantee to freedom from discrimination to more classes of people, but also in the sense that they actually provide positive rights serving to mitigate economic and social inequalities.

The second difference between today's concept of human rights and eighteenth-century natural rights is that today's human rights are less individualistic. Recent rights manifestos have tempered the individualism of classical theories of natural rights. They continue to protect individual rights and liberties, but they often conceive of people as members of families and communities, not as isolated individuals (Glendon 2001: 93). And the human rights movement has produced treaties and declarations that forbid genocide and protect the rights of women, minorities, and indigenous peoples.

Thirdly, today's human rights differ from eighteenth-century natural rights in being internationally oriented and promoted. Not only are they prescribed internationally – which is nothing new – but they are also seen as appropriate objects of international action and concern. Although eighteenth-century natural rights were viewed as rights of all people, they served mainly as criteria for justifying rebellion against existing governments. International organizations with power to investigate, expose, and adjudicate human rights problems were not yet on the horizon. While states remain jealous of their sovereignty and anxious to prevent outsiders from interfering in their affairs, the principle that international inquiries and interventions are justifiable in cases of large-scale violations of human rights is now well established.

The International Protection of Human Rights

This section offers a description of how human rights are promoted and protected by governmental and nongovernmental institutions in 2006. An annually updated version of this section is available in the "human rights" entry in the online Stanford Encyclopedia of Philosophy (<http://plato.stanford.edu/entries/rights-human/>).

The agencies involved in the effort to bring about international respect for human rights today include the United Nations, various regional governmental organizations such as the Council of Europe and the Organization of African Unity, nongovernmental organizations, and individual nations acting alone or in concert with others. This section offers brief descriptions of each of these mechanisms for promoting and enforcing human rights as well as some of the most important treaties that have been enacted. Readers with limited interest in international organizations and human rights treaties are invited to skim this section and move on to Chapter 2. Treaties and declarations dealing with the rights of minorities are discussed in Chapter 10.

The United Nations

United Nations human rights treaties

After the approval of the Universal Declaration in 1948, efforts to create international human rights treaties were handicapped by the Cold War but went ahead anyway. The Genocide Convention was approved in 1948, and as of 2003 has more than 130 participating countries (United Nations 1948a). It defines genocide and makes it a crime under international law.

It also calls for action by UN bodies to prevent and suppress acts of genocide and requires states to enact national legislation prohibiting genocide, to try and punish persons or officials who commit genocide, and to allow extradition of persons accused of genocide. The International Criminal Court, which was created by the Rome Treaty of 1998, is authorized to prosecute genocide, along with crimes against humanity and war crimes, at the international level (see Schabas 2001).

The plan to follow the Universal Declaration with analogous treaties also went ahead, but at a glacial pace. Drafts of the International Covenants were submitted to the General Assembly for approval in 1953. To accommodate those who believed that social rights were not genuine human rights or that they were not enforceable in the same way as civil and political rights, two treaties were prepared, the Civil and Political Covenant and the Social Covenant.

Between the Universal Declaration of 1948 and the General Assembly's approval of the two Covenants in 1966, many African and Asian nations, recently freed from colonial rule, entered the United Nations. These countries were generally willing to go along with the human rights enterprise, but they modified it to reflect their own interests and concerns, such as ending colonialism, apartheid in South Africa, and racial discrimination around the world. The two Covenants reflect these concerns. They assert the rights of peoples to self-determination and to control their own natural resources, give rights against discrimination a prominent place, and omit the Universal Declaration's rights to property and to remuneration for property taken by the state.

A country ratifying a UN human rights treaty agrees to respect and implement the rights the treaty covers. It also agrees to accept and respond to international scrutiny and criticism of its record. The Civil and Political Covenant, which has been ratified by 152 countries, illustrates the standard UN system for implementing an international bill of rights. It created an agency, the Human Rights Committee, to promote compliance with its norms. The 18 members of the Committee serve in their personal capacity as experts rather than as state representatives. The Committee can express its views as to whether a particular practice is a human rights violation, but it is not authorized to issue legally binding judgments (Alston and Crawford 2002).

Participating states are required to prepare and present periodic reports on their compliance with the treaty, and the Human Rights Committee has the job of receiving, studying, and commenting critically on these reports (Boerefijn 1999; McGoldrick 1994). While doing so, the Committee holds meetings in which it hears from nongovernmental organizations such as Amnesty International and meets with representatives of the state making the report. At the end of this process the Committee publishes "Concluding Observations" which evaluate human rights compliance by the reporting country. The reporting procedure is useful in encouraging countries to identify their major human rights problems and to devise methods of dealing with them over time. But the reporting system has few teeth to deal with countries that stonewall or fail to report, and the Human Rights Committee's conclusions often receive little attention (Bayefsky 2001).

In addition to the reports on compliance that the treaty requires of all participating countries, the Civil and Political Covenant has an optional provision requiring separate ratification that authorizes the Human Rights Committee to receive, investigate, and mediate complaints from individuals alleging that their rights under the Civil and Political Covenant have been violated by a participating state (Joseph, Schultz, and Castan 2000). By June 2004, 104 of the 152 states adhering to the Covenant had ratified this optional provision. The United States has ratified the Covenant but not its first protocol.

Overall, this system for implementing human rights is limited. It does not give the Human Rights Committee the power to order states to change their practices or compensate a victim. Its tools are limited to persuasion, mediation, and exposure of violations to public scrutiny.

Many other UN human rights treaties are implemented in roughly the same way as the Civil and Political Covenant. These include the International Convention on the Elimination of All Forms of Racial Discrimination (United Nations 1965), the Convention on the Elimination of All Forms of Discrimination against Women (United Nations 1979), the Convention on the Rights of the Child (United Nations 1989), and the Convention against Torture and Other Cruel, Inhuman or Degrading Treatment or Punishment (United Nations 1984).

Other human rights agencies within the United Nations

Human rights treaties are only one part of the UN's human rights program. There are a number of UN agencies that are charged with promoting human rights independently of the requirements imposed by human rights treaties. These bodies include the UN High Commissioner for Human Rights, the Human Rights Council, and the Security Council.

The High Commissioner for Human Rights is charged with coordinating the many human rights activities that go on within the UN. The High Commissioner receives complaints about human rights violations, assists in the development of new treaties and procedures, sets the agenda for human rights agencies within the UN, and provides advisory services to governments. Most importantly, the High Commissioner serves as a full-time advocate for human rights within the United Nations (Korey 1998: 369).

The Human Rights Council is a standing body of the United Nations that replaced the Human Rights Commission in 2006. Its role is to examine serious human rights problems in all parts of the world and make recommendations. It has 47 members who are elected by the General Assembly. They serve for three years and for no more than two consecutive terms. The main purpose of the 2006 reforms was to keep representatives from countries with bad human rights records from serving on the Council.

The Security Council's mandate under the UN Charter is the maintenance of international peace and security. The 15-member body can authorize military interventions and impose diplomatic and economic sanctions (Bailey 1994; Rodley 1999; Ramcharan 2002). During the Cold War the Security Council tended to avoid human rights disputes other than apartheid in South Africa. But since the early 1990s the Security Council has dealt with many issues pertaining to human rights and war crimes. It authorized the use of military force in Somalia, the former Yugoslavia, Rwanda, Haiti, and East Timor, and sponsored a number of peacekeeping missions (Katayanagi 2002). It also established international criminal tribunals for Rwanda and Yugoslavia.

Regional systems

The Council of Europe and the European Convention on Human Rights

In 1949 the countries of Western Europe founded a political organization, the Council of Europe, that sought, among other things, to promote human rights. The European Convention on Human Rights, agreed to a year later, contained a list of civil and political rights similar to that found in the Universal Declaration. Social rights were later treated in a separate document, the European Social Charter (Council of Europe 1961). With the end of the Cold War in the early 1990s, many countries in Eastern Europe, including Russia, have joined the Council. In 2004, the Convention covered 46 countries and 800 million people.

Countries that ratify the Convention agree to respect and implement the rights enumerated in the treaty, but they also agree to the extra-national investigation, mediation, and adjudication of human rights complaints. The Convention establishes the European Court of Human

Rights, to which complaints about human rights violations can be made and in which remedies for them can be pursued. It is the most effective system currently operating for protecting human rights at the international level. The Court, based in Strasbourg, France, has one judge from each participating state – although the judges are appointed as independent jurists rather than as state representatives. Individuals from the participating countries with human rights complaints who have been unable to find a remedy in their national courts are able to petition the European Court of Human Rights. Complaints by governments about human rights violations in another participating country, though rarely made, are also permitted. If the Court agrees to hear a complaint, it investigates and adjudicates it. The Court first attempts to mediate the dispute, but if conciliation fails, it will issue a judgment and impose a remedy (McKaskle 2005). Through this process a large body of international human rights jurisprudence has developed (Janis, Kay, and Bradley 1995; Jacobs and White 1996). Governments almost always accept the Court's judgments. Compliance occurs because governments are committed to human rights and because their membership in good standing in the European Community would be endangered were they to defy the Court.

The Inter-American and African Systems

There are two regional systems outside of Europe. One is the Inter-American System operating in North, Central, and South America under the auspices of the Organization of American States; the other is the African System sponsored by the African Union.

The Inter-American System, which includes almost all countries of the Americas, is broadly similar to the European System. It includes a human rights declaration, the American Declaration of the Rights and Duties of Man (Organization of American States 1948); a treaty, the American Convention on Human Rights (Organization of American States 1969); a commission; and a court. The Commission receives, investigates, and attempts to resolve individual complaints and prepares reports on countries with severe human rights problems. The Inter-American Court of Human Rights interprets and enforces the Convention (Davidson 1997). It may submit cases to, or request advisory opinions from, the Inter-American Court of Human Rights, which was established in 1979. The Court's jurisdiction is limited to cases brought by the state parties and the Commission. The Court issued its first decision in 1980, and to date has decided more than 65 cases.

The African System, which covers the countries of the African continent, has a human rights treaty and a human rights commission. The treaty, created by the African Union (formerly the Organization of African Unity), is the African Charter on Human and Peoples' Rights (African Union 1981). The African Commission on Human and Peoples' Rights, created in 1986, promotes human rights in Africa and monitors compliance with the treaty. Countries must submit regular reports to the Commission on their human rights problems and efforts to address them. An effort to create a court, the African Court on Human and Peoples' Rights, is currently under way. The African System has enormous human rights problems to address, frequently faces non-cooperation by governments, and has inadequate resources to play a major role (Evans and Murray 2002; Flinterman and Ankumah 2004).

Promotion of human rights by states

States sometimes act, individually or jointly with other states, to promote or protect human rights in other countries. The methods used include diplomacy, publishing reports and statements, conditioning access to trade or aid on human rights improvements, economic sanctions, and military intervention. For example, Portugal attempted to defuse the 1999 crisis concerning East Timor's independence from Indonesia, and Australia led the military effort that created an independent state of East Timor.

These efforts by states add some real power to the international human rights system. The historic pillars of the human rights establishment have been the countries of Western Europe plus Australia, Canada, and (less consistently but still importantly) the United States. They have lent their considerable support and clout to the system, keeping it going during hard times and helping it expand and flourish in better times. Although they have not always risen to the challenge of human rights emergencies, they have sometimes done so at considerable cost to themselves in money and lives (see Power 2002). In doing this, they have often worked closely with the Security Council. They do not, however, have a standing legal commitment to do this, except their commitment in the UN Charter to support the actions of the Security Council (Steiner and Alston 2000: 987–8).

Nongovernmental organizations dealing with human rights

Many nongovernmental organizations are active at the international level in the areas of human rights, war crimes, and food and medical assistance.

Examples include Amnesty International, Human Rights Watch, the International Commission of Jurists, Doctors without Borders, and Oxfam. NGOs are seen everywhere in the international human rights system. They attend and often participate in the meetings of UN human rights bodies, and they provide information about human rights violations through the reports they publish and the testimony they give. They also shape the agendas, policies, and treaties of the UN through their participation and lobbying, and provide links between the international human rights system and politics at the domestic level (Korey 1998).

Modest achievements?

The human rights regime within international law is still under construction. So far it has developed a substantial body of norms and a variety of international institutions to promote and protect them. Outside of the European System, it relies more on encouragement, consciousness-raising, persuasion, exposure, and shaming than it does on imposing sanctions. Legal enforcement of human rights at the national level – in countries where it is actually available – continues to be the main vehicle for the effective implementation of human rights.

The fact that the international human rights system only rarely forces recalcitrant violators to change their practices leads many people to view it as ineffectual and hypocritical. There is truth in this, but the system has helped to create an international climate in which most countries are willing to discuss and address human rights issues. Powerful countries such as China and the United States can resist its demands. Still, the system creates continuous pressure on all countries, including powerful ones, to take human rights seriously.

--- **Overview** ---

Human rights as we know them today are the (specific and numerous) rights of the lawyers, not the (few and abstract) rights of the philosophers. They comprise families such as security rights, due process rights, basic liberties, and social rights. Human rights today are internationally oriented and promoted. Most countries have ratified international treaties that list specific human rights and that create courts and other bodies to scrutinize national practices and conditions.

———————————— **Further Reading** ————————————

Burgers, J. 1992. "The Road to San Francisco: The Revival of the Human Rights Idea in the Twentieth Century." *Human Rights Quarterly* 14: 447.

Glendon, M. 2001. *A World Made New: Eleanor Roosevelt and the Universal Declaration of Human Rights*. New York: Random House.

Goodman, R., and Jinks, D. 2004. "How to Influence States: Socialization and International Human Rights Law." *Duke Law Journal* 54: 621.

Lauren, P. 1998. *The Evolution of International Human Rights*. Philadelphia: University of Pennsylvania Press.

Morsink, J. 1999. *Universal Declaration of Human Rights: Origins, Drafting, and Intent*. Philadelphia: University of Pennsylvania Press.

Chapter 2

Human Rights as Rights

Historic documents limiting governmental abuses were often formulated in the language of rights. Examples include the English Bill of Rights (1689, in Ishay 1997), the French Declaration of the Rights of Man and the Citizen (1789, in Ishay 1997), and the US Bill of Rights (1789, in Urofsky and Finkelman 2002). Because of these influential precedents, it is not surprising that the authors of the Universal Declaration chose the concept of rights to express international standards of government conduct. This chapter explains what it means to say that human rights are rights.

Before turning to that, however, a qualification is in order. The political project of creating international standards regulating how governments should treat their citizens and residents does not stand or fall with the concept of rights. That project can be pursued using other normative concepts. Indeed, human rights documents do not use the language of rights exclusively. They often issue prohibitions such as "No one shall be subjected to torture or to inhuman or degrading treatment or punishment" (European Convention, article 3). They sometimes issue requirements such as "Anyone who is detained shall be informed of the reasons for his detention and shall be promptly notified of the charge or charges against him" (American Convention on Human Rights, article 7.4). And they occasionally declare general normative principles such as "All human beings are born free and equal in dignity and rights" (Universal Declaration, article 1). These alternative vocabularies offer both normative and philosophical flexibility. The importance of the concept of rights to the human rights movement can be recognized while avoiding a fetishism of rights.

Elements of Rights

One way to analyze a concept is to look at its elements or parts and the relations between them. For example, if we analyze "biological mother" in this way the elements would include female, parent, and offspring. Because rights often involve complex relationships concerning who has the right and when it can be applied, it is helpful to have a detailed analysis of the parts of a fully specified right.

First, rights have rightholders, parties that possess and exercise the right. For example, I am the holder of the rights conferred by my retirement plan. And the human right to freedom of religion has all persons as its rightholders.

Second, a right is to some freedom, power, immunity, or benefit, which is its scope or object. "Fair trial" roughly identifies the object of the right to a fair trial. This right prescribes that a person charged with a crime must have available a full and genuine opportunity to have a fair trial. It does not require, however, that each accused person actually be given a trial. The accused can waive his or her right to a trial by pleading guilty or accepting a plea bargain. The scope of a right often contains exceptions excluding items that might otherwise be expected to be included. If, for example, the constitutional right to freedom of speech in the United States does not include protection for speeches made from the visitors' gallery during sessions of Congress, this exception could be specified in, or be a consequence of, a full statement of the right's scope.

Third, almost all human rights are or include claim-rights, and such rights identify a party or parties (the addressees or dutybearers) who must act to make available the freedom or benefit identified by the right's scope. (Besides claim-rights there are immunity-rights, power-rights, and privileges (see Hohfeld 1964 and Wenar 2005).) Rights are commonly classified as negative or positive, according to whether the right requires the addressees merely to refrain from doing something or instead to take some positive action they might not otherwise take. Many rights impose on their addressees both negative and positive duties.

Finally, the weight of a right specifies its rank or importance in relation to other norms. Weight pertains to whether a right can be overridden by other considerations in cases of conflict. A prima facie right is a nonabsolute right whose weight is not fully specified. Describing a right as prima facie does not imply that it is only an apparent right but rather asserts that it a genuine right that can sometimes be outweighed by other considerations.

Rights range from abstract to specific (or from general to precise) according to how fully their parts are specified. Indeterminacy can occur in any of the elements of a right. There may be lack of clarity about the identity of the rightholders and addressees. The scope of the right, what it offers its holder(s) and requires of its addressee(s), may be imprecisely defined. And we may lack a clear view of the right's weight in competition with other considerations. One of the confusing things about rights is that they have differing degrees of abstractness. A right under a business contract is likely to be quite specific while constitutional and human rights are usually abstract (and therefore somewhat vague). Abstract rights are just as important as specific rights, so we should not repudiate them simply to achieve some philosophical ideal of precision.

Rights and Goals

Suppose that instead of formulating a bill of rights the human rights movement had formulated high priority goals in areas such as civil liberties, security of the person, due process, and social justice, and had recommended that these goals be pursued by all nations. This vocabulary would have lent itself to formulating a long list of things that it was desirable for governments to do and not do. The resulting "Universal Declaration of High Priority Goals" could have been even more expansive than the Universal Declaration.

A declaration of high priority goals might have had much the same effect, and many of the same problems, as the Universal Declaration. These goals might have served as international standards for governments and led to familiar sorts of disputes about the phrasing, relative priorities, and ambitiousness of the goals. Defenders of these high priority goals might have justified them by appeal to considerations of human welfare, dignity, and equality. Their critics might have charged that high priority goals for such things as civil liberties and due process are Western ideas with few roots in non-Western cultures.

This comparison of goals and rights should help us to recognize some of the distinctive features of rights. I have spoken of high priority goals in order to match an apparent feature of rights, namely, that they are typically very important or high priority considerations. In Ronald Dworkin's phrase, rights are "trumps" (Dworkin 1977). What Dworkin means to suggest with this metaphor is not that rights always prevail over all other considerations but rather that rights – or at least constitutional rights – are strong considerations that generally prevail in competition with other concerns such as national prosperity or administrative convenience. Dworkin proposes "not to call any political aim a right unless it has a certain threshold weight against collective goals; unless, for example, it cannot be defeated by appeal to any of the routine goals of political administration" (Dworkin 1977). Part of the rhetorical appeal of the concept of a right is that having a right to something usually means having a strong claim that can outweigh competing claims.

The assertion that rights are powerful normative considerations does not imply that their weight is absolute or that exceptions cannot be built into their scope. And the weight of a particular right is relative to other considerations at work in a given context. Some rights involve matters that are not of earthshaking importance (for example, the repayment of a small loan). Such rights are powerful in comparison with other considerations normally at work (for example, in the context of a small loan, the debtor's convenience).

The vocabulary of goals, if it had been chosen for the Universal Declaration, would have yielded more flexible standards of government behavior. Even high priority goals can be pursued in various ways and can be deferred when prospects for progress seem dim or when other opportunities are present. Rights, however, are more definite than goals; they specify who is entitled to receive a certain mode of treatment (the rightholders) and who must act on specific occasions to make that treatment available (the addressees).

Rights are more suitable for enforcement than goals because they have identifiable holders, scopes, and addressees. But a theorist who wished to equate rights with some subset of goals might respond that rights are just those goals that are both high priority and definite in the sense of having specific beneficiaries and addressees.

It is not clear, however, that having these two characteristics will make a goal into a right. Suppose that a family chooses as a high priority goal making available to its only child the resources needed to fund a university education. It is clear that such a high priority goal is a lesser commitment than giving the young person a right to the resources needed to attend university. The mandatory character of a right is still missing. As long as providing the resources is merely a high priority goal, the parents would do no wrong if they decided to use their resources to pursue some other project such as providing for their retirement by taking advantage of a very attractive investment opportunity. But if they had given their child a moral right to the resources for a university education through an explicit promise, such a decision would be morally wrong. The mandatory character of a right provides a basis for complaint that a high priority goal may not.

Rights are distinctive not only in their high priority and definiteness but also in their mandatory character. It is these three features – high priority, definiteness, and bindingness – that make the rights vocabulary attractive in formulating minimal standards of decent governmental conduct. This character would be lost if we were to deconstruct rights into mere goals or ideals.

To avoid exaggeration here, however, two qualifications need to be stated. First, rights are never perfect guarantees. To return to our example, a young person who has been given a right to university expenses may face not only deliberate noncompliance with that right but also the parents' inability to pay when the time arrives or even a conflicting, higher priority claim on those resources such as expensive medical treatments for a sibling.

The second qualification concerns the fact discussed above that rights vary greatly in degree of specificity, ranging from very specific, such as a right to reside in a particular apartment under a rental contract, to grand constitutional rights such as due process of law. Abstract rights are much less definite in their requirements than specific rights; indeed, very abstract rights may function in a way not too different from high priority goals. Rights do not always imply clearly who must do what, and hence actions to comply with and implement them are subject to considerable discretion. But when abstract rights can be made concrete in particular cases, they differ from priority goals by conferring on the guidance they provide a binding character that high priority goals lack and cannot confer.

Claiming One's Rights

Some theorists have emphasized the usefulness of rights in claiming things as one's due. By facilitating claiming things as one's due, rights provide especially firm support for dignity and self-respect. Joel Feinberg states this as follows:

> Even if there are conceivable circumstances in which one would admit rights diffidently, there is no doubt that their characteristic use and that for which they are distinctively well suited, is to be claimed, demanded, affirmed, insisted upon . . . Having rights, of course, makes claiming possible, but it is claiming that gives rights their special moral significance . . . Having rights enables us to "stand up like men," to look others in the eye, and to feel in some fundamental way the equal of anyone. (Feinberg 1973; see also Hart 1955; Gewirth 1981; and Pogge 2002)

Moral and legal guarantees of important freedoms, benefits, and powers do seem to support people's self-respect. And we can readily concede that the identification of rightholders to whom the addressees have duties (or other normative burdens) gives rights a more definite meaning than goals. It is less clear, however, that the activity of claiming is somehow central to the meaning of the rights vocabulary or the maintenance of self-respect.

One problem with this assertion is that the notion of claiming a right is very ambiguous: it can involve (1) insisting that one has a right to something (as when civil rights protesters claimed that they had a right to use segregated public libraries); (2) triggering an already recognized right (as when one invokes or triggers one's right to a fair trial in a criminal case by entering a not guilty plea and demanding a trial); (3) demanding compliance with a recognized right in the face of a threatened violation (as when a member of a minority group insists on nondiscrimination from a realtor who is giving him or her the runaround). The assertion that all rights can be claimed in the first and third senses is not very interesting because any norm can be asserted and compliance with it demanded. The second sense is the more interesting one, but not all rights require triggering to be engaged. A person's right not to be tortured can be engaged even if the person is too weak to invoke it.

Another problem concerns the claimant. Must it be the rightholder? Or can claiming by an interested party other than the rightholder serve as well? This difference is important since a self-effacing society might rely almost entirely on an interested party claiming.

These questions show how imprecise it is to say that the distinctive feature of rights is found in the activity of claiming one's due. A further problem with this thesis is that we can easily imagine the concept of a right functioning in cultures where actions such as demanding, claiming, and protesting are frowned on as discourteous. If we generalize from the close connection between rights and claiming in many Western societies, we risk giving an ethnocentric account of the functions of rights – one which overemphasizes social and legal procedures for bringing about the recognition of rights and which suggests that other cultures cannot have or adopt the concept of rights unless they are or become pushy and litigious.

Finally, it is not necessary to identify some particular speech act – claiming or anything else – as the single act which it is the special role of the rights vocabulary to perform. Most words can be utilized in a great many speech acts. Just as the word "good" can be used to perform many speech acts besides commending, the statement that someone has a right can be used to perform many speech acts besides claiming a right to something.

Besides claiming rights, we can recognize them, question them, take them into account, disregard them, respect them, and use them as a basis for decision. Since these other activities give the rights vocabulary a functional role, perhaps all we should say about the connection between rights and claiming is that claiming things as someone's due is one of the characteristic things done by rights talk.

——— Rights and Duties in Morality and Law ———

Rights are found in various normative systems, such as moralities; the regulations of organizations; and local, state, national, and international legal systems. It is common to classify rights by the kind of normative system in which they are rooted. A positive legal right is one that is recognized and implemented within some legal system. A moral right is one that exists within a morality.

Moral rights can be divided into those that exist in actual moralities and those that exist as constructs in critical or justified moralities. An accepted moral right is one that exists within the actual morality of some group or groups. For example, a group's moral code may give people a right not to have their clothes forcibly removed by other persons. Such a right may exist prior to the group's having a formal legal system, and it may be recognized and enforced by the formal legal system once such a system comes into being. Rights often exist both as accepted moral rights and as positive legal rights.

When a right is part of a group's actual morality, it is used as a standard of argument and as a guide to the evaluation of conduct and social policy. Those who refuse to comply may be scolded, shamed, ostracized, exiled, beaten, or even killed. For some rights such recognition and implementation at the moral and social level may be all that is possible or desirable. Legal or governmental implementation may be impossible (as with, say, a right to revolt against repressive governments), or it may be inappropriate because it would be too costly or because its enforcement would require unacceptable violations of other norms.

Many people believe that their moral rights include not only those accepted within their society but also some unrecognized rights they believe to be justifiable. This belief suggests that some rights exist as justified moral rights. A justified morality may be a philosophical reconstruction of morality, of the sort one finds in Kant and Mill, or it may simply be an actual morality that has had some deficient norms replaced with ones believed to be better.

Legal positivists and skeptics hold that we should take legal rights as our exclusive paradigms of rights and thus treat moral rights as degenerate or spurious. Closely connected issues here are whether it should be definitional that rights are constituted by the duties or other normative burdens of the addressees, and whether legal and moral rights are rights in the same sense of the word.

Three broad positions can be taken in response to these questions, corresponding to three stages in the evolution of a legal right. The first stage is the recognition that it is very important for people to have some good available to them – that people are somehow entitled to that good. The second stage involves identifying moral duties, disabilities, and liabilities of some parties that, if they are complied with, will result in the availability of that good. The third stage involves constructing parallel legal duties, disabilities, and liabilities and providing measures for their enforcement; at this stage a legal right emerges.

Each stage corresponds to a position on when it is appropriate to speak of a right. The first, which I call the entitlement theory, endorses a liberal use of the language of rights and holds that it is proper to speak of rights whenever one can justify on moral or legal grounds the proposition that people are entitled to enjoy specific goods – even if we cannot say who should bear the burden of making these goods available or how these entitlements should be implemented and enforced. A more restrictive view, which I call the entitlement-plus theory, holds that entitlements alone cannot constitute full-fledged rights and must be supplemented by the identification of addressees who have appropriate moral duties, disabilities, or liabilities. These burdens on the addressees are the "plus" added to the entitlement to yield a full-fledged right. The third and narrowest position, which I call the legally implemented entitlement theory, agrees with the previous theory in holding that genuine rights are more than mere entitlements, but it holds that this "something more" must include legal implementation. In this view, it is not proper to speak of rights at the earlier stages; the real thing does not emerge until one has effective legal implementation.

The entitlement theory

Broadly, this theory holds that a right is a very strong moral reason why people should have a certain freedom, power, protection, or benefit. H. J. McCloskey puts forward a theory of this kind; he believes that rights are best "explained positively as entitlements to do, have, enjoy, or have done, and not negatively as something against others . . ." (McCloskey

1976). McCloskey's view implies that a full-fledged right need not specify who bears the burden of making available what the right is to; a right is not to be equated with claims against other parties. Of course, rights do often give rise to duties, but McCloskey wishes to emphasize the logical priority of entitlements to the duties they generate. An entitlement might be a strong set of reasons, rooted in the nature of human beings, for ensuring that a certain good is available to people. Since McCloskey believes that entitlements – and thus rights – can exist even when it is not feasible to implement them, he finds no difficulty in saying that a right to medical care, for example, is a universal human right.

The entitlement theory has the advantage of accounting for the wide range of actual uses of the rights vocabulary. McCloskey emphasizes that people often speak of rights when it is unclear who must bear the burdens of these alleged rights. Thus McCloskey would have no objection on linguistic grounds to reformers who declared a new right even though they were unable to specify who would bear the burdens of this right, what exactly these burdens would be, or whether resources were available to meet such burdens. Such rhetorical uses of the rights vocabulary are very common, but a key issue here is whether we should endorse them.

A second advantage of the entitlement theory is that its notion of rights is readily exportable. Talk of entitlements is tied neither to possibly parochial activities such as claiming things as one's due or seeking remedies for wrongs nor to legal implementation. Thus the vocabulary of rights can easily be put to use in diverse cultures.

Viewing rights as mere entitlements, however, is likely to have inflationary results. A moral right will exist whenever there are strong moral reasons for ensuring the availability of a certain good. Hence there is danger that the list of entitlements will be nearly as long as the list of morally valuable goods. To extend the economic metaphor, this conception has no built-in assurance that the demand side of rights will not outrun the supply side.

The entitlement theory is insufficiently penetrating because it is unable to distinguish between rights and high priority goals. It dilutes the mandatory character of rights by cutting out essential reference to their addressees.

The entitlement-plus theory

These problems can be remedied, it seems, by adding essential reference to specific addressees and burdens to our conception of a full-fledged right. This is what the entitlement-plus theory does. It holds that a right cannot be constituted by an entitlement alone, that moral or legal norms directing the behavior of the addressees are essential to the existence of moral or legal rights and must be added to an entitlement to constitute a right.

A version of the entitlement-plus theory of rights is put forward by Joel Feinberg, who makes a useful distinction between "claims-to" benefits and "claims-against" parties to supply those benefits (Feinberg 1973). A claim-to is what I call an entitlement, and a claim-against is the "plus" that can be added to an entitlement. Feinberg's position is that a full-fledged claim-right is a union of a valid claim-to and a valid claim-against. He allows, however, that rights in a weaker, "manifesto," sense can be constituted by a claim-to or entitlement alone. Feinberg's approach makes clear that justifying a right requires one to justify not only an entitlement (or claim-to) but also a claim-against, that is, the burdens that the right will impose on at least one other party.

The entitlement-plus theory fits well with the traditional view that claim-rights are simply duties seen from the perspective of one to whom a duty is owed. In this view the difference between A's right against B and B's duty to A is mainly the difference between the active and the passive voice. From B's perspective the normative relation is a duty and from A's perspective it is a right, but the relation is really the same.

The entitlement-plus theory need not require all full-fledged rights to have precisely specified scopes, weights, and addressees. The vocabulary of rights is used in abstract as well as in specific normative discourse, and one cannot expect abstract rights to be fully specified. The description of an abstract right often identifies only key ideas and leaves specific elements to be worked out at the implementation stage. But even when rights are stated abstractly, as they typically are in human rights documents, there must at least be some general idea of what normative burdens are imposed by the right and who the dutybearers are.

The entitlement-plus theory has important advantages over the entitlement theory. First, it is a more accurate and penetrating analysis in recognizing an essential feature of rights, the burdens they impose on their addressees, which the entitlement theory leaves out. Its penetration comes from its ability to distinguish rights from high priority goals and to explain how both moral and legal rights are rights. Because the entitlement-plus theory holds that even justified moral claim-rights must generate norms that place burdens on addressees, it sees similar normative structures in all kinds of claim-rights, which makes it easier to see that they are all rights in the same sense. Second, the entitlement-plus theory is noninflationary in that it denies that mere entitlements are full-fledged rights.

Still, some will say that the entitlement-plus theory is insufficiently accurate and penetrating because it ignores practices of legal recognition and enforcement and thus fails to emphasize what is practically most important about rights and also fails to mark the very significant difference between legal rights and moral demands. I now turn to this charge, which is central to the third theory of rights.

The legally implemented entitlement theory

It is often claimed that a "right" is mainly a legal notion, that practices of legal enforcement are central to the existence of rights, and that non-legal rights are phony rights. To the nineteenth-century philosopher Jeremy Bentham, the idea of rights not created by positive law was nonsense. Bentham might have been willing to allow that entitlements, in the sense defined above, can exist as conclusions to utilitarian arguments and can serve as grounds for wanting corresponding legal rights. But he held that such entitlements are not rights just as "hunger is not bread" (Waldron 1987).

Bentham held that talk of moral and natural rights is politically dangerous and ultimately unintelligible. An advocate of Bentham's view might point out that when, for example, the right to leave one's country is not legally recognized, respected, or enforced, we sometimes say that people in that country do not have the right to leave or that this right does not exist there. But this mode of speaking proves nothing. One may mean by these statements that the right to leave is not a legal or effectively implemented right in that country without at all wanting to deny that it exists as an accepted or justified moral right. Indeed, it is precisely to demand reform in cases like these that we may wish to appeal to independently existing moral or human rights.

Bentham viewed appeals to nonlegal rights as mere rhetorical ploys, and held that without a court of law to determine who has the right and what it means, talk of rights is merely "a sound to dispute about," allowing argument from undefended premises. But an appeal to rights is no bar to further argument. Underlying assumptions are always open to challenge. Bentham was eager to settle political questions by appeal to what would maximize utility, but there is no system of courts and judges to answer the question of whether a particular policy maximizes utility. Thus, if we accept Bentham's premise that a normative concept without an adjudication procedure merely gives us a sound to dispute about, we must conclude that nothing more is given by the principle of utility that he favored. Subtract Bentham's exaggerated claims about the determinacy of his preferred standard, and it becomes clear that Bentham's attack on the vocabulary of his opponents undermines his own appeals to utility.

A third argument against nonlegal rights is that recognition and enforcement are such important features of our paradigm that unenforced rights cannot be said to be rights in the same sense as enforced rights. According to this view, only by saying that nonlegal rights are rights in a different or phony sense can we adequately reflect the importance of recognition and enforcement to what rights are all about. But important differences often exist within a single generic category. There are huge differences between small economy cars and giant long-distance trucks, but this does not require us to say that they are vehicles in a different sense of "vehicle."

Although noninflationary, the equation of all rights with enforced legal rights excludes talk of important moral rights and severely limits the exportability of the concept of rights. Another disadvantage is that restricting full-fledged rights to legal ones gives important argumentative advantages to defenders of existing social, political, and legal arrangements.

Overview

Rights are high priority mandatory norms that typically have rightholders, addressees, scopes, and weight. They focus on the rightholder and thereby emphasize the freedom or benefit to be obtained or enjoyed. Unlike goals, claim-rights impose moral or legal duties on the addressees. Rights can exist in actual and justified moralities and in national and international legal systems. Legal enforcement is generally important to making rights effective, but is not essential to the existence of rights.

Further Reading

Feinberg, J. 1970. "The Nature and Value of Rights." *Journal of Value Inquiry* 4: 243–51.

Glendon, M. 1991. *Rights Talk: The Impoverishment of Political Discourse.* New York: Free Press.

Hart, H. 1955. "Are there Any Natural Rights?" *Philosophical Review* 64: 175–91.

Wellman, C. 1975. "Upholding Legal Rights." *Ethics* 86: 49–60.

Wenar, L. 2005. "The Nature of Rights." *Philosophy & Public Affairs* 33: 223–52.

Chapter 3

Making Sense of Human Rights

A general explanation of the concept of a right, like the one in Chapter 2, does not tell us what human rights are. An account of the nature of rights explains the genus, but we still need an understanding of the particular species, human rights. The explanation of the genus is helpful, however, because it identifies relevant questions. It shows that we need answers to questions such as what areas of life are covered by human rights, who has human rights, which parties have duties under human rights, how weighty human rights are, and how human rights exist. If we had good answers to these questions, then we would have a general conception of human rights. Questions would remain about the justification, existence, and lists of human rights, but at least we would understand the general idea.

In Chapter 1, human rights were defined as being:

- mandatory norms with rightholders, addressees, and scopes;
- universal in the sense of protecting all people;
- high priority norms with strong justifications;
- not dependent for their existence on recognition by particular governments or on legal enactment at the national level;
- international standards of evaluation and criticism that are not restricted by national boundaries;
- political norms whose primary addressees are governments rather than interpersonal standards;
- numerous and specific norms dealing with matters such as security, due process, liberty, equal citizenship, and basic welfare;
- minimal standards that constrain rather than replace legislation and policy-making at the national level.

This chapter explains and qualifies these characterizations of human rights. Let's begin with the last.

Human Rights as Minimal Standards for Governments

When a widespread human problem is recognized the question arises of whether its remedy should be conceived as a human right. This is not just a political question; it includes the foundational question of whether the problem is serious enough to be a matter of human rights. To answer this question we need to appeal to fundamental values and norms. Discomfort due to hot weather is a widespread human problem, and a right to air conditioning might be proposed as its remedy. But this problem is not serious enough (discomfort does not generally get one into the realm of human rights), and its universal remedy is not feasible enough, to support a universal human right. We can think of the emergence of a human right as the coming together of the recognition of a problem; the belief that the problem is very severe; and optimism about the possibility of addressing it through social and political action at national and international levels. Judgments about the severity of a problem are hard to make because different people are impacted differently by problems and because of the vagueness of the boundary between problems that are severe enough to be matters of human rights and ones that are not. Still, we have strong reasons for limiting international human rights to minimal standards.

Human rights aim at avoiding the terrible rather than achieving the best. Their modality is "must do" rather than "would be good to do." Henry Shue suggests that human rights specify the "lower limits on tolerable human conduct" rather than "great aspirations and exalted ideals" (Shue 1996). As minimal standards they leave most legal and policy matters open to democratic decision-making at the national and local levels. Minimal standards can accommodate a great deal of cultural and institutional variation. Human rights block common threats to a decent or minimally good life for human beings. There are many such threats, however, and we need several dozen specific rights to address them.

As a political morality of the depths, human rights do not attempt to prescribe a general theory of distributive justice or give an account of optimal democratic institutions. Instead they prescribe equality in areas where inequality would be entirely unacceptable, and demand that countries allow political participation and have regular elections.

There are four strong reasons why international human rights should be minimal standards. First, it is by insisting that human rights address very severe problems that we ensure their high priority and universality. If human rights are created to deal with problems such as smoking and the unavailability of holidays with pay, this may undermine the claim of human rights to have great importance.

Another reason is to leave ample room for democratic decision-making at the national level. It is appropriate for a country's citizens and legislators to have the power to shape laws, institutions, and practices to fit popular desires, the country's cultures and traditions, and physical and economic circumstances. Globalization is already producing excessive uniformity around the world. Human rights should not contribute to such uniformity except in a few important areas where only one way is the acceptable way.

The third reason why human rights should be minimal standards is that this helps make them acceptable to countries who prize their independence and self-determination. The requirements of widespread and ongoing participation by sovereign states in human rights institutions need to be taken seriously (see the discussion of national self-determination in Chapter 6). Limiting the scope of international human rights is such a requirement.

The final reason is that by limiting human rights to minimal standards we make them more likely to be feasible in the vast majority of the world's countries. Human rights will do little work if they are so expansive that many countries can see them only as distant ideals to be realized some time in the future.

Who Has Human Rights?

A simple answer to this question is "Humans!" – all human beings everywhere and at all times. That human rights apply to all people without distinction has been a major theme of the human rights movement. Nevertheless, reflection on the idea that the holders of human rights are simply all people reveals that this answer is too broad.

First, some rights are held only by adult citizens, not by all persons. The clause of the Civil and Political Covenant dealing with political participation begins not with "Everyone" but with "Every citizen" (article 25). Further, the rights of people who are very young, severely retarded, comatose, or senile are justifiably limited. Although these people have important rights such as life, due process, and freedom from torture, it would be implausible to argue that they have rights to vote, run for political office, or travel freely on their own. These latter rights presuppose a greater degree of rationality and agency than some human beings possess.

Furthermore, some human rights cannot be universal in the strong sense of applying to all humans at all times, because they assert that people are entitled to services tied to relatively recent social and political institutions. Specific human rights are only as timeless as the specific problems they address. Some human rights problems have been with us for millennia, such as violence related to getting or retaining political power. Others have emerged in the last few centuries with the arrival all over the globe of the modern state, with its associated legal, penal, bureaucratic, educational, and economic branches (on the spread of modern political institutions see Morris 1998; see also Donnelly 2003: 92, 117). Human rights deal with security, liberties, fair trials, political participation, equality, basic welfare, and perhaps even the natural environment.

Due process rights, for example, presuppose modern legal systems and the institutional safeguards they can offer. Social and economic rights presuppose modern relations of production and the institutions of the redistributive state. My point here is not merely that people living 10,000 years ago would not have thought to demand these rights but rather that the scope of these rights can be defined only by reference to institutions that did not then exist (on "embracing temporal relativity" see Tasioulas 2002b: 87). Human rights could be formulated in much broader terms to avoid this objection, but the result would be very abstract rights, subject to a variety of interpretations and hence less useful in political criticism and less suitable for legal implementation.

Assigning Responsibilities for Human Rights

Rights have identifiable addressees – people or agencies who have responsibilities related to the realization of the right. This connection between rights and the assignment of responsibilities is a basis for a frequently voiced question: who bears duties in regard to human rights? On hearing, for example, that people have rights to food and education, one may wonder whether individuals have duties to try to provide these things out of their own resources.

The primary addressees of human rights are the world's governments. Human rights are not ordinary moral norms applying mainly to interpersonal conduct. Rather they are political norms dealing mainly with how people should be treated by their governments and institutions. The political focus of human rights is very clear in the human rights treaties. The European Convention, for example, requires participating governments to "secure to everyone within their jurisdiction the rights and freedoms defined [in] this convention" (article 1). It also requires that "Everyone whose rights and freedoms as set forth in this Convention are violated shall have an effective remedy before a national authority notwithstanding that the violation has been committed by persons acting in an official capacity" (article 13). This requirement presupposes that governments are often both addressees and violators. The struggle to gain respect for a human right must often attempt to get the government both to restrain its own agencies and officials and to use its legal powers to restrain others.

If Almeida is a citizen or permanent resident of Brazil, the government of Brazil has the heaviest duties to respect and uphold Almeida's human rights. Brazil has duties not just to refrain from violating Almeida's human rights; it also has duties to uphold them through actions such as implementing them legislatively, protecting them with police work, providing legal remedies in the courts, and providing services such as food assistance. But we should not conclude from this that all of Almeida's rights are against the government of Brazil, or that all of the human rights duties of the Brazilian government are duties to its citizens.

Some of Almeida's human rights are against people and governments in other countries who at least have duties not to kill or imprison him without trial. When Almeida is standing peacefully on the Brazilian side of the Brazil/Bolivia border, a Bolivian police officer standing nearby on the other side of the border has the same human rights duty not to shoot Almeida as he has not to shoot a peaceable Bolivian citizen as she walks along the Bolivian side of the border.

Further, people and governments in other countries, along with international organizations, may have back-up responsibilities for Almeida's human rights when the government of Brazil is unwilling or unable to respect or uphold them. The United Nations and the World Bank, for example, may have duties to monitor human rights conditions in Brazil and to promote compliance with human rights. International corporations operating there may also have responsibilities (Weissbrodt 2005).

Because of the failures of many states to respect and uphold the rights of their residents, it is tempting to assign these tasks to international organizations such as the United Nations or to hope that a world federation or government will soon emerge to assume them. International organizations, however, have limited authority and power to enforce rights around the world. And a world federation or government currently seems at best a distant possibility. At present no alternative exists to assigning sovereign states the main responsibility for upholding the rights of their residents. This is a hard saying since many governments are corrupt and weak, and reform and development have proven hard to bring about through outside pressure and assistance.

Saying that the primary addressees of human rights are governments is not the end of the story, however. Individuals also have responsibilities generated by human rights. This view is suggested by the Universal Declaration. Its preamble suggests that human rights have implications for the conduct of individuals when it says that "every individual and every organ of society, keeping this Declaration constantly in mind, shall strive by teaching and education to promote respect for these rights and freedoms and by progressive measures national and international to secure their universal and effective recognition and observance." Clearly, the authors of the Universal Declaration believed that both states and individuals have obligations in regard to human rights. A rationale for this view is that if the justifying reasons for human rights are substantial enough to override domestic law and justify risks of international conflict, those grounding reasons are also likely to generate obligations for individuals in matters subject to their control.

Further, people participate as individuals in human rights abuses such as racial discrimination, slavery, domestic violence, and political killings (Cook 1994). When article 4 of the Universal Declaration asserts, "No one shall be held in slavery or servitude, slavery and the slave trade shall be prohibited in all their forms," the main violators of this right are not governments. Slaveholders have generally been individuals, although governments have often supported and institutionalized slavery. The right to freedom from slavery obligates individuals and governments not to hold slaves and further requires governments to pass legislation making slavery illegal. When article 11 of the Convention on the Elimination of All Forms of Discrimination against Women (United Nations 1979) commits ratifying countries to "take all appropriate measures to eliminate discrimination against women in the field of employment," it is clear that this requires governments to pass legislation prohibiting discrimination by private businesses, firms, and corporations.

One approach to explaining how and why citizens share in the duties generated by human rights views the citizens of a country as having ultimate responsibility for the human rights duties of their government. If their government has a duty to respect or implement the right to a fair trial, or a duty to aid poor countries, its citizens share in that duty. They are required as voters, political agents, and taxpayers to try to promote and support their government's compliance with its human rights duties. This principle of shared responsibility is particularly attractive in democratic societies where the citizens are the ultimate source of political authority. This view makes individuals back-up addressees for the duties of their governments. Thomas Pogge has taken a related but slightly different approach to generating individual duties from human rights that have governments as their primary addressees (Pogge 2002: 67). Pogge emphasizes Universal Declaration article 28 which says that "Everyone is entitled to a social and international order in which the rights and freedoms set forth in this Declaration can be fully realized." Pogge sees in this article a plausible norm, namely that both countries and individuals have duties not to be complicit in an international order that unfairly disadvantages poor countries and the people in them.

The complex view of the addressees of human rights sketched above can be illustrated using the right against torture (Nickel 1993a). Duties to refrain from engaging in torture can feasibly be borne and fulfilled by all persons and agencies, so this duty can be addressed to all. An adequate response to people's entitlement not to be tortured also requires finding individuals or institutions that can protect people against torture. The right to protection against torture can be universal without all of the corresponding duties being against everyone, or against some single worldwide agency. What is required is that there be for every rightholder at least one agency with duties to protect that person from torture. This agency will typically be the government of one's country of citizenship or residence. The duty not to torture falls on everyone; the duty to protect against torture falls primarily on governments.

There may also be secondary addressees who bear back-up or monitoring responsibilities connected with the right against torture. The people of a country are secondary addressees with respect to fundamental rights. They bear the responsibility of creating and maintaining a social and political order that respects and protects the right to freedom from torture. International institutions are also secondary addressees. They bear the responsibility of assisting, encouraging, and pressuring governments to refrain from torture and to provide effective protections against torture. If national or international institutions are unable to fulfill this responsibility there is the possibility of reforming them or creating new ones (Shue 1996: 166).

--------------- **Scope, Weight, and Trade-Offs** ---------------

Human rights are both mandatory and high priority. As mandatory norms, they are not mere goals. Meeting their demands is obligatory, not merely a good thing. As high priority norms, they generally prevail in competition with other considerations – including advancing utility, prosperity, national security, and good relations with other countries. To have high priority they must be supported by strong moral and practical reasons.

It is not plausible, however, to suggest that all human rights are absolute, that they can never be suspended or sacrificed for other goods. As James Griffin says, "The best account of human rights will make them resistant to trade-offs, but not too resistant" (Griffin 2001: 314). At least some civil and political rights can be restricted by public and private property rights, by restraining orders related to domestic violence, and by legal punishments. Further, after a disaster such as a hurricane or earthquake, freedom of movement in the area is often appropriately suspended to keep out the curious, to permit free movement of emergency vehicles and equipment, and to prevent looting. The Civil and Political Covenant permits rights to be suspended during times "of public emergency which threatens the life of the nation" (article 4). Yet it excludes some rights from suspension including the right to life, the prohibition of torture, the prohibition of slavery, the prohibition of ex post facto criminal laws, and freedom of thought and religion.

Human rights and their exercise are generally subject to regulation by law. For example, rights to freedom of speech, religious practice, assembly, movement, and political participation require substantial qualification and regulation so that they harmonize with each other and with other important considerations. A system of human rights must adjust the scopes and weights of its rights so that they can coexist with each other and form a coherent system (Rawls 1971, 1993). The right to privacy, for example, must be adjusted to coexist with the right to a fair trial. And the right to security against crimes has to be accommodated to rights to due process of law.

The scope of a right is the benefit, freedom, power, or immunity that it confers upon its holders. For example, specifying the scope of the right to freedom of religion involves describing a set of freedoms in the area of religious belief and practice that the holders of the right enjoy. Weight concerns the ranking or priority of a right when it conflicts with other considerations. To be exceptionless is a matter of scope, and to be absolute is a matter of weight. Nevertheless, it is often difficult to know whether the failure of a right to outweigh competing considerations and to dictate the result that should be followed, all things considered, in a particular case is best described as an instance of its containing an implicit qualification (scope) or as an instance of its being overridden (weight).

Suppose that Kim wants to exercise her right of free speech by marching into the courtroom in which Lee is on trial and telling the jury some fact that is barred from them by the rules of evidence (for example, about

Lee's criminal record). Here Kim's right to speak would conflict with Lee's right to a fair trial. Suppose further that we agree that Kim should not be allowed to speak to the jury and that the relevant rights do not, all things considered, require that she be allowed to do this. There are two possible ways of describing the failure of Kim's right to freedom of speech to prevail here. One approach says that the right to free speech, properly understood, does not include within its boundaries a right to enter a courtroom and tell the jury things about the defendant they are precluded from knowing. Here the matter is treated as one of scope. The other description says that Kim's right of free speech applied in this situation would normally have required that she be allowed to speak, but it was outweighed in this unusual case by Lee's right to a fair trial, which is of higher priority. Here the matter is treated as one of weight.

In this instance it is probably best to see the matter as one of scope. One might hope that all conflicts between norms could be dealt with as they arose by redrawing boundaries and inserting exceptions. Boundaries would eventually be adjusted to minimize or eliminate conflicts, and the relative priority of different norms would be reflected in the expansion or retraction of their boundaries when they covered contiguous areas.

All the same, at least three barriers stand in the way of this program. One is that we cannot anticipate all conflicts between rights and with other norms, and we are often uncertain about what we should do in the cases we can imagine. A second barrier is that a right containing sufficient qualifications and exceptions to avoid all possible conflicts would probably be too complex to be generally understood. Third, relieving a conflict by building in an exception will sometimes incorrectly imply that the overridden right did not really apply and that we need feel no regret about our treatment of the person whose right was overridden. The most awful moral dilemmas are conflicts not at the edges of rights or duties but at their very centers. Adding exceptions to cover such cases may lead us to see what is happening as nontragic, rather than as calling for regret, apology, and – if possible – compensation. Retaining the vocabulary of weight and overriding may help us to remember that not all moral dilemmas can be anticipated or resolved in advance and that in hard cases even our best efforts may result in serious harm or unfairness (Ignatieff 2004).

When we describe human rights as prima facie rights because we cannot provide in advance adequate accounts of how to deal with conflicts between human rights and other important considerations, we render irrelevant the sorts of objections that could be made if we claimed that human rights are absolute or near absolute. Prima facie rights are far easier to defend, but their implications for practice are often unclear. If no substantial competing values are present, a prima facie right will tell us what to do. But when substantial competing considerations are present, as they often are, prima facie rights are silent. The danger is that prima facie rights will provide no guidance in the cases where guidance is needed most.

Two responses can be made to this objection. First, there is no reason why the scopes of prima facie rights cannot be defined in considerable detail or principles for ranking them in relation to competing considerations worked out. Classifying a right as prima facie implies not that this sort of work cannot be done, but that we recognize that the work will always remain partially unfinished. Second, appeals to human rights should be seen as part of moral and political argument, not as the whole of it. The presence of claims about human rights does not mean that less specialized forms of moral and political argument cannot be invoked.

Are Human Rights Inalienable?

We say that human rights are universal to avoid leaving the oppressed noncitizen, minority group member, or social outcast without rights to stand on. We claim that human rights are inalienable so that oppressive governments cannot say their subjects have forfeited or voluntarily given up their rights. Further, the idea that human rights are inalienable fits nicely with the idea that governments are not the ultimate source of human rights. What governments do not give they also cannot take away.

Inalienability means that a right cannot be permanently forfeited or given up entirely. The inalienability of a right implies that the rightholder's attempts to repudiate that right permanently, or attempts by others to take that right away, will be without normative effect. If people and government agencies lack the moral power to eliminate permanently a right of their own or others, that disability makes the right inalienable. And since the right cannot be eliminated, those who act as if it had been eliminated will violate it.

One problem with the claim that human rights are inalienable is that some of the rights in the Universal Declaration are forfeitable in many legal systems upon conviction of serious crimes. Most systems of criminal punishment use incarceration as a penalty, and thereby suppose that criminals forfeit at least temporarily their right to liberty. In spite of such examples, advocates of human rights often worry that the idea of forfeiture, if admitted, could consume too many rights. Admitting the possibility of forfeiture seems to invite oppressors to say that unpopular groups have forfeited their rights to life, liberty, or decent treatment. Nevertheless, this possibility is not sufficient to show that all human rights are immune to forfeiture. Most normative concepts are susceptible to rhetorical abuse.

The claim that human rights cannot voluntarily be repudiated wholesale is also problematic. Some eighteenth-century rights theorists asserted the inalienability of natural rights because they wanted to counter the Hobbesian claim that people had agreed to give up all their rights when they left the state of nature and entered civil society (Hobbes 1981). And perhaps we can agree that some minimal rights to security and liberty are inalienable and hence that individuals lack the power to permanently waive those rights.

I doubt, however, that we can plausibly say that every human right is immune to repudiation. People choose to give up many basic liberties when they voluntarily enter monasteries or military service, yet we would not forbid these actions. Likewise, people may accept permanent limits on what they can say and publish about certain topics in order to receive a security clearance for government intelligence work. As a general conclusion about the inalienability of specific human rights I suggest that they are hard to lose but that few are strictly inalienable (for a stronger view of inalienability see Donnelly 2003: 10).

The Existence of Human Rights

Human rights are often held to exist independently of acceptance or enactment as law. The attraction of this position is that it permits critics of repressive regimes to appeal to human rights whether or not those regimes accept human rights or recognize them in their legal systems. Yet the contention that human rights exist independently of acceptance or enactment has always provoked skepticism. If human rights were mere wishes or aspirations, we could say that they exist in people's minds. In order to be norms that are binding on all people, however, human rights must be far more than wishes or aspirations.

It is possible to sidestep skeptical doubts about the independent existence of human rights by pointing to their place in international law. For example, the right to leave a country is found in article 12 of the Civil and Political Covenant, a treaty that is now part of international law. Under this treaty a person who wishes to leave her country (and who is not fleeing debts or criminal prosecution) has in this right a strong justification, and her government has a corresponding obligation to allow her to go. As this example suggests, human rights can exist as legal rights within international law.

When human rights are implemented in international law, we continue to speak of them as human rights; but when they are implemented in domestic law we tend to describe them as civil or constitutional rights. It is possible, however, for a right to be instantiated within more than one normative system at the same time. For example, a right to freedom from torture could be a right within a justified morality, a right within the domestic legal system, and a right within international law. This kind of congruence is an ideal of the human rights movement, which seeks broad conformity between various levels of law, existing moral codes, and the standards of enlightened moralities.

Because human rights are now enacted within many national and international legal systems, the worries of legal positivists about unenforced moral rights are no longer fatal to taking human rights seriously. As Louis Henkin observes, "Political forces have mooted the principal philosophical objections, bridging the chasm between natural and positive law by converting natural human rights into positive legal rights" (Henkin 1978: 19). This view is much more plausible today than when Henkin wrote it because nearly all countries have by now committed themselves to human rights treaties and because mechanisms for protecting human rights at the international level have become more powerful and better accepted.

Still, it would be better for the general applicability and stability of human rights if their availability as standards of criticism were not dependent on enactment or acceptance. Many have followed this line of thought, and thus human rights are commonly characterized as *moral rights*. A right is a moral right if it exists as a norm within an actual or justified morality.

Accepted moral rights are rights that are recognized and mostly respected in actual human moralities today. These rights can exist before a formal legal system is established and may later become legal rights. Perhaps most actual moralities confer some rights on individuals, but it is not clear that accepted norms are adequate to support rights of international applicability. If human rights are to be generated by the various accepted moralities that exist around the world, these moralities must share a commitment to principles of the sort found in the Universal Declaration. It is not clear that enough moral agreement exists worldwide to support anything like the full range of rights declared in contemporary manifestos (but see Chapter 11 below), and ordinary interpersonal moralities usually have little to say about matters such as fair trials and equality before the law.

A human rights advocate who asserts that human rights are binding on governments independently of acceptance and international law will probably construe human rights as existing within *justified moralities* rather than within all accepted moralities. A justified morality is one that is well supported by appropriate reasons. John Stuart Mill, a nineteenth-century advocate of what we now call human rights, would have allowed that there is little agreement worldwide in accepted moralities about basic rights (Mill 2002b). But he would have claimed nonetheless that human rights exist within justified moralities – which in his view would all give a prominent place to the principle of utility.

Viewing justified moralities as the ultimate home of human rights requires strong epistemological and metaphysical and moral commitments. It requires believing that moral and political reasons of worldwide applicability exist and that most humans have the epistemological capacities required to recognize and apply them. It requires believing that the grounds of human rights are in some sense objective. I find these propositions believable, and think that plausible metaethical grounds can be found for them. But I do not attempt a defense of them here. I should say, however, that viewing the human moral capacity as competent, in principle, to permit the recognition of universal human rights does not warrant moral arrogance. Human moral capacities, like other cognitive and emotional capacities, are extremely fallible. Further, shared moral capacities need not yield uniform principles if circumstances in different societies are substantially different. The universality of norms must be defended by showing that problems and circumstances in different cultures are sufficiently similar as to permit broad underlying principles to yield similar specific principles.

The analysis of rights offered in Chapter 2 held that a full-fledged right is an entitlement-plus, which implies that for a justified moral right to exist, two things must obtain. First, there must be a justifiable entitlement to a freedom or benefit. Second, it must be possible to justify the duties or other burdens that require making this freedom or benefit available to all. A justified moral right, in this view, is an entitlement with holders, scope, weight, and addressees that is supported by strong moral reasons. At the level of theory, the identification of these elements may be fairly abstract, with many details left unspecified. Nonetheless, at least a vague conception of the content of these elements must be present for one to have a full-fledged right.

A justified morality does not need to be accepted or practiced by anyone, nor does it necessarily have a social or institutional dimension. Thus the question arises: are the principles and rights that constitute such a justified morality sufficiently robust and determinate to be binding in actual situations here and now? What the knowledge of human rights comes to in this view is – at a minimum – knowledge of strong reasons for adopting and following a certain set of norms. The Universal

Declaration can accordingly be seen as an international attempt to specify the content of such a justified morality in the area of relations between people and their governments.

Legal positivists doubt that the principles of justified moralities are sufficiently knowable to be worth talking about or whether it is worthwhile, in our contemporary Babel with its many competing voices and views, to talk about principles everyone would be justified in adopting. They prefer the cold steel of legally implemented rights to the hot air of justified human rights. One who sees human rights as existing most fundamentally as justified moral rights may have the same preference but believe that, in those areas where we lack international agreement on norms that can be implemented everywhere through domestic and international law, we should continue discussing, and trying to identify, define, and promote justifiable norms. Human rights declarations and treaties are usefully seen as an attempt to formulate some fixed points in this discussion, to identify some rights that are widely accepted and strongly supported by good reasons. The belief that it is possible to formulate such a list rests on the belief that human beings have a substantial capacity for moral understanding and progress, but the need for such a list presupposes that the unaided consciences of government officials will not reliably provide fully adequate beliefs about how people ought to behave and how society ought to be organized.

──────── ## How Human Rights Guide Behavior ────────

Some of the ways in which human rights can guide behavior are obvious; in other areas the guidance they provide is complicated or problematic. In the obvious cases, full-fledged rights direct the behavior of their addressees through negative and positive duties. For example, a right to freedom from torture guides behavior by defining torture (see Levinson 2004), forbidding everyone to engage in it, and imposing a duty on governments to protect people against it. Still, the prohibition of torture is likely to be vague, and adjudication may be needed to refine its meaning.

Many issues about dealing with torture are not directly covered by a right against torture. Formulations of the right against torture are likely to provide little guidance about (1) what actual and potential victims of torture may do to defend themselves; (2) how ordinary citizens should relate to those they suspect of being engaged in torture (for example, do they have a duty to try to interrupt torture sessions, or a duty not to sell groceries to torturers?); (3) how citizens and officials should respond when the right to be free from torture is not legally recognized; and (4) how people and governments from other countries should respond to known cases of torture. Determinate answers to these questions cannot usually be found by appeal to human rights alone. Other moral and political principles must play an ongoing role. It is often necessary to look back to the abstract moral principles that underlie specific human rights, sideways to moral considerations other than rights, and forward to likely consequences. A list of human rights is only a partial guide to, and not a substitute for, moral and political deliberation.

Guidance from rights that are not accepted or implemented

Even when a human right is not generally recognized or legally implemented in a country, it can guide the behavior of those who believe it is morally justified. Suppose that Fariz is an adherent of the Baha'i faith – which is unpopular in some countries – and that she sincerely believes in the right to freedom of religion for herself and others. The validity of this norm is confirmed, she thinks, by its international recognition in the Universal Declaration and human rights treaties. As a holder of this justified moral right, Fariz has the moral liberty to hold Baha'i beliefs, to engage in Baha'i religious practices, and to instruct her children in the Baha'i faith. It is clear that Fariz's recognition of these norms – whether or not they are socially or legally recognized – can guide her behavior. This right can also guide the behavior of its addressees. As one of these addressees, Fariz will have a moral duty not to interfere with the religious beliefs and practices of others. Fariz would do wrong to disrupt a religious meeting by Jehovah's Witnesses, and if she were a public official, she would do wrong to sponsor legislation to outlaw the Jehovah's Witnesses from proselytizing or to force the children of its members to undergo instruction in the Baha'i faith.

Rights can guide behavior not only by directing it with duties and other normative elements (the stronger and more usual case) but also by providing reasons or justification for it (the weaker case). For example, a violation of one's right to freedom of religion, or the likelihood of such a violation, may provide a reason or justification for such actions as refusing to obey a law, engaging in public protest, or seeking to emigrate. Not all the guidance obtainable from a human right is found in its scope.

What to do about violations of human rights

Governments have dual and conflicting roles in relation to human rights. On the one hand their sponsorship is needed to make many rights effective, and on the other hand they are often the most significant potential source of violations. The struggle to gain respect for a human right must often attempt to get a government both to restrain itself and to use its legal powers to restrain others. Where human rights violations are deep and systematic, rights advocates must devise strategies for political change that are not in the scope of human rights. Here respect for and implementation of human rights becomes a goal, and means–end or strategic reasoning must be used to pursue this goal.

Similarly, we generally cannot deduce from the content of a human right alone the best strategies for promoting and protecting that right at the international level. How large a role countries should play in promoting human rights abroad cannot be settled by appeal to human rights alone. Other relevant considerations include the means chosen (for example, diplomacy, pressure, intervention), the likelihood of success, the weight assigned to the principle of nonintervention in the domestic affairs of other countries, and competing claims on national energy and resources. As before, these additional considerations do not seem to be part of the rights themselves but must rather come from general moral and political principles. Human rights do not provide complete guidance to political action – not even to political action directed at human rights violations.

Legal guidance

The paradigm of legal implementation at the national level for a human right has two parts: (1) enactment in abstract terms in a constitution or bill of rights, and (2) enactment in more specific terms in statutes that become part of the day-to-day law of the realm. To protect freedom of religion, a constitutional norm might commit a country to religious freedom and tolerance, separation of church and state, and state neutrality between different religious groups. For example, article 4 of the Constitution ("Basic Law") of Germany prescribes religious freedom in the following terms:

> Freedom of faith and of conscience, and freedom to profess a religious or philosophical creed, shall be inviolable. The undisturbed practice of religion shall be guaranteed. No one may be compelled against his conscience to

render military service involving the use of arms. Details shall be regulated by a federal law.

As the last sentence of this article suggests, legislation will usually be needed to apply these general principles to specific national problems, which might include the institutional status of the dominant religious group, tax exemptions for religious organizations, the policy toward parochial schools and toward religious education in the public schools, and exemptions from military service for conscientious objectors.

Enactment in effective national or international law is perhaps the most important means of implementing human rights. But legal enactment is neither necessary nor sufficient for the realization of human rights. Legal enactment is not always necessary because in some lucky societies the attitudes of the public and of government officials are so supportive of particular rights that no enforcement is necessary. And it is not always sufficient because legal enactment in a showcase bill of rights does little or nothing to realize a right.

Persuasion and legislation are obviously not mutually exclusive. In fact, education of the population in sound moral and political principles is often one of the main goals of human rights legislation. Most compliance with human rights must be voluntary and based on acceptance.

Overview

To make sense of human rights it is necessary to qualify them. Human rights are minimal standards. They deal with severe political abuses that undermine fundamental interests and deprive people of dignity. Accordingly, their content is as varied as those abuses. Human rights are primarily against governments but secondarily against individuals and international organizations. Secondary addressees play a back-up role; they are required to step in when the primary addressees are unwilling or unable to fulfill their responsibilities. Human rights are high priority norms that are universal and hard to lose. To say that human rights are high priority norms is not generally to say that they are absolute. Universality is qualified by restriction to current times; specific human rights are not transhistorical. Further, human rights are sometimes rights of citizens rather than of all people. Human rights provide direct guidance to their holders and addressees. Fundamental rights do not, however, provide complete guidance as to details of implementation, appropriate responses to noncompliance, and strategies for promoting compliance. A list of rights cannot serve as an alternative to political thought and deliberation.

Further Reading

Beitz, C. 2004. "Human Rights and the Law of Peoples." In Deen Chatterjee (ed.), *The Ethics of Assistance*, 193–214. Cambridge: Cambridge University Press.
Henkin, L. 1978. *The Rights of Man Today.* Boulder, CO: Westview Press.
Pogge, T. 2001a. "How should Human Rights be Conceived?" In P. Hayden (ed.), *The Philosophy of Human Rights*, 187–210. St. Paul, MN: Paragon House.
Rawls, J. 1999. *The Law of Peoples.* Cambridge, MA: Harvard University Press.

Chapter 4

Starting Points for Justifying Human Rights

Human rights need strong grounds. If we think of human rights as justified moral rights, they simply do not exist apart from their grounds. But even when the human rights in question are national or international legal rights, existence in law alone will not ensure us that they are powerful and compelling. If a human rights declaration or treaty tells us that a right is important enough to be a human right we will not believe it unless we think that suitably strong supporting reasons for that right are likely to be available. And we need to know how strong the grounds of rights are to have accurate views of their weights, and of how much energy and other resources it is appropriate to spend on their implementation.

This chapter offers a pluralistic justificatory framework for human rights. It endorses several kinds of justifications of human rights: (1) prudential arguments, that is, one's claiming that people will have better prospects for a good life when they live under a political system that recognizes, respects, and protects their human rights; (2) utilitarian and pragmatic justifications; and (3) arguments from plausible moral norms and values, including fairness, dignity, minimal well-being, security, and liberty. Also endorsed (in Chapter 5) are linkage arguments that show that one right is necessary to the effective implementation of another.

The approach taken here does not pursue a highly parsimonious set of starting points because that pursuit often requires one to leave aside plausible justifications. If human dignity, for example, is not one of the fundamental values or norms of the theory it is likely to disappear, never to be seen again. It will not do any work in justifying human rights, even if it is well suited to do so. Simplicity is a valuable aspiration in some theoretical contexts, but if we adhere to it while trying to justify human rights the result may be that they seem less justifiable than they actually are. When one pushes good ways of justifying human rights off the stage and puts one's own single favored way in the limelight, one's justification may look thin and vulnerable. Alone under the spotlight, its weak spots are likely to be apparent. Readers may think that if this is the best justification for human rights, those rights are really shaky.

James Griffin, for example, justifies human rights entirely by reference to the values of "personhood" (or autonomy) and "practicalities." He takes this to be the "best philosophical account of human rights":

> What seems to me the best account of human rights is this. It is centered on the notion of agency. We human beings have the capacity to form pictures of what a good life would be and to try to realize these pictures. We value our status as agents especially highly, often more highly even than our happiness. Human rights can then be seen as protections of our agency – what one might call our personhood. (Griffin 2000: 4)

Autonomy by itself does not seem likely to be able to generate due process rights, or rights to nondiscrimination and equality before the law. To compensate, Griffin accordingly relies heavily on "practicalities" in allowing these rights. The result, in my view, is to make the justification of rights other than liberties appear shaky and derivative. This could have been avoided by introducing some other fundamental values or norms. Viewing the claim to life as fundamental makes it unnecessary to try to derive it from autonomy. And taking as basic a requirement of fair treatment when very important interests are at stake would be no more controversial than autonomy as a starting point for human rights, and it would allow due process rights to be as central and nonderivative as liberty rights (for discussion and criticism of Griffin's justification of human rights see Tasioulas 2002b).

Prudential Reasons for Human Rights

In this section I present and discuss a prudential justification for human rights. It views good reasons for accepting and complying with rights as prudential reasons – reasons relating to a person's own prospects for a good life. Here, the basic premises pertain to what norms a prudent person, fully aware of her own status as a person and of the circumstances in which she lives, would find it reasonable to accept and live by (see Schulz 2001 for another attempt to offer prudential grounds for international rights).

The general idea of a prudential justification is that I (or you) will have better chances for a good life in a society that respects and protects human rights. Security rights, fundamental freedoms, and the other families of rights all contribute to making society safer, more harmonious, and more productive. In terms of my (your) own interests, I am (you are) likely to be better off, and hence I (you) have good reason to accept and support human rights.

Instead of focusing on the global effects of respecting and protecting human rights, a prudential argument could focus on particular interests that are general and strong. Let's say that a *fundamental interest* of a person is an interest in conditions necessary to surviving during a normal lifespan or to developing and exercising central features of human personality. Survival during a normal lifespan is a fundamental interest in this sense. It generates more specific interests such as access to food and water, security against murderous attacks, and to assistance when injured or sick. Other examples of fundamental interests include some degree of freedom of action, and access to social interaction and cooperation. Fundamental interests are general in the sense that almost everyone has them, and strong in the sense that they will generally outweigh other interests. As conditions of having a life as a person, they will generally prevail over interests within a person's life. A prudential argument from fundamental interests attempts to show that it would be reasonable to accept and comply with a system of rights – when most others are likely to do so – because these norms are part of the best means for protecting one's fundamental interests against actions and omissions that endanger them. We can illustrate this with the following prudential argument for legal protections of basic liberties such as freedom of thought and communication, freedom of association, and freedom of movement.

1   I have a fundamental interest in enjoying the basic liberties, but these liberties are vulnerable to infringement by the government and by other individuals. There are widely experienced threats to people's basic liberties that pose dangers to me.

2   The only way to protect this interest in enjoying the basic liberties includes – whatever else it may involve – getting government to create, and most other people to support, a system of legal protections of my basic liberties that I can invoke as a matter of enforceable personal right.

3   If something is an indispensable means to protecting my fundamental interests, then I have a fundamental interest in the availability of that means.

4   (Subordinate conclusion) I have a fundamental interest in getting government to create and other people to respect legal protections of my basic liberties that I can invoke as a matter of enforceable personal right.

5   Most other people's interests in having such protections enacted, respected, and protected are very similar to mine and have roughly the same strength.

6   Others are unlikely to support such protections unless both I and the government recognize their claims to the same protections that I find desirable. To provide such protections will be expensive for government, and government will pass some of those costs on to me in the form of taxes. And I will be subject to restraints on abilities that I might otherwise have to interfere with the freedoms of others. But the burdens involved in complying with and supporting this system of legal protections will be tolerable, and hence these burdens are insufficient to outweigh my fundamental interest in the availability of the protections.

7   Conclusion: when government and my fellow citizens will support a system of legal protections for my basic liberties, I have good prudential reasons for supporting and complying with that system.

This form of argument works equally well for fundamental interests other than liberty. Substituting "security" for "liberty" turns it into something like Thomas Hobbes's argument for a legal regime to protect security rights (Hobbes 1981, originally published 1651).

The argument's second and third premises assert that necessary means of protecting one's basic liberties include creating enforceable legal norms. Since other people need to be willing to accept the norms for the project to succeed, I cannot hope that the norms and protections will be ones enormously favorable to me and unfavorable to other people.

The last premise deals with costs or burdens. One issue here concerns how much the protections of the basic liberties should be qualified to make its costs bearable. A system of unqualified protections of liberty might harm my interests more than it helped them if it failed to allow the legal prohibition of actions of others that cause significant harm to me. This illustrates the general possibility of making the cost of a system of rights more bearable by building in exceptions for areas where their operation would do more harm than good to my fundamental interests.

Another issue related to costs concerns the time frame. There are likely to be cases in which other people use their basic liberties to do things and promote causes that I detest. Genuine conflicts of this kind occur frequently and cannot be wished away. It may be possible to navigate around most of them, however, by taking a longer-term view. If one surveys legal institutions from the perspective of a person who expects to live a long life, with the consequent uncertainties about what may happen over several decades, the benefits and costs of legal protections of the basic liberties are likely to even out. This does not mean that there will not be substantial costs along the way, merely that the overall balance is likely to be favorable.

Worries about the cost of rights arise when one considers whether to accept the moral and legal duties that go with a system of rights. From a prudential perspective, success in justifying rights depends on a favorable balance of benefits and costs. One must get more benefits – direct and indirect – from living under a system of rights than one loses by fulfilling one's obligations under the system.

One problem with prudential arguments for general moral principles is the possibility that a powerful group of people will create a system that serves its interests while victimizing a less powerful group. Although it may be advantageous for the members of the powerful group to recognize rights among themselves, it may not be advantageous for them to recognize the rights, or the full range of rights, of members of the weaker group. If it is certain that the system of subordination and exploitation will endure for one's lifetime and that the members of the weaker group or their sympathizers will not be able to retaliate through violence or the refusal of cooperation or aid, then it may not be in the interests of the members of the powerful group to accept principles that confer rights on the members of the weaker group.

This kind of objection points out a structural weakness of the prudential approach, namely, that it makes one's claim to rights dependent on one's bargaining power or ability to influence the welfare of others. But this weakness may not make much difference in practical reasoning, since from the perspective of long-term prudence one has good reasons to worry that a system of exploitation will not endure during one's entire lifetime and that the victims or their sympathizers will find ways of retaliating. This is particularly true today, when people are less likely to accept the idea that someone's place at the bottom of the social and economic order is naturally or divinely ordered.

Prudential reasoning may not yield universal human rights, but it gets us somewhere in the vicinity. Further, it helps show how it is psychologically possible for creatures with strong interests of their own to adopt a perspective requiring concern for strangers. If human rights generally serve people's most basic prudential interests, and generate widely available secondary benefits as well, this helps explain why people have good reasons to respect them and to demand that their governments respect and protect them.

Utilitarian and Pragmatic
Justifications for Human Rights

Discussing moral and political questions in prudential terms is distasteful to many (Perry 1998). The approach of the previous section, where the demand for justification was taken to be a demand for prudential reasons, may therefore seem to start on the wrong foot. A different, but complementary, approach interprets a demand for justification as a request for moral reasons, for a case to be made that fundamental principles of morality require one to accept and comply with human rights. Here the presupposition is that the people to whom the argument is directed are moral beings who have transcended total preoccupation with their own interests and are prepared to accept arguments that appeal directly to what is reasonable from the moral point of view.

Transforming prudential into moral reasons

In moving to the moral point of view, one may wish to carry along some of the considerations revealed by a prudential approach. If reflection on my fundamental interests revealed that I, as a fairly normal person, have fundamental interests in security and liberty, say, then perhaps almost all people have such fundamental interests. The results of reflection on the fundamental interests of oneself and others can be used in any justificatory approach that takes such interests to be relevant. Utilitarians, ideal observer theorists, Rawlsians, and fairness-constrained consequentialists can all appeal to these interests in defining notions of harm, crime, fairness, and welfare. Considerations that were formerly part of prudential arguments are now appealed to within a structure representing some conception of the moral point of view. Arguments identifying strong interests that it would be prudent for individuals to protect now become moral arguments identifying basic interests of all that warrant moral and legal protections. Insofar as the prudential approach was successful in identifying fundamental interests of people in all countries and cultures, these interests become focal points of interpersonal concern.

Utilitarian and pragmatic justifications

A familiar and indispensable way of reasoning about norms and institutions considers how well they work in producing societies in which the average level of welfare is high. Pragmatic considerations attract many people to human rights. Such people judge norms and institutions by their results for people everywhere, and support human rights because they think that countries that respect and protect human rights are likely to be more peaceful, stable, welfare-promoting, and prosperous.

Utilitarianism is a theory in philosophical ethics that celebrates this way of thinking. It holds that we should judge norms and institutions entirely on the basis of their likely consequences for the general welfare (see Lyons 1992). The principle of utility, when applied to norms and institutions, advises that we should accept the ones whose acceptance and implementation will best promote the general welfare. If a society with legally protected due process rights, for example, is likely to have higher levels of welfare than one without such rights, then we have good reason to support due process rights. If the utilitarian case for due process rights is extremely strong in every country, then the utilitarian has good reasons to support due process rights as human rights within international law.

Satisfaction of fundamental interests is a large part of people's welfare, so if human rights contribute greatly to the satisfaction of most people's fundamental interests, the utilitarian will take this to be a strong argument in support of human rights. Effective protections of life and of basic liberties, for example, are likely to promote people's welfare by blocking major sources of damage to welfare. The utilitarian will always insist, however, that costs and secondary consequences be considered.

Another way in which human rights support the general welfare is by making governments less dangerous. By requiring governments to protect people's fundamental interests, and to refrain from ruling with an iron fist, successfully implemented systems of human rights help make people feel secure and respected.

An effectively implemented system of human rights that includes democratic institutions is likely to make governments attentive and responsive to the desires and needs of the people – thereby promoting better government and higher levels of welfare. A defense of universal human rights offered by William Talbott argues that these rights provide a remedy for a universal problem of governments, namely knowing what things are good for human beings and having the motivation to act to improve the availability of those goods:

> In order for a government to be able to effectively promote the well-being of its citizens, it must obtain reliable feedback from them on how well its policies promote this and be appropriately responsive to this feedback . . . The reliable feedback problem and the appropriate responsiveness problem are only problems for societies that have the capacity to improve, which is

to say they are problems for all human societies. Once it is recognized that they are problems of all human societies, it can be seen that there is a consequentialist justification for basic human rights to be universal. (Talbott 2005: 134)

The solution to these two problems is to design a "self-improving, self-regulating [political] system." And basic human rights "are the rights necessary for a government so to function" (Talbott 2005: 37).

The good consequences of human rights at the international level can also be taken into account. As noted earlier, the authors of the Universal Declaration thought that a necessary condition of a peaceful world was an international order in which future Hitlers would be deterred from persecuting domestic minorities and invading neighboring countries. They said that the effective protection of human rights would make it unnecessary for people to resort to "rebellion against tyranny and oppression" and would "promote the development of friendly relations between nations" (1948b: preamble). John Rawls has argued that constitutional democracies, unlike authoritarian regimes, seldom go to war with each other (Rawls 1999).

Like prudential arguments, utilitarian arguments are attractive because they display a robust practicality. And one can take these arguments seriously without claiming that they are the only valid kind of arguments for human rights.

A second use of utilitarian arguments is to boost the weight of rights that are already justified or nearly justified on other grounds. Joseph Raz has argued that the weight of a right is often boosted by its indirect effects, including its production of collective goods. By using legal rights to protect the fundamental interests of each person we create collective goods such as security, stability, and a culturally rich society:

The right of free expression serves to protect the interest of those who have it and who may wish to use it to express their views. It also serves the interest of all those who have an interest in acquiring information from others. But here again the right serves the interests of those who are neither speakers nor listeners. Everyone who lives in a democracy is affected by the fact that this is a society enjoying a free exchange of information. One may go one step further. If I were to choose between living in a society which enjoys freedom of expression, but not having the right myself, or enjoying the right in a society which does not have it, I would have no hesitation in judging that my own personal interest is better served by the first option. (Raz 1994: 39)

Raz thinks that the small direct contribution that civil liberties make to a person's own good helps explain why many people undervalue civil liberties:

> Many people judge [the value of civil and political rights] by their contribution to their well-being, and it is not much. Their real value is in their contribution to a common liberal culture. (Raz 1994: 40)

I suspect that Raz underestimates the direct usefulness of civil and political rights to individual welfare, but the general point is well taken. In justifying human rights, secondary benefits need to be considered. Further, we should not think about the justification of rights as a one-by-one matter. Some of the secondary benefits we receive from rights we receive from the operation of families of rights (for example, security and due process rights play a major role in producing the rule of law) and from the entire system of rights.

A worry about utilitarian arguments is that perhaps they only support human rights in those circumstances where compliance with them is practically useful. As Lyons suggests, "utilitarian arguments for institutional design . . . do not logically or morally exclude direct utilitarian arguments concerning the exercise of, or interference with . . . rights" (Lyons 1982). In an emergency, for example, the utilitarian may support suspending or ignoring important rights if that seems likely to have the best consequences for the general welfare in the circumstances. In order to give human rights greater power to resist folding when applied in nonstandard circumstances, it may be necessary to support them directly with deontological moral considerations such as fairness or dignity. It is to an approach offering this possibility that we now turn.

Four Secure Claims

In this section I propose a nonconsequentialist framework for justifying human rights. Choosing abstract norms to use in justifying human rights is a difficult matter. They should have the features necessary to do the job – such as universality, ability to support duties, and high priority. They should be widely accepted as part of people's moralities so that one does not have to make a case for them before moving on to use them in defending human rights. And they should be reliable in the sense that rational, reflective, and morally sensitive people continue over time to find them appealing and do not discover good reasons for rejecting them (Griffin 1996).

As a simple framework for justifying human rights, I propose that we take as basic the idea that people have secure, but abstract, moral claims in four areas:

- a secure claim to have a life;
- a secure claim to lead one's life;
- a secure claim against severely cruel or degrading treatment;
- a secure claim against severely unfair treatment.

These four abstract rights with associated duties are "secure" in the sense that they do not have to be earned through membership or good behavior (although claims to liberty, for example, can be forfeited by criminal behavior). They are also "secure" in the sense that their availability to a person does not depend on that person's ability to generate utility or other good consequences.

These four principles ascribe abstract obligations to everyone – whether individuals, government officials, or corporate entities – to respect and protect them. Some of the duties involved are obviously positive; negative duties are not given a privileged position.

A unifying idea for these four secure claims is that, perfectly realized, they would make it possible for every person living today to have and lead a life that is decent or minimally good. This is a substantial but limited commitment to equality. Because these principles prescribe a secure floor of respect, protection, and provision for each person, they hold a prospect of grounding the universality of specific human rights. No person is to be denied respect, protection, or provision except on grounds of impossibility, unacceptably high costs to the basic interests of others, or as a reasonable punishment for a serious crime.

This theory of the supporting reasons for human rights is modest. It sets a low standard, namely a life that is decent or minimally good. This fits the proposition advanced earlier that human rights attempt to specify a morality of the depths, not of the heights. They are concerned with avoiding misery and great injustices. Second, it recognizes that there are many sources of misery in human life that humans do not control such as natural disasters, diseases, and genetic misfortunes. Third, it recognizes that the specific human rights to be generated from these abstract rights will mainly address the standard threats in various areas to a decent or minimally good life. Perfect protection is not envisioned. Finally, it does not claim to offer a complete moral or political theory.

It will be useful to say more about each of these secure claims and the specific human rights that they are likely to support under contemporary conditions. How one gets from these abstract claims to specific human rights is treated in the next chapter.

The secure claim to have a life

As we saw earlier, a central human interest is security against actions of others that lead to one's death or loss of health. The secure claim to life is partially constituted by negative duties of all agents not to murder, use violence except in self-defense, or harm negligently or maliciously. It includes a claim to freedom and protection from murder, violence, and harm. Thus it includes positive duties to assist people when they need help in protecting themselves against threats of murder and violence. In today's world these duties to protect and provide will be mostly be discharged through the creation and funding of legal and political institutions at the local and national levels.

Having a life, however, requires more than merely being free from violence and harm. One's body must be capable of most normal functions, and to maintain these capabilities people must satisfy physical needs for food, water, sleep, and shelter. People can usually supply these things for themselves through work. But everyone goes through periods when self-supply is impossible – typically, childhood, illness, unemployment, disability, and advanced old age. During such periods people have claims upon others to assistance. As with claims against others to assistance in protecting a person's security, these claims will mostly be discharged through the creation and funding of legal and political institutions at the local and national levels.

The secure claim to lead one's life

Normal adults are autonomous agents, and put great value on continuing to be such. They evaluate, choose, deliberate, and plan. They recognize and solve practical problems. They make plans for the future and attempt to realize them. Evaluation, choice, and efforts at reform often extend to a person's own character. When one's life is significantly shaped by one's own evaluations, choices, plans, and efforts, it becomes one's own.

Agency is found in animals other than humans. For example, birds, dogs, chimps, and apes are capable of evaluating food and places to sleep, and can solve practical problems in realizing their desires. They devise ways of digging a hole or building a nest so as to have a comfortable and safe place to sleep and reproduce. The autonomous agency of humans is souped-up agency – the agency of nonhuman animals to which many additional cognitive, practical, and emotional capacities have been added (on autonomy and its near-relatives see Haworth 1986; Meyers 1991; Rawls 1993; and Raz 1987). Further elaboration of the idea of autonomous agency is found in Chapter 8 below.

The claim to lead one's life yields claims to freedoms from slavery, servitude, and the use of one's life, time, or body without one's consent. It also yields claims to liberties in the most important areas of choice such as occupation, marriage, association, movement, and belief. And it yields claims to the liberties of a moral being – liberties to participate in social relations involving roles, duties, and responsibilities, and liberties to learn, think, discuss, criticize, decide, and act. As this suggests, specific freedoms are mainly selected as fundamental and therefore as protected under the liberty principle by showing their importance to the realization and use of autonomous agency. The claim to lead one's life is strongest in regard to actions that structure or set the direction for one's life, and involve matters that take up much of one's time such as work, marriage, and children. The secure claim to liberty is not just a claim to respect for or noninterference with one's liberty. It is also a claim to assistance in protecting one's liberty, and for the creation and maintenance of social conditions in which the capacity for agency can be developed and exercised. The right to education, for example, receives support from the claim to lead one's life.

A system of unqualified respect for liberty would license other people to act in harmful ways; such a normative system would harm one's fundamental interests more than it helped them. The solution is to build restrictions into the principle of liberty. Some of these follow, obviously, from the restrictions on violence already discussed. In deciding which liberties to include or exclude we will have to ask whether a particular liberty is essential to our status as persons and agents and whether the costs of respecting and protecting it are likely to be so high that it is not worth protecting.

The secure claim to liberty is not just a claim to respect for or noninterference with one's liberty. It is also a claim to assistance in protecting one's liberty, and for the creation and maintenance of social conditions in which the capacity for agency can be developed and exercised. Duties of assistance to others carve an exception into the claim to liberty. Within limits that prevent excessive burdens and severe unfairness, people can be called on to expend their time and resources in protecting and provisioning others and in supporting institutions that provide such assistance in regular and efficient ways.

The secure claim against severely cruel or degrading treatment

A simple form of cruelty imposes severe pain on another person thoughtlessly or gleefully. This type of cruelty can degrade a person because it suggests that he has no feelings or that his suffering does not matter. More complicated forms of cruelty are calculated to degrade a person by suggesting, or bringing it about, that she is something that she and others will think base or low. Slavery is degrading because it treats slaves as if they lack the agency needed to lead lives of their own. Rape is degrading because it treats a person as a mere sexual resource to be used without consent, or because in many cultures it destroys a woman's social standing as a virtuous and pure person. Degradation may deprive a person of the respect of self and others. A secure claim against severe cruelty forbids these sorts of actions and requires individual and collective efforts to protect people against them. The severity of cruelty depends on how degrading it can reasonably be taken to be, its duration and frequency, the degree of malicious intent, and the amount of harm that it is likely to cause.

The secure claim against severely unfair treatment

Humans are keenly attuned to unfairness, particularly when it takes the form of doing less than one's fair share in collective enterprises. Here we are concerned with severe unfairness because being subject to lesser forms of unfairness is probably compatible with having a minimally good life. For present purposes we are concerned with forms of unfairness so severe that they are matters of ruinous injustice. The severity of unfair treatment depends on the degree of unfairness, its duration and frequency, whether or not malicious intent is present, and the amount of harm or degradation that the unfairness causes. The claim against severely unfair treatment is a claim to freedom from such treatment and a claim to individual and collective efforts to protect people against it. For example, governments have a duty not to imprison innocent people and to protect people against being imprisoned while innocent of crimes by providing them with fair trials. The claim against unfair treatment plays an important role in supporting the universality of human rights.

All four principles protect aspects of human dignity

The Universal Declaration speaks of the "inherent dignity . . . of all members of the human family" and declares that: "All human beings are born free and equal in dignity and rights. They are endowed with reason and conscience." The four grounds of human rights that I have proposed provide an interpretation of these ideas. We respect a person's dignity when we protect her life and agency and when we prevent others from imposing treatment that is severely degrading or unfair.

All four principles should be thought of as requirements of human dignity. We can speak of dignity with reference to any particular feature of persons that has distinctive value (for example, their ability to suffer, their lives, their agency, their consciousness and reflective capacities, their use of complicated languages and symbolic systems, their rationality, their individuality, their social awareness). I reject the view of many that human dignity is found exclusively in human agency or autonomy.

The secure claim to have a life prevents others from treating one's health and survival as if it had little or no value, as if ending a human life were morally equivalent to uprooting a carrot. The secure claim to lead one's life prevents others from treating one's agency or practical reason as if it were an unimportant part of being a person. The secure claim to freedom from cruel, degrading treatment protects one from being treated as a thing that is unable to feel pain or whose pain does not matter. The secure claim against severely unfair treatment protects one from the indignity of having one's interests ignored or severely discounted in social and political practices.

Conflicts between these principles

These four principles are strongly supportive of each other. They work together to protect a decent life for all people. For example, the secure claim against treatment that is severely cruel or degrading works together with the claim to life to support a specific right against torture. But conflicts between these principles are possible and even familiar. For example, aggressive uses of the criminal law to deter crime and to protect claims to life frequently conflict with fundamental freedoms and with the prohibition of cruel treatment. The conflict between security and liberty is a familiar one in contemporary politics.

There is no simple formula for resolving such conflicts, and no straightforward priority ranking of the four principles seems plausible. The four secure claims have roughly equal weight or priority. Conflicts between their cores will have to be avoided whenever possible and compromised when avoidance is impossible. Saving people's lives will often have special priority, but life loses much of its value if the other requirements of making it decent are not met.

Are there too many or too few principles?

If someone proposed that one or more of these principles is derivable from one or two of the others, or from some other single principle, I would not be opposed to the possibility. For example, one might attempt to derive the right to life, and the right against severe cruelty, from the requirements of leading one's life. If such derivability were shown, it would not matter to the framework.

On the other side, the theory proposed may be too simple for the job at hand. Even a morality of the depths is a complex thing, and the four principles I have proposed may fail to capture all of that complexity. Implementing human rights will require a conception of personal and institutional responsibility, a doctrine of consent, and a justification for punishment. But if most of the justificatory work for human rights can be done by these four, they will have served my purpose. They will have provided good starting points, even if they are not the only ones we need. The goal here is not to provide a comprehensive theory of normative ethics.

There are other attractive principles that I have left out. Desert is neglected, except insofar as it is covered by fairness. Part of the unfairness of being punished for a crime one did not commit is that one does not deserve the punishment. Property is not taken to be a fundamental principle. A specific human right to property will be defended, however, in Chapter 8.

Where do we get these claims?

These four principles do not answer all of the questions that philosophically minded people are likely to have about human rights. In particular, they are not accompanied by a metaethical theory that explains or justifies the status of fundamental moral and political principles such as these. Accepting them as a basis for human rights is compatible with several positions in metaethics including the view that we know moral principles through some sort of intuition (Smith 1979; Huemer 2005), a view like Gewirth's that these principles themselves can be justified in terms of some deeper and less controversial starting point (Gewirth 1982), and the Rawlsian theory that these principles summarize and unify our firmest and most carefully considered moral beliefs (Rawls 1971, 1993). Allegiance to these principles does not commit one to the view that all arguments somehow stop with them.

For these principles to serve as a basis for universal human rights there is one view of them that must be rejected, however. This is the view that one's having these fundamental claims depends on their being conferred by one's society or country (Lukes 1993). Whatever status human rights turn out to have, an explanatory theory must give them transnational force, something independent of particular governments and societies. Otherwise our account will fail to support a fundamental feature of human rights, namely that they are rights that one simply has as a person.

Are these four principles too demanding?

Orienting claims and duties by reference to interests leaves us with the problem of how much should be done to promote and protect people's interests. The broad answer is that the nature and level of protections and provisions to be supplied are to be chosen rationally in the light of the threats present and the institutions and resources available. Social and political justification will therefore always need to look in two directions: backward to the most fundamental interests of persons as the source of claims to restraint, protection, and assistance; and forward to institutions, costs, and resources. Extreme scarcity of resources will not extinguish one's claims but will badly cramp the responses to them.

These principles are binding on all agents, including organizations and groups, but the discharge of their positive responsibilities to provide and protect will need to be mediated by available social and political structures. In the contemporary world, this means that the implementation of human rights will rely on the international system of separate sovereign states. The governments of these states are the only organizations presently capable of providing protection and other services to people all around the world. Hence, appropriate ways of upholding human rights will reflect the prevailing international system, which divides the earth into distinct territories and assigns primary responsibility for the people in each territory to its government.

At least some of the limits to the burdens imposed by these principles are to be found in the principles themselves. The burdens should not destroy people's lives, enslave them or otherwise make it impossible to lead one's life, subject them to severely degrading treatment, or be severely unfair. The positive duties of states to respect and uphold the rights of all residents will often strain their resources severely. But these duties are limited by the principle that the costs of respecting and upholding human rights must not be so large as to undermine the levels of human development, the economic productivity, and the social and political institutions that are necessary over the long run to maintain respect for and implementation of a system of human rights.

Overview

Starting points for human rights are underlying values or norms that support the importance or high priority of these norms. From the perspective of individual prudence, the protections human rights provide for one's fundamental interests are very desirable if their costs are not too high. Prudential reasoning may not reach universal human rights, but it gets one somewhere in the vicinity. When we move to the moral point of view, utilitarian arguments defend human rights in terms of their good consequences for the general welfare. Another attractive approach to justifying human rights appeals to secure moral claims to have a life, to lead one's life, against severe cruelty, and against severe unfairness.

Further Reading

Gewirth, A. 1982. *Human Rights: Essays on Justification and Applications.* Chicago: University of Chicago Press.

Griffin, J. 2000. "Discrepancies between the Best Philosophical Account of Human Rights and the International Law of Human Rights." *Proceedings of the Aristotelian Society* 101: 1–28.

Lyons, D. 1982. "Utility and Rights." In J. Pennock and J. Chapman (eds.), *Ethics, Economics, and the Law*, 107–38. New York: New York University Press.

Lyons, D. 1992. "Utilitarianism." In L. Becker (ed.), *The Encyclopedia of Ethics.* New York: Garland Publishing.

Nussbaum, M. 2001. *Women and Human Development: The Capabilities Approach.* Cambridge: Cambridge University Press.

Rawls, J. 1971. *A Theory of Justice.* Cambridge, MA: Harvard University Press.

Rawls, J. 1993. *Political Liberalism.* New York: Columbia University Press.

Rorty, R. 1993. "Human Rights, Rationality, and Sentimentality." In S. Shute and S. Hurley (eds.), *On Human Rights: The Oxford Amnesty Lectures.* New York: Basic Books.

Schachter, O. 1983. "Human Dignity as a Normative Concept." *American Journal of International Law* 77: 848–54.

Chapter 5
A Framework for Justifying Specific Rights

The starting points discussed in Chapter 4 only get us started. To justify a specific human right additional premises are needed. This chapter suggests that the justification of a specific human right, such as the right to a fair trial when charged with a crime, requires six steps. Each step requires satisfying a particular justificatory test that is necessary to a successful outcome. The first step requires showing that people today regularly experience problems or abuses in the area protected by the proposed right. The second step is to show that this norm has the importance or high priority that is a key feature of human rights. We do this by showing the right protects things that are central to a decent life as a person. The starting points sketched in Chapter 4 play a central role in this test. The third step in justifying a specific human right involves seeing if the proposed norm fits the general idea of human rights explained earlier. For example, can it be formulated as a right of all people that they have independently of recognition or enactment at the national level? The fourth test requires showing that a norm as strong as a right is needed to provide this protection, that no weaker measures will be sufficiently effective. The fifth criterion is that the burdens the right imposes are neither excessive nor severely unfair. The sixth and final test requires that human rights be feasible to implement in an ample majority of countries today.

Six Tests for Specific Rights

Substantial and recurrent threats

People's recognition of a human right may not begin with abstract principles; it is more likely to start with the experience, direct or indirect, of indignities and injustices. An early step in justifying a specific right as a human right involves showing that important interests or claims are significantly threatened in the area that the right would protect. If we recognized specific rights at every point where an essential condition of a decent life is present, whether or not it is threatened at each of those points, we would have more claims and potential rights than we could remember, much less implement.

(1) *Shue on threats among contemporary human rights theorists* Henry Shue was the first, to my knowledge, to use the intuitively attractive idea of threats or dangers in explaining the content of human rights (Shue 1996, originally published 1980). He defined a right as "a rationally justified demand for social guarantees against standard threats," and emphasized that "People are neither entitled to social guarantees against every conceivable threat nor entitled to guarantees against ineradicable threats." Shue also held that the discovery of threats is a "largely empirical question," and that what is eradicable may change over time (Shue 1996: 17, 32–3).

Evidence for the idea that experienced dangers and injustices play a large role in the formulation of human rights is found in the fact that bills of rights often begin with a list of recently experienced injustices that make imperative the proposed rights. For example, the English Bill of Rights (1689, in Ishay 1997) includes the following complaints against King James II:

- And excessive bail hath been required of persons committed in criminal cases to elude the benefit of the laws made for the liberty of the subjects;
- And excessive fines have been imposed;
- And illegal and cruel punishments inflicted.

Similar complaints are found in the United States Declaration of Independence (1776). And Johannes Morsink has demonstrated in detail how the Universal Declaration of Human Rights was "born out of the experience of the war that had just ended," and particularly "the connection between the Holocaust and the Declaration" (Morsink 1999: 37–8).

(2) *Dershowitz on experienced injustices* Alan Dershowitz has recently proposed that our formulations of constitutional and human rights arise from the experience of injustice (Dershowitz 2004). That experience may be direct (when one endures the injustice oneself), or indirect (when one learns of the injustice from those who endured it, or from journalists or historians). The development of lists of rights to be protected through

political action represents a kind of social learning. People gradually learn the most severe wrongs and injustices that human psychology and political institutions produce and develop means of protecting themselves and their fellow citizens against those injustices. Dershowitz expresses his view as follows:

> Rights come from human experience, particularly experience with injustice. We learn from the mistakes of history that . . . certain fundamental rights . . . are essential to avoid repetition of the grievous injustices of the past. Working from the bottom up, from a dystopian view of our experiences with injustice . . . , we build rights on a foundation of trial, error, and our uniquely human ability to learn from our mistakes in order to avoid replicating them. In a word, rights come from wrongs. (Dershowitz 2004: 9)

As examples of such wrongs Dershowitz mentions "the Holocaust, the Stalinist mass murders, the Cambodian and Rwandan genocides, slavery, lynchings, the Inquisition, or the detention of more than 100,000 Japanese Americans" (Dershowitz 2004: 7). Note that this list of experienced injustices would make for a very short list of human rights. Further, it says nothing about women's rights (see Binion 1995). Still, the experienced injustices theory of rights has the potential to be open-minded about new human rights. It allows for the possibility that humankind will experience new forms of severe injustice, and relies on moral sensitivity and democratic institutions to decide whether new injustices require new rights. Dershowitz's version fails, however, to offer an account of how we should evaluate alleged injustices and proposals for new rights to deal with them. It needs an account of how to test experienced injustices to determine whether they are so severe and so likely to reoccur that defining, enacting, and implementing a constitutional right at the national level or a human right at the international level is warranted.

(3) *Donnelly on threats from the modern state* Jack Donnelly also stresses the importance of threats to the justification of rights, but puts the focus on threats from the modern state (Donnelly 2003). The world's 200 or so countries now use similar sorts of political and legal institutions including centralized political power; a legal system including legislators, courts, and prisons; police and armed forces; large bureaucracies; media of mass communication; a monetary system; a mixture of public and private property; and tax systems (on the modern state see Morris 1998). These institutions, used around the world, give countries shared problems and lead to the adoption of similar remedies for those problems. If

all countries use the same basic institutions, and if these institutions pose some distinctive threats to values that most peoples share, then human rights will often float free of cultural differences.

Donnelly holds that human rights are needed in all countries because the modern state is now used everywhere and international human rights are socially learned remedies for its built-in dangers (Donnelly 2003: 46; see also p. 92). The forms these threats take and how to deal with them are gradually learned, emerging "from the concrete experiences, especially the sufferings, of real human beings and their political struggles to defend or realize their dignity" (Donnelly 2003: 58). Once the dangers and remedies have been learned, the lessons ought to be shared with all the users.

Donnelly describes the threats that make specific rights necessary as "widespread, systematic, and egregious" (Donnelly 2003: 226). "Widespread" means that the threat occurs with some frequency, although this frequency may be low. Seriously unfair criminal trials may be a daily or only an occasional problem. "Systematic" means that the danger is built-in or inherent. The danger that jails will be used to confine and incapacitate the political opponents of those in power is inherent in having law, punishment, and jails. Finally, "egregious" means that the threat or danger must be seriously harmful, degrading, or unjust for political rights and international rights to be appropriate remedies.

The modern state evolved from earlier systems of government, law, and property, and it is implausible to suggest that none of the dangers of the modern state were present in the earlier versions. The dangers of the reckless and corrupt use of political power, of food scarcity due to systems of private agricultural property, and the dangers of democracy have been known and discussed for more than 2000 years. Still, the modern state has dimensions that are new. Morris emphasizes this:

> Our states are different from earlier forms of political organization . . . [T]hey claim a variety of special powers, and their authority is rather sweeping. Their governance . . . is territorial in relatively new ways. Government is now more centralized and hierarchical than in earlier, pre-modern times. In a variety of ways, the sorts of allegiances that are now expected of us and the ways in which our state affects our identities are new. (Morris 1998: 17)

It is doubtful that Donnelly's theory supports all families of human rights. Not all of the problems that human rights address derive from abuses of political institutions. For example, spousal and child abuse are human rights problems, but the threats involved do not come mainly from governments.

Human rights deal with threats that are regularly present and dangerous. We need historical knowledge to identify threats that have long been
present and that seem to accompany the use of familiar institutions. And
we need knowledge of current social and political institutions to recognize new threats and to determine the levels at which old and new threats
are present. Since human rights are universal rights, the identification of
serious threats needs to be done in a worldwide way. At the implementation stage, however, particular countries can take local conditions into
account in formulating their constitutional and legal rights.

(4) *Threats to distinctive groups*   In applying the experienced threats
idea the emphasis is on threats to all or most people. It is imperative,
however, not to neglect the distinctive problems of different parts of the
human population. Elderly people may not suffer much from violations
of due process rights, but may be strongly interested in access to political participation and access to social security and medical care. Young
women may experience threats to their sexual and reproductive freedoms,
along with the danger of rape, whereas middle-aged women may worry
about domestic violence and dangers to their children (see Binion 1995).
Young men may disproportionately experience threats of military draft
and of violations of due process. People with disabilities may disproportionately experience denial of access to educational and productive opportunities. The selection of threats to be addressed through human rights
must be done with equal concern for all and with systematic empirical
knowledge.
    A general human rights document that lists only a few dozen rights
can only go so far in addressing the distinctive threats faced by various
parts of the human population. This is the reason why specialized treaties
and declarations have been developed to address threats to racial, ethnic,
and religious minorities, women, children, and indigenous peoples. See,
for example, the Genocide Convention (United Nations 1948a), the
International Convention on the Elimination of All Forms of Racial Discrimination (United Nations 1965), the Convention on the Elimination
of All Forms of Discrimination against Women (United Nations 1979),
and the Convention on the Rights of the Child (United Nations 1989).
These treaties are discussed in Chapter 10.

The importance of what is protected

It is not always easy to distinguish between threats of discomfort and
threats of serious indignity and injustice. To justify a human right we need

to decide if a threat is sufficiently egregious – to use Donnelly's word. Chapter 4's normative framework is designed to provide assistance with this decision. If someone proposes, say, that government toleration of smoking violates human rights, we can ask whether failing to penalize smoking seriously threatens any of the four abstract claims (to have a life, to lead one's life, against severely cruel and degrading treatment, and against severe unfairness). The standard of important needs to be set quite high because, as suggested in Chapter 2, human rights are minimal standards. They do not promise the good life and the great society; the vision is rather of a decent life for all and of societies that can count as civilized.

The six justificatory steps proposed in this chapter are independent of the starting points proposed in Chapter 4. People who have different views of the starting point(s) for justifying human rights can still accept and use these six tests. All they need to do is substitute their account of the starting points when the question of the egregiousness of threats is being decided.

Can it be a universal right?

The idea that a human right has to fit the general conception of human rights that prevails today will rule out many possible norms. Human rights have people as their holders and beneficiaries, so rights of artworks or ecosystems cannot be human rights (this is not to prejudge the question of whether they can be justified rights of some other sort). Human rights have governments as their primary addressees, so a right of a child that is exclusively against her parents cannot be a human right. Human rights have high priority, so a right that deals with a trivial matter cannot be a human right. Human rights apply around the world, so a right that makes sense only within the context of a particular country's institutions cannot be a human right.

Would some weaker norm be as effective?

When the first three tests have been passed by a proposed right to something, some sort of restraint or assistance from others in regard to that thing is appropriate. The norm prescribing such restraint or assistance could be weaker than a right, however. It could be a goal or a duty of charity. Conceivably a society could rely on collective aspirations or goals, together with feelings of love and solidarity, to ensure that all people enjoy minimally good lives. This vision, dear to many utopians, suggests that an emphasis on specific legal or constitutional rights is not inescapable (see Buchanan 1989). The third test requires showing that such alternatives would provide inadequate protections.

Specific legal rights have some important advantages as protections because of their characteristic firmness and definiteness. First, the individuated character of rights ensures that identifiable parties will be charged with providing these protections, rather than leaving them to the good will of volunteers. Second, the obligations or responsibilities that attach to rights are mandatory and fairly definite; they require identifiable parties to respond in specified ways to the rightholders. And third, rights are usually claimable. In addition to the pleas for compliance that can accompany any appeal to a norm, specific rights generally give a special place to steps that rightholders or others can take to bring special procedures or protections into play. For example, legal rights often permit injured parties to sue for cessation of a violation or compensation, and sometimes empower an official or citizens to monitor compliance and invoke protections. Beyond this, established political rights provide useful focal points for political action, especially among actors who are otherwise uncoordinated. Government invasions of freedom of religion may occasion unease and discontent among many people, but without a recognized norm dealing with religious freedom their responses may be diffuse.

These general advantages of rights need to be weighed in relation to the distinctive advantages and disadvantages of other forms of protection and provision. The alternatives I will consider are self-help, voluntary aid, and structural modifications that eliminate the threat or make the basic good available in abundance.

(1) *Self-help* One of the most important ways of providing and protecting fundamental interests is for people to help themselves by seeking, finding, and defending their own goods. Whether the goods are liberties, opportunities, services, or commodities, people will often gain and defend these things through their own efforts. The "selves" that engage in self-help need not be isolated individuals but may rather be families or communities.

(2) *Social aid* The use of voluntary aid to supply protection and other goods to those unable to supply their own provides an option intermediate between relying on protected self-help alone and governmental provision of goods or services. Families, friends, neighbors, and charitable organizations are often willing to help provide protection, shelter, and food to those who are unable to satisfy their own needs. This aid may be forthcoming out of sympathy or as a response to socially recognized duties

of charity. Duties of charity, however, leave the giver discretion about when, where, and how much to give. They do not confer corresponding rights.

This discretion creates the danger that aid through charity will produce only an irregular and spotty supply. Because of this danger, people often organize charitable institutions to enable them to discharge their duties to aid others more effectively. Within these institutions, hired or voluntary workers encourage giving and distribute funds to some target group of needy persons. Gifts are stimulated by campaigns; supply is more regular because funds can be accumulated, budgeted, and spread; there is scope for large projects; and coverage of people in need is broader. The agency is able to seek out people with certain sorts of need, so that assistance does not entirely depend on a needy person's being in the vicinity of someone willing and able to help.

In some areas, protected self-help together with formal charitable organizations may be an adequate response to a claim that passes the first two tests. But when significant numbers of people are left without protection or aid by these measures, mandatory legal norms are appropriate. State police and welfare systems require everyone to contribute through taxes and offer services to all who need them. The great advantage of a general governmental supply is a substantial increase in regularity and comprehensiveness over random or organized charity. Disadvantages include greater bureaucratic rigidity, higher costs, and the possible loss of a sense of community if personalized or community-based forms of mutual aid are abandoned. Whether charitable systems need to be supplemented with rights to a supply in a particular area depends on whether self-help together with charity can respond adequately to the justified claims of all.

(3) *Structural changes*   Specific legal rights might be unnecessary if we could change the social and economic systems of countries around the world to create an abundance of goods and eliminate most threats to life, freedom, and fairness. We might call these possibilities, respectively, the abundance strategy and the threat-elimination strategy. These can be combined with self-help and mutual aid; when supplies are abundant and threats few, self-help and mutual aid may be effective enough to make specific political rights unnecessary.

An advocate of the abundance strategy might note that we seldom speak of a right to air because an adequate supply is freely available. We do, of course, recognize a right not to be smothered as an aspect of the right to life, and we do have standards in many countries for clean air, but in general people can get the air they need simply by breathing. One might hope to achieve something similar in other areas by generating a very large productive capacity that would make supplies of needed goods and services so plentiful that no one would find it impossible to get an adequate supply. But this level of abundance has been reached nowhere, and most countries are very far from it.

The threat-elimination strategy has sometimes been advocated by those who think it possible to transform human motivation and consciousness through religion or other modes of enlightenment. They hope that such a transformation will eliminate selfishness, greed, conflict, and corruption. But it is fair to say, I think, that successful transformations have been limited to small groups.

Marxists sometimes advocate a combination of the two strategies. Their hope is that an abundant economy resulting from successful industrialization can be combined with social and distributive structures that promote solidarity and mutual aid, thereby eliminating the need for rights guaranteed by the state. They hoped that getting rid of rights would abolish the bureaucratic rigidity of many rights-bound institutions and the egoistic character of a rights mentality that always insists on getting its due. These are attractive goals, but efforts to achieve them have not been conspicuously successful and prospects for the foreseeable future seem slim.

The burdens are justifiable

The fifth step in justifying specific rights requires showing that the burdens imposed by a proposed right are justifiable. Each person is both a holder and an addressee of human rights. As rightholders we may want the most extensive list of human rights possible; but as addressees and taxpayers we will want to limit the size of the burdens that human rights impose and ensure that those burdens are not distributed in ways that are severely unfair or economically destructive. The four secure claims sketched in Chapter 4 both support and limit human rights. They limit them by requiring that the normative burdens they impose on people not be ones that are destructive of life or health, that deprive people of fundamental freedoms, or that treat people in ways that are severely cruel or unfair.

Feasible in a majority of countries

The final test is feasibility. A necessary condition for the justification of a specific human right is the possibility of successfully implementing it in an ample majority of countries today. When this test is failed the putative human right may simply fail to be a human right, or it may be a justifiable human right whose scope is narrower (and hence less demanding) than we initially thought. An unsuccessful candidate for the status of human right may nonetheless be a justifiable constitutional right in some countries. Further, if the right satisfies all the tests except feasibility, and if it partially satisfies feasibility, then it will be an international norm of considerable importance even though it is not (quite) a human right.

Resources and Rights

Rights are not magical sources of supply. Costs have to be taken into account in formulating and evaluating specific rights. Holmes and Sunstein are surely right in saying that "a theory of rights that never descends from the heights of morality into the world of scarce resources will be sorely incomplete, even from a moral perspective" (Holmes and Sunstein 1999: 18). Even if affordability is not used to draw a boundary between justified specific rights and not yet justified rights, it will still have to be used to draw a boundary between operative and nonoperative rights. If we do not face the issue of feasibility at the justification stage, we will face it at the application stage.

The authors of human rights documents faced great difficulties with regard to feasibility. On the one hand, they needed to formulate rights that are specific enough to give clear guidance; on the other hand, they wanted their formulations to apply to countries that had very different levels of human, institutional, and financial resources. The approach these authors took in the Universal Declaration and subsequent treaties was to formulate a single high standard for the whole earth. As a result, today's lists of human rights presuppose the financial, institutional, and human resources needed to construct democratic political institutions, a fair and humane legal system, and a system of provision for subsistence, education, and at least rudimentary health care. The result is a list of fairly demanding rights that is useful as a standard of criticism for richer countries. If a much lower level of resources had been assumed, many of the requirements would have been extremely easy for the richer countries to meet and thus would have had little practical significance for them.

The authors of early human rights documents such as the Universal Declaration may have hoped that the implications for poorer countries of the idea of human rights would be spelled out in regional documents to be created by representatives of countries in those regions. The regional bills of rights could take into account the traditions, problems, institutions, and resources found in particular parts of the world. But regional systems for the international promotion and protection of human rights, as found in the African Union, the Council of Europe, and the Organization of American States, have produced little innovation in lists of human rights, priority ranking, and how to deal with feasibility. Rights documents written by regional bodies have avoided the problem of what to do about rights under extreme scarcity and have been nearly as ambitious in their demands as the Universal Declaration and the UN treaties. Given the severe poverty and instability of a number of African countries, one might have expected the African Charter on Human and Peoples' Rights (African Union 1981) to be especially sensitive to the problems of implementing human rights in the context of scarcity and political turmoil, but it formulates most of its rights in the same manner as the Universal Declaration. For example, article 16 declares that every person has a "right to enjoy the best attainable state of physical and mental health." Perhaps the reason why the problem of scarcity has been skirted in regional human rights documents is that variation in levels of resources and development within these regions is often nearly as large as the variation within the world as a whole. What is possible for Nigeria may not be possible for Mali, and what is possible for Brazil may not be possible for Haiti.

The feasibility standard

Three broad propositions are helpful in understanding how rights are linked to abilities and resources.

(1) *Inability to fulfill a moral or legal duty is generally an excuse from that duty*   If an ambulance driver has a duty to assist car accident victims, and if the driver is unable to get to a particular accident in time to assist because of a flat tire, we do not say that the driver's duty did not exist in that case. We rather say that the duty existed, that the driver failed to fulfill it, and that the driver had a good excuse and therefore is not to blame. Ability to fulfill a duty means ability to do so while also fulfilling one's higher priority duties and continuing to survive.

(2) *The genuine inability of the addressees to fulfill their duties does not generally cancel a pre-existing right*   If a person accused of armed robbery has a right to a fair trial within a certain period, and if hurricane damage to government buildings makes it impossible for the government to

provide trials during that period, the government has a valid excuse and has not violated the person's right even though the person's right was not satisfied or fulfilled. But the person's right to a fair trial has not disappeared; it is still present and must be satisfied by the government as soon as possible. Inability may render a duty temporarily or permanently inoperative, but it does not eliminate the duty. The idea that "ought implies can" is too simple. Duties, and the rights they support, can be present and guide behavior in cases where they have been made inoperative by valid excuses or justifications.

(3) *The duties imposed by rights should be ones that a majority of the addressees are able to fulfill*   Rights should be selected and formulated so that they can be effectively implemented. Neither morality nor law is advanced by rights that are stated so idealistically that most of their addressees will be excused most of the time on grounds of inability. The language of goals and ideals is available for stating aspirations that go beyond our current capabilities. Further, goals can be made more like rights by specifying beneficiaries, addressees, and scopes, resulting in what I call "rights-like goals."

When human rights call for legal recognition and implementation, the duties imposed by those rights should be ones that can be complied with or fulfilled by most of the addressees of the right. Human rights enacted in national and international law should not be mere showcase rights. They should be rights that can become operative and effective if the addressees are generally willing to comply. If only a minority of countries is able to implement a human right it will end up being a showcase right in most countries. Willingness to comply will not lead to its becoming operative and effective.

Consider an analogy. In most countries parents are legally responsible for caring for their children. They are legally liable if they neglect their children, if they fail to provide them with adequate food, clothing, and care. The duty of providing adequately for one's children is very burdensome for many people, but most parents satisfy it. Some parents are exceptionally capable; most have adequate capabilities; a few are marginally capable; and a few are simply incapable. The inability of some parents to provide and care for their children is not dealt with by lowering standards of provision and care across the board to inadequate levels. The abilities of the least capable third of parents are not used as the reference point for norms that apply to all parents.

Further, legal enforcement of standards of parental care is not abandoned because some people are incompetent or unable to perform as parents. Courts and judges are active in this area, and their work is supplemented by social workers. Parents may have legal duties to accept government assistance or intervention if refusing it would cause their children to go unfed and uncared for. Finally, inability relieves one from blame (unless one is to blame for the inability); it provides one with an excuse for noncompliance. One's parental responsibilities do not just disappear at that point, however. A person who becomes incapacitated as a parent still has duties to seek substitute care for his or her children, to do the best he or she can until substitute care becomes available, and to resume care when possible.

Chapter 3 sketched a complex view of the addressees of human rights which held that (1) governments are the primary addressees of the human rights of their citizens and permanent residents with duties both to respect and to uphold their human rights; (2) governments have negative duties to respect the rights of people from other countries; (3) individuals have negative responsibilities to respect the human rights of people at home and abroad; (4) individuals have responsibilities as voters and citizens to promote human rights in their own country; and (5) governments, international organizations, and individuals have back-up responsibilities for the fulfillment of human rights around the world. This view of responsibilities for human rights means that estimating the feasibility of a right is a complex matter because it needs to look at the abilities of all of these addressees to fulfill their regular and back-up responsibilities. To simplify matters for current purposes I will focus solely on the abilities of governments to respect and uphold the human rights of their citizens and permanent residents.

Identifying and counting costs

This section offers a taxonomy of the costs of rights. The idea of "costs" is used here in a very broad sense, and hence it is unlikely that we will be able to represent all of these costs in monetary terms. Because of this it may not be possible to bring together all kinds of costs on the same scale.

(1) *Conflict costs*   When a new right is introduced, conflicts with other norms, including other rights, may arise. Losses to other norms from recognizing, complying with, or implementing a right can be called conflict costs. Here the cost is what the right requires us to give up from our normative system which we would otherwise keep. For example, a possible conflict cost of a strong right to privacy is that respecting and implementing this right would require us to carve important exceptions into the right of freedom of the press.

An especially severe form of conflict cost is involved when a right cannot be implemented without imposing such severe burdens on some people that the imposition violates other important norms, for example, avoiding severe unfairness in the distribution of burdens. We would reject the idea that people who need kidney transplants have a right to them if we knew that the only way to obtain the kidneys needed for these transplants would be by a national lottery in which the persons selected by chance were forced to donate one kidney to a national kidney bank.

As this example suggests, the problem of unacceptable conflict costs will be most severe when the costs of implementing a right cannot be spread among most members of society through taxation but must rather be met through extremely burdensome contributions by a small number of people. In general, however, the costs of human rights can be met by imposing modest tax burdens on most members of society and thereby generating the resources needed to provide the right to all (see Holmes and Sunstein 1999). The development in the last few centuries of government institutions that can efficiently spread large costs through income and other taxes has made it possible to add costly items such as welfare rights to contemporary lists of human rights without incurring unacceptable conflict costs. We should note, however, that in low-income countries the use of taxation to support the implementation of human rights is more difficult for two reasons. One is that there is less wealth to tax since there is not a large middle class with good salaries. The other is that taxation systems are less likely to be efficient and relatively free of cheating and corruption.

Conflict costs, like some of the other costs of rights, can be direct or indirect. A direct conflict cost exists when there is a contradiction between the descriptions of the scopes of two rights (or norms) or between descriptions of what is involved in normal exercise or enforcement of those rights (or norms). Indirect conflict costs occur when the conflict is mediated by an extended causal linkage.

(2) *The costs of using weaker means* An account of the costs of rights needs to acknowledge a distinction between duties not to infringe people's rights and duties to uphold or protect people's rights. The former duties are negative in that they involve only restraints; the latter are positive in that they require one to act so as to provide or protect a good. The right against torture, for example, implies negative duties for both individuals and governments; they are not permitted to use torture as a means to their ends. But governments also have positive duties to uphold this right and to protect against torture people who are threatened by government or private agents.

The costs of upholding rights are obviously often high, but it is sometimes suggested that the costs of noninfringement – because they involve merely not doing something – are always low. The truth is that the costs of not being able to act in a certain way, of not being permitted to take a certain course of action when it is the only or most effective means to a desired goal, are often substantial. We might call these kinds of costs the costs of using weaker means.

To illustrate this kind of cost, consider the case of torture. Forbidding governments to use torture will deny some of them a preferred method of criminal interrogation. Human rights are often controversial precisely because they forbid political tactics that are dirty but effective (at least in the short term). In the case of torture this cost does not in my opinion call into question the right against torture, but it does illustrate that the loss of effective means to public goals can become a significant cost. Negative duties are not always costless or low in cost.

(3) *Implementation costs*   When people think of the costs of rights they usually think of implementation costs. Human rights impose duties to uphold, as well as to respect. Duties to provide protection are paradigms of duties to uphold. Protection may be provided directly through criminal laws and sanctions and through procedures that permit individuals to sue for cessation of violations of their rights or compensation for them. Protection of rights can also be produced indirectly through institutional mechanisms such as checks and balances, executive control of police and military, civil service systems, and regular elections.

Implementing a right often requires providing not just protection but other goods as well. Thus governments may be obligated to provide opportunities (to vote or to attend school), services (medical care or occupational guidance), or payments (a minimum income during unemployment, disability, or old age). When a good is made available as a matter of legal right, government may become the main supplier of the good or it may serve only as a supplier of last resort. Even when something is available as a matter of right, many people may still prefer to supply the good for themselves, and many will want a higher quantity or quality of the good than is guaranteed by right. The expense of implementing a right will generally depend on how many people will continue to create or pay for their own supply after the right is implemented. Upholding rights, where either protecting or providing is involved, is often enormously expensive, and thus cost estimates, as well as cost reduction proposals, usually focus on implementation.

Like conflict costs, implementation costs can be divided into those that are direct and those that are indirect. Direct implementation costs are the immediate costs of providing the services that uphold a right. Indirect implementation costs are negative consequences that follow by an extended causal chain from the activity of implementing a right. For example, collecting the taxes necessary for implementing a right may decrease the supply of venture capital and retard productivity, and implementing a right may use up resources that could have been used to achieve other desirable goals.

Counting the costs

Because of the number and variety of costs just surveyed, we seldom have a precise idea how much it costs to respect and implement a right. Cost estimates are often hard to make, particularly because they require comparisons with hypothetical alternatives and count different kinds of costs that are difficult to bring together on a single scale. There is often controversy about how much weight should be attached to particular kinds of costs. Finally, it is hard to determine a country's level of resources or what portion of these resources should be used to comply with and implement the human rights of all residents.

In spite of these problems, people regularly assess the affordability of rights, and it will be useful to sketch what is involved. A budgeting process for rights at the national level might begin with an estimate of the resources available for implementing rights. I suggested earlier that this level of overall expenditure on rights should be a portion of national resources that is small enough to avoid putting severely unfair and destructive burdens on particular individuals and to avoid undermining the institutions and levels of economic productivity needed to provide for the general welfare and implement rights effectively over time. Once we have some idea of the resources available (given these criteria) and a preliminary ranking of the rights candidates, together with their costs, we can cut and prune these candidates so as to make the final list of rights compatible with national resources.

What happens to otherwise justified rights that fail the feasibility test?

Let's consider a potential human right that has passed the first five justificatory steps, but fails the test of being feasible in most of the world's countries. Let's also stipulate that the right comes close to passing the feasibility test because it is feasible in some of the world's countries, but not in most. It is not utopian in the sense that we do not know how to implement it anywhere. Let's say that this is an almost justified human right. A plausible example is the right to health care when it is thought of as guaranteeing the things provided by a good government health system in Europe.

First, we should ask whether the countries in which it is not feasible would find it possible to implement a pruned version of the right that preserves services that are most crucial to protecting people's survival and functioning. A pruned version might focus on public health measures such as inoculations and clean water, services to pregnant mothers and infants, fighting infectious diseases, and emergency services for the severely injured. This right to rudimentary health care would still be very expensive, but it is probably feasible to implement in most of the world's countries, particularly if international assistance is called upon and accepted.

What if even this pruned version is too costly to be affordable in most of the world's countries? Failing to be feasible in a majority of countries does not cause an almost justified human right to disappear. It is based on powerful normative considerations that have important implications for how governments should behave when they are able to. Countries that are able to recognize and implement this right should do so, even though it is not justifiable for most countries. A nearly justified right might also guide the behavior of governments not currently able to implement it. When a right is nearly justified, considerations of fairness – which help support the universality of a fully justified right – have already come into play. They make it appropriate to treat the object of the nearly jus-tified right with special concern for fair distribution. A nearly justified right tells countries unable to implement it what their responsibilities will be when their capacities increase, and it makes clear that health problems need to be addressed to the extent that they can do so at present. It may also suggest that governments of low-income countries seek international assistance for the implementation of human rights and avoid putting reg-ulatory or other obstacles in the way of that assistance being effectively used.

It is entirely possible for fully justified specific human rights to slide back into being almost justified or even unjustified. Severe and widespread economic depression, ecological disaster, or epidemics of disease could have this effect. By my lights, this happens when an already stripped-down right moves from being feasible in an ample majority of countries to being feasible in only some countries.

——— Deriving Rights from Other Rights ———

An arduous process of justification that begins with fundamental norms and then works its way through the six steps proposed above might be avoided in some cases if we could justify a specific right by deriving it from another human right that is already accepted as justified. We might attempt to justify the right to freedom of movement, for example, by showing that movement is a part of, or necessary to, the exercise of other rights such as freedom of association and freedom of political participation.

There are at least three ways in which one right can imply a second. The first right may be a general or abstract right that implies a second, more specific, right. For example, the general right to freedom of expression implies the more specific right to distribute pamphlets on public streets. The scope of the former includes the scope of the latter. Second, the effective implementation of the first right may require the implementation of the second, even though the second right is not normally thought to be included in the scope of the first. For example, the effective implementation of the right to freedom of assembly may require the implementation of a right to security against violence. Third, the second right may serve to make violations of the first less likely, even though the two rights operate in different spheres. For example, if the right to freedom of the press is regularly used to expose official misconduct, it will help to deter officials from violating the right to due process in criminal trials. My interest here is in the last two kinds of implication.

For one right to imply another in either of these two ways, the second right must provide support for the implementation or enjoyment of the first. The support the second right provides can, at one end of the spectrum, be essential to the effective implementation of the first or, at the other end, be merely helpful to the successful implementation of the first. The effective implementation of due process rights, for example, is at least mildly helpful to the successful implementation of many other rights. The more essential the second right is to the implementation of the first, the stronger the justificatory support that the first right provides for it.

We can think of this kind of justification as involving a consistency test, as asking whether the successful implementation of the first right is inconsistent with the nonimplementation of the second. For this test to be adequate, however, we must count not only logical inconsistency between the implementation of the first right and the nonimplementation of the

88

second but also practical inconsistency, which holds when it is logically possible but extremely unlikely that one can successfully implement the first right without implementing the second.

Whether implementation of some right is consistent in practice with the nonimplementation of a second right will sometimes depend on the degree of implementation we have in mind. Very rudimentary protections for the first right may be consistent with the absence of the second, while full or elaborate implementation of the first is inconsistent with the absence of the second. The degree of justificatory support that the first right provides for the second is likely to depend on how essential the second right is to some particular degree of implementation of the first.

Consistency tests are best suited for use at the implementation stage, when we already know what resources are available and the levels at which rights will be implemented. But these tests can also be used earlier if dependency relations can be detected in more abstract formulations of rights. For example, even without information about specific problems in a country, one can see that the right to freedom of assembly will require for its effective implementation a right to freedom from violence. Suppose that a country purported to implement a right to freedom of assembly without implementing a right to freedom from violence. When an unpopular group attempts to exercise its right of assembly in that country, it may be possible to prevent it from doing so by threats of violence since it knows that no government help will be available to meet those threats.

In *Basic Rights*, Henry Shue appealed to such connections between rights in order to defend rights to subsistence, security, and liberty (Shue 1996: 11–88). Shue argued that someone who allows that there is at least one human right will have to admit that there are also human rights to security, subsistence, and basic liberty. A key premise in this argument is that these rights are basic, in the sense that no other rights can be effectively implemented if they are not effectively implemented. Shue's starting point is the proposition that there is at least one universal right that ought to be effectively implemented. He then tries to show that whatever this right is, its effective implementation will require the implementation of universal rights to security, subsistence, and liberty.

In his defense of a right to subsistence, Shue is not merely making the point, sometimes made by Marxists, that guarantees of security or political participation are not very valuable if one must constantly worry about where one's next meal is coming from. Instead, he is making the much stronger claim that a person who does not have an effectively implemented right to subsistence can enjoy no rights at all. In Shue's view, a person does not really "enjoy" a right (or, alternatively, a right is not effectively implemented) unless there are social guarantees to protect the substance of the right against the most common threats. Basic rights protect against threats to the enjoyment of any right; they are defined as rights that are necessary to the enjoyment of any other rights.

Shue insists that there is a small group of rights one must enjoy if one is to enjoy any others: "[R]ights are basic in the sense used here only if enjoyment of them is essential to the enjoyment of all other rights" (Shue 1996: 19). It follows that a basic right cannot be sacrificed to promote other rights: to sacrifice a basic right would be to sacrifice all rights. Shue's argument has an important limitation, however. Sacrifice of some people's subsistence or security rights might supply the means to implement rights to paid holidays or to medical care for others. Shue's arguments therefore do not show that a society without subsistence rights for everyone cannot provide other effectively implemented rights to some people. At most they show that such a society cannot provide any other effectively implemented rights to everyone.

An important question about Shue's arguments concerns the strength of the supportive relationship between security or subsistence and other rights. I worry that these relationships are not as strong as Shue suggests. Security against violence is a basic right, he says, "because its absence would leave available extremely effective means for others, including the government, to interfere with or prevent the actual exercise of any other rights that were supposedly protected" (Shue 1996: 21). Here Shue goes beyond the true and important claim that effective protections of security are strongly supportive of many other rights to make the stronger claim – which I think is an exaggeration – that general protections of security are strictly necessary to the implementation of every other right.

Consider, for example, the right to asylum. Suppose that there is severe persecution of Hindus by Muslims in one country and that a number of Hindus manage to flee to a neighboring country where there is less persecution. They present themselves to the border guards, request asylum, and ask for safe passage to a third country. The officials of the second country take seriously their obligations under international law to provide asylum to endangered refugees, and with the assistance of international organizations or other governments they provide asylum and safe passage to these refugees. It would be quite possible to do all of this, I contend, even if the general right to security against violence was not effectively implemented in the second country. As long as these refugees can be provided security by special arrangements, their right to asylum can be effectively upheld. Because the right to asylum can be upheld in such cases without a general right to security against violence, it follows from Shue's strict definition that the right to security against violence is not a basic right.

Because of examples of this sort, I doubt whether there are implicative relationships among rights as broad and strong as those Shue claims to identify. It is clear, however, that a variety of supportive relationships is likely to exist within complex systems of rights, and thus many rights may be wholly or partially justified because of the support they provide for other rights that are already accepted as justified. Shue focuses on cases in which one right is strictly necessary to the implementation of another, but the weaker category of being strongly supportive of the other right seems just as serviceable here.

Many rights can be supported by arguments of this type. If other justifications are available, linkage arguments can provide complementary support and, perhaps, justify additional content or weight. For example, the right to education is often defended by showing how educated people are better able to understand and protect their rights. Successful implementation of a system of rights requires that people know what rights they have and what they can do if those rights are threatened or violated. But this knowledge will not be sufficiently widespread in a society where many people are illiterate and uneducated. Upholding a right to education seems to be strongly supportive of, and even perhaps practically necessary to, the successful implementation of many other rights.

Similarly, many rights associated with democracy (for example, rights to speak, protest, assemble, and vote) receive at least part of their justification from their roles in preventing abuses of human rights. If malfeasance by public officials can be exposed, and if officials are regularly held accountable to the electorate in meaningful elections, these officials will find it much riskier to engage in systematic abuses of human rights.

Deriving a right from another right provides no escape from the feasibility test. If we discover that the effective implementation of one right requires the implementation of a previously unrecognized right, the costs of the second have to be added to those of the first and feasibility reassessed.

Overview

Justifications for human rights begin with starting points like those discussed in Chapter 4 and end with the conclusion that a specific right is justified. The justification of a specific human right requires satisfying six tests: (1) the norm responds to severe and widespread threats; (2) it protects something of great importance; (3) it can be formulated as a right of all people today; (4) a specific political right, rather than some weaker norm, is necessary to provide adequate protection against the threat; (5) the normative burdens imposed by the right are tolerable and can be equitably distributed; and (6) the specific political right is feasible in an ample majority of countries.

Further Reading

Donnelly, J. 2003. *Universal Human Rights in Theory and Practice*, 2nd edn. Ithaca, NY and London: Cornell University Press.

Holmes, S., and Sunstein, C. 1999. *The Cost of Rights: Why Liberty Depends on Taxes*. New York: W. W. Norton.

Shue, H. 1996. *Basic Rights*, 2nd edn. Princeton, NJ: Princeton University Press.

Chapter 6

The List Question

The Universal Declaration and the human rights treaties that followed are lists of rights that address particular problems such as imprisonment without trial and suppression of political dissent. As noted earlier, today's human rights are the specific and numerous rights of the lawyers, not the abstract and general rights of the philosophers. Although the Universal Declaration asserts that "All human beings are born free and equal in dignity and rights," it is not mainly a declaration of abstract political principles. To make sense of human rights we need to know whether the Universal Declaration's list of human rights, which provided the pattern for the most of the human rights treaties that followed, is a plausible one. This chapter addresses that question. Specialized treaties dealing with the rights of minorities, women, and children are discussed in Chapter 10.

Determinacy through Law

The Universal Declaration and the treaties that followed achieved what philosophical reflection cannot, namely, the establishment of a largely settled list of human rights. Within international law and politics, the selection and enactment of an authoritative list of human rights seems to have been substantially completed and to have found widespread acceptance. By 2000 the main human rights treaties had been ratified by a large majority of the world's countries. As Ann Bayefsky writes, "Every UN member state is a party to one or more of the six major human rights treaties. 80% of states have ratified four or more" (Bayefsky 2001). This is not to say, of course, that all or most states largely comply with these treaties.

The idea that law can achieve what morality cannot is found in John Locke's *Second Treatise of Civil Government* (Locke 1986, originally published 1689). In spite of Locke's belief that people can have knowledge of natural rights such as "life, liberty, and property," he says that without positive law they lack "an established, settled, known law, received and allowed by common consent to be the standard of right and wrong, and the common measure to decide all controversies" (Locke 1986: ch. 9, sec. 126). Not only does a system of positive law provide established and knowable legal standards with canonical formulations, it also provides adjudication and enforcement. Legal systems provide "a known and indifferent judge, with authority to determine all differences according to the established law" and "power to back and support the sentence" and to "give it due execution."

Beginning during World War II, the human rights movement undertook to create international human rights law and institutions that provide international standards, adjudicate complaints and controversies, and promote compliance. The human rights treaties that emerged in the 1970s and 1980s established legal standards for how governments should treat their citizens and residents. The treaties have also created international means of adjudicating, promoting, and enforcing human rights. These measures were surveyed in the first chapter.

Before pursuing the list question it will be helpful to review the various families of human rights that international human rights law includes. First, there are security rights that protect people against crimes such as murder, massacre, torture, and rape. For example, article 2 of the European Convention sets out the following right to life:

> Everyone's right to life shall be protected by law. No one shall be deprived of his life intentionally save in the execution of a sentence of a court following his conviction of a crime for which this penalty is provided by law. Deprivation of life shall not be regarded as inflicted in contravention of this article when it results from the use of force which is no more than absolutely necessary: (a) in defense of any person from unlawful violence; (b) in order to effect a lawful arrest or to prevent escape of a person lawfully detained; (c) in action lawfully taken for the purpose of quelling a riot or insurrection.

Second, there are due process rights that protect against abuses of the legal system such as imprisonment without trial, secret trials, and excessive punishments. Article 5 of the European Convention, for example, says that people facing criminal charges are "entitled to a fair and public hearing within a reasonable time by an independent and impartial tribunal established by law." Due process rights are discussed in Chapter 7.

Third, there are liberty rights that protect fundamental freedoms in areas such as belief, expression, association, assembly, and movement. For example, article 11 of the European Convention says that "Everyone has the right to freedom of peaceful assembly and to freedom of association with others, including the right to form and to join trade unions for the protection of his interests."

Fourth, there are rights of political participation that require a democratic political process in which people can participate through actions such as voting, serving in public office, communicating, assembling, and protesting. The African Charter is typical in setting out that "Every citizen shall have the right to participate freely in the government of his country, either directly or through freely chosen representatives in accordance with the provisions of the law" (African Union 1981). The American Convention goes further, saying that every citizen shall have the right to "vote and to be elected in genuine period elections, which shall be by universal and equal suffrage and by secret ballot" (Organization of American States 1969).

Fifth, there are equality rights that guarantee equal citizenship, equality before the law, and nondiscrimination. For example, article 24 of the American Convention says that: "All persons are equal before the law. Consequently, they are entitled, without discrimination, to equal protection of the law."

Sixth, there are social rights that require governments to ensure that each person has access to subsistence, health care, and education. For example, the Social Covenant sets out a "right of everyone to an adequate standard of living for himself and his family, including adequate food, clothing, and housing" (United Nations 1966b). Social rights are defended in Chapter 9 below.

Finally, there are rights addressing the problems of distinctive groups including women, children, minorities, and indigenous peoples. Human rights treaties place great emphasis on the right to freedom from discrimination, but they go beyond it to require specific protections for distinctive groups. For example, article 27 of the Civil and Political Covenant says that "In those States in which ethnic, religious, or linguistic minorities exist, persons belonging to such minorities shall not be denied the right, in community with the other members of their group, to enjoy their own culture, to profess and practice their own religion, or to use their own language." The Universal Declaration does not include group rights, but several human rights treaties do, beginning with the Genocide Convention. Group rights include protections of ethnic groups against genocide and the ownership by countries of their national territories and resources.

This classification of human rights into seven families is much more fine-grained than the familiar division of human rights into civil and political rights and social rights. It is also more discriminating than Karel Vasek's classification of human rights in terms of three generations. (The first generation of rights was civil and political rights; the second was social rights; and the third was "solidarity rights" which include group rights and rights to peace and development (Vasek 1977; see also Wellman 1999).)

Liberty rights, together with rights of political participation, incorporate the liberal and democratic dimensions of contemporary human rights. Equality rights, along with social rights, comprise the egalitarian dimension of contemporary lists of human rights. And minority and group rights embody the communitarian commitments of international human rights.

In deciding which specific rights are human rights it is possible to make too little or too much of international documents such as the Universal Declaration and the European Convention. One makes too little of them by proceeding as if drawing up a list of important rights were a new question, never before addressed, and as if there were no practical wisdom to be found in the choices of rights that went into the historic documents. It was an amazing achievement to produce a legally established list of international human rights. And one makes too much of them by presuming that those documents tell us everything we need to know about human rights. The latter approach involves a kind of fundamentalism: it holds that if a right is on the official lists of human rights that fact settles its status as a human right ("If it's in the book, that's all I need to know"). Writing human rights documents in the United Nations and elsewhere was a heavily political process with plenty of imperfections. There is little reason to take international diplomats as the most authoritative guides to which human rights are justifiable. And even if a treaty could settle the issue of whether a certain right is a human right within international law, a treaty cannot settle its weight. If a treaty created a legal right to free entrance to national parks in one's country, this would establish the right as a "human right" in a legal sense, but it would not settle the question of whether free entrance to national parks merits treatment as a human right.

Rights Expansion and the Devaluation of Rights

If the human rights movement has created through law a determinate and accepted list of rights, why should we worry about the list question? There are several reasons why the list question is still worth pursuing. One, which was just mentioned, is that it is worth considering whether there really are strong supporting reasons for all of the rights in the Universal Declaration and the human rights treaties. Perhaps lists of human rights have gotten too long. It is also worth considering whether new human rights are needed. Finally, it will be interesting to consider whether there is any significant unity among the two dozen or more rights that we find in the international treaties.

The human rights movement has reflected – and perhaps even led – the expansion in the use of the idea of rights within moral and political discourse. To the rights found in historic bills of rights, it has added social rights, women's rights (see the Convention on the Elimination of All Forms of Discrimination against Women, 1979), children's rights (see the Convention on the Rights of the Child, 1989), and rights of peoples to self-determination and control over their natural resources (see the International Covenants, 1966a and 1966b).

Many political movements would like to have their main demands recognized as rights. It is easy to repackage a political movement's agenda in terms of rights, and the temptation to do so is sometimes strong. In the popular mind the idea of a right suggests a high priority norm that you can do something about by litigating or protesting (standing up for your rights). Stating a movement's agenda as a matter of rights suggests its importance and the possibility of realizing it through legal or political action. Further, gaining recognition as a human right for a key item on a group's agenda will help legitimate and promote that item. If international recognition of the right is achieved, bodies such as the United Nations and the Council of Europe will include the right in declarations and treaties, promote it with their organizational resources and personnel, and pressure countries to comply with it.

Rights expansion has led many theorists to call for quality control and serious critical evaluation. A prominent worry, first expressed by Maurice Cranston, is that positing too many rights will lead to rights inflation, to the devaluation of the currency of rights. Rhetorical excess in the positing of human rights will, he suggested, "push all talk of human rights out of the clear realm of the morally compelling into the twilight world of utopian aspirations" (Cranston 1967). He worried that if we put a right to "periodic holidays with pay" onto the human rights agenda (as the Universal Declaration did in article 24), people may think that the human right to a fair trial when charged with a crime is no more important than the right to holidays with pay.

Other worries about heavy reliance on the language of rights include the following. First, rights emphasize benefits to the rightholder rather than social responsibilities, thereby promoting egoism and self-centeredness. Second, it would be bad if rights talk replaced a normative focus on love, trust, and community that may be far more useful in ensuring good lives for vulnerable people. Third, emphasizing rights promotes litigiousness since rights are thought of as claims that you can take to court. Finally, inflated claims about rights are utopian in the sense of making demands that exceed our moral, institutional, and financial resources.

These worries about rights expansion have led some to oppose all or most of the rights introduced in the last century, to advocate treating civil and political rights (or "first generation" rights) as the only genuine human rights. These worries have led others into deeper reflection on the nature and justification of human rights in the hope that such reflection will lead to useful criteria for the evaluation of controversial rights. It is the latter path that I try to follow in this book. Chapter 5 proposed a framework that puts six demanding tests on the justification of specific human rights. The idea is to restrain rights inflation not with a single master criterion but to have a number of tests that must be passed as we make our way through the justification for an existing or proposed right.

I believe that this approach allows us to be both tough-minded and open-minded about new families of human rights. It is important to be open-minded to new rights because justifiable lists of specific human rights depend on the problems, institutions, and resources of particular places and times. Increased productivity, stability, and democracy in many countries make it possible to take seriously claims of injustice that would once have been thought hopelessly utopian. The emergence of large human populations, dangerous technologies, and increased international interaction and trade can generate new problems and injustices. And international organizations that did not exist a century ago make it possible to address these problems and injustices at the international level.

To pursue briefly the issue of rights expansion, consider environmental rights. Conceived as rights of animals or of nature itself, environmental rights do not fit our general idea of human rights because the rightholders are not humans. But narrower formulations are possible; environmental rights can be understood as rights of humans to an environment that is healthy and safe. Such a right is human-oriented: it does not cover directly issues such as the claims of animals, biodiversity, or sustainable development (Nickel 1993b).

The right to a safe environment can be sculpted to fit the general idea of human rights by conceiving it as primarily imposing duties on governments and international organizations. It calls on them to regulate the activities of both governmental and nongovernmental agents to ensure that environmental safety is maintained. Citizens are secondary addressees. This right sets out a minimal environmental standard, safety for humans, rather than calling for higher and broader standards of environmental protection. Countries that are able to implement higher standards are of course free to enact those standards in their national law or bill of rights.

A justification for this right must show that environmental problems pose serious threats to fundamental human interests, values, or norms; that governments may appropriately be burdened with the responsibility of protecting people against these threats; and that an ample majority of the world's governments actually have the ability to do this. This last requirement – feasibility – may be the most difficult. Successful environmental protection is expensive and difficult, and many governments will be unable to do very much of it while meeting other important responsibilities.

Rawlsian Ultraminimalism

John Rawls did not discuss international human rights until the last decade of his life. Shortly before his death he published *The Law of Peoples*, which sketches a normative philosophy of international relations (Rawls 1999). One of the eight principles of international justice proposed is that countries "honor human rights" (Rawls 1999: 37). Rawls agrees with most theorists in viewing human rights as high priority norms that are international and universal. He also accepts that human rights set out minimal rather than optimal standards for how countries should treat people. But Rawls's view of human rights is distinctive in holding that human rights play a "special role" in limiting a country's autonomy and in specifying when intervention by other countries is permissible (Rawls 1999: 79).

Rawls thinks that human rights are more plausible internationally if they are kept to an ultraminimal list list (for an even more minimal view, which focuses human rights activism on security rights alone, see Ignatieff 2000: 173; see also Cohen 2004). One reason for keeping the list minimal is to accommodate "decent peoples" – countries which reject or ignore many liberal and egalitarian rights but which are not so oppressive and dangerous as to be considered "outlaw" states. Rawls believes that such countries are sufficiently just (or "acceptable") to merit the respect of countries that are democratic, liberal, and egalitarian ("liberal peoples"). Denial of such respect "may wound the self-respect of decent nonliberal peoples" and "lead to great bitterness and resentment" (Rawls

1999: 61). Further, there are strong reasons for respecting "a people's self-determination" even when the country's human rights record is poor by the standards of liberal peoples (Rawls 1999: 61, 85). To respect decent peoples requires refraining from "condemnation" and "intervention" (Rawls 1999: 81).

Since serious violations of human rights make permissible international condemnation and intervention, the only way to ensure that "decent" peoples will not be condemned and invaded is to have a very short list of human rights. Rawls worries that the list of rights we get from the Universal Declaration is too liberal, democratic, and egalitarian to find widespread acceptance and to give appropriate tolerance and respect to decent but nonliberal peoples.

Rawls offers the following broad description of the international human rights he endorses: (1) "the right to life (to the means of subsistence and security)"; (2) the "right of emigration" and "freedom from slavery, serfdom, and forced occupation, and to a sufficient measure of liberty of conscience to ensure freedom of religion and thought)"; (3) "property (personal property)"; and (4) "formal equality as expressed by the rules of natural justice (that is, that similar cases be treated similarly)" (Rawls 1999: 65, 74).

The biggest differences between Rawls's conception of human rights and the one found in the Universal Declaration are in three areas: liberty rights, political rights, and equality rights.

(1) *Liberty rights* Rawls proposes a far more restricted conception of "fundamental freedoms," than the one found in the Universal Declaration. A large number of the fundamental freedoms found in the Universal Declaration and human rights treaties are excluded by Rawls's short list of freedoms. These include freedom of opinion and expression (articles 18–19); peaceful assembly and association (article 20); and freedom to choose one's own marriage partner (article 16).

(2) *Political rights* Rawls does not endorse the view of political rights found in articles 20–21 of the Universal Declaration. Those articles declare rights to peaceable assembly and association (which allows one to hold political rallies and to form and join political parties), to participate in one's country's governance, to equal access to public service, and to periodic and genuine elections with universal suffrage. Rawls replaces these commitments to democracy with a requirement that political leaders receive petitions from and consult with the leaders of the country's constituent groups. He says that to deserve toleration countries must at least have a "decent consultation hierarchy" with "a family of representative

bodies whose role in the hierarchy is to take part in an established procedure of consultation" (Rawls 1999: 71–2).

(3) *Equality rights* Rawls believes that human rights require that
rulers govern rationally and with concern for the common good, but that
international human rights should not forbid political hierarchy or the
political subordination of women and minority religious groups. A legal
system that fulfills human rights must display "formal equality as expressed
by the rules of natural justice" (Rawls 1999: 65), but this does not exclude
hierarchical and group-based differences. Rawls allows that one religious
group may be favored, that there may be "inequality of religious
freedom," and that there may be religious (and presumably therefore
gender) discrimination in access to higher political and judicial appoint-
ments (Rawls 1999: 74–5). Women's place in society need not be equal,
but he imagines that "dissent has led to important reforms in the rights
and role of women" (Rawls 1999: 78).

Rawls's minimal list of human rights fails to address many severe injustices. True, it does protect people's security, and thus if it were respected
it would block some of the worst and most dangerous sorts of human
rights violations. Nevertheless, it has substantial deficits in regard to
liberty, democracy, and equality. It would not have been thought adequate in 1948 when the Universal Declaration was being authored since
it fails to incorporate areas of important political progress in the last two
centuries. And it does not reflect the fact that nearly all countries today
have ratified human rights treaties committing them to the full range of
human rights. Rawls clearly did not believe that a country that fulfilled
his minimal list of human rights would thereby be a just society. The
deficits in liberty, equality, and democracy were deliberately selected, not
an accident. But clearly they did not represent Rawls's own political
beliefs. So why did he choose this ultraminimal list?

There are two main reasons. The first is that Rawls accepted a broad
and strong doctrine of tolerance for the self-determination of countries
as long as they were not "outlaw states." He believed that liberal constitutional democracies had strong duties of tolerance towards countries
that were "decent" even though they were illiberal, undemocratic, and
hierarchical. National self-determination certainly deserves respect, but
assigning this principle extremely high priority in relation to other international norms is inadequately defended by Rawls.

Second, Rawls held that a defining role of human rights is to help
specify when outside intervention in a country is permissible. He says that
human rights "specify limits to a regime's internal autonomy" and that
their fulfillment "is sufficient to exclude justified and forceful intervention

by other peoples, for example, by diplomatic and economic sanctions, or . . . by military force" (Rawls 1999: 79–80). A country that "fulfills" human rights, along with the other principles of international justice, is entitled to tolerance, which Rawls takes to mean that other countries are required to recognize that country as an equal member in good standing in the international community and to refrain from coercion and force in their dealings with that country. Negatively, if a country does not fulfill human rights, then it is permissible (if often unwise) for other countries to use coercion and force to try to get that country to change its practices. For Rawls, human rights are norms that can justifiably be imposed on countries even when they reject them on principle. The means of imposition, whose appropriateness depends on the severity of the violation, are diplomatic, economic, and military sanctions.

Tying the definition of human rights so closely to what standards it is justifiable to impose with coercion and force is not very plausible. In fact, human rights serve *many* international roles, some of them unconnected to enforceability. First, they serve as standards for noncoercive international persuasion. They say to countries: "Here are the standards for good government that the world community endorses. Consider adopting them!" Second, they serve as standards for domestic aspiration and criticism, as rights to enact and implement nationally. Citizens who appeal to them in domestic political debate can defend them as internationally endorsed and widely accepted. Third, they function as operative norms within international treaties that are voluntarily accepted. Fourth, they serve as standards to be promoted within international organizations using methods of persuasion and criticism that are noncoercive, or that involve very low levels of coercion. Finally, some of them serve as standards for permissible international intervention using coercion and force (the function that Rawls takes to be central).

As human rights function today within international organizations it is simply untrue to say that they are mainly about intervention using coercion and force. A better description of their main role is that they are used to persuade and encourage governments to treat their citizens humanely with respect for their lives, liberties, and equal citizenship. The human rights system puts this emphasis on persuasion and encouragement because of the high costs and dangers of strongly enforcing public norms within the international system we currently have. Because enforcement efforts are costly and dangerous it is reasonable to restrict their use to the most severe human rights crises. These tend to be situations in which large numbers of people are being killed. To avoid narrowing the human rights agenda to such crises, means for promoting human rights have been devised that do not require intervention or the imposition of heavy diplomatic or economic sanctions. These means are weaker, but they allow human rights to cover a wider but still very important set of issues. If not all rights are going to be imposed by force, many cultural differences can be accommodated without slashing the list.

Rawls's proposal to sacrifice many important human rights is hard to swallow. An alternative is to keep the Universal Declaration's list of human rights – with some trimming – while easing enforcement of human rights that conflict with practices of decent societies that are mildly authoritarian, undemocratic, or hierarchical. Broadly, the rights that Rawls wants to keep will sometimes be enforced through international sanctions, but the ones he want to cut will be saved but generally promoted through persuasion, encouragement, mild pressure, and reporting schemes such as those the UN uses to implement its treaties. As suggested above, I believe that this is what the human rights movement has actually done.

Rawls has a very simple view of the relation between tolerance and human rights. If a national practice does not comply with his minimal list of human rights, then other countries are not required to tolerate that practice. Use of coercion or force is permissible. On the other hand, when a national practice complies with his minimal list it must be tolerated. Human rights define the limits of tolerance by defining the standards that the international community is permitted to enforce. Rawls takes the boundary of tolerance to be exactly the same as the boundary between human rights issues and problems that do not involve human rights. The realm of tolerance does not overlap with the realm of human rights.

On the alternative view proposed here, noncompliance with human rights norms is sometimes deliberately tolerated. I endorse toleration, combined with disapproval and criticism, in some cases of deliberate noncompliance with human rights. This stance allows the international community to accommodate at least temporarily the fact that a country does not respect and protect the full range of fundamental freedoms, that its political institutions are not democratic, or that its social and political institutions are very hierarchical and sexist, without giving up the demand that these human rights failures eventually be remedied (for a fuller elaboration of this alternative, see Nickel 2006). This approach reduces the dangers of causing great resentment in response to diplomatic condemnation and intervention, and helps accommodate human rights to political realism and the value of national self-determination. Following Rawls in sharply cutting the list of human rights is unnecessary.

This is not to say, however, that no cuts in the Universal Declaration's list of rights are appropriate. Chapter 9 argues that the only social rights that should be considered international human rights are subsistence, basic health care, and basic education (the Vance Conception). And

Chapter 5 argues that the justification of any human right requires satisfying a fairly demanding test of feasibility. I do not, of course, expect that these cuts will actually be made as formal amendments to human rights declarations and treaties. But we can use these ideas about proposed cuts to decide which human rights to take less seriously.

Unity and Diversity among the Families of Human Rights

A look at the families of human rights described above suggests that human rights are a diverse lot. There are at least three sources of this diversity. The most important is that humans are vulnerable to abuse and injustice in a wide variety of ways. Humans are needy and vulnerable creatures; there are lots of ways in which people can be harmed and mistreated. It is for this reason that human rights documents include seven families of rights covering various kinds of problems such as torture, unfair trials, exclusion from political participation, the subordination of women, and extreme poverty. Another source of diversity, I think, is that the underlying values are several, not unitary. As suggested in Chapter 4, they include having a life, leading one's life, avoidance of severe unfairness, and avoidance of severe cruelty. Prudential and utilitarian reasons play a role as well. And the fundamental value of having a life, for example, quickly branches into concerns for security, the material conditions of survival, and health. A third source of diversity is that the institutions needed to protect the underlying values against the standard threats and abuses are various. A workable system of rights needs various institutions including the criminal law and law enforcement, due process rights, democratic institutions, and educational institutions.

I may be wrong in thinking that there is no single master value such as utility or autonomy that is the ultimate source of human rights. But even if there is such a value, the fact that there are two other sources of variety among human rights (diversity of abuses and diversity of institutional remedies) means that deep unity will not produce surface unity. Consider an analogy. Imagine a (very idealized) hospital was totally governed by the value of health and thus had unity at a deep level. And suppose that all of the hospital workers were ultimately guided by the same value (however much they might have to be guided as well by subordinate values such as careful record keeping or using the best surgical techniques). Still, there would be hundreds or thousands of different kinds of diseases and treatments, and the hospital would be divided into different departments such as surgery, obstetrics, infectious diseases, housekeeping, etc. And there would still be plenty of opportunities for conflicts between these units over space, prestige, and budgets. I suspect that being rooted in a single ultimate value would do no more for the unity of human rights than it does for the unity of health care.

Should we be troubled by the diversity of human rights? Not if there is some significant unity that exists in the midst of the diversity. One source of unity is the existence of a functional role that ties together human rights even though it does not provide their foundations. As suggested earlier, I think that there are two plausible and closely related candidates for this idea. One is that all human rights identify types of treatment that are incompatible with human dignity. The other idea is that human rights try to identify the conditions of a minimally good life as a person.

Harmony is another kind of unity that we might hope for. Harmony is compatibility and complementarity within difference. It requires the absence of deep and total conflict. I believe that the seven families are harmonious in this sense – or at least can be if the particular rights within them are properly chosen and shaped. The fact that some countries have substantially succeeded in implementing all seven families of human rights provides evidence for the claim that human rights are harmonious.

A final kind of unity is *intersupport* (discussed in Chapter 5 in connection with Shue's idea of basic rights). Intersupport exists when the effective implementation of one family of rights helps with the implementation of some or all of the others. The interdependence of human rights is an official doctrine of the United Nations, supported both by the General Assembly and by the Office of the High Commissioner for Human Rights. The UN General Assembly's 1977 endorsement of interdependence provides a representative formulation:

> All human rights and fundamental freedoms are indivisible and interdependent; equal attention and urgent consideration should be given to the implementation, promotion, and protection of both civil and political, and economic, social, and cultural rights.   (United Nations 1977)

This resolution rightly emphasizes that the supporting relations between rights extend but are not restricted to the supporting relations between civil and political rights and social rights (that is, between the human rights in the two generic UN human rights treaties). Mutual support exists, in varying degrees of strength, between all of the families of rights.

Overview

The Universal Declaration and the treaties that followed provide an established list of human rights. That list gives more determinate meaning to human rights than normative reasoning alone can hope to establish. Normative theory seldom produces general agreement, especially when we get down to details. Most countries have ratified the treaties creating these lists. Nevertheless, the catalogs of human rights found in these treaties merit critical scrutiny. One obvious question is whether the lists are too long and include rights of insufficient importance and universality. Although some cuts would be appropriate, the lists are not excessively long. Despite Rawls's views to the contrary, we do not need to shorten the lists drastically to accommodate cultural diversity. Another question is whether there is significant unity among the various human rights. One source of unity is that all the rights protect people's dignity. Another is that the various families of rights form an intersupportive system.

Further Reading

Nickel, J. 1993b. "The Human Right to a Safe Environment." *Yale Journal of International Law* 18: 281–95.

Silverstein, H. 1996. *Unleashing Rights: Law, Meaning, and the Animal Rights Movement.* Ann Arbor: University of Michigan Press.

Sunstein, C. 2004. *The Second Bill of Rights: FDR's Unfinished Revolution and Why We Need It More than Ever.* New York: Basic Books.

Vasek, K. 1977. "A 30-Year Struggle: The Sustained Efforts to Give Force of Law to the Universal Declaration of Human Rights." *Unesco Courier* 10: 29–30.

Wellman, Carl. 1999. *The Proliferation of Rights: Moral Progress or Empty Rhetoric?* Boulder, CO: Westview Press.

Chapter 7

Due Process Rights and Terrorist Emergencies

Due process rights protect people against being imprisoned for alleged crimes without being given the opportunity for a fair and public trial. This chapter discusses the grounds for due process rights and the permissibility of suspending them during national emergencies. The two topics are profitably treated together because due process rights – along with freedom of movement, expression, and political participation – are often suspended or restricted when national emergencies occur. Although I present a strong case for due process rights as human rights, this justification does not settle their priority during emergency situations. That requires further argument – which I attempt to provide. The overall thrust of the chapter is to defend the importance of respecting due process rights during troubled times.

Due Process Rights

Tyrants throughout history have used the institutions, personnel, and sanctions of the criminal law as means of imposing their arbitrary and unjust rule. They throw their enemies and political opponents into jail, have them executed, or take away their property. The authors of historic and contemporary bills of rights were well aware of these dangers and accordingly gave due process rights a prominent place. For example, Magna Carta included due process provisions such as:

> 38. No bailiff for the future shall, upon his own unsupported complaint, put anyone to his "law," without credible witnesses brought for this purpose.

39. No freemen shall be taken or imprisoned or disseised or exiled or in any way destroyed, nor will we go upon him nor send upon him, except by the lawful judgment of his peers or by the law of the land. (1215, in Urofsky and Finkelman 2002)

The US Bill of Rights devotes more space to due process rights than to any other family of rights. Of the original ten amendments to the US Constitution, five of them (4–8) deal with due process. For example, the Sixth Amendment prescribes:

In all criminal prosecutions, the accused shall enjoy the right to a speedy and public trial, by an impartial jury of the state and district wherein the crime shall have been committed . . .; to be informed of the nature and cause of the accusation; to be confronted with the witnesses against him; to have compulsory process for obtaining witnesses in his favor, and to have the assistance of counsel for his defense. (1791, in Urofsky and Finkelman 2002)

Due process rights also play a prominent role in contemporary human rights declarations and treaties. For example, the Civil and Political Covenant deals with due process issues in articles 6–15. Article 9.4 (habeas corpus) is representative:

Anyone who is deprived of his liberty by arrest or detention shall be entitled to take proceedings before a court, in order that [the] court may decide without delay on the lawfulness of his detention and order his release if the detention is not lawful.

A central role of due process rights is to prevent summary punishments in which a person believed guilty of a crime is killed, tortured, beaten, or thrown into jail solely on the basis of a unilateral and unreviewed decision of a politician or police officer. Due process rights require that decisions to impose criminal punishments be reviewed and confirmed by other decision-makers. As Magna Carta says, a police officer's "own unsupported complaint" is insufficient (1215, in Urofsky and Finkelman 2002).

If a criminal case is prosecuted and no plea bargain is reached, subsequent review will occur in a trial. The criminal trial is an organized inquiry – one could also say "ritual" or "pageant" – which involves assembling needed participants, systematically collecting and presenting evidence, considering the arguments for and against the defendant's guilt, and judging appropriate penalties. The deliberate pace of a trial allows passions to cool and greater objectivity to emerge. And the judge, who serves both as master of ceremonies and as interpreter of the law, is charged with impartial application of both law and evidence (see Duff 1986).

——————— **The Grounds of Due Process Rights** ———————

This section offers a normative justification of due process rights. It uses the justificatory tests proposed in Chapters 5 and 6 above to argue that due process rights are human rights.

Have people experienced many violations in the area of due process?

Criminal punishment is used and abused in every country; this is an area of widely experienced injustices. Threats or abuses include using the criminal law system to intimidate or destroy the enemies of those in power and to victimize unpopular minorities (or even majorities). The unpopular, the troublesome, and the powerless are especially vulnerable to being denied fair trials, but anyone can be a victim of the incompetence or laziness of judges and other officials.

Is due process sufficiently important?

Chapter 5 proposed four "secure claims" as central grounds of human rights: (1) having a life, (2) leading one's life, (3) not being subjected to severely cruel or degrading treatment, and (4) not being subjected to severely unfair treatment. Let's consider how due process rights protect these claims.

(1) *Security of life and liberty* Due process rights protect both life and liberty against threats from government. Suppose that we have been persuaded by the arguments in Thomas Hobbes's *Leviathan* that without a strong government to protect us against the predations of our neighbors it will be impossible to have adequate levels of order and productivity and that consequently we will have a poor chance of avoiding a miserable life and early death (Hobbes 1981). Greedy or hungry neighbors who will raid, kill, steal, dispossess, kidnap, and rape pose what I call the First Problem of Insecurity. To protect ourselves from them we create law, property, and government. We enact criminal laws, create courts and jails,

and proceed to convict and punish offenders. We thereby solve – or at least ameliorate – the First Problem of Insecurity. The system of law and government is dangerous, however, and we still have reason to be fearful, but now our fear is of the government's predations, corruption, and ineptitude. This is the Second Problem of Insecurity.

A common worry about governments is that they will throw us in jail or execute us because some official suspects us of committing a crime, wants to neutralize us as a political opponent, finds us troublesome, or wants our property. In response to this worry we come up with the idea of not permitting the government to impose severe punishments without justifying a person's punishment before an impartial and independent tribunal. Law is the remedy – or at least a key part of it – to both problems of insecurity. Just as we imposed law and its potential sanctions on ourselves and our neighbors to solve the First Problem, we now impose legal restrictions on our government to solve the Second Problem. Both projects are difficult and may never be fully successful. Still, due process rights give us important protections for our lives, liberty, and property. Like the criminal law itself they protect our security. But instead of protecting us against private criminals they protect us against government.

Due process rights protect us not only directly when we are personally accused of crimes, but also indirectly by serving as checks on governmental power. They make less available tempting but tyrannical ways of governing, and thereby promote good government. They do this by requiring that a number of procedural steps be taken before sentencing someone to jail. They also make tyrannical ways of governing less available by making criminal procedure transparent. Public trials give citizens a view of how the criminal justice system is working. Oppression, if it is occurring, is more likely to be open to public view. An attractive feature of trials by jury is that they bring randomly selected members of the public into the criminal justice system as participants, and test legal judgments against their consciences and common sense. Democratic practices, and the rights to campaign, protest, and vote that go with them, make transparency more valuable and due process rights more stable.

One way that due process rights protect people's liberty is by requiring legal justification for incarceration – a justification that shows that the accused person violated a law that was already in existence and knowable at the time the alleged criminal offense occurred. Suppose that the police, as well as some of the citizenry, do not like the styles and activities of certain teenagers, or the door-to-door witnessing of certain religious groups. Police in many countries harass such people by arresting them for minor or imaginary offences and by beating them up during or after arrest. Due process rights protect such people by making conviction of a criminal offense more difficult since they require a fair trial in which it is shown that the person violated a valid law. Further, by opening arrest, interrogation, abuse, and detention to judicial and public scrutiny they help make it dangerous for police to use unauthorized violence.

(2) *Cruelty*   Due process rights protect people against severe cruelty by reducing the incidence of police violence during arrest and interrogation (as in the example in the previous paragraph). They also prohibit cruel punishments and torture (for an excellent collection of essays on torture see Levinson 2004). Article 7 of the Civil and Political Covenant prescribes:

> No one shall be subjected to torture or to cruel, inhuman or degrading treatment or punishment.

The prohibition of torture also helps to protect people's ability to lead their lives since it blocks use of a powerful means of forcing people to do and say things they do not want to do or reveal.

(3) *Unfair treatment*   The secure claim against severely unfair treatment plays a large role in grounding the importance of due process rights. After all, the centerpiece of due process rights is the right to a fair trial. The claim to fairness requires trials that improve accuracy in the determination of guilt. A trial is a fair process, one that anyone would choose if they did not know if they were going to be a suspect, a prosecutor, or a victim. And by offering greater accuracy than summary punishments a trial yields a better chance of reaching a substantively fair result.

Can due process be a universal right?

There is no difficulty in formulating due process rights as rights of all people. The primary addressee is any government that takes a person into custody for purposes of detention or criminal prosecution.

Would some weaker norm be as effective?

Neither structural improvements in legal regimes, self-help, nor charitable assistance will eliminate the possibility of unfair trials in criminal proceedings. Individuals frequently lack the competence to gain good treatment for themselves within a complex legal system. High priority legal guarantees that can be invoked by the defendant are needed to protect people against the dangers imposed by the coercive powers of criminal justice systems. Important members of the due process family are provisions for proof of guilt in public before an impartial tribunal, assistance of effective counsel, habeas corpus, and review of convictions on appeal.

Are the burdens on government excessive?

The costs of implementing a general right to a fair trial are substantial. Providing those accused of crimes with fair trials requires an expensive infrastructure of courts, judges, lawyers, record-keepers, and buildings. But a majority of countries successfully bear these costs. The necessary resources can be collected from citizens and businesses through a fair tax scheme. And the burdens imposed on jurors and witnesses can be limited and distributed so as to avoid severe unfairness.

Are due process rights feasible in most countries?

Due process rights may seem to be negative rights, ones that merely require their addressees to refrain from certain actions. But in fact they are more like positive rights, ones that require their addressees to provide a service to the rightholders. In my view they are best classified as conditionally positive. They say that if the government plans to punish someone then it must give that person various procedural protections and legal services along with the opportunity to have a trial. The if-clause of this conditional is sure to be continuously satisfied because governments need to threaten and carry out punishments in order to govern, and thus governments will have duties to provide due process services in many cases. From a practical point of view due process rights impose unavoidable duties to provide, just like positive rights. Ask government officials whether the system of courts and trials is a discretionary expenditure and they will laugh at you. Due process rights require governments to provide expensive legal services that require large, fragile, and expensive bureaucracies and infrastructures.

Criminal justice is expensive, and providing the personnel and infrastructure for fair criminal trials is part of that cost. Because of the size of these costs and the unpopularity of spending money on suspected or convicted criminals, many countries skimp on criminal justice and have horrible prison conditions and long delays in providing trials. This is, however, more a problem of attitudes than of resources. An ample majority of the world's countries have the resources necessary to respect and implement due process rights.

Emergencies in International Human Rights Law

The moral and practical case for due process rights is very strong, but that does not settle the question of whether such rights may be suspended during emergencies. For that, further discussion and argument is required. Let's begin with a discussion of emergencies.

National emergencies are extremely troubled times in the life of a country. They typically result from wars, threats of attack, rebellions, terrorist attacks, famines, plagues, major industrial accidents, and natural disasters. During national emergencies extremely harsh measures are sometimes warranted because the problems are immense, resources and personnel are severely strained, and it is imperative to take the most effective actions. We think of emergencies as temporary, as bounded on both sides by times that are normal. But sometimes emergencies endure for a long time and the measures adopted during emergency rule become the standard political and legal practices of the country.

The most severe emergencies are ones in which most parts of the country have high levels of physical devastation, loss of life, loss of home and livelihood, economic crisis, and institutional breakdown. The presence of imminent invasion or threatened attack also contributes to the severity of an emergency. We can also categorize emergencies in terms of the harshness of the measures their management is thought to require. These might range from temporary curfews and restrictions on movement, to declaring a state of siege and imposing martial law, to full-blown military occupation and pacification. It is common for restrictions of rights to fall on freedom of movement and residence, freedom of assembly, freedom of expression and protest, democratic rights, and due process rights.

In a serious national emergency such as an armed foreign invasion or an extended series of terrorist attacks, governments have the responsibility of minimizing damage to people and property, stopping the invasion or attacks, restoring security and services, and repairing the most disruptive damage. In order to do these things, certain emergency powers are sometimes justified. First, governments need powers to control the location and movement of people, to move them from the most dangerous areas and into areas where security and rudimentary services (food, shelter, and medical care) can be provided. Rights to freedom of movement and to choice of residence may be severely infringed during such emergencies. Second, governments need powers to reestablish rudimentary services. Doing this may involve commandeering public and private buildings and supplies to feed, house, or care for people, and requiring that citizens, particularly those with special skills, assist in the provision of these services. Thus rights to property and against forced labor may need to be restricted during emergencies. Third, governments need powers to reestablish security. In a natural disaster this may be mainly a matter of preventing looting. In a war, insurrection, or terrorist onslaught it may also involve preparing defenses against additional attacks. People who are believed to be dangerous may be detained in circumstances where it is impossible to file charges or hold hearings quickly. Thus due process rights may need to be qualified or their application postponed.

Severe national emergencies are dangerous for human rights because they provide ample opportunities to rationalize gross violations. For example, the wars that occurred during the break-up of Yugoslavia involved large-scale massacres, the use of murder, torture, and rape to terrorize people, and the use of ethnic cleansing to redraw national boundaries. Because of the dangers that national emergencies pose to human rights it is important that human rights declarations and treaties provide some guidance as to what governments may and may not do during such periods.

Fortunately, three major treaties – the European Convention, the American Convention on Human Rights, and the Civil and Political Covenant – undertook this difficult task. They allow that during severe national emergencies most rights can be suspended if doing so is genuinely necessary, but that a few of the most important rights cannot. Article 15 of the European Convention gives a representative formulation:

> In time of war or other public emergency threatening the life of the nation any [country that has ratified the Convention] may take measures derogating from its obligations under this Convention to the extent strictly required by the exigencies of the situation . . . No derogation from Article 2 [right to life], except in respect of deaths resulting from lawful acts of war, or from Articles 3 [right against torture and degrading treatment], 4 (paragraph 1) [right against slavery and servitude] and 7 [right against ex post facto laws] shall be made under this provision.

This clause makes several especially important rights immune to suspension, permitting the remaining rights to be set aside only as far and for as long as is indispensable, or at least highly useful, to managing the emergency. Further, other countries that are parties to the treaty must be informed of any suspensions. According to the three treaties, most human rights – including due process of law, personal liberties, and democratic rights – may be suspended in national emergencies when the country's security and survival requires it. If there are compelling goals of security and survival that a country cannot reasonably hope to reach without suspending some right, then its suspension is permissible as long as it is not on the short-list of rights whose suspension is forbidden in all circumstances.

It is not quite accurate to say that the three treaties simply make due process rights subject to suspension because the right to life in these treaties is formulated so as to require that capital punishment may be imposed "pursuant to a final judgment rendered by a competent court and in accordance with a law establishing such punishment, enacted prior to the commission of the crime" (American Convention, article 4.2). The effect of this clause is to forbid summary executions. It also suggests an attractive principle, namely that due process rights are most imperative when the most fundamental interests and rights are at stake.

Many scholars and human rights bodies have advocated making due process rights immune to suspension during emergencies. The Inter-American Court of Human Rights and the United Nations Human Rights Committee (established under the Civil and Political Covenant) have made substantial efforts in their interpretations and rulings to give due process rights more protected status during emergencies (Oraa 1992; Jinks 2001: 359; see also the Siracusa Principles, United Nations 1985). The necessity test recognizes the weight of human rights by requiring that what is on the other side of the scale be the security and survival of the country during a period of great danger. The American Convention requires a "war, public danger, or other emergency" that is sufficiently large to threaten a country's "independence or security." The European Convention and the Civil and Political Covenant require a time of war or other public emergency threatening the life of the nation.

The approach to emergencies found in the three treaties uses a simple emergency versus nonemergency approach. I believe that we will think more clearly about human rights during emergencies if we work with four categories instead of just two. I present these four categories as ideal types, recognizing that reality is often messier than neat categories suggest. First, there are *normal times*, periods when a country is not facing severe and dramatic problems. The problems that do exist are perennial problems such as crime, unemployment, inflation, inequality, prejudice, and political discontent, and these problems are not at crisis levels. Further, no major emergencies are occurring in the home territory, although there may be floods, hurricanes, recessions, and crime waves. The country may be involved in small-scale wars and peacekeeping operations in other countries, but it is not experiencing major war or insurrection. Britain and the United States, for example, were in normal times during the year 2000.

Second, there are *troubled times*. In such a period the country is experiencing the problems of normal times plus engaging in a war outside of the homeland, experiencing occasional terrorist attacks (victims in the hundreds or few thousands), having very serious domestic unrest, or trying to recover from a major natural disaster or industrial accident. Rebellion and resistance may also be present, provided that they are not large-scale. Large natural disasters may create troubled times through their political and economic impacts. Britain, for example, was in troubled times after the 2001 terrorists attacks on New York, because terrorist attacks on Britain were reasonably thought to be likely – and eventually occurred.

Third, in *severe emergencies* the country is experiencing war, armed rebellion, or regular and severe terrorist attacks in some parts of the homeland, with resulting economic problems and political instability. If attacks have not yet occurred, they are imminent and likely to be large. Conducting a large war outside of the homeland may also create a severe emergency. The emergency may be having a very negative impact on the domestic economy and on foreign relations. Still, basic institutions are functioning in most parts of the country. In the *Greek Case* the European Human Rights Court held that for an emergency to justify derogation from the requirements of the European Convention, it must have the following characteristics:

1   It must be actual or imminent
2   Its effects must involve the whole nation
3   The continuance of the organized life of the community must be threatened
4   The crisis or danger must be exceptional, in that the normal measures or restrictions, permitted by the convention . . . are plainly inadequate (European Human Rights Court 1969; see also *Lawless* v. *Ireland*, European Human Rights Court 1959, and Hartman 1981)

Fourth and finally, there are *supreme emergencies* (or "extremely severe emergencies") which literally threaten the survival of the country as independent and whole (Walzer 1977; Rawls 1999). A major war or insurrection is occurring in the homeland, causing widespread death and devastation. In many areas political and economic institutions are not functioning, or are functioning at low levels. The economic and institutional strain is enormous, and there is a serious risk that the war or insurrection will end in disastrous defeat. Britain, for example, was in a supreme emergency during the worst years of World War II.

If we use the four categories suggested above to classify the countries such as France, Spain, the United Kingdom, and the United States which experienced terrorist attacks between 2001 and 2006, the most plausible view is that actual and threatened terrorist attacks have put these countries into troubled times but not into the category of severe national emergency (Ackerman 2004: 1044). I recognize, of course, that in late 2001 it was not foreseeable that terrorist attacks would not continue to occur regularly in the United States, and we do not know what the future holds. Still, if no severe emergency exists at present, then under the three treaties these countries are not permitted to suspend due process rights. The British Lords of Appeal reached exactly this conclusion in the Belmarsh Case (House of Lords 2005), quashing the government's derogation from the European Convention – taken in the wake of the New York terrorist attacks. Human rights standards apply without restrictions during normal and troubled times.

Detention without Trial in the War against Terror

The American and British governments responded to the 2001 terrorist attacks on New York and Washington by adopting a policy of detaining suspected terrorists without trial and other due process protections (on terrorism see Jaggar 2005). Many detainees were denied access to counsel, habeas corpus, and the right to a fair trial. This section addresses the justifiability of setting aside due process rights as part of a war on terrorism.

Defining the issue

Under international law it is permissible to detain without trial captured enemy soldiers. The Geneva Conventions, which govern the law of war, permit prisoners of war to be held without trial until the end of hostilities. Prisoners of war who were lawful combatants are not regarded as criminals unless they participated in war crimes. In order to incapacitate them and prevent their return to the war effort they may be imprisoned without trial. They are entitled to some sort of administrative review of the grounds for their imprisonment, but this need not be a trial. The rationale for detention without trial of enemy soldiers during wartime includes the costs and difficulties of conducting trials for thousands of prisoners, the fact that the captives are not generally accused of crimes, and the temporary nature of the detention. If detained combatants are charged with crimes rather than simply being held until the end of hostilities, they must in most circumstances be given a trial or court martial with full due process protections (see Hamdan v. Rumsfeld, US Supreme Court 2006).

The issue to be discussed here is not about combatants like Hamdan captured in a war zone outside of the national territory. It is rather whether human rights permit the holding without trial of persons suspected of terrorism but captured outside of any war zone. After the 9/11 attacks, both Britain and the United States held without trial suspected terrorists who had been apprehended domestically. An example is Jose Padilla, who was born in Brooklyn to a Puerto Rican family. Padilla is a convert to Islam who traveled to Egypt, Saudi Arabia, Afghanistan, Pakistan, and Iraq. Upon return to the United States in 2002, Padilla was arrested at the Chicago airport and initially held as a material witness. Suspected of planning to detonate a "dirty bomb" in the United States, he was subsequently designated an enemy combatant and imprisoned in a military brig in South Carolina. In 2005 Padilla was finally indicted on charges of conspiring to wage and support international terrorism. Padilla's trial in civilian court is scheduled for late 2006.

Detention without trial of fighters apprehended in a war zone may raise questions of fairness, but it does not pose much threat of undermining the domestic system of due process rights. A case like Padilla's, however, poses such a threat as he is a citizen arrested within the national territory. The danger in countries like the United States and Britain is not that the whole system of trials and due process rights will be abandoned. It is rather the opening of a second track dedicated to people thought to pose a threat to national security. This track would operate largely out of the public view, without habeas corpus or other forms of judicial scrutiny, and without the requirement that the people held be brought to trial quickly. In this track the forms of interrogation used may often be severe enough to border on torture.

When government officials believe that a detained person is seriously dangerous but doubt that they have the evidence needed for a conviction, they may find the possibility of detention without trial attractive. It permits incapacitating a person through incarceration without having to bring him or her to trial and thereby risking acquittal and release.

Detention without trial is often justified as a kind of quarantine, a way of keeping dangerous people from doing harm. It might be argued that when we impose what amounts to house arrest on a person who has been discovered to have a contagious and dangerous disease we do not think a trial is necessary. If a statute prescribes that infectious bearers of the disease be quarantined, and if a physician has determined that a person has the disease and is infectious, then the health department can order and supervise the person's quarantine. No procedural guarantees are provided.

More analogous to detention without trial of a suspected terrorist for several years or more would be the practice of sending lepers to remote and isolated leper colonies. (This practice is now largely abandoned because leprosy – Hansen's disease – is less contagious than once thought and can be treated with antibiotics.) Quarantine in a leper colony is such a long and large deprivation of liberty that if there were a significant possibility of mistakes in the diagnosis of leprosy, some form of review of decisions to send people to leper colonies would be appropriate. If a person is being subjected to long-term detention or quarantine, and if there is a significant error rate (false positives) in selection for the kind of detention or quarantine in question, then some sort of process involving second-party review of the case for detention or quarantine must be available.

The Three Options Argument

Since I do not believe that human rights are absolute, and since I think that personal security is itself an important ground for some human rights, I cannot simply dismiss the possibility of using detention without trial in a special national security track. An argument for detention without trial, which I call the "Three Options Argument," relies on four premises. The first premise is that a suspected terrorist can be treated in only three ways: (1) released; (2) brought to trial; or (3) detained without trial for an extended period.

Premise two is that the first option (releasing the suspect) is unacceptably risky. If the government is right in believing that the suspect is involved in terrorist activities, releasing him risks severe harm to public safety as the person returns to terrorist activity.

Premise three is that the second option (bringing the suspect to trial) is also unacceptably risky. The cases in question are ones where the government believes its evidence may well be insufficient to convict at trial. Thus, a criminal prosecution may well result in his release, risking severe harm to the country as the person returns to terrorist activities. And even if the person is convicted of something, it will often be on lesser charges, such as immigration violations, and thus impose only a short period of detention. Bringing the suspect to trial may also risk revealing the government's undercover agents and other sources of intelligence. Further, if torture or near-torture was used in interrogating the suspect or witnesses, allowing them to participate in a trial runs the risk of embarrassing the government by exposing that fact.

Premise four is that the third option carries no comparable risks. Detaining the person without trial for an extended period eliminates any risk that he will return to terrorist activities.

If there are only three options, and if the first two are unacceptably risky while the third is not, then the third would seem to be the best option. The argument concludes that long-term detention without trial is the best option for protecting society against suspected terrorists when it is doubtful whether the evidence available will support conviction of serious charges at trial.

An objection to this argument is that the first premise is false, that there are more than three options. One additional option is reducing or eliminating the need for detention without trial by making it easier for the government to gain convictions of those suspected of terrorism when it brings them to trial. This could be accomplished by making it easier for law enforcement officers to engage in effective surveillance. Another way of doing this is passing special terrorism laws which make it easier to convict people of engaging in a terrorist conspiracy or belonging to a terrorist organization. There could also be special tribunals for those accused of terrorism in which some due process protections are not available. The United States Supreme Court, in dealing with citizens who are detained as "enemy combatants," allowed that "enemy combatant proceedings may be tailored to alleviate their uncommon potential to burden the Executive at a time of ongoing military conflict. Hearsay, for example, may need to be accepted as the most reliable available evidence from the Government in such a proceeding." It also allowed that "once the Government puts forth credible evidence that the habeas petitioner meets the enemy-combatant criteria, the onus should shift to the petitioner to rebut that evidence with more persuasive evidence that he falls outside the criteria" (United States Supreme Court 2004). A different approach attempts to make detention without trial less objectionable by using milder methods of control such as house arrest and electronic bracelets. This sort of approach was used by the Blair government in response to the "Belmarsh decision" by the Law Lords that the use of incarceration without trial was incompatible with European human rights norms which Britain has adopted (House of Lords 2005). These additional options may be useful in some cases, but none of them makes the problem go away entirely.

An objection to premise two is that the dangers in releasing suspected terrorists are the same ones we face when we release criminals suspected of being dangerous because we have failed to convict them at trial. For this worry to have special force in the case of suspected terrorists we have to be persuaded that the damage they are likely to do once released is far greater than that done by ordinary criminals whom we fail to convict at trial. This seems far from obvious. First, upon release they will surely be subjected to heavy police surveillance both in order to protect society and in hopes that they will lead police to other members of terrorist networks. The likelihood of surveillance will also lead other terrorists to stay away from them. Second, after release they will not be trusted by other terrorists because of the worry that in order to gain freedom they have switched sides and become informers.

Another objection to this argument rebuts premise four by holding that detention without trial also has great risks to the public's safety. It poses the danger of undermining the protections against government abuses that due process rights provide. Abandoning due process protections puts at risk protections that are valuable to us all. If this objection is correct then none of the three options is good for the public's safety.

A final objection is that what we do cannot be decided entirely on the basis of public safety. The severity of unfairness also has to be considered. Long-term detention without trial has the features of summary punishment. It increases the risk of incarcerating people who are neither dangerous nor guilty of crimes. Estimating how dangerous a person is turns out to be extremely difficult. Still, if precautionary detention without trial were limited to a few months, done in accordance with authorizing legislation, and required justification before a judge early on, these measures would help reduce its unfairness and its danger of undermining security against the government. This is not, however, how precautionary detention has been practiced in the United States in response to the 2001 terrorist attacks.

The Priority Shift Argument

Another argument for detention without trial is the "Priority Shift Argument." Its key idea is that in severe emergencies people downgrade the importance of liberty and fairness. Emergency conditions can be bad enough for reasonable people, at least temporarily, to shift their priorities in the direction of greater concern for security – a concern for saving one's life and health. If this shift occurs in the priorities of rational people, then an impartial legislator could reasonably be guided by it in deciding which rights are immune to suspension.

Does the Priority Shift Argument help justify long-term detention without trial of suspected terrorists in severe emergencies? One reason for doubting that it does is that the shift does not occur, I believe, in regard to fairness in the distribution of the most important goods. The downgrading of fairness-based rights is not rational when a person's most important interests are at stake. This is why the three treaties forbid capital punishment without full due process. For another example, in a severe natural disaster citizens will be very concerned that greatly needed government assistance is provided to people and neighborhoods in ways that are fair. Thus concern for fair distribution of the measures that protect people against government abuses of the criminal justice system may survive the Priority Shift.

A related reason to believe that due process rights will survive the Priority Shift is that they are themselves protections of security. Recall that a major justification for due process rights given above was in terms of security against abuses by government. Thus the trade-off is security versus security, not just security versus fairness. Recall also that one of the objections to the Three Options Argument above was that the third option, long-term detention without trial, threatened public security by undermining historically hard-won due process protections.

Still, ordinary citizens may not much fear being suspected of terrorism. They may say that they will not be troubled if the government decides to restrict or suspend the due process rights of suspected terrorists. Ordinary citizens find it hard to believe that they could be mistaken for criminals, much less for terrorists. Thus they cannot see that protecting the due process and other rights of accused terrorists does much to protect the security of ordinary people. The security argument for due process rights leaves them cold. This coldness applies particularly to noncitizen detainees, but it applies as well to citizen detainees who seem to have been involved in terrorism. This outlook is a great practical barrier to the maintenance of due process rights during emergencies and troubled times. Its roots are not necessarily egoism, a concern only for oneself. More commonly they are a matter of limited sympathies, a willingness to dismiss the claims of people who seem threatening or alien.

One response to this worry is to try to persuade ordinary citizens that the risks of mistakes in the detention and prosecution of terrorists are real, that those mistakes have severely bad consequences, and that some ordinary law-abiding citizens are vulnerable to those risks. The best means of persuasion here may take the form of plausible stories that illustrate how various sorts of people would be at risk if governments could detain and punish without providing trials and procedural protections. But such attempts at persuasion also need to invoke fairness, to remind people that one of the most important reasons for having due process rights is to avoid severe unfairness (R. Dworkin 2002).

Conclusion

The Three Options Argument showed that detention without trial of suspected terrorists has some attractions. It allows a country to detain and incapacitate extremely dangerous people whom it is unable to convict of crimes. If a terrorist emergency is severe enough (thousands of domestic terrorists at work with large weekly attacks) it may be justifiable to enact a system of detention without trial of suspected terrorists arrested in the national territory. If detention without trial were used, the authorizing legislation should require initial approval and periodic review of a person's detention by a judicial or quasi-judicial agency outside of the executive branch. The most important conclusion, however, is that creating through legislation a special regime of preventative detention for suspected terrorists is extremely dangerous to people's security and to the universality of hard-won protections for due process. Further, such a system is not warranted at the present time in Britain and the United States because neither country is in a severe emergency.

Further Reading

Ackerman, B. 2004. "The Emergency Constitution." *Yale Law Journal* 113: 1029.

Duff, R. 1986. *Trials and Punishments.* Cambridge: Cambridge University Press.

Dworkin, A. 2005. "Military Necessity and Due Process: The Place of Human Rights in the War on Terror." In D. Wippman and M. Evangelista (eds.), *New Wars, New Laws? Applying the Laws of War in 21st Century Conflicts.* Ardsley, NY: Transnational Press.

Dworkin, R. 2002. "Terror and the Attack on Civil Liberties." *New York Review of Books* (February 28): 50.

Gross, O. 2003. "Providing for the Unexpected: Constitutional Emergency Provisions." *Israel Yearbook on Human Rights* 33: 13–43.

Jaggar, A. 2005. "What is Terrorism, Why is it Wrong, and Could it Ever be Morally Permissible?" *Journal of Social Philosophy* 36: 202–17.

Jinks, D. 2001. "The Anatomy of an Institutionalized Emergency: Preventive Detention and Personal Liberty in India." *Michigan Journal of International Law* 22: 311–70.

Oraa, J. 1992. *Human Rights in States of Emergency in International Law.* Oxford: Oxford University Press.

Chapter 8

Economic Liberties as Fundamental Freedoms

Contemporary human rights documents address many problems in the economic realm, including slavery, employment discrimination, property, and access to food. But formulating international norms in this area is not easy. The fact that some countries are rich and others are shockingly poor makes uniform worldwide standards problematic. And contemporary political ideologies disagree substantially over the appropriate economic role of the state. Capitalists emphasize property rights and free trade. Socialists no longer reject market mechanisms, but emphasize social rights and worry about poverty in developing countries.

The human rights movement has generally prescribed both property rights and welfare rights. It has done this by endorsing a generic right to hold and use property while also endorsing social rights such as the right to an adequate standard of living and the right to basic education. This chapter argues the importance of economic liberties, which, broadly described, include the liberty to buy and sell labor, to engage in independent economic activity, to hold both personal and productive property, and to buy, sell, use, and consume goods and services. I argue that these liberties are necessary to promoting and protecting fundamental human interests, and to the enjoyment of other important families of human rights. No claim is made, however, that economic liberties should have unbounded scopes or that their exercise cannot be regulated by law. Chapter 9 defends a limited set of social rights.

Property and Economic Liberties

The Universal Declaration states that "Everyone has the right to own property alone as well as in association with others" and prohibits arbitrary deprivations of property (article 17). The American Declaration of the Rights and Duties of Man (1948, article 23) and the American Convention on Human Rights (1969, article 21) also endorse qualified rights to private property. A 1952 amendment to the European Convention added a right to property:

> Every natural or legal person is entitled to the peaceful enjoyment of his possessions. No one shall be deprived of his possessions except in the public interest and subject to the conditions provided for by law and by the general principles of international law. The preceding provisions shall not, however, in any way impair the right of a State to enforce such laws as it deems necessary to control the use of property in accordance with the general interest or to secure the payment of taxes or other contributions or penalties. (Protocol 1, article 1)

The right to property is also found in the African Charter on Human and Peoples' Rights (1981, article 14). The Civil and Political Covenant and the Social Covenant are exceptional in not containing rights to personal property. They do, however, contain identical clauses protecting the property rights of peoples or nations. Article 1 of each treaty states:

> All peoples may, for their own ends, freely dispose of their natural wealth and resources without prejudice to any obligations arising out of international economic co-operation, based upon the principle of mutual benefit, and international law. In no case may a people be deprived of its own means of subsistence.

As this suggests, the right to hold and use property can be held by groups and corporate bodies as well as by individuals (Halstead 2002). Property, which many consider a paradigm of an individual right, also turns out to be a group right (Anaya and Williams 2001).

There are some things that it is impermissible to own. Rights to property do not include a right to own people or to force them to give you their labor. Immediately after the Universal Declaration's statement of a generic right to liberty, "Everyone has the right to life, liberty and security of person" (article 3), a categorical prohibition of slavery appears: "No one shall be held in slavery or servitude; slavery and the slave trade shall be prohibited in all their forms" (article 4; see also the European Convention, article 4). A similar clause is found in the Civil and Political Covenant (article 8). The Social Covenant includes a right to free choice of occupation (article 6). These clauses clearly reflect underlying views about the importance of being able to lead one's own life, of not being totally subject to the will of another.

It is common to categorize all economic liberties under the right to property. If property is conceived dynamically as something that one can use for production, consumption, and exchange, then perhaps all economic liberties can be subsumed under the idea of property. But it is useful for our purposes to identify more specifically which freedoms are included under basic economic liberties. I propose that ample freedom should be available in the following (overlapping) areas:

- *Using and consuming, including eating, drinking, inhabiting, and wearing* Negatively, these liberties allow one to refuse to follow ways of living and consuming of which one disapproves.
- *Transacting and contracting, including buying, selling, lending, investing, giving, and contracting* Included here are liberties to sell and buy labor and products, to save and invest, to enter into market competition, and to profit from transactions. Also included are liberties to start, run, and shut down a business, professional practice, factory, farm, or other enterprise. Negatively, these liberties prohibit slavery and servitude and permit people to decline to engage in economic activities they dislike or disapprove of.
- *Acquiring, holding, and alienating, including legitimate acquisition and possession, of property, and using property for commercial and productive purposes* Inventing and working are included as means of creating property, as when people work at paid jobs, write songs or books, or build their own houses. Also included is freedom from expropriation without due process and compensation. These freedoms apply to both personal and productive property. Negatively, they permit people to get rid of property that they do not wish to have.

Taken together, these basic economic liberties enable a person to be an economic agent, to have and lead an economic life as a consumer, householder, producer, business person, investor, and property-holder. These liberties are most secure when they are legally defined and protected. None of them is conceived as unlimited or immune to regulation and taxation. "Private" economic transactions often have large spillovers or externalities. In endorsing the liberty to hire workers, for example, I do not wish to rule out legislation to protect the health and safety of workers, to prevent discrimination, to facilitate and regulate collective bargaining, or even to require some sort of industrial democracy in large enterprises.

─────────────── **Justifying Economic Liberties** ───────────────

In recent decades countries in all parts of the world have become much more friendly toward economic liberties for individuals and families. Theories of economic development now put less emphasis on government development schemes and more on facilitating production and exchange at many levels – including microenterprises. This historic change was driven in large measure by changed beliefs about what works, that is, what sorts of economic arrangements lead to development and prosperity. Trying to impose government control over all economic activity does not produce prosperity and innovation. Stimulating people's energy and creativity in the economic arena requires giving them considerable space for independent economic activity. Granting such space also avoids forcing independent economic activity into an underground economy (de Soto 1989). But even if we accept that economic liberties are in many circumstances conducive to prosperity, we may still wonder whether economic liberties have deeper roots. Can basic economic liberties be justified as human rights? Is it an impermissible violation of human rights to deprive people of basic economic liberties? In this section I defend affirmative answers to these questions. Rather than going through all the justificatory steps identified in Chapter 5, I shall focus on the central question of whether these liberties are sufficiently important to be human rights.

Liberties and the claim to lead a life

Economic liberties, like most other liberties, rely heavily for their justification on the claim to lead one's life. It is useful here to review and supplement the explanation of the secure claim to lead one's life that was given in Chapter 4. This is a claim of a person on social and political institutions to meaningful opportunities for choice, endorsement, and refusal within the life they have and are developing. The metaphor of leading (rather than following) suggests that one has control over the direction and path of one's life. Individuals have distinctive preferences, perspectives, and dreams, and are equipped with capacities for evaluation and choice. As they encounter the world they – individually and jointly – deliberate, plan, evaluate, set goals, discuss, choose, act, monitor outcomes, and rethink. Life offers goods to be realized, sets problems, provides opportunities, and requires choices. As people deal with these through time they define who they are and decide what they want to become and be (Raz 1987).

The claim to lead one's life has to be realized in lives where much is already determined or constrained by nature and culture. The accidents of birth preclude many choices by determining matters such as parents, family, gender, era, nationality, culture, language, talents, health, and disabilities. And respect for the rights of others requires us to accommodate their lives, needs, and choices. In spite of these limits, there is still much to choose – and life often takes surprising turns. Under poor conditions many people will be limited to filling in the details within patterns of life that they did not choose and only partially endorse. Under good circumstances, people can set the main direction of their lives as well as choosing many of the details.

To lead one's life it is necessary to be able to plan it, monitor it, discuss it, evaluate it from various perspectives, and modify or reform it. People typically do these things in social contexts where consultation with others is part of the process. Conformity to familiar patterns is more common than doing something unusual or unique. In order to plan, discuss, evaluate, and act, people need liberties to inquire, reflect, choose and reject, communicate, discuss, criticize, demand, explain, apologize, negotiate, blame, forgive, and pursue moral duties and ideals. These sorts of activities are covered by human rights to basic liberties such as freedom of belief and conscience, freedom of religion, freedom of communication, and freedom of association.

The scope of the claim to lead one's life has to be worked out on the ground by discovering which liberties really are important to being able to lead a life under contemporary conditions, which freedoms are threatened, and which liberties are ones that can reasonably and affordably be extended to all people. Lists of human rights do not purport to set out a complete list of valuable human liberties, nor do they suggest that these are exactly the same for every person and for all countries. What lists of human rights do is set out in fairly abstract terms some very basic liberties thought to be valuable for everyone.

Freedoms in regard to major life decisions such as marriage, children, career, and religious affiliations are especially important in leading one's life. These decisions structure and set directions for one's life and other projects, have long-term impacts, and involve large portions of one's time. Another important part of leading one's life is being able to control things, persons, and activities that are close to or parts of one's body, thought, and personal identity. Here basic liberties allow one to seek, explore, and adopt ways of living that fit the person one is and that are appropriate to the sort of life one is trying to lead. Areas of liberty relevant here include sex and reproduction, personal relations, the clothing one wears, food and drink, household effects, religious and philosophical beliefs, and how one spends one's time apart from work.

People's activities as workers, producers, and consumers typically require much of their time, impose limits on and set directions for other parts of their lives, and shape their identities. Having no control over economic activity keeps one from leading one's economic life and makes it difficult to control one's life in the social, religious, and political realms (see the linkage arguments below). The fact that economic activity is necessary to most people's survival and flourishing means that most humans engage in it and take participation and success to be important. Consequently, economic activity has long been an important area for the development and exercise of choice. Economic struggle has been the game that almost all humans have had to play. Accordingly, many people find meaning and value in this area. This fact helps explain why unwanted unemployment is generally a bad thing. The claim to engage in historically and culturally meaningful economic activities obviously applies as well to particular professions or careers. Free choice of occupation – the liberty to choose the life of a farmer, teacher, builder, singer, or cook – draws support from these considerations.

Economic liberties are at least as important under harsh conditions as they are during prosperity. If jobs are few and one's government is failing to provide assistance, saved assets can be used to survive while looking for work. They also allow one to start a little business to support one's life and that of one's family. Millions of people in developing countries survive in this way. Of course, endorsing basic economic liberties is no substitute for endorsing effective social rights. But since the right to subsistence is not effectively implemented by governments in many developing countries, economic liberties provide an important alternative path to survival.

Economic liberties are also important to people who are peculiar or distinctive, who because of their unusual beliefs, tastes, habits, or origins do not fit well in the economic roles that society makes available. Economic liberties make it possible for such people to start and run economic activities of their own and thereby escape employers and co-workers who would attempt to force them into standard molds. Having some basic economic liberties gives one a chance to create a new occupational path to suit oneself better.

We can imagine a world in which economic problems have been solved, in which automation, centralized production, and free services make it unnecessary for most people to engage in economic activity except as consumers and householders. Perhaps in such a world most people will not have jobs, or will work only part-time. If such a world were to emerge, and be reliable and sustainable, people would not need all of the basic economic liberties. As I have emphasized, specific human rights are not timeless. They are closely related to the institutions and problems of particular eras. But we are still in a situation in which most adults need to make an economic contribution. Until a workless utopia arrives and proves reliable, there are strong reasons for insisting on basic economic liberties.

Linkage arguments for economic liberties

Linkage arguments are based on the idea of consistency testing explained in Chapter 5. In this section I argue that rejecting basic economic liberties is practically inconsistent with endorsing less controversial rights such as freedom of religion, freedom of communication, freedom of association, and political freedoms. Thus economic liberties are tied to respecting these basic liberties.

Many activities protected by freedom of religion have important economic dimensions. Restricting economic activities in a wholesale way will accordingly restrict freedom of religion. Religious people frequently engage in activities such as (1) buying, renting, or constructing buildings for religious activities; (2) starting and running religious enterprises such as churches, schools, and publishing houses; (3) hiring employees to serve as religious leaders, editors, teachers, office workers, and janitors; (4) soliciting donations for religious causes; (5) saving, managing, and spending the funds coming from donations and the proceeds of religious enterprises; and (6) abandoning work or career to pursue religious study and callings.

The economic activities of religious organizations are not immune to government regulation. But if these economic activities are entirely or largely blocked, then important religious activities will be severely limited. A political system that does not respect economic liberties may allow people to have religious beliefs and to pursue them in their leisure time, but it implies that people should never let their religious activities interfere with their work, and that their religious activities should be conducted without having property or enterprises and without use or management of financial resources. Freedom of religion is not totally demolished by this, but it is substantially restricted – particularly in its collective dimensions.

Economic liberties are also important to freedom of speech and expression. Activities covered by freedom of speech and press often have large economic and commercial dimensions. If economic activities and enterprises are severely limited, freedom of communication will also be substantially limited. Those who communicate on behalf of a cause frequently engage in activities such as (1) producing and distributing printed material, which requires having access to paper, ink, editorial services, printing, and transportation; (2) employing full-time workers such as writers, editors, artists, printers, and truck drivers; (3) seeking donations and memberships to support communicative efforts; and (4) saving, managing, and spending funds. If actions required for large-scale communication are substantially blocked as economic activities, the result will be to block substantially the freedom to communicate. A system that purports to grant communicative freedoms but heavily restricts economic activities is inconsistent in practice. It suggests that people can communicate as they wish, but that they should do so without offices and equipment, without starting organizations with a commercial dimension, and without acquiring and spending substantial resources.

Similar points apply to activism on behalf of a political party or cause. Activities that are central to political freedom often have large economic and commercial dimensions. Because of this, wholesale restrictions on economic liberties will restrict political freedoms. Attempts to communicate with and persuade large numbers of people are core parts of political freedom, so all points made about freedom of communication also apply here. And political organizations and parties, like religious organizations, frequently need full-time employees, buildings, and equipment. Creating and supporting these require managing and expending funds as well as consuming resources.

Links to freedom of association can also be found. Central dimensions of freedom of association such as forming, joining, and participating in ethnic organizations have economic dimensions. Major restrictions on economic activities will limit freedom of association, particularly in its organized and large-scale manifestations. Religious association is one important form of association, so some of the links between religious activities and economic activities are also relevant here. Social organizations are often organized to provide services to members of particular ethnic groups and to provide opportunities for engaging in games or group activities (for example, creating basketball courts for a neighborhood or organizing a music festival). To pursue their goals social organizations often engage in economic activities such as (1) renting, buying, or building a facility in which the association's activities can be organized and held; (2) seeking dues-paying members to support the activities of the organization; (3) communicating with present and potential members through newsletters and other media; and (4) managing, saving, and spending funds from memberships and donations. When a political system grants freedom of association but substantially restricts economic activities, the restrictions on economic activities inevitably restrict important areas of freedom of association.

There are also strong links to freedom of movement. Key parts of freedom of movement require economic activity. To illustrate this point we can use one particularly important type of movement, namely internal or external migration to escape famine, severe poverty, or persecution. At the individual level success in such a migration requires quitting one's job (if any), converting any assets one has to money or things that can be carried or shipped, and buying supplies. If the process of traveling is extended, survival along the way will require finding places to sleep, eat and drink, and work or donations. Substantial restrictions on economic activities can impose restrictions on migration. A political system that does not recognize economic liberties within some substantial range but claims to protect freedom of movement will tell people that they are free to move and flee but that they should do so without control over the resources and activities needed for successful movement. Freedom to flee a country, for example, is practically incompatible with forbidding people to sell their belongings in order to pay for the journey.

Objections to Economic Liberties

Objection 1: Economic liberties are of little use to the impoverished

Marxists often assert that civil and political rights – and particularly economic liberties – are of little or no value to people who are severely impoverished. And Henry Shue holds that it is impossible to enjoy any rights in the absence of guarantees of the availability of food (Shue 1996: 19). In opposition to these views, I maintain that even hungry and malnourished people have strong interests in respect for their economic liberties, along with respect for their civil and political rights generally. These strong interests are present even when social rights are not respected and implemented. Liberties that allow impoverished people to engage in self-help include liberties to engage in economic activities such as working, farming, buying and selling, and the liberty to move to locations where economic opportunities or aid are more available.

Shue holds that subsistence rights are "essential to the enjoyment of all other rights" (Shue 1996: 19). If he means that subsistence rights are very useful to the enjoyment of all other rights I would not disagree. But he intends something stronger, namely that no other right can be effectively implemented without the effective implementation of a right to subsistence. If this were true it would be impossible to enjoy the right to freedom of movement if one did not enjoy a right to subsistence. But it is easy to find examples that show this is not impossible. People fleeing the Texas–Oklahoma "dustbowl" in the 1930s generally enjoyed a well-respected right to freedom of interstate movement even though there was no implementation of a right to food or subsistence. The right to freedom of movement can be widely accepted by the public and by government officials, and many threats to it can be blocked by legal measures, in the absence of a right to subsistence. It is certainly true that having no food assistance programs in a famine situation can make it harder to migrate since it will be difficult to acquire food for and along the journey. But "harder" does not mean impossible, especially if sure starvation is the price of not moving. And, as argued above, making use of the freedom to migrate requires economic liberties to finance the migration. Assets need to be sold and ways of moving found. And it is often necessary to find temporary work or gather food along the way. Moving in order to escape famine and war may seem something out of the past, but it is still extremely common in developing countries.

Objection 2: Economic liberties allow some people to block the liberties of others

Although economic liberties are important to those who end up having money and property, these liberties may seem dangerous to the poorest people in society. Economic liberties pose the danger that economically less-favored persons will end up being dominated by the property rights, disproportional political influence, and purchasing power of the economically powerful.

One response to this objection is to emphasize – as I have done – the great importance of economic liberties to people in poverty. For example, the liberty to start and run small farms and businesses has been the path to survival for impoverished people around the world. Economically disadvantaged people are often capable of self-help, and it is important for both moral and practical reasons not to deny or overlook this capability (Nickel 1995: 180). More generally, the linkage arguments given above show the importance of economic liberties to everyone's enjoyment of other basic liberties. But these responses may be insufficient by themselves to overcome the objection. Perhaps economic liberties are valuable but not valuable enough to outweigh their costs and risks.

There are, however, many measures available to reduce the power over other people that is conferred by wealth. First, a country can implement a system of provision for basic needs that is available to all who need it. Chapter 9 defends a conception of social rights that does exactly this. Measures ensuring that unemployment does not mean starvation give people the liberty to quit abusive or unpromising jobs and to undertake economic ventures (van Parijs 1998). Second, a right of access to education on a nondiscriminatory basis helps ensure that ordinary people will be able to develop the skills needed for economic and political participation. Third, nondiscriminatory access to economic opportunities helps ensure that ordinary people will not be locked out of favored positions. Fourth, ample protection for the full range of basic liberties enables people to think, discuss, associate, protest, choose their occupations, and more. These liberties help enable ordinary people to understand, protest, and protect themselves against domination by the wealthy. Fifth, the scale of holdings protected by the right to property can be limited. To protect the property rights most valuable to ordinary people one does not have to protect immense concentrations of wealth. But neither can one restrict legitimate property rights to household or personal property (Nickel 2000). Finally, measures to ensure the fair value of political liberties can be enacted. These include such things as public financing of political campaigns and limits on the size of political contributions.

Objection 3: Basic liberties do not permit regulation within their scopes

One may be persuaded by arguments for the importance of economic liberties and yet resist declaring them to be basic liberties or matters of human rights on the grounds that a great deal of regulation is necessary in the economic realm. After all, if economic liberties are so important, should not they be near-absolute in the exceptions they allow? The objection might continue as follows: "Look, I can see declaring a human right to freedom of thought and belief, because efforts to regulate thoughts and beliefs coercively are almost always unjustifiable. But since you endorse the regulation of economic liberties, you should not claim that liberties in this area are fundamental freedoms or human rights."

This objection might go on to note that when the right to property was added to the European Convention by amendment, a broad qualification clause was included:

Every natural or legal person is entitled to the peaceful enjoyment of his possessions. No one shall be deprived of his possessions except in the public interest and subject to the conditions provided for by law and by the general principles of international law. The preceding provisions shall not, however, in any way impair the right of a State to enforce such laws as it deems necessary to control the use of property in accordance with the general interest or to secure the payment of taxes or other contributions or penalties. (Protocol 1, 1950)

It is a mistake, however, to think that the fundamental freedoms are generally immune to regulation. In all of the human rights treaties, key liberties are accompanied by generous (by my lights often too generous!) qualifications. For example, the right to freedom of association in article 11 of the European Convention has the following limitation clause:

1. Everyone has the right to freedom of peaceful assembly and to freedom of association with others, including the right to form and to join trade unions for the protection of his interests.   2. No restrictions shall be placed on the exercise of these rights other than such as are prescribed by law and are necessary in a democratic society in the interests of national security or public safety, for the prevention of disorder or crime, for the protection of health or morals or for the protection of the rights and freedoms of others. This article shall not prevent the imposition of lawful restrictions on the exercise of these rights by members of the armed forces, of the police or of the administration of the State.

As a general matter, most of the liberties we find in historic bills of rights need substantial qualification and regulation (Rawls 1993: 295). Consider freedom of movement. First, there are regulations to make movement in the streets more efficient, such as different lanes for pedestrians, bicycles, and cars; one-way streets; and stoplights. These restrict movement but if well designed result in greater ease of movement for most people. Second, there are regulations to make movement safer, such as crosswalks, turn restrictions, and speed limits. Third, there are restrictions of entry into private property such as homes and businesses and public property such as government offices and military installations. These limit where one can go and where one can stop. Finally, there are prohibitions of movements that are parts of crimes, such as interstate flight to escape prosecution.

Similar points can be made about freedom of communication, freedom of association, and freedom of assembly and protest. It is not inconsistent to hold that basic economic liberties are human rights while prohibiting some activities in the economic sphere as crimes or misdemeanors (for example, fraud, discrimination in hiring, operating an unsafe workplace, or eliminating competition by murder or arson).

Objection 4: Many areas of economic liberty are not important enough to be human rights

The economic realm is an extremely large area of human activity; it contains thousands of specific action-types. For example, buying can be directed to thousands of kinds of goods and services. Is it really plausible to claim that all kinds of buying are matters of basic liberty? The problem is not that some kinds of buying, such as buying people, are deeply immoral. We remove buying persons from the scope of the liberty to buy things, just as we remove human sacrifice from the freedom of religion. The problem is rather that many instances of buying – such as buying sand, carrots, or pencils – just do not seem important enough to be matters of basic liberty. True, people have substantial liberty interests in not being blocked from buying these things. Sand, carrots, and pencils are things that people often find useful to be able to get through purchase, and important projects would be blocked if one could not buy these things. Still, if a government blocks the buying and selling of sand, this does not seem as unjust as blocking prayers or speeches.

It is easy, however, to find analogous cases in the standard basic liberties. Within freedom of religion it is important that people be free to build temples, churches, and mosques, but not as important that they be free to create religious buildings that are skyscrapers. Within freedom of communication it is important to be free to protest economic hardship but not as important to be free to send Valentine's Day cards to one's friends. Within freedom of movement it is important that one be free to move about to obtain food and other necessities but not as important that one be free to make late-night excursions to buy ice cream. It is simply a general fact about basic liberties that not all the specific things they cover are of equal importance.

Giving a basic liberty ample scope does not require us to say that every part of that scope is equally important. The boundary of importance may be one of scale, as it would be if we said that small-scale economic activity is more important in terms of personal liberty than very large-scale economic activity. Or the boundary of importance may be in terms of specific action-types, as when we suggest that the liberty to buy books is more important than the liberty to buy sand. Or the boundary may be the context or situation, as it would be if we said that the liberty to hire children as workers is less weighty than the liberty to hire adults.

Overview

Human rights include many fundamental freedoms. Among those freedoms are some basic economic liberties. They include the liberty to buy and sell labor, to engage in independent economic activity, to hold both personal and productive property, and to buy, sell, use, and consume goods and services. It is not plausible to suggest, however, that these liberties should have unbounded scope or that they cannot be legally regulated.

Further Reading

de Soto, H. 1989. *The Other Path*. New York: Harper & Row.

Halstead, P. 2002. "Human Property Rights." *Conveyancer and Property Lawyer* 66 (March–April): 153–73.

Hayek, F. 1960. *The Constitution of Liberty*. Chicago: University of Chicago Press.

Henkin, L. 1994. "Economic Rights under the United States Constitution." *Columbia Journal of Transnational Law* 32: 97–132.

Nozick, R. 1974. *Anarchy, State, and Utopia*. New York: Basic Books.

Chapter 9

Social Rights as Human Rights

The Universal Declaration differs importantly from earlier lists of human rights in that it includes rights to social benefits and services. The parties to the UN Charter committed themselves to promoting "higher standards of living, full employment, and conditions of economic and social progress and development" (United Nations 1945). The American Declaration of the Rights and Duties of Man, the Universal Declaration, and the subsequent International Covenant on Economic, Social and Cultural Rights all asserted rights to an adequate standard of living, health services, education, support during disability and old age, employment and protection against unemployment, and limited working hours.

It is difficult to find a good name for rights like the ones just listed. Following the United Nations nomenclature in calling them "economic and social rights" is awkward, and risks confusing them with the economic liberties treated in Chapter 8. Calling them "welfare rights" associates them too closely with being on the dole, and does not apply very well to opportunities to earn a living and the right to education. Calling them "social rights" (as in "social security") is better, but not very descriptive. Of these options, I prefer and shall use the latter.

The idea that social rights are fully justifiable human rights remains controversial. These rights are often alleged to be desirable goals but not fullfledged rights. The European Convention did not include them, although it was amended in 1952 to include the right to education. Instead social rights were put into a separate treaty, the European Social Charter (Council of Europe 1961), which calls them rights but treats them much like goals. When the United Nations began the process of putting the rights of the Universal Declaration into international law, it followed the model of the European system by treating social standards in a treaty separate from the one dealing with civil and political rights. This treaty, the Social Covenant, treated these standards as rights – albeit rights to be progressively realized. More than 140 countries have ratified this treaty.

The Social Covenant's list of rights includes nondiscrimination and equality for women (articles 2 and 3), freedom to work and opportunities to work (article 4), fair pay and decent conditions of work (article 7), the right to form trade unions and to strike (article 8), social security (article 9), special protections for mothers and children (article 10), the right to adequate food, clothing, and housing (article 11), the right to basic health services (article 12), the right to education (article 13), and the right to participate in cultural life and scientific progress (article 15).

In Chapter 8 I defended basic economic liberties as human rights, and thus it may be thought that I have left no room for social rights. But there is no deep incompatibility between economic liberties and social rights. The experience of many countries in the last 80 years has shown that the taxation and regulation needed to implement basic social rights are compatible with respecting basic economic liberties. There are areas of conflict, but conflict between important rights is familiar and manageable. And there are numerous ways in which economic liberties and rights support each other. Having secure access to food, minimal health services, and basic education allows one to participate in the economic sphere and to use one's economic liberties. And having economic liberties means that people can promote their own survival and flourish through employment, agriculture, and commerce.

The Vance Conception of Social Rights

Human rights are not ideals of the good life for humans; they are rather concerned with ensuring the conditions, negative and positive, of a minimally good life. If we apply this idea to social rights it suggests that these standards should not be concerned with promoting the highest possible standards of living or with identifying the best or most just form of economic system. Rather they should attempt to address the worst problems and abuses in the economic area. Their focus should be on hunger, malnutrition, preventable disease, ignorance, and exclusion from productive opportunities. To put this in a different way, human rights should not attempt to provide a full account of the requirements of distributive justice. Instead they should set out the most imperative requirements of distributive fairness and equal citizenship while leaving countries considerable space to work out their own standards of social and economic equality through democratic decision-making (see generally Buchanan 2005).

Some philosophers have followed this line of thought to the conclusion that the main social right is "subsistence." Henry Shue, John Rawls, and Brian Orend make subsistence the centerpiece of their concern for social rights. Shue defines subsistence as "unpolluted air, unpolluted water, adequate food, adequate clothing, adequate shelter, and minimal preventative health care" (Shue 1996). Orend's definition is very similar: "Material subsistence means having secure access to those resources one requires to meet one's biological needs – notably a minimal level of nutritious food, clean water, fresh air, some clothing and shelter, and basic preventative health care" (Orend 2001). Rawls includes "subsistence" on his very short list of human rights, treating it along with security as part of the right to life. Rawls interprets "subsistence" as including "minimum economic security" or "having general all-purpose economic means" (Rawls 1999: 65).

The idea of subsistence alone offers too minimal a conception of social rights. It neglects education, gives an extremely minimal account of health services, and generally gives too little attention to people's ability to be *active* participants and contributors, to be producers as well as consumers (see Sen 1999a, 1999b; Nussbaum 2001). It covers the requirements of having a life, but neglects the conditions of being able to lead one's life.

If Shue, Rawls, and Orend err by making social rights too minimal, international human rights documents make them excessively grandiose by including desirable goals and ideals. They view social rights as prescriptions for prosperity and an ample welfare state. For example, the European Social Charter includes human rights to vocational guidance, annual holidays with pay, and "protection of health" that aspires "to remove as far as possible the causes of ill-health" (articles 9, 2, 11, and 26). I recognize, of course, that these are good things that political movements legitimately promote at the national level. As a resident of a rich country I would vote for them. But these standards go far beyond the conditions of a minimally good life. Further, it would not be plausible to castigate a country as a human rights violator because it fails to fund occupational guidance, to require employers to provide employees with holidays with pay, or to mount an antismoking campaign (smoking is surely one of the main causes of ill health). The point is not merely that poorer countries should be excused from these requirements. It is that these formulations do not have a good fit with the idea of human rights as minimal standards even when we are thinking about rich countries.

In the next few paragraphs I advocate a conception of social rights that goes beyond subsistence to include health care and education. I call it the "Vance Conception" because it conforms to the list advocated by former US Secretary of State Cyrus Vance in his 1977 Law Day speech at the University of Georgia (Vance 1977). In that speech Vance set out a view of human rights that included "the right to the fulfillment of such vital needs as food, shelter, health care and education." Although this list is more expansive than subsistence alone, it adheres to the idea that social rights, like other human rights, are concerned with the conditions of having a minimally good life. It thereby avoids the excesses of contemporary declarations and treaties. This conception suggests that social rights focus on survival, health, and education. It obligates governments to so govern that the following questions can be answered affirmatively:

- *Subsistence* Do conditions allow all people to secure safe air, food, and water as well as environmentally appropriate shelter and clothing if they engage in work and self-help insofar as they can, practice mutual aid through organizations such as families, neighborhoods, and churches, and procure help from available government assistance programs? Do all people capable of work enjoy access to productive opportunities that allow them to contribute to the well-being of themselves, their families, and their communities?
- *Health* Do environmental conditions, water and sewer systems, public health measures, and available health services give people excellent chances of surviving childhood and childbirth, achieving physical and mental competence, and living a normal lifespan?
- *Education* Do available educational resources give people good opportunities to learn the skills necessary for survival, health, functioning, citizenship, and productivity?

The Vance Conception of social rights identifies three broad and interlocking rights whose fulfillment is needed for all people to have minimally good lives. The definition of the right to subsistence used in this conception is much like Shue's, except that health is moved to a separate category. Health-related concerns remain within subsistence, however, since air, food, and water must be safe for intake, and shelter and clothing are required to be environmentally appropriate where that includes protections needed for health from cold, heat, and precipitation. Further, it includes access to economic opportunities and thus incorporates some aspects of the right to work (see Arneson 1990).

The Vance Conception views the right to health services in a broader way than Shue's "minimal preventative health care." It covers prevention through public health measures such as sanitation systems and inoculation programs. But it goes beyond these preventative measures to include emergency reparative services such as help in setting broken bones and dealing with infections. And it covers minimal services related to pregnancy and birth. These health services are costly, but they are necessary to many people's ability to have a minimally good life. Further, addressing major health problems promotes people's ability to pursue education and work in an energetic way (on the right to health, see Chapman 2002).

The right to basic education focuses on literacy, numeracy, and preparation for social participation, citizenship, and economic activity. It helps orient social rights towards action, choice, self-help, mutual aid, and social, political, and economic participation. The Universal Declaration emphasizes that basic education should be both free and compulsory. Families do not have the liberty to keep children uneducated and illiterate. But they do have qualified liberties to control the kind of upbringing and education their children receive (article 26).

The Vance Conception has at least two advantages. It views social rights as minimal standards without limiting their requirements to subsistence and while expecting these standards to be exceeded in most countries. Keeping social rights minimal also makes their realization a plausible aspiration for poorer countries and makes it more likely that social rights can pass the test of feasibility.

Several of the articles in the Social Covenant conform to the Vance Conception. The treatment of food and of an adequate standard of living in article 11 mostly fits. That article commits the countries ratifying the Covenant to ensure for everyone "an adequate standard of living for himself and his family, including adequate food, clothing and housing," and to "the continuous improvement of living conditions." The Vance Conception interprets "adequate standard of living" as requiring a level adequate for a minimally good life, not for an excellent life. It rejects the demand for "continuous improvement of living conditions" as a confusion of the desirable with the imperative.

There is also a fairly good fit with the statement of the right to education in the Social Covenant. Article 13 requires free and compulsory primary education for all children, that secondary education be generally available, and that higher education be equally accessible to those equally talented. The idea of giving priority to primary education is a good one. On the Vance Conception, higher education is not directly a matter of human rights. The European Convention's formulation is better, although arguably too vague: "No person shall be denied the right to education" (Protocol 1, article 2). A still better formulation might describe a right of all persons to basic education, available free to all and compulsory for children, to achieve literacy, numeracy, and the knowledge and skills necessary for health, economic competence, citizenship, and social life.

Not all of the articles conform to the Vance Conception. For example, article 12 of the Social Covenant puts forward a right to health that recognizes "the right of everyone to the enjoyment of the highest attainable standard of physical and mental health." This article departs from the idea of human rights as minimal standards in demanding optimization of health rather than setting a threshold.

Implementing Social Rights

This section considers the objection that social rights are deficient as rights because they cannot – or perhaps should not – be implemented by judges alone. It might be argued, for example, that judges have the powers necessary to implement the right to freedom of religion or the right to a fair trial, but that they do not and should not have the powers necessary to implement the right to basic education. Judges, after all, cannot create or fund a school system – and in a democracy they should not try to.

When a country has accepted a right to freedom of religion by putting the right in its constitution or by ratifying an international human rights treaty, judges can proceed to implement it. If the legislature passes a law forbidding the beliefs and practices of Jehovah's Witnesses, and a practitioner of that religion is convicted under that law, judges can on appeal overturn the conviction and declare the law unconstitutional or incompatible with the country's obligations under international treaties. Judges can implement freedom of religion.

Now suppose, in contrast, that a country has accepted a right to basic education by putting the right in its constitution or by ratifying an international human rights treaty. Perhaps the formulation of the right goes like this:

> Children have a right to education. Accordingly, the legislature shall create and fund a system of free public schools open to all children and available in all parts of the country. Free public education shall be available for at least eight years of schooling.

Suppose further that the legislature ignores this right and neither creates nor funds schools. A group of parents who want free public education to be available file suit, asking a judge to order the legislature to perform its constitutional duties. A judge might issue such an order, but cannot enforce it by overturning a law because there is no law to overturn. Judges cannot do anything to implement the right until the legislature has created and funded a system of public schools. Beyond this, in a democracy it would be wrong for a judge to take over the role of legislator by designing and creating a school system and appropriating the necessary funds. It is not a judge's proper role to take money from bridge construction or prisons and divert it to school funding.

The conclusion drawn from these contrasting examples might be that judicial implementation works only when judges can overturn laws or decisions, and accordingly that real rights are ones that are strictly negative, that forbid governments from suppressing any religion or infringing people's speech.

The trouble with this argument is that it implies that due process rights are not real rights. To see this, consider an example analogous to the one on the right to education. Suppose that a country has accepted a right to a fair trial by putting the right in its constitution or by ratifying an international human rights treaty. Perhaps the formulation of the right goes like this:

> In all criminal prosecutions, every accused person has the right to a fair and public trial, by an impartial jury. At trial, all accused persons have the right to the assistance of counsel, provided at public expense if necessary.

Suppose further that the legislature ignores this right and allows the police to continue putting in jail without trial people who they believe to have committed crimes. There are no criminal prosecutions, no legislative provision for them, and no system to provide free legal counsel. Accordingly, judges play no role in punishing criminals, although they play many other legal roles. Suppose now that a person who has been put in jail without prosecution or trial files suit, asking a judge to order the police to release him or bring him to trial. A judge may issue such an order, but cannot enforce it by overturning a law because there is no law to overturn. Judges cannot do anything to implement the right until the legislature has created and funded a system of criminal prosecution and trial. The judges can order the police to stop imprisoning people without a fair and public trial, but the police would simply scoff at the order, jesting that judges have very few weapons. Beyond this, in a democracy it would be wrong for a judge to take over the role of legislator by creating a criminal justice system and appropriating the necessary funds. It is not a judge's proper role to take money from bridge construction or schools and allocate it to courts and lawyers.

Because of the prominent place of due process rights in historic bills of rights, and the strong case that was made for them in Chapter 7, the argument that due process rights are not genuine human rights is implausible. It is more plausible to assume that there is something wrong with the argument against the right to education.

Claims about what judges can do to implement rights are relative to a background of institutions and practices. We think of judges as capable of implementing due process rights because we presuppose practices giving judges significant power over criminal prosecutions. But take away that presupposition and judges are no more able to implement rights to due process than they are able to implement the right to education when the legislature has never been willing to do anything about education. In general, the effective implementation of rights requires a joint effort by legislatures and courts.

To return to the example of the right to education, judges can play a significant role in implementing that right once a system of education has been created and funded. If parents in a region where no public schools have been provided file suit demanding that their children's right to education be fulfilled, a judge can order the commissioner of education to create a school in that region. Similarly, judges can deal with complaints of discriminatory exclusion of some students, or failures to provide eight years of instruction. The same is true for rights to subsistence and to basic health care. Once they have been legislatively defined and funded, judges can implement these rights. With social rights, however, it is probably more efficient to put implementation in the hands of specialized bureaucracies, leaving to judges the job of dealing with appeals from the decisions of those agencies.

Justifying Social Rights

Since social rights remain controversial in some quarters, it will be useful to make a strong case for them. In sketching this case I shall presuppose the Vance Conception of social rights. We can begin by sketching some linkage arguments similar to the ones that were used to defend economic liberties. After that I shall use the justificatory framework sketched in Chapters 4 and 5 to defend social rights.

Linkage arguments

Henry Shue pioneered the use of linkage arguments to defend the right to subsistence:

> No one can fully . . . enjoy any right that is supposedly protected by society if he or she lacks the essentials for a reasonably healthy and active life . . .

Any form of malnutrition, or fever due to exposure, that causes severe and irreversible brain damage, for example, can effectively prevent the exercise of any right requiring clear thought.   (Shue 1996: 24–5)

As noted earlier, it is important to guard against exaggerated claims about the impossibility of enjoying any other rights without enjoying subsistence rights. But Shue's point here can be stated in a more probabilistic form. We can say that without protections for subsistence, basic health care, and basic education, people in severe poverty will frequently be marginal rightholders. They will be unlikely to know what rights they have or what they can do to protect them, and their extreme need and vulnerability will make them hard to protect through social and political action. If you want people to be capable rightholders who can effectively exercise, benefit from, and protect their rights then you must ensure their enjoyment of basic social rights.

Direct justifications

Let's now turn to the justificatory tests sketched in Chapter 5. For each of these tests I will explain briefly how basic social rights can meet its requirements.

(1) *Recurrent threats?*   Inadequate access to subsistence, basic health care, and basic education is a major problem in many countries today. Countries that do not have political programs to ensure the availability of these goods to all parts of the population have high rates of hunger, disease, and illiteracy (Pogge 2002). People who recognize their responsibility to provide for themselves and their families may nevertheless find that limited abilities, harsh circumstances, or a combination of both make it impossible for them to gain sufficient access to subsistence. A drought may make it impossible to grow food, for example, or severe illness may make one unable to work, or the wages paid for working may be insufficient to cover basic needs.

(2) *Are social rights sufficiently important?*   It is sometimes alleged that social rights do not have the importance that civil and political rights have (Cranston 1973; see also the discussion in Beetham 1995). If the objection is that some formulations of social rights in international human rights documents are too expansive and go beyond what is necessary to a minimally good life, that point can be conceded and those formulations rejected. But if the objection is that core social rights do not protect very important claims and interests it is utterly implausible.

One way of showing the importance of basic social rights has already been provided, namely, the linkage arguments given above. They show that effectively implementing other human rights for all is difficult or impossible in situations where many people's basic social rights are unprotected and insecure.

Chapter 4 proposed a pluralistic conception of the norms and interests underlying human rights, suggesting that people have secure, but abstract, moral claims on others in four areas: (1) a secure claim to have a life; (2) a secure claim to lead one's life; (3) a secure claim against severely cruel or degrading treatment; and (4) a secure claim against severely unfair treatment. These four principles impose on all agents abstract obligations to respect and protect people's claims. Some of the duties involved are obviously positive; negative duties are not given a privileged position. Costs matter, but not whether those costs result from trying to fulfill a negative or a positive duty.

The secure claim to life plays a central role in justifying social rights. Without safe food and water, life and health are endangered and serious illness and death are probable. The connection between the availability of food and basic health care and having a minimally good life is direct and obvious – something that is not always true of other human rights. Education also promotes the fundamental interest in life by teaching health-related knowledge and skills as well as ways of supporting one's life through work.

The secure claim to lead a life – to be able to develop and exercise one's autonomous agency – also supports the importance of basic social rights. Developing and exercising agency requires a functioning mind and body as well as options and opportunities. The availability of food and basic health care promotes and protects physical and mental functioning. And the availability of basic education promotes knowledge of social, economic, and political options. In the contemporary world, lack of access to educational opportunities typically limits (both absolutely and comparatively) people's abilities to participate fully and effectively in the political and economic life of their country (see Hodgson 1998; Coomans 2002).

The secure claim against severely unfair treatment supports social rights. It is severely and ruinously unfair to exclude some parts of the population (rural people, women, minorities) from access to education and economic opportunities. Basic social rights protect against that kind of unfairness.

(3) *Do social rights fit the general idea of human rights?* Guarantees of access to subsistence, basic health care, and basic education are easily

formulated as rights – norms with rightholders who have claims, powers, and immunities; addressees who have duties and liabilities; and scopes or objects specifying a liberty, protection, or benefit that the rightholder is to enjoy.

It is sometimes objected, however, that we cannot identify the addressees of social rights. Let's discuss this with reference to the right to food. People are often perplexed by the idea of an international right to adequate food because they are not sure what it means for them. Does it mean that they have an obligation to feed some fair share of the world's hungry? Earlier I proposed a complex view of the addressees of human rights, that (1) governments are the primary addressees of the human rights of their residents with duties both to respect and to uphold their human rights; (2) governments have negative duties to respect the rights of people from other countries; (3) individuals have negative responsibilities to respect the human rights of people at home and abroad; (4) individuals have responsibilities as voters and citizens to promote human rights in their own country; and (5) governments, international organizations, and individuals have back-up responsibilities for the fulfillment of human rights around the world. This view is easily applied to social rights.

(4) *Would some weaker norm be as effective?* Social rights may be unnecessary if people participated in self-help, assistance to family members, and charitable giving to those in need. This proposal suggests that we can recognize that people have moral claims to assistance in regard to subsistence, health care, and education without having to view these claims as generating rights or as requiring political action.

A harmonious combination of self-help and voluntary mutual assistance is certainly to be encouraged, but such a mixture offers little prospect of providing adequately for all of the needy and incapacitated if it is viewed as a substitute for, rather than as a supplement to, politically implemented social rights. First, some people are unable to help themselves because they are sick, disabled, very young, or very old. Second, some people lack families to assist them, and impoverished people often come from low-income families with limited abilities to assist their members. Third, there are obvious limits on charitable giving as a source of aid to the needy. There are often too few donors for the needs present. Further, provision for the needy is likely to be spotty rather than comprehensive. This may be because no capable donor is within call or because the capable donors that are within call have used their discretion and given to other causes. This spottiness was noted by John Stuart Mill, who remarked that "Charity almost always does too much or too little: it lavishes its bounty in one place, and leaves people to starve in another" (Mill 1848).

(5) *Are the burdens justifiable?*   A familiar objection to social rights is that they are too burdensome. Frequently the claim that social rights are too burdensome uses other, less controversial human rights as a standard of comparison, and suggests that social rights are substantially more burdensome or expensive than liberty rights, for example. Liberty rights such as freedom of communication, association, and movement require both respect and protection from governments. And people cannot be adequately protected in the enjoyment of liberties such as these unless they also have security and due process rights. The costs of liberty, as it were, include the costs of law and criminal justice. Once we see this, liberties start to look a lot more costly. In order to provide effective liberties to communicate, associate, and move, it is not enough for a society to make a prohibition of interference with these activities part of its law and accepted morality. An effective system of provision for these liberties requires a legal scheme that defines personal and property rights and protects these rights against invasions while ensuring due process to those accused of crimes. Providing such legal protection in the form of legislatures, police, courts, and prisons is very expensive.

Further, we should not think of social rights as simply giving everyone a free supply of the goods these rights protect. Guarantees of subsistence will be intolerably expensive and will undermine productivity if everyone simply receives a free supply. A viable system of social rights will require most people to provide for themselves and their families through work as long as they have access to appropriate opportunities, education, and infrastructure. Government-implemented social rights provide guarantees of availability (or "secure access"), but it should not be necessary for governments to supply the requisite goods in more than a small fraction of cases. Basic health care and education may be exceptions to this since many believe that governments should provide free health services and education irrespective of ability to pay.

Countries that do not accept and implement social rights still have to bear somehow the costs of providing for the needy. If government does not supply food, clothing, and shelter to those unable to provide for themselves, then families, friends, and communities will have to shoulder much of this burden. It is only in the last century that politically implemented social rights have taken over a substantial part of the burden of providing for the needy. The taxes associated with social rights are partial replacements for other burdensome duties, namely the duties of families and communities to provide adequate care for the unemployed, sick, disabled, and aged. Deciding whether to implement social rights is not a matter of deciding whether to bear heavy burdens, but rather of deciding whether to continue with total reliance on systems of informal provision that provide insufficient assistance and whose costs fall very unevenly on families, friends, and communities.

Once we recognize that liberty rights also carry high costs, that intelligent systems of provision for social rights need to supply the requisite goods to people in only a small minority of cases, and that these systems are substitutes for other, more local ways of providing for the needy, the difference between the burdensomeness of liberty rights and the burdensomeness of social rights ceases to seem so large.

Even if the burdens imposed by social rights are not excessive, they may still be wrong to impose on individuals. Libertarians think that social rights are unacceptable because they require impermissible taxation. This view is vulnerable to an attack on two grounds. First, taxation is permissible when used to discharge the moral duties of taxpayers, as when it is used to support government-organized systems of humanitarian assistance that fulfill more effectively than charity duties of assistance that all individuals have (Beetham 1995: 53). Second, one can recognize the importance of property rights without believing that they are so weighty that they can never be outweighed by the requirements of meeting other rights.

(6) *Feasibility* The test of feasibility proposed earlier for international human rights is that an ample majority of countries in the world today are able to implement the right in question. Feasibility is a challenging test for basic social rights because some of the world's countries are too impoverished, troubled, and disorganized to respect and implement them effectively. This is particularly true in "low income" countries (ones in the lowest quartile in terms of average individual income). These are countries such as Burundi, Cambodia, and Haiti, where the average income is less than US$600 per year, the average lifespan is slightly under 60 years, childhood immunization is near 65 percent, and illiteracy rates are about 30 percent for men and nearly 50 percent for women (see World Bank 2006).

The abilities and resources of the least capable countries are not an appropriate standard of feasibility. The legal duties of parents, for example, are not keyed to the least capable parents. Rather we should ask whether an ample majority of countries can comply, whether countries in the top two quartiles and some of those in the third have the resources and capabilities to implement basic social rights. Countries in the top quartile clearly can. They include countries such as Canada, Denmark, Greece, Japan, and Singapore. So can "upper middle income" countries (the second quartile). They include countries such as Chile, Mexico, and Poland. Average personal income in these countries ranges from a low of about US$2,400 to a high around US$8,000; the average lifespan is around 70 years; and illiteracy rates are under 6 percent (World Bank 2006). Most of them already have programs to promote and protect basic social rights, although the quality and efficiency of these programs is often poor.

But what about "lower middle income" countries (the third quartile)? If some of them are able to implement basic social rights, the feasibility test will be passed. Countries near the top of the third quartile include Colombia, Samoa, and Swaziland. The average personal income in these countries near the top of the third quartile is around $2,000; the average lifespan is around 70; and illiteracy is near 10 percent. Many of the countries in the third quartile already have programs to reduce hunger, promote health, and provide education, but those programs are often underfunded and fail to cover all regions and parts of the population. But it seems likely that at least the top third of them are able to implement basic social rights. Thus, if we use the Vance Conception of social rights it seems that the feasibility test can be met.

If all of the appropriate justificatory tests can be met by social rights, this means that these rights are justified for the whole world. A majority of countries can implement them and have no excuse on grounds of resources for not doing so as quickly as possible. In countries that are genuinely unable to implement them, these rights exist as justified international norms, but their governments and peoples are excused on grounds of inability for their failure to make them available. This does not render the rights irrelevant, however. They stand as norms to be realized as far and as soon as possible and whose lack of realization is an appropriate matter of regret. Further, those rights call upon secondary and back-up addressees to come forward and provide meaningful assistance.

The Social Covenant commits its signatories to progressive rather than immediate implementation. Article 2.1 requires a ratifying country to "take steps, individually and through international assistance and co-operation . . . to the maximum of its available resources, with a view to achieving progressively the full realization of the rights recognized in the present Covenant." Here the duties associated with social rights are seen as duties to try – to make a good-faith effort progressively over time to implement these rights for all of the population in all parts of the country. This allows countries to be in compliance with their legal duties even though subsistence, minimal health care, and basic education are not available to all of their people.

The use of the idea of progressive implementation to deal with problems of resources is not an entirely happy solution. It gives the illusion that the problem of feasibility has been dealt with when in fact it has only been massaged. Second, it suggests that the problem of feasibility arises only in regard to social rights when in fact it is a serious problem for civil and political rights as well. Third, it does not do anything to obligate international organizations and countries around the world to assist low-income countries. Fourth, it produces human rights that are undersupported by their associated duties and hence misleadingly formulated. If we proclaim a specific right to food or education, but support it only with duties to try to ensure the availability of food or education, the right is undersupported. A more accurate description of the right would be to say that people have a right that their governments *try* to provide food or education.

A better approach, perhaps, would have been to use the same commitment clause found in article 2 of the Civil and Political Covenant, namely to "respect and to ensure to all individuals within its territory . . . the rights recognized in the present Covenant." A supplemental statement could have said that countries genuinely unable to implement social rights are temporarily excused but have duties to implement these rights as soon and as far as they can. Beyond this, duties of richer countries to assist low-income countries in realizing basic social rights should have been specified abstractly but explicitly (see Rawls 1999: 37).

The UN committee that administers the Social Covenant, the Committee on Economic, Social and Cultural Rights, has tried to deal with some of the problems with progressive implementation by introducing the supplemental ideas of making a good faith and measurable effort and of meeting minimum standards. "[W]hile the Covenant provides for progressive realization and acknowledges the constraints due to the limits of available resources, it also imposes various obligations which are of immediate effect" (United Nations 1991). The duty to make an immediate, good-faith, and measurable effort may be understood to require the making of plans, the establishment and funding of agencies, and the setting of measurable timetables or "benchmarks." To facilitate the monitoring of compliance the country may be required to collect data regularly concerning realization of the goals, make periodic reports, and allow its citizens to complain to the monitoring body about failures to pursue the goals energetically. This general idea is found in article 14 of the Social Covenant which states that a ratifying country that has, at the time of ratification, not been able to provide to all its children free primary education "undertakes, within two years, to work out and adopt a detailed plan of action for the progressive implementation, within a reasonable number of years, to be fixed in the plan, of the principle of compulsory education free of charge for all."

Social rights can be further strengthened by adding duties to satisfy without delay feasible minimal standards while making efforts to realize the right fully over a longer term. This is often described as a "minimum core" (Eide 1989; United Nations 1991; Chapman and Russell 2002). A right of this sort can be thought of as having two objects. One, the minimal object, is set at a level that almost all countries can meet and requires nearly immediate compliance. In regard to food, the minimum core may be a duty to prevent famines, while the outer core is secure access to adequate food for all. It sets a more demanding goal which provides a broader focus for the right and which is supported by a duty to try.

Overview

This chapter defended social rights as human rights and as an attractive approach to addressing world poverty. A modest conception (the Vance Conception) of social rights was proposed which includes rights to subsistence, basic health care, and basic education. These three rights were defended by starting with abstract norms pertaining to life, leading one's life, avoiding severely cruel treatment, and avoiding severe unfairness. The justification for social rights continued by applying the six tests proposed in Chapter 5. Social rights are not excessively burdensome on their addressees and they are feasible worldwide in the appropriate sense.

Further Reading

Aiken, W., and LaFolette, H. (eds.) 1996. *World Hunger and Morality*. Upper Saddle River, NJ: Prentice-Hall.

Arneson, R. 1990. "Is Work Special? Justice and the Distribution of Employment." *American Political Science Review* 84: 1127–47.

Beetham, D. 1995. "What Future for Economic and Social Rights?" *Political Studies* 43: 41–60.

Fabre, C. 2000. *Social Rights under the Constitution: Government and the Decent Life*. Oxford: Clarendon Press.

Howard, R. 1987. "The Full-Belly Thesis: Should Economic Rights Take Priority over Civil and Political Rights?" *Human Rights Quarterly* 5: 467–90.

Peffer, R. 1978. "A Defense to Rights to Well-Being." *Philosophy & Public Affairs* 8 (1): 65–87.

van Parijs, P. 1998. *Real Freedom for All*. Oxford: Oxford University Press.

Chapter 10
Minority Rights

Minorities are particularly vulnerable to human rights violations. For example, religious minorities sometimes endure restricted liberty to practice their beliefs. Ethnic and racial minorities are often subject to discrimination and second-class citizenship. Indigenous peoples are often deprived of their traditional lands and resources. The human rights movement has made serious efforts to deal with these problems, beginning with the minority rights treaties established by the League of Nations (see Stone 1932) and continuing with specialized treaties such as the International Convention on the Elimination of All Forms of Racial Discrimination (CERD; United Nations 1965), and the Convention on the Elimination of All Forms of Discrimination Against Women (CEDAW; United Nations 1979). This chapter describes those efforts and asks whether and how minority rights can be human rights.

Talk of minority rights can be ambiguous. It is sometimes unclear whether we are talking about rights of individual members of the minority group or rights of the group itself. And if it is the former, are we talking of general rights that play an important role in protecting minorities or are we talking of rights that specifically mention and target the problems of minorities? To avoid confusion it will be helpful to distinguish three categories. First, Universal Rights Applied to Minorities (URAMs) are ordinary human rights of all people in one of their roles, namely protecting minority persons. URAMs do not name types of minorities or mention specific problems of minorities. When the Civil and Political Covenant asserts in article 27 that minorities have a right "to profess and practise their own religion" this is a URAM at work since everyone has a right to profess and practice their religion. URAMs are often used as reminders that minorities have all the standard human rights. URAMs are not problematic as human rights. They may, however, be problematic as minority rights because they say so little about minorities and have no minority-specific content. This does not show that they are unimportant as minority rights but only that they are not the whole story, that they need to be supplemented with Minority Rights or Group Rights that identify types of minorities and address their distinctive human rights problems (Henrard 2000).

Second, there are minority rights proper (which I shall refer to as "Minority Rights," using initial capital letters to indicate this definition of the term). These are rights that refer to and are formulated specifically to meet the vulnerabilities and problems of minorities. Minority Rights are group-differentiated in that they are rights of particular minorities or types of minorities, not rights of all humans (Kymlicka 1995a). When the Civil and Political Covenant says in article 27 that persons belonging to ethnic, religious, or linguistic minorities shall not be denied the right "to use their own language," this is a Minority Right since the right to use one's own language, unlike the right to practice one's religion, is not a right that human rights treaties attribute to all people. Rather, it seems to be group-differentiated, to be a right that minority group members have but that mainstreamers do not. It is not, however, a Group Right since the right to use one's own language is a right held by individuals. We will return to this example below to consider whether these appearances are misleading.

The third category of minority rights is group rights (again, I shall refer to these as "Group Rights" to indicate my defined meaning). These are rights held by a group rather than by individuals who are members of the group. Like Minority Rights, Group Rights are group-differentiated. They are rights of some, not rights of all. They refer to a minority group or groups, and that reference is used to attribute the right to the group, to make the group the rightholder. Group rights may be exercised by authorized group leaders, through other forms of collective action, or by individuals. Group Rights often accompany "autonomy regimes," political systems that authorize control by ethnic or religious groups over family law, education, or territory (Hannum 1990; Steiner and Alston 2000). Familiar group rights include rights against genocide, forced assimilation, and ethnic cleansing, to semi-autonomous status, territory, control over resources, recognition as distinctive and/or oppressed; recognition of a group's language as one of the official languages of the country; subsidies to help keep a culture alive; expanded educational and economic opportunities; political participation as groups; self-determination; and secession (Nickel 1997). The items on this list are extremely varied. Which Group Rights, if any, are appropriate to a particular minority group depends greatly on the group's nature and circumstances.

────── The Rights of Minorities: 1948–2006 ──────

The treatment of minority rights within the United Nations moved gradually from an URAM approach emphasizing the nondiscriminatory possession and enjoyment by minorities of all human rights, to an approach that also includes Minority Rights and Group Rights. Some Group Rights – particularly autonomy rights that give groups some degree of political control over territory – continue to be controversial within the international community.

The Universal Declaration of Human Rights

The Universal Declaration emphatically included minority persons among those who have and should enjoy universal human rights without discrimination. The Universal Declaration begins with the principle that "All human beings are born free and equal in dignity and rights" (article 1). It prohibits slavery and servitude (article 4), and says that "Everyone is entitled to all the rights and freedoms set forth in this Declaration, without distinction of any kind, such as race, colour, sex, language, religion, political or other opinion, national or social origin, property, birth or other status" (article 2). Note that this nondiscrimination clause contains an ample list of suspect classifications – things like race, sex, and religion which are presumptively not to be used in making distinctions relating to rights. The Universal Declaration also declares the equality of persons before the law, equal protection of the law, and a right to legal protection against discrimination (articles 6 and 7). It was a great achievement to gain international recognition of these principles at a time (1948) when colonialism was still overtly practiced and racial segregation still legally entrenched in a number of countries, including South Africa and the United States.

The Universal Declaration's approach to minority rights in terms of equal rights and nondiscrimination for all has several advantages. First, it does not have to devote much energy to naming or defining minority groups. Whichever they are, their members all have equal human rights. Second, since it does not ascribe special rights to endangered groups it does not need to address the possibility that these special rights will be seen as discriminatory by people not belonging to these groups. And third, it can enlist mainstreamers in the cause of minority rights by suggesting that by supporting minority rights they are thereby making more secure the principles and practices that support their own rights.

The Genocide Convention

An early exception to the emphasis on equal rights and nondiscrimination was the Genocide Convention (United Nations 1948a). It can be seen as establishing a Group Right which directly protects ethnic and religious groups. It is notable, however, that the Genocide Convention does not say that the right against genocide is a human right, nor does it anywhere use the phrase "human rights." Genocide is referred to as a crime, and the Convention calls upon its signatories to enact in their countries criminal legislation prohibiting genocide. The crime of genocide is defined as acts such as killing, injuring, and preventing births "with intent to destroy, in whole or in part, a national, ethnical, racial, or religious group, as such." The prohibition of genocide provides protection to groups as groups. It is largely negative in the sense that it requires governments and other agencies to refrain from destroying groups; but it has positive elements requiring enactment of legislation at the national level to prohibit and punish genocide. The prohibition of genocide is now enforced within the criminal law of many countries and (in a back-up role) by the International Criminal Court (United Nations 1998).

Other human rights treaties

Human rights treaties in the 1950s and 1960s generally used the URAM approach. The European Convention, the American Convention, and the Civil and Political Covenant all emphasized equality of rights and nondiscrimination as a way of protecting the rights of minorities. But the two UN Covenants established new patterns in two ways. First, their identical first article declares that "peoples" have rights to self-determination and to control over their national resources. Although vague in meaning, these norms are clearly Group Rights. Second, the Civil and Political Covenant explicitly included some Minority Rights in article 27:

> In those States in which ethnic, religious or linguistic minorities exist, persons belonging to such minorities shall not be denied the right, in community with the other members of their group, to enjoy their own culture, to profess and practise their own religion, or to use their own language.

The minorities listed are ethnic, religious, and linguistic minorities – ones that have a distinctive culture, religion, or language that they wish to use, teach, and preserve.

Specialized treaties

Beginning in 1966, the United Nations produced a series of specialized minority rights treaties and declarations. These treaties include the International Convention on the Elimination of All Forms of Racial Discrimination (CERD), the Convention on the Elimination of All Forms of Discrimination against Women (CEDAW), the Convention on the Rights of the Child (United Nations 1989), the Declaration on the Rights of Persons Belonging to National or Ethnic, Religious and Linguistic Minorities (United Nations 1992), the Draft Declaration on the Rights of Indigenous Peoples (United Nations 1994), and the Declaration on the Elimination of All Forms of Religious Intolerance (United Nations 1995). Similar declarations were produced by other international organizations such as the Organization of American States and the Organization for Security and Co-operation in Europe.

This list of treaties and declarations suggests the large variety of groups that a conception of minority rights could try to cover. An even longer list might include children; the disabled; gays, lesbians, bisexuals, and transgendered people; the elderly; ethnonational groups; immigrants; indigenous peoples; linguistic minorities; the mentally troubled and ill; racial groups; refugees; the retarded and educationally challenged; religious groups; and women (on the definition of "minority," see Gurr 1993: 3–33; Henrard 2000: 16–55). Because of the great differences between and within these groups it is unlikely that any single diagnosis of minority problems and their sources or any single normative or political remedy will be plausible. This is not an area where a "one size fits all" approach will work.

The International Convention on the Elimination of All Forms of Racial Discrimination

The first specialized minority rights treaty within the United Nations was the International Convention on the Elimination of All Forms of Racial Discrimination. It requires signatories to outlaw racial discrimination and apartheid and to protect and promote the advancement of racial minorities. CERD's provisions cover groups defined by "race, colour, descent, or national or ethnic origin" (article 1). This broad scope has allowed CERD to serve as a generic minority rights treaty. CERD followed the Universal Declaration in approaching minority rights by emphasizing equal enjoyment of universal rights, but recognized and dealt with the possibility of group-differentiated measures to protect and assist particular groups:

Special measures taken for the sole purpose of securing adequate advancement of certain racial or ethnic groups or individuals requiring such protection as may be necessary in order to ensure such groups' or individuals' equal enjoyment or exercise of human rights and fundamental freedoms shall not be deemed racial discrimination, provided, however, that such measures do not, as a consequence, lead to the maintenance of separate rights for different racial groups and that they shall not be continued after the objectives for which they were taken have been achieved.   (article 1.4)

This clause recognizes the fact that when Minority Rights and Group Rights are attributed to some but not all groups, there is a danger that members of excluded groups will view these special minority rights as discriminating against them. After all, differences in fundamental rights that are drawn along group lines are normally viewed as discriminatory (on the affirmative action debate, see Cahn 2002).

CERD is implemented by a system in which participating states make periodic reports on measures taken to comply with the treaty to a committee which receives, evaluates, and writes responses to these reports. State complaints may be received, investigated, and mediated by the committee. Individual complaints may be authorized by states under an optional protocol (article 14). This type of implementation system is used for many UN human rights treaties.

The Convention on the Elimination of All Forms of Discrimination against Women

Women are a majority rather than a minority, but it is illuminating to consider women's rights in the context of this chapter. The UN Convention on the Elimination of All Forms of Discrimination against Women was prepared by the UN Commission on the Status of Women. CEDAW is an interesting mixture of an equal rights–nondiscrimination approach with an approach that identifies specific problems and vulnerabilities of women and proposes distinctive rights as remedies for them. CEDAW often sets equality with men's treatment as the standard to be achieved, and it follows earlier documents in focusing on discrimination as the generic threat to women's equality of rights. But CEDAW transforms this approach in several ways. First, it deepens the understanding of the threat of discrimination by recognizing the role of stereotypes and beliefs in male superiority in fostering discrimination against women. Article 5 calls on governments to take measures to eliminate "prejudices . . . based on stereotyped roles for men and women." Second, CEDAW mentions numerous areas in which women face distinctive problems. For example, the preamble notes that "in situations of poverty women have the least access to food"; article 6 deals with "traffic in women and exploitation of prostitution of women"; and article 10, which concerns the right to education, calls for "reduction of female student drop-out rates." Reproductive and maternity issues receive ample attention. Article 14 calls on states to take measures "to assist rural women in areas such as access to health care facilities, agricultural credit and loans, marketing facilities . . . and equal treatment in land and agrarian reform."

CEDAW is implemented by a system in which participating states make periodic reports on measures taken to comply with the treaty to a committee that receives, evaluates, and writes responses to these reports. Under an optional protocol, individual complaints may be received and investigated by the committee. The UN has also used international conferences, such as the ones in Cairo in 1994 and in Beijing in 2000, to promote women's rights.

The Convention on the Rights of the Child

Children are an odd "minority." Like women, they are found in all countries, cultures, religions, and income categories. But they do have some distinctive problems and vulnerabilities that the Convention on the Rights of the Child attempts to address. Like CEDAW, the Convention on the Rights of the Child uses an approach that mixes URAMs and Minority Rights. This treaty has turned out to be very popular; it has been adopted by almost all of the world's countries. In addition to identifying various human rights that children have and should enjoy without discrimination, it identifies special problems and vulnerabilities of children and proposes normative remedies for them. For example, it addresses issues of custody (article 9), adoption (article 14), parental responsibilities (article 27.2), and the sexual exploitation of children (article 34).

The Draft Declaration on the Rights of Indigenous Peoples

As we have seen, the general pattern of UN minority rights treaties is to emphasize the universality of human rights and the equal enjoyment of rights through freedom from discrimination; to refer to minority rights as the rights of members of minority groups; and to address the special problems of the group in question through Minority Rights. This pattern is largely abandoned in the Draft Declaration on the Rights of Indigenous Peoples where group rights are wholeheartedly embraced. It speaks of both "individuals" and "peoples." This Declaration has not been approved by the General Assembly as of 2006.

The Draft Declaration contains all three kinds of minority rights. URAMs are seen in article 1 where indigenous peoples are said to have all of the human rights that other people have. Minority Rights are seen in article 13: "Indigenous peoples have the right to manifest, practice, develop and teach their spiritual and religious traditions, customs and ceremonies"; and in article 11: "Indigenous peoples have the right to special protection and security in periods of armed conflict." These articles would have a better fit with our earlier definition of Minority Rights, however, if they had begun with "members of indigenous groups" instead of "indigenous peoples."

Group Rights are found throughout the document. Examples include: "Indigenous peoples have the right of self-determination" (article 3); "Indigenous peoples have the collective and individual right not to be subjected to ethnocide and cultural genocide" (article 7); and "Indigenous peoples have the right to own, develop, control and use the lands and territories . . . which they have traditionally owned or otherwise occupied or used" (article 26).

Minority Rights as Human Rights

This section undertakes to show how many minority rights fit into the family of human rights and can be supported by the same considerations that support human rights generally. As defined above, Minority Rights are individual rather than group rights. But they are rights of minority individuals, not rights of all persons. Minority Rights raise the problem of how rights that are group-differentiated and hence not rights of all people can be human rights. Further, it is definitional of human rights that people have them independent of membership in any particular nation or group. But whether one has minority rights is not independent in that way, since people do not have Minority Rights unless they belong to certain groups.

In many cases, however, this seems true only at a superficial level. Consider the right of minority individuals to use their own native language. This right is arguably derivable from the universal right to freedom of expression or communication. If Kim wants to communicate with Lee, Kim is free to use whatever language she and Lee know or prefer. Kim should be free to practice her Swahili whenever she talks to Lee (as long as Lee is willing). It is probably possible to justify as a human right the freedom to use whatever language both a speaker and listener are able and willing to use. As with other liberties, this liberty may require some qualifications. There may be justifiable limitations in areas where it is very important for everyone to use a single language (for example, aircraft control). If the right of everyone to use their own language is derivable from other human rights, or justifiable using the same grounds and steps as other human rights, then in its application to minorities it is just an unproblematic URAM.

More difficult cases arise when the special rights or protections prescribed by Minority Rights are literally not ones that all citizens can enjoy. For example, article 6 of CEDAW requires states to "suppress all forms of traffic in women and exploitation of prostitution of women." Superficially, at least, this right is group-differentiated; it does not protect men and boys. One option here is the one just explained in the case of the right to use one's own language. We could say that a right of men and boys against trafficking, exploitation, and prostitution is also justifiable. If men and boys face this problem (as, of course, boys and young men sometimes do), they are equally protected. The right is only superficially group-differentiated. It focuses on women because they are so much more exposed to these threats than men are, but at a deeper level it is universal.

Another option is to say that trafficking, exploitation, and coerced prostitution are distinctive problems of women requiring distinctive norms that do not apply to men. This latter approach is most plausible in cases where the right is to something that men literally cannot enjoy. Women's right to prenatal care is an example, since men simply cannot bear children. Let's say that these sorts of rights are strongly group-differentiated.

Even here the strategy of seeing group-differentiated rights as implications of universal rights seems available. Standing behind the right to prenatal care during pregnancy is the universal right to basic medical care. The right to prenatal care necessary to the health and survival of mothers and babies is derivable from that general right, and hence even strongly differentiated Minority Rights can turn out to be URAMs. The right to basic medical care is interesting in this regard because it is strongly need-based. If Kim needs penicillin and Lee does not, Lee is not justified in complaining that his rights have been violated when a state-funded physician refuses to give him penicillin. The right to a fair trial is also need-based: one's human rights do not entitle one to a fair trial (a fancy legal ceremony that some may enjoy starring in) unless one is charged with a crime. One's particular entitlements under human rights are often need-based.

To sum up, I claim that when Minority and women's rights are human rights, they are only superficially group-differentiated. They can all be explained as URAMs. Accordingly, I propose the following test for whether a Minority Right (to some good I shall call "A") is a human right. The Minority Right to A is a human right if it is derivable (using plausible additional premises) from a universal human right.

Minority Rights spell out the implications of universal rights for people who face distinctive problems. Minority Rights pick out the threatened kinds of groups and propose specific rights and remedies. Different kinds of minorities face distinctive problems or abuses along with those that afflict all minorities. The distinctive problems of religious minorities, for example, are somewhat different from the distinctive problems of racial minorities. This is why there are separate treaties for racial groups, religious minorities, women, and children. To formulate a treaty on the rights of religious minorities one has to find out what the problems of religious minorities are, and which of these are plausibly seen as human rights problems. Then one has to relate them to the general human rights and to the underlying values and norms. One also has to look for plausible remedies and check to ensure that they are consistent with the general human rights framework.

Special remedies and protections can be prescribed generally for all minorities or on a "where appropriate" basis. The UN Declaration on the Rights of Persons Belonging to National or Ethnic, Religious and Linguistic Minorities (United Nations 1992) illustrates this distinction. Article 4.2 says that "States shall take measures to create favourable conditions to enable persons belonging to minorities to express their characteristics and to develop their culture, language, religion, traditions and customs," whereas article 4.4 says that "States should, *where appropriate*, take measures in the field of education, in order to encourage the knowledge of the history, traditions, language and culture of the minorities existing within their territory" (my emphasis). The former declares a general obligation of states, whereas the latter depends on a judgment of appropriateness. It says that states should do this if in their territory it is appropriate or useful. Formulation on a "where appropriate" basis allows useful practices and institutions to be recommended by human rights documents without being prescribed everywhere or having to be categorized as general duties or rights.

Do Human Rights Include Group Rights?

Group Rights are like Minority Rights in naming types of minorities and addressing their typical problems. But Group Rights are unlike Minority

Rights in attributing rights to groups rather than to members of groups. They are rights of peoples rather than of persons. Because of this they do not have a good fit with the general idea of human rights, which concerns rights that people have independently of group or national membership. In this section I suggest that Group Rights are not human rights in the standard sense because they are not rights that people simply have as humans rather than as members of some state or group. This is not to deny, however, that group rights may appropriately be included in human rights treaties and in other areas of international law. Nor does it deny that Group Rights may sometimes be justifiable by reference to the same sorts of considerations as justify human rights.

Groups often have interests that are different from, and even conflict with, the interests of some of their members. If a group has an organized decision-making structure that gives some members the power to make decisions for the group, those decisions can select goals that then create interests for the group (Nickel 1997). For example, if the leaders decide to invest a large proportion of an indigenous group's assets in a casino, the group thereafter has an interest in the casino's success. And this can be true even if the casino's success works against the interests of some of the individual members (for example, those who live across the road from it and have to endure its traffic and noise).

It is useful to distinguish three kinds of Group Rights: (1) group security rights; (2) group representation rights; and (3) group autonomy rights. Group security rights protect the existence and safety of minority groups as groups. The right against genocide is an example of a group security right, as are rights against ethnocide, deprivation of group property, and forced relocation. Group representation rights attempt to give groups secure access to meaningful political participation. These might take the form of a guaranteed number or percentage of seats in parliament, or a share in ministerial positions. And group autonomy rights give minority groups formal powers to rule themselves in some areas. These areas may be family and property law, education, or – most grandly – semi-autonomous rule over a territory.

Of these three categories of Group Rights, group security rights are the least controversial and the most easily justified. The fundamental interests of many minority individuals are tightly tied to the survival and safety of their groups. Article 6 of the Draft Declaration on the Rights of Indigenous Peoples says that "Indigenous peoples have the collective right to live in freedom, peace and security as distinct peoples and to full guarantees against genocide." Like the right against genocide generally, this is a right held by peoples. This Group Right protects directly the interests of indigenous groups in security and continued existence and protects indirectly the interests of indigenous individuals in the security and continued existence of their groups. Perhaps some hardy individuals could survive and flourish after the destruction of their ethnic or national group (assuming that they did not die in the assault on the group), but many would succumb to alcoholism, depression, and suicide. Still, even when a Group Right is justifiable on the same grounds as human rights, that does not turn it into a human right in the standard sense.

Group Rights are often used to protect people's "identity" or group membership. Many people care passionately about their ethnic, national, or cultural identity. It forms part of their self-conception, structures their lives and social relations, and is interwoven with their well-being. Harm to the group is harm to them. Accordingly, we can sometimes say that justified Group Rights are instrumental to a minimally good life for group members. Perhaps we can also say something stronger, namely that living within one's cultural group is a constituent part of some people's good (and not merely a means to that good). If so, for such people the survival of their group may have the same value as their own survival.

Group representation rights are often called for and used in circumstances where minority group members cannot get a fair share of political offices through undifferentiated electoral politics (see Young 1989; Lijphart 1995; Phillips 1995). Such representation rights have not been broadly endorsed by human rights treaties and declarations, and some theorists worry that they will permanently freeze ethnic divisions (Glazer 1983; W. Wilson 1987).

Group autonomy rights are the most controversial Group Rights. Minimally they give groups formal control over and funding for their educational and religious institutions. They may also give groups control over the legal regime governing families, religion, and property. National and religious minorities often enjoy these sorts of arrangements, particularly in the Middle East. Or they may give groups control over semi-autonomous territories (Hannum 1990). This is most common when the historic territories of indigenous peoples – or some parts of them – are recognized as reserves in which indigenous groups have a substantial degree of self-rule. James Anaya has argued persuasively that respect for the territories and prerogatives of indigenous peoples has received sufficient recognition and acceptance to be a norm of customary international law (Anaya 2004).

The idea behind both Minority Rights and Group Rights is that the special problems of minorities often require special remedies. The prerogatives that Group Rights offer are group-oriented, but their rationales may still come back to the minority individuals whose fundamental interests are dependent upon and woven together with the survival, security, resources, representation, and autonomy of their groups.

It might be objected that the approach to Group Rights taken in this chapter is too oriented towards individuals and does not take groups seriously enough. Since groups can have agency and interests, including an interest in continued existence, would it not be better to say that they have moral claims analogous to those of individual persons? An argument for this point of view might run as follows. Human groups, if organized so that they have a decision-making structure, an executive, goals and interests, memory and records, and a physical platform such as a population, land, and buildings, are artificial persons and artificial agents. (Their capacities are assembled, as it were, from the capacities of their human and other parts.) These artificial persons have genuine agency, interests, plans, and norms, as well as some moral capacities. They are capable of discussing and negotiating, contracting, having rights and powers, committing crimes and other violations of norms, being held responsible for actions, and being punished. Artificial persons can hold and exercise rights. Just as natural persons have intrinsic value, artificial persons have intrinsic value. The intrinsic value of artificial persons is not derivable from the intrinsic value of their members who are natural persons. Just as natural persons are worthy of equal moral respect, artificial persons are worthy of equal moral respect. Thus, if artificial persons avoid criminal behavior, they are entitled to security (not to be killed or harmed), non-interference, freedom from theft and fraud, and tolerance. These entitlements do not depend on or derive from the entitlements of their human members.

This argument is interesting but ultimately unpersuasive. If the destruction of an artificial person would in no way harm or frustrate the interests of its members it is doubtful that it has any moral claim to continue to exist. Suppose that a wealthy family incorporated legally a charitable organization 75 years ago, but now all the family members have died, all the funds have been spent, and the organization's only employee is about to take retirement with an ample annuity. Learning of this situation, a government agency cancels the organization's charter and thereby destroys an artificial person. Since no individual human persons are harmed, it seems that no moral wrong has been done. Even if the organization's charter declared that the organization was to exist in perpetuity, any associated corporate interest would carry no weight after being detached from the interests of live persons. If this were correct, group rights must connect with individual interests and claims if they are to have moral weight.

Overview

This chapter distinguished three types of minority rights. First there are ordinary human rights serving the role of protecting members of minorities (URAMs). Second, there are Minority Rights proper. These are rights that refer to and are formulated specifically to meet the vulnerabilities and problems of minorities. They are "group differentiated" in that they are rights of particular minorities or types of minorities, not rights of all people as people. Third, there are Group Rights. These are rights held by a group rather than by individuals who are members of the group. Over the last half-century the United Nations has moved from an approach to minority rights that emphasized nondiscrimination and URAMs to an approach that includes Minority Rights and Group Rights. There is some difficulty in viewing these latter categories of rights as human rights because they are rights of some people or groups, not rights of all people. Still, Minority Rights can often be reformulated as rights of all. And the idea behind both Minority Rights and Group Rights is that the special problems of minorities often require special remedies.

Further Reading

Anaya, S. J. 2004. *Indigenous Peoples in International Law.* Oxford: Oxford University Press.

Baker, J. 1994. *Group Rights.* Toronto: University of Toronto Press.

Henrard, K. 2000. *Devising an Adequate System of Minority Protection.* The Hague: Martinus Nijhoff.

Kymlicka, W. 1989. *Liberalism, Community, and Culture.* Oxford: Clarendon Press.

Okin, S. 1998. "Feminism, Women's Human Rights, and Cultural Differences." *Hypatia* 13: 32–52.

Chapter 11

Eight Responses to the Relativist

Planet Earth is wonderfully varied in its peoples, cultures, religions, and national traditions. Put all those differences together with the idea of universal human rights and the combination may not seem very plausible. How can a single set of rights be appropriate to such a diverse world? Accordingly, the universality and justifiability of human rights are sometimes challenged by appeal to cultural differences, using some notion that a society's norms inevitably are, or should be, relative to its culture and circumstances. The defender of universal human rights may be accused of insensitivity, arrogance, and cultural imperialism (Talbott 2005). *Insensitivity* may be found in failing to recognize differences in values and traditions. *Arrogance* may be found in considering one's own values to be better without having thought deeply about the matter. *Cultural imperialism* may be seen in being prepared to impose one's own culture's values and norms coercively. This chapter begins by explaining cultural relativism, and then proceeds to offer eight responses to the relativist. My goal is less to refute relativists than to get them to moderate their views and endorse at least some human rights.

Relativism and Human Rights

When the Universal Declaration was being formulated in 1947, the Executive Board of the American Anthropological Association warned of the danger that the Declaration would be "a statement of rights conceived only in terms of the values prevalent in Western Europe and America," and condemned an ethnocentrism that translates "the recognition of cultural differences into a summons to action." The main concern of the Board was to condemn intolerant colonialist attitudes and to advocate cultural and political self-determination. The Board allowed that "freedom is understood and sought after by peoples having the most diverse cultures" and suggested that in attempting to influence repressive regimes "underlying cultural values may be called on to bring the peoples of such states to a realization of the consequences of the acts of their governments, and thus enforce a brake upon discrimination and conquest" (American Anthropological Association 1947).

In addition to these sensible suggestions the AAA Board also made some stronger assertions. One was that "standards and values are relative to the culture from which they derive" and thus "what is held to be a human right in one society may be regarded as anti-social by another people." The Board also asserted that "respect for differences between cultures is validated by the scientific fact that no technique of qualitatively evaluating cultures has been discovered" (American Anthropological Association 1947). This bizarre argument attempts to justify a norm of tolerance by asserting that there is no way of justifying moral and legal norms. If norms are impossible to justify, so are norms that prescribe diversity and tolerance.

Globalization and its accompanying set of transnational influences create unlikely combinations of beliefs, practices, and commitments. The world's countries and cultures are not isolated, insulated, and homogeneous. Most of them have not been so in recent centuries, but they are even less isolated and homogeneous today than they once were. The walls separating countries are battered and breached not only by trade and other forms of economic interaction but also by global media and communications systems, legions of travelers, extensive migration, international organizations, and global governance systems – including, of course, the international human rights system. The world long ago ceased to be comprised of separate "culture gardens" that are homogeneous, coherent, and integrated (Preis 1996: 288–9). Instead, cultures are bombarded by outside influences that lead to internal conflict and debates. Disagreement and conflict are part of culture (Preis 1996: 305). This is not to deny, of course, that there are dominant patterns of culture within most countries which help constitute a country's traditions, practices, and institutions.

I shall argue below that there is much more agreement worldwide about human rights than one might initially expect. But there is no doubt that there exists today significant normative disagreement about various features of human rights. Important areas of disagreement include:

- the importance of and appropriate qualifications to fundamental freedoms such as freedom of religion, expression, and association;

- the importance of rights of political participation and regular elections;
- whether social rights are genuine human rights;
- whether concern for social and economic equality is an appropriate concern of human rights;
- whether women's rights to nondiscrimination and social and economic equality are important human rights requiring immediate realization through government action;
- the importance of the rights of groups in thinking about human rights.

It is safe to say that in every country there is diversity of opinion about these questions. In particular countries one perspective on these questions may be by far the most popular, however, and it may be influenced by political and religious traditions or by economic circumstances. Countries with authoritarian political traditions may have political elites or popular majorities that are unenthusiastic about individual liberties and democratic institutions. Countries with very hierarchical religious traditions may have elites or popular majorities that are unenthusiastic about women's rights, rights of religious and ethnic minorities, and concern for social and economic equality. Countries whose traditions put great emphasis on the importance of community and belonging, particularly at the national level, may have political elites or popular majorities that are enthusiastic about democratic rights and group rights, but unenthusiastic about the fundamental freedoms (which they may consider excessively individualistic).

We now turn to eight arguments directed towards the cultural relativist. The first three responses attempt to attract the relativist to a human rights perspective. The second set continues that effort by showing how international human rights norms can accommodate a great deal of cultural and political diversity. The last two suggest that substantial acceptance of human rights now exists around the world, and that this acceptance makes irrelevant many relativist worries.

First Response: Human Rights Yield Far ——— Stronger Protections of Tolerance and ——— Security than Relativism can Support

Many people are attracted to cultural relativism because they think that it promotes tolerance, rejects imperialism and colonialist practices, and shows respect for other countries and cultures. After all, if people restrict the application of their own norms to their own countries or cultures, then they will not find any justification for imposing their own values and norms upon other cultures. Relativism produces tolerance. There may be some truth in this if we are looking at relativism and tolerance from a psychological perspective. It seems likely that people who are keenly aware of cultural and national differences, and who do not see any basis for extending norms across borders, will be inclined towards more tolerant attitudes than universalistic moral absolutists.

But from a logical perspective, relativism provides no support for tolerance across borders. If the culture of A-land fosters very intolerant attitudes towards the practices of other peoples, and citizens of A-land act intolerantly towards people from B-land, the A-landers are just following their own traditions and cultural norms. To the relativist, that is normal. Suppose that B-land has cultural and political traditions that are tolerant of other countries and cultures, and that our relativist is a native of B-land. Our relativist will not find it appropriate to criticize the intolerance of citizens of A-land because they are just following their longstanding cultural norms. To criticize the A-landers, people from B-land will have to endorse or presuppose a transnational principle of tolerance (see Talbott 2005: 43). And that transnational principle will go against the cultural traditions of some peoples and countries.

If relativists committed to tolerance recognize that there are likely to be occasions on which they will find it necessary to engage in transnational moral and political criticism, they should find attractive international human rights norms that prohibit genocide, prescribe security and nondiscrimination for minority cultures, endorse the self-determination of peoples, and combat racism.

Second Response: The Milder Forms of —— Relativism are Compatible with Thinking that —— at Least Some Human Rights are a Good Idea

A relativist does not need to be a total moral skeptic. She can believe that humans have some reliable abilities to arrive at useful practical norms. Neither the weak nor the strong forms of moral skepticism are proven true by the existence of important moral, political, and legal differences. The nonskeptic can respond that disagreement only shows that some people hold justified moral beliefs and others unjustified ones or, more plausibly, a mixture of the two. Disagreement does not show that reliable and rational methods of settling moral, political, and legal questions are unavailable or impossible. Some people may not know good methods, or they may be incapable of using them well because of bias, irrationality, or lack of knowledge about relevant facts.

Interestingly, the existence of complete agreement on moral issues worldwide would not disprove moral skepticism. That view could still be correct if agreement derived from irrational grounds and was impossible to justify by appeal to rational ones. Skeptics appeal to disagreement and nonskeptics to agreement as evidence for their views, but neither appeal is conclusive. The issue must be argued on other grounds.

One may hope to settle the matter in favor of skeptical relativism by arguing that if there were a rational method for settling moral disagreements everyone would know it or, at least, that moral philosophers would be able to specify its steps adequately. This argument does not work. It took millennia for human beings to develop rational methods for deciding disputes in scientific matters, and even now there are very significant disputes about the methods of physical sciences. Further, philosophers have offered numerous accounts of the grounds of practical knowledge and argumentation, one of which may be correct.

Cultural relativists tend to prefer that moral and legal norms be decided at the cultural or national level, but this preference is sure to require exceptions. Otherwise the relativist would have to disapprove of having a general criminal law in a multicultural society, and would have to object not just to international human rights but to international law generally. The superiority of indigenous standards is often exaggerated. We know from our own cultures that indigenous institutions often work badly and become outdated. Social and technological changes often make older norms and practices ill-suited to a group's needs. For example, when education and wide availability of electronic media make people more knowledgeable about politics and less willing to have no influence on important political decisions, the absence of even rudimentary democratic institutions becomes a problem. Further, one cannot assume that the existing norms and practices that violate human rights are in fact indigenous. They may themselves have been imported from other authoritarian or hierarchical countries.

The claim that imported standards generally function poorly or not at all is also an exaggeration. Many transplanted institutions and norms can function successfully, especially if a transition period is planned. The parliamentary institutions created in Japan after World War II are one striking example of successful transplantation. Borrowing between countries occurs constantly and ranges from social movements (for example, environmentalism, feminism), political institutions and law (for example, civil service systems, judicial review, ombudsmen, income tax, environmental law) to technology and economics (for example, assembly line production, computers, air transportation).

Third Response: A Strong Case for International Human Rights can be Made by Appealing to Widely Recognized Problems and Widely Shared Values

Many human rights problems come from the dangers of contemporary political and economic institutions. As we saw in Chapter 5, human rights are needed in all countries because the institutions of the modern state are now used everywhere and many human rights are socially learned remedies for the built-in dangers of these institutions. As Jack Donnelly says, "[T]he special threat to personal autonomy and equality presented by the modern state requires a set of legal rights, such as the presumption of innocence and rights to due process, fair and public hearings before an independent tribunal, and protection from arbitrary arrest, detention, or exile" (Donnelly 2003: 46 and 92). Differences in values and social traditions are less important than one might think.

As a humble analogy consider the rotary lawnmower, a motorized device with wheels that spins a blade parallel to the ground in order to cut grass. Rotary lawnmowers sometimes injure the operator's feet. The danger is inherent in the device and is realized everywhere the device is used. And people everywhere find cut-up feet to be a bad thing. So, if people in all countries use rotary lawnmowers, their dangers and remedies need to be taught everywhere. If this social learning first occurred in the countries where rotary mowers were first introduced, it was or would have been appropriate to spread its lessons around the world as soon as use of the device began to spread. This is analogous to the modern state, with its built-in dangers which need to be learned and remedied. Once the dangers and remedies have been learned, the lessons ought to be shared with all the users. Indeed, since the European colonial powers both developed and promoted the spread of the modern state, they have responsibilities to address its dangers. A recall of the product is not possible, but sharing the lessons about its dangers and remedies is.

This response to the relativist, with its focus on problems caused by the modern state, may not be useful in defending human rights that address problems that are more social or cultural than political. For example, many of the rights in the Convention on the Elimination of All Forms of Discrimination against Women address problems that are not primarily caused by the state. Parties to this treaty agree in Article 5 to "modify the social and cultural patterns of conduct of men and women, with a view to achieving the elimination of prejudices and

customary and all other practices which are based on the idea of the
inferiority or the superiority of either of the sexes or on stereotyped roles for
men and women." Doing this requires states to deal with problems such as
discrimination, trafficking in women, and denial of educational opportunities. The state's role here is as regulator rather than as the primary
source of the problems.

Fourth Response: Intervention is Not the Main Means of Promoting Human Rights

This is the first of three responses focusing on the ability of international
human rights norms to accommodate cultural and political diversity. This
response turns to the issue of imperialism. The ugliness and frequent inef-
fectiveness of international intervention to protect human rights often
leads people to its wholesale rejection (see Talbott 2005: 107). I agree
that coercive intervention is often likely to be unsuccessful, and emphasize that its costs are very high. It is because of the costs, dangers, and
low success rate of coercive intervention that the international human
rights movement has predominantly relied on persuasion and pressure
rather than coercion to promote human rights. I cannot, however,
endorse a wholesale rejection of international intervention to protect
human rights. I believe that some interventions have been necessary and
successful. These include sanctions against apartheid in South Africa, the
NATO intervention in Kosovo, and the intervention led by Australia in
East Timor. And I believe that some interventions did not occur when
they should have, a notable example being intervention to stop the 1994
genocide in Rwanda.

Still, as human rights function today within international organizations
it is just untrue to say that they are mainly about intervention. A better
description of their main role is that they encourage and pressure governments to treat their citizens humanely with respect for their lives, liberties, and equal citizenship. They use social pressure and acculturation
to promote acceptance and compliance with human rights norms (see
Goodman and Jinks 2004).

Because enforcement efforts are costly, dangerous, and often fail to work
it is reasonable to restrict their use to the most severe human rights crises.
These tend to be situations in which large numbers of people are being
killed. To avoid narrowing the human rights agenda to such crises, means
for promoting human rights have been devised that do not require intervention or the imposition of sanctions. These weaker means include educat-

ing governments and publics about international human rights standards, treaties that commit countries to human rights norms and require governments to make reports on their progress in realizing them, and nagging and shaming governments by NGOs, other governments, and international officials such as the UN High Commissioner for Human Rights.

Fifth Response: Human Rights —————— are Compatible with Great Cultural —————— and Political Diversity

Human rights are minimal standards open to interpretation at the national level. At the implementation stage countries can take local conditions into account in formulating their constitutional and legal rights. Formulations of human rights use broad language that allows considerable flexibility to interpretation and implementation at the national level. When human rights are enforced by courts, as they are under the European Convention on Human Rights (Council of Europe 1950), the scope allowed to local interpretation is constrained. But even there, accommodation is promoted by the "margin of appreciation" doctrine. It allows the Court to defer to national authorities in matters that are culturally sensitive (see Hartman 1981).

Human rights standards have a number of features allowing them to accommodate diversity. Perhaps the most obvious and important is limited scope – they provide minimal standards in a limited number of areas. For example, the rights one has as a homeowner, teacher, or union member depend not on human rights but on the morality, laws, and customs of one's country. It is possible, of course, that some of the rights found in the Universal Declaration and other human rights documents are insufficiently basic, and that if one wanted to preserve local flexibility against international human rights one would set the criterion for a "minimal standard" or "basic right" rather high (recall the discussion of Rawls in Chapter 6).

Second, the terms used in formulating human rights are often broad or abstract enough to allow considerable latitude to local interpretation. For example, article 10 of the Civil and Political Covenant requires that people in prison be "treated with humanity and with respect for the inherent dignity of the human person." This permits the operation of varying conceptions of human dignity. What counts as an indignity depends somewhat on how most people live and are treated and on what the local culture finds repulsive. If many people work in the fields pulling plows because there are no tractors or beasts of burden, then a punishment involving such work would be no indignity. But if such work is normally done by tractors, and only prisoners are required to pull plows, this may amount to a substantial indignity by suggesting that prisoners are mere beasts or machines.

Third, the possibility of overriding some human rights in emergency situations is explicitly allowed by major human rights treaties. For example, the European Convention allows countries to suspend some rights during "time of war or other public emergency threatening the life of the nation." These derogation clauses were discussed in Chapter 7.

Finally, the human rights movement has supported diversity within a structure of basic principles by endorsing the principle of self-determination and, in the UN Charter, the principle of nonintervention in matters essentially within the domestic jurisdiction of a state. It should be understood, however, that these principles are subject to some important qualifications. The domestic jurisdiction clause does not relieve a country of obligations undertaken in international law even if they pertain to domestic matters.

Sixth Response: Human Rights Collide ——— with Culture and Religion Much Less than ——— One Might Expect

Two beliefs that can collide, in the sense of one contradicting or excluding belief in the other, may fail to do so, or collide only rarely. Let's call this non-collision. For example, a Muslim immigrant to the United States may believe, as a religious ideal, that the US Constitution should be replaced by an Islamic constitution which makes Islamic law central to American life. But this ideal is so unlikely to be realized in the foreseeable future that he consigns it to the realm of things that are desirable in theory but which do not have much relevance to daily practice. Indeed, he may admire the US Constitution as a good, practical second best.

There are a number of sources of non-collision. One, just mentioned, is psychological or practical compartmentalization. People often put potentially conflicting beliefs in different realms. Many religious norms and ideals will be placed in the categories of religion and home and family, but be viewed as having limited relevance to current politics and business. Political and legal matters are often kept in their own realm. For example, a requirement that people receive fair trials when charged with a crime does not generally conflict with cultural values or religious beliefs since those values are unlikely to be focused on criminal trials.

A second explanation of why non-collision occurs is that people can agree on human rights without agreeing on the grounds of human rights. A libertarian may endorse the fundamental freedoms because they take seriously the separateness of persons, while a communitarian who rejects the separateness of persons may also endorse the basic liberties because he thinks they are as important to groups as they are to individuals (Buchanan 1989). And many people will not have fancy theoretical grounds for believing in human rights; they subscribe to them because their friends do or because they seem to work. Rawls's notion of an "overlapping consensus" is based on this; it allows people to support political principles for reasons that are rooted in their own religions, philosophies, and worldviews (Rawls 1993). But this is too ordinary a matter to require a fancy name. It is a commonplace of politics that people support beliefs and policies for different reasons. For most people, agreement on human rights is not agreement on a philosophy of human rights or a liberal political ideology. Just as people from different ideologies often accept the same political institutions with varying degrees of enthusiasm, people from different ideologies can accept most of the same human rights norms.

A third explanation of why non-collision occurs is that the cultural and religious views of many people are loosely organized rather than tightly systematized, held with the understanding that some competing considerations have to be accommodated, and viewed as ideals or duties with lots of exceptions rather than as categorical requirements. Another explanation of why non-collision occurs has already been mentioned. It is that human rights cover only a few areas of social and political practice and use terms that allow for local interpretation. They provide minimal standards in a limited number of areas.

If most human rights exhibit non-collision in relation to cultural and religious views, then the diversity of those views does not present a direct problem for most human rights. It will not be possible to infer rejection of human rights from the presence of widely accepted cultural and religious beliefs and practices that seem contrary to human rights. For example, the Buddhist belief that the self is ultimately illusory can often fail to collide with the view of human rights advocates that governments should respect the personal freedoms of their citizens.

It may be alleged that non-collision works only in liberal societies where politics and religion are separated. I doubt this, while allowing that non-collision is more likely when a significant degree of psychological and institutional separation exists between politics and local religions. Even in religiously ordered countries the limitations that religion places on political practices allow considerable flexibility in constitutional arrangements and in matters such as criminal law, due process, and punishment. Further, it cannot be assumed that people in strongly religious countries have no commitment to tolerance or want their religious leaders to be their political leaders.

Seventh Response: Human Rights Treaties Have Been Ratified by Most Governments

This is the first of two responses focusing on the acceptance of human rights by people and governments in all parts of the world. As of 2006, the Civil and Political Covenant has been ratified by 155 countries (out of a total of about 200), and the Social Covenant by 152. The Convention on the Elimination of All Forms of Discrimination against Women has been ratified by 180, and the Convention on the Rights of the Child by 192. Part of the explanation for these ratifications is the desire to look good internationally and the absence – in most cases – of irresistible pressure to comply with United Nations human rights treaties. But governments would not have accepted these treaties if they regarded their content as outlandish or totally alien to their visions of the future. Countries that ratify a treaty consent thereby to scrutiny and discussion of their practices.

Many countries have gone beyond ratifying international treaties to incorporate international human rights norms in their national constitutions, bills of rights, and legislation.

Eighth Response: Human Rights are Widely Accepted by Ordinary People Around the World

The best way to find out how much agreement and disagreement there is about international human rights is empirical; it involves, among other things, asking people what they think. I have lost confidence in our ability to project beliefs about human rights from what we think we know about people's cultures, religions, or national traditions. There are several reasons why such projections are risky. First, it may be that only part of the population holds those beliefs or adheres to those traditions. It's easy to exaggerate the uniformity of culture or religion. Second, people care about their culture, religion, and traditions, but these are not their only big concerns. Third, as we saw above, religious and cultural norms are often loosely applied; full and exact compliance may be unnecessary or too demanding for most people. Fourth, and also mentioned above, different areas of life are somewhat compartmentalized institutionally and psychologically. Fifth, most people know about the dangers of mixing religion and politics.

Polling and other empirical studies are needed to find out what people think about human rights. Such polling is starting to be done worldwide, and its results are sometimes surprising. For example, in a 2002 opinion poll in eight Arab countries, respondents were asked to rank, in order of importance, ten different political issues. "Civil and personal rights" received the highest score in all eight countries, coming in ahead of health care and Palestine (Zogby International 2002; see also Pew Research Centre 2003).

If we wanted to find out empirically whether human rights are accepted worldwide, what exactly would we need to investigate? One large question here is exactly what a person who accepts human rights must accept. This problem is analogous to the problem of determining the percentage of people in a country who accept a particular religion. How many of the religion's theological beliefs does an ordinary person need to endorse in order to accept the religion? Understanding worldwide acceptance requires us to analyze what acceptance is, which people must accept human rights, and what propositions about human rights they must endorse. In order to explain worldwide acceptance it will be necessary to explain *acceptance by a person* and *acceptance by a country.*

To accept a norm is to believe in its validity or to have favorable attitudes towards its adoption and use. Sincere acceptance is compatible with having some worries about the norm, or with limited enthusiasm for it. Opinion polls accommodate this by allowing people to choose between strongly agree and agree. Acceptance of a norm is not the same as always complying with a norm. As those who have struggled against temptation know, people frequently violate norms that they sincerely accept. And accepting a norm does not require that one has any particular reasons for one's acceptance.

How many people need to accept human rights for worldwide acceptance? We could give a simple majoritarian answer requiring that more than 50 percent of the world's competent adults accept human rights. But this answer would allow for the possibility that there is one-half of the world where nearly everyone accepts human rights and another half where few people do. To avoid that possibility, let's use a country-by-country approach and require that a majority of people in almost all countries accept human rights. Acceptance in a country exists when the appropriate number of people in the country agree with human rights norms. And acceptance in the world exists when almost all of the world's countries accept human rights.

One could answer the "Which people?" question by giving a special place to the opinions of people, such as political leaders and public intellectuals, who are well placed to influence government policies on human rights, or to officials, such as soldiers and police officers, who are in position to violate human rights. I will not take this approach since acceptance by an elite, however influential or practically important, does not constitute general acceptance. Nevertheless, it will be useful for many purposes to have statistics about which subgroups within society accept and reject human rights.

It is hard to decide which beliefs about human rights a person needs to have to be counted as believing in human rights. There are limits to what ordinary people can be expected to understand about human rights. Articulate acceptance of a complex conception of human rights by ordinary people is not a plausible expectation. Most people have never thought about what a right is, how rights relate to duties and powers, who the addressees of human rights are, or about the high priority of rights. If the acceptance of human rights requires that ordinary people have complicated understandings of human rights and their place in morality and international law we will find that few ordinary people accept human rights.

Suppose we could ask a person about a dozen questions to determine if she accepted human rights. Which questions should we ask? I propose two sorts of questions. The first kind pertains to the general idea of human rights. For example, does the person have the idea that there should be minimal international standards that apply to people everywhere? The second kind of question pertains to whether a person accepts the kinds of specific norms that are found in contemporary human rights declarations and treaties.

Let's start with the general idea of human rights. I propose to represent this general idea with questions pertaining to (1) universality; (2) high priority; and (3) associated duties. Universality might be tested by propositions such as:

- All people everywhere ought to enjoy decent treatment by governments and societies.
- Rights to life and security are protections that nobody should be denied.

To these propositions people would be asked to indicate whether they strongly disagree, disagree, agree, strongly agree, or have no opinion.

The idea that human rights are mandatory or duty-generating may be tested by propositions such as:

- It is generally wrong for governments to violate human rights such as the right against torture and the right to a fair trial.
- The responsibilities of governments include respecting and protecting people's human rights.

Belief in the high priority of human rights will be tested by formulating propositions about specific rights, or families of rights, as questions about importance. For example, a question about the right to life would be formulated as: "It is very important that people enjoy protections against being killed without trial by agents of the state."

Next we can turn to testing for beliefs about specific human rights. The requirement I propose is that we test for acceptance of representative examples of rights from all of the six families of human rights. These six families are security rights, due process rights, liberty rights, rights of political participation, equality rights, and welfare rights. To illustrate this, here are five propositions to which people could indicate that they strongly disagree, disagree, agree, strongly agree, or have no opinion.

- It is very important that governments refrain from and protect all people against arbitrary execution and torture.
- It is very important that governments ensure that all people charged with crimes receive a fair trial.
- It is very important that governments respect and protect everyone's rights of political participation such as voting and engaging in political movements and campaigns.
- It is very important that governments respect and protect everyone's equality before the law and freedom from discrimination on grounds such as race, sex, or religion.
- It is imperative that governments take steps to ensure that all people have access to basic material needs such as food and shelter and that all children have access to education.

My proposal, then, is that our questions include some that concern the general idea of human rights, and others that are about the main families of particular human rights.

To accept human rights a person would need to accept most of the items in each group. Thus, if a person agreed to most of the dozen propositions about human rights, including most of the ones about the general conception of human rights and most of the ones about specific rights, I would count that person as accepting human rights.

It is obvious that certain questions are more important than others in determining belief in human rights. Believing in the right to life, for example, is more important than believing in the right to freedom of political participation. But I propose not to make any one question the touchstone of believing in human rights. It is hard to identify such propositions, and it is even harder to formulate questions in such a way that a person who believed in human rights might not nevertheless find things in them to disagree with. For example, a person much preoccupied with crime might disagree with "It is generally wrong for governments to violate human rights such as the right against torture and the right to a fair trial" because it contains no exception permitting the severe punishment of rapists and murderers.

Note that under this sketch of what acceptance means there are lots of things that people do not need to accept in order to accept human rights. They do not have to accept any particular reasons for human rights, much less a liberal political ideology. They do not have to accept any precise conception of what a right is. They do not have to distinguish between moral and legal norms. And they do not need to have views about the international enforcement of human rights. But the formulation of the test does incorporate the universality, mandatory character, and high priority of human rights.

If a person agreed to most of the dozen propositions about human rights in the way described above, I would count that person as accepting human rights. If, apart from those with no opinion, a majority of competent adults in a country were like the person just described, then I would count that country as accepting human rights. And if almost all countries accepted human rights, then worldwide acceptance of human rights would exist. Note that this describes a world in which there could – and probably would – still be lots of disagreement about human rights among intellectuals, politicians, and ordinary people.

Statistical representations of the results of conducting in all countries an opinion poll similar to the one described above would be much more informative than the simple notion of general acceptance that I have defined. Polling data would tell us which rights, and ideas of rights, were accepted by what percentage of people in each country, and would correlate acceptance of each item with variables such as religion, age, sex, ethnicity, religion, level of education, occupation, and political outlook. The data would also tell us about acceptance of human rights by intellectual and political elites.

One might think that the world has far too many human rights problems for worldwide acceptance, or some near approximation of it, to exist. If most people in almost all countries accepted human rights in the sense defined, surely there would not be the political and human rights problems that we have at present. This overlooks the fact that rejection of human rights is not the only obstacle to their realization. Even in countries where a majority now accepts human rights, severe social and political problems can remain. Acceptance of human rights, in the sense defined, can exist in countries in which large and influential minorities of people and leaders do not accept human rights. Because large numbers of people do not participate in the consensus, they may be sources of rejectionist ideas, political insurgencies, ethnic hatreds, terrorism, and the like. Higher levels of acceptance diminish but may not remove this possibility.

Further, large gaps between accepted norms and actual practices may exist. People and governments frequently fail to live up to their human rights beliefs, just as they often fail to live up to their religious and ethical beliefs. And government leaders often fail to bring political and legal institutions into line with human rights. Beyond this, all sorts of disagreements about matters not fully covered by human rights may exist among those who accept human rights. Big disagreements about territory, historic injustices, terrorism, and various political and economic arrangements may still exist.

Finally, many countries will still be poor and troubled. Perhaps their problems will take more peaceful forms if most people accept human rights, but not necessarily. Thugs who do not believe in human rights may still be able to take over the government of a country, loot its resources, and kill and rape its people.

Even though worldwide acceptance of human rights is unlikely to solve many of the world's problems, there are clearly ways in which worldwide acceptance will improve matters. First, political discourse among governments and peoples will often be guided by shared norms, and democratic support will more often be available for government actions to respect, protect, provide for, or promote human rights. Policies such as genocide and ethnic cleansing will be off the table in most countries, particularly those in which 80 or 90 percent of people accept human rights. Second, efforts to promote and protect human rights by international organizations are less likely to be blocked by deep disagreements (as they were during the Cold War) and more likely to be based on consensus. Third, worries about the legitimacy of international efforts to promote and protect human rights will be reduced. Finally, it will be harder to demonize countries and peoples if we know that large majorities in them accept human rights.

Overview

The argument of this chapter has been, first, that there is much in today's lists of human rights that should be attractive to people, including those inclined towards relativism, who care deeply about the survival and independence of distinctive cultures and peoples. Second, it was shown how international human rights norms can accommodate a great deal of cultural and political diversity. Finally, it was suggested that relativists and others take seriously the possibility that substantial acceptance of human rights already exists around the world.

Further Reading

Baderin, M. 2005. "Human Rights and Islamic Law: The Myth of Discord." *European Human Rights Law Review* 2: 165–85.

Bauer, J., and Bell, D. (eds.) 1999. *The East Asian Challenge for Human Rights*. Cambridge: Cambridge University Press.

Bell, D. 2000. *East Meets West: Human Rights and Democracy in East Asia*. Princeton, NJ: Princeton University Press.

Brackney, W. (series editor) 2004. *Human Rights and the World's Major Religions*, vol. 1: *The Jewish Tradition*, ed. P. Hass; vol. 2: *The Christian Tradition*, ed. W. Brackney; vol. 3: *The Islamic Tradition*, ed. M. Abd al-Rahim; vol. 4: *The Hindu Tradition*, ed. H. Coward; vol. 5: *The Buddhist Tradition*, ed. R. Florida. Westport, CT: Praeger.

Cowan, J., Dembour, M., and Wilson, R. (eds.) 2001. *Culture and Rights: Anthropological Perspectives*. Cambridge: Cambridge University Press.

Evans, M., and Murray, R. (eds.) 2002. *The African Charter on Human and People's Rights: The System in Practice, 1986–2000*. Cambridge: Cambridge University Press.

Preis, A. 1996. "Human Rights as Cultural Practice: An Anthropological Critique." *Human Rights Quarterly* 18: 286–315.

Talbott, W. 2005. *Which Rights Should be Universal?* Oxford: Oxford University Press.

Wilson, R. (ed.) 1997. *Human Rights, Culture and Context: Anthropological Perspectives*. London: Pluto Press.

Chapter 12

The Good Sense in Human Rights

This book has defended the contemporary conception of human rights by arguing that the human rights found in the Universal Declaration and subsequent treaties are generally plausible and are supported by attractive and widely accepted values. Human rights draw on historic ideas of justice and natural rights, but they are applications of those and other ideas in service of the contemporary project of preventing governments from doing terrible things to their people and thereby promoting international peace and security. They limit national sovereignty by making how a state treats its residents a matter of international scrutiny and concern. Widespread, if not worldwide, acceptance of human rights has occurred.

Is Talk about Human Rights Just Empty Rhetoric?

Because rights are usually powerful considerations, the language of rights is attractive to people engaged in political argument. Many theorists have worried that the extensive use of the concept of rights in exaggerated political rhetoric would soon destroy the concept's usefulness. But susceptibility to exaggeration and distortion is a frailty found in all normative concepts, not just the concept of rights. For example, repressive regimes on both the left and the right frequently offer reinterpretations of the idea of democracy to support their practices. The concept of democracy, like most normative concepts, is vague and open to distortion. But it is far from useless nonetheless. Vagueness is not emptiness, and it is possible to resist wholesale extensions of important concepts. Legal formulations of rights help do this.

Viewing human rights as protections of a decent or minimally good life provides another way of resisting exaggerations. Human rights do not require everything that might contribute to making a life good or excellent. Other concepts are available for talking about the requirements of excellence and for dealing with issues that human rights do not cover. The concept of human rights does not need to encompass every important dimension of social and political criticism.

Another way to resist exaggerated claims about rights is to insist that a right is an entitlement-plus. Justifying a right to something requires more than merely showing the great importance of people's having access to a good. It also requires showing the availability of a feasible and morally acceptable way of imposing duties and constructing institutions that will make it possible to supply that good to all people. A broad notion of feasibility must restrain the formulation and implementation of specific human rights. In estimating feasibility, not all existing economic relations need be taken as given; indeed, implementing human rights often requires changes in economic structures. When an internationally recognized human right is implemented at the national level, its costs must be considered in determining the scope of the associated legal right and the sorts of enforcement or other forms of implementation provided for it.

Do We Have a Plausible List of Human Rights?

Different people (and peoples) often have different conceptions of the threats that specific rights should address and different views about the underlying normative grounds for human rights. To overcome that disagreement theorists work up views of the grounds for human rights. I have attempted to do that in this book. But normative theory seldom produces general agreement, especially when we get down to details. Law helps settle through enactment and convention what abstract reasoning leaves in dispute. The Universal Declaration and subsequent treaties provide an established and largely settled list of human rights. Although there is no reason to view that list as sacrosanct, it gives more determinate meaning to the contemporary idea of human rights than normative theory alone can provide. The theoretical and practical approaches come together when lawyers and politicians achieve a result that is within the range that normative theory can endorse. This book has defended the optimistic view that the Universal Declaration and subsequent treaties provide us with a list of human rights that, for the most part, is normatively defensible.

The Universal Declaration's list of human rights has often been criticized for including social rights. Although I believe that the Universal Declaration's list of social rights is too long, this is no reason for jettisoning all social rights. What the Universal Declaration got right, in my view, is that people have a strong claim to assistance in obtaining the material conditions of a decent life when their own reasonable efforts prove insufficient. I proposed a modest conception of social rights – the Vance Conception – and argued that rights to subsistence, basic medical services, and basic education are justifiable as human rights

Human rights also include minority rights. Minority rights emphasize that minorities have human rights like everyone else, but they do not stop there. They also focus on specific problems that particular groups suffer and prescribe specific rights as protections on either a general or "when appropriate" basis. There is no barrier to viewing minority rights of this sort as part of the family of human rights so long as they are rooted in the same values as other human rights and prescribe similar sorts of remedies.

Are Legal Rights the Only Genuine Rights?

Rights are complex norms with holders, addressees, scopes, and weights. Because they are mandatory and have addressees, rights are the sorts of norms that can be demanded or claimed by their holders and others. Fully specified rights are capable of giving precise guidance to behavior; this capacity makes them very useful in law and well suited to legal enforcement.

Many people take legal rights as their paradigms of rights. If legal rights provide the model, moral rights may be thought of as phony rights, as lacking key features that real rights have. Prior to the implementation of human rights in international law, this view might have led to their rejection. Today, however, human rights exist in international law through widely accepted treaties, which makes it possible for those who deny the existence of nonlegal rights to endorse human rights as legal rights. A stronger account of the universality of human rights views them as existing, most fundamentally, as moral rights within justified moralities. Human rights are norms that we have good reasons for retaining in or adding to existing moralities. Legal enforcement is often essential to the effectiveness of human rights, but such enforcement is not essential to their existence.

Can Human Rights be Justified?

Today's human rights are descendants of, but different from, the broad natural rights of the eighteenth century. Not only are contemporary human rights more specific than natural rights and clearly international in their reach; they are more egalitarian and less individualistic as well. They function as middle-level norms, derived from more basic and abstract moral and political considerations. They identify specific areas in which powerful normative considerations impose responsibilities on governments, international institutions, and individuals.

Defending this conception of human rights requires at least two steps. One involves arguing that there are plausible abstract grounds for human rights. The second step involves showing that these abstract grounds support specific human rights such as the right to a fair trial or a right to freedom of assembly.

The first step was addressed in Chapter 4, where I argued that human rights can be defended from several starting points. From the perspective of individual prudence, protections for one's fundamental interests are attractive if their costs are not too high. This mode of reasoning may not reach universal human rights, but it gets one somewhere in the vicinity. When we move to the moral point of view, providing protections for each person's most fundamental interests is a central concern. I interpreted the idea of fundamental human interests as giving every person secure moral claims to have a life, to lead one's life, against severe cruelty, and against severe unfairness.

The second step, namely showing that these abstract considerations support specific human rights, was addressed in Chapter 5, where it was suggested that the derivation of a specific political right requires satisfying six tests. The first two tests require showing that the specific right protects something of great importance against significant threats. Third, we need to decide whether the proposed norm can be formulated as a right of all people today. Fourth, we need to show that a specific political right, rather than some weaker norm, is necessary to the protection of the important interest against some substantial threat. Fifth, we need to show that the normative burdens imposed by the right are tolerable and can be equitably distributed. Finally, we need to show that a specific political right is feasible in an ample majority of countries.

———— Can Human Rights Guide Behavior? ————

The scopes of human rights often provide fairly clear guidance to their addressees but usually do not specify what victims of violations may do to defend themselves, how persons other than the addressees should respond to violations, or how governments should respond to violations in other countries. In deciding what should be done in these instances, considerations about relevant rights play a central but partial role. These decisions require looking back to the abstract moral considerations that underlie specific human rights, sideways to moral considerations other than human rights, and forward to the likely consequences of actions and policies designed to promote respect for human rights. Human rights provide guidance to thoughtful policy deliberation, but they are not a substitute for it.

———— Do Human Rights Make Any Difference? ————

People who thought that the Universal Declaration and the subsequent human rights treaties would transform the world into a far better place within, say, 50 years would have been badly disappointed at the turn of this century. Human rights problems existed in every country, and many countries had very severe problems. Large-scale genocide had been repeated in Rwanda, and the wars following the break-up of Yugoslavia involved ethnic cleansing and other horrible war crimes. And many governments today are oppressive, undemocratic, corrupt, disorganized, and inefficient.

The first 50 years of the human rights movement were much less than ideal for making progress since 45 of those years coincided with the Cold War. With the end in the early 1990s of that ideological struggle, the development of human rights institutions accelerated. Still, a reasonable worry is that the human world on planet Earth is too tough a place for human rights to do much good. Further, the limits of using international law to force countries to behave well are apparent. In most areas, countries can defy international human rights law without facing intolerable pressure from international institutions or other countries.

A reply to this worry should not minimize the world's problems or the difficulties of achieving the political and social reforms human rights require. A tough situation is nothing new. The people who created the human rights movement after World War II were in an even tougher situation, yet they believed that they had a chance to create a better-organized international society that would promote better government, respect for people's rights, and diminish the chances of major war.

The human rights project continues and has not failed. Human rights have become part of the currency of international relations, and most countries participate in treaty arrangements that nudge them in the direction of addressing their human rights problems. The European and Inter-American human rights courts have shown that it is possible to enforce human rights internationally through adjudication. The role of the United Nations in promoting human rights and dealing with human rights crises has expanded and improved. And in nearly all countries there are non-governmental organizations, international and local, that promote respect for human rights, criticize violations, and help to ameliorate human rights crises.

Without denying that the human rights project could ultimately fail, I am moderately optimistic. The human rights movement has come much farther since 1948 than I would have dared to predict 30 years ago. Almost all countries now participate in international human rights treaties. Human rights ideas, including equal rights for women and minorities, have gained acceptance in many parts of the world. Realizing human rights is a project for centuries, not decades, and there will always be human rights problems. Still, the widespread acceptance and realization of human rights has ceased to be a utopian idea.

Appendix 1

Universal Declaration of Human Rights

Preamble

Whereas recognition of the inherent dignity and of the equal and inalienable rights of all members of the human family is the foundation of freedom, justice and peace in the world,

Whereas disregard and contempt for human rights have resulted in barbarous acts which have outraged the conscience of mankind, and the advent of a world in which human beings shall enjoy freedom of speech and belief and freedom from fear and want has been proclaimed as the highest aspiration of the common people,

Whereas it is essential, if man is not to be compelled to have recourse, as a last resort, to rebellion against tyranny and oppression, that human rights should be protected by the rule of law,

Whereas it is essential to promote the development of friendly relations between nations,

Whereas the peoples of the United Nations have in the Charter reaffirmed their faith in fundamental human rights, in the dignity and worth of the human person and in the equal rights of men and women and have determined to promote social progress and better standards of life in larger freedom,

Whereas Member States have pledged themselves to achieve, in co-operation with the United Nations, the promotion of universal respect for and observance of human rights and fundamental freedoms,

Whereas a common understanding of these rights and freedoms is of the greatest importance for the full realization of this pledge,

Now, Therefore THE GENERAL ASSEMBLY proclaims THIS UNIVERSAL DECLARATION OF HUMAN RIGHTS as a common standard of achievement for all peoples and all nations, to the end that every individual and every organ of society, keeping this Declaration constantly in mind, shall strive by teaching and education to promote respect for these rights and freedoms and by progressive measures, national and international, to secure their universal and effective recognition and observance, both among the peoples of Member States themselves and among the peoples of territories under their jurisdiction.

Article 1

All human beings are born free and equal in dignity and rights. They are endowed with reason and conscience and should act towards one another in a spirit of brotherhood.

Article 2

Everyone is entitled to all the rights and freedoms set forth in this Declaration, without distinction of any kind, such as race, colour, sex, language, religion, political or other opinion, national or social origin, property, birth or other status. Furthermore, no distinction shall be made on the basis of the political, jurisdictional or international status of the country or territory to which a person belongs, whether it be independent, trust, non-self-governing or under any other limitation of sovereignty.

Article 3

Everyone has the right to life, liberty and security of person.

Article 4

No one shall be held in slavery or servitude; slavery and the slave trade shall be prohibited in all their forms.

Article 5

No one shall be subjected to torture or to cruel, inhuman or degrading treatment or punishment.

Article 6

Everyone has the right to recognition everywhere as a person before the law.

Article 7

All are equal before the law and are entitled without any discrimination to equal protection of the law. All are entitled to equal protection against any discrimination in violation of this Declaration and against any incitement to such discrimination.

Article 8

Everyone has the right to an effective remedy by the competent national tribunals for acts violating the fundamental rights granted him by the constitution or by law.

Article 9

No one shall be subjected to arbitrary arrest, detention or exile.

Article 10

Everyone is entitled in full equality to a fair and public hearing by an independent and impartial tribunal, in the determination of his rights and obligations and of any criminal charge against him.

Article 11

(1) Everyone charged with a penal offence has the right to be presumed innocent until proved guilty according to law in a public trial at which he has had all the guarantees necessary for his defence.
(2) No one shall be held guilty of any penal offence on account of any act or omission which did not constitute a penal offence, under national or international law, at the time when it was committed. Nor shall a heavier penalty be imposed than the one that was applicable at the time the penal offence was committed.

Article 12

No one shall be subjected to arbitrary interference with his privacy, family, home or correspondence, nor to attacks upon his honour and reputation. Everyone has the right to the protection of the law against such interference or attacks.

Article 13

(1) Everyone has the right to freedom of movement and residence within the borders of each state.
(2) Everyone has the right to leave any country, including his own, and to return to his country.

Article 14

(1) Everyone has the right to seek and to enjoy in other countries asylum from persecution.
(2) This right may not be invoked in the case of prosecutions genuinely arising from non-political crimes or from acts contrary to the purposes and principles of the United Nations.

Article 15

(1) Everyone has the right to a nationality.
(2) No one shall be arbitrarily deprived of his nationality nor denied the right to change his nationality.

Article 16

(1) Men and women of full age, without any limitation due to race, nationality or religion, have the right to marry and to found a family. They are entitled to equal rights as to marriage, during marriage and at its dissolution.
(2) Marriage shall be entered into only with the free and full consent of the intending spouses.
(3) The family is the natural and fundamental group unit of society and is entitled to protection by society and the State.

Article 17

(1) Everyone has the right to own property alone as well as in association with others.
(2) No one shall be arbitrarily deprived of his property.

Article 18

Everyone has the right to freedom of thought, conscience and religion; this right includes freedom to change his religion or belief, and freedom, either alone or in community with others and in public or private, to manifest his religion or belief in teaching, practice, worship and observance.

Article 19

Everyone has the right to freedom of opinion and expression; this right includes freedom to hold opinions without interference and to seek, receive and impart information and ideas through any media and regardless of frontiers.

Article 20

(1) Everyone has the right to freedom of peaceful assembly and association.
(2) No one may be compelled to belong to an association.

Article 21

(1) Everyone has the right to take part in the government of his country, directly or through freely chosen representatives.
(2) Everyone has the right of equal access to public service in his country.
(3) The will of the people shall be the basis of the authority of government; this will shall be expressed in periodic and genuine elections which shall be by universal and equal suffrage and shall be held by secret vote or by equivalent free voting procedures.

Article 22

Everyone, as a member of society, has the right to social security and is entitled to realization, through national effort and international co-operation and in accordance with the organization and resources of each State, of the economic, social and cultural rights indispensable for his dignity and the free development of his personality.

Article 23

(1) Everyone has the right to work, to free choice of employment, to just and favourable conditions of work and to protection against unemployment.
(2) Everyone, without any discrimination, has the right to equal pay for equal work.
(3) Everyone who works has the right to just and favourable remuneration ensuring for himself and his family an existence worthy of human dignity, and supplemented, if necessary, by other means of social protection.

(4) Everyone has the right to form and to join trade unions for the protection of his interests.

Article 24

Everyone has the right to rest and leisure, including reasonable limitation of working hours and periodic holidays with pay.

Article 25

(1) Everyone has the right to a standard of living adequate for the health and well-being of himself and of his family, including food, clothing, housing and medical care and necessary social services, and the right to security in the event of unemployment, sickness, disability, widowhood, old age or other lack of livelihood in circumstances beyond his control.
(2) Motherhood and childhood are entitled to special care and assistance. All children, whether born in or out of wedlock, shall enjoy the same social protection.

Article 26

(1) Everyone has the right to education. Education shall be free, at least in the elementary and fundamental stages. Elementary education shall be compulsory. Technical and professional education shall be made generally available and higher education shall be equally accessible to all on the basis of merit.
(2) Education shall be directed to the full development of the human personality and to the strengthening of respect for human rights and fundamental freedoms. It shall promote understanding, tolerance and friendship among all nations, racial or religious groups, and shall further the activities of the United Nations for the maintenance of peace.
(3) Parents have a prior right to choose the kind of education that shall be given to their children.

Article 27

(1) Everyone has the right freely to participate in the cultural life of the community, to enjoy the arts and to share in scientific advancement and its benefits.
(2) Everyone has the right to the protection of the moral and material interests resulting from any scientific, literary or artistic production of which he is the author.

Article 28

Everyone is entitled to a social and international order in which the rights and freedoms set forth in this Declaration can be fully realized.

Article 29

(1) Everyone has duties to the community in which alone the free and full development of his personality is possible.
(2) In the exercise of his rights and freedoms, everyone shall be subject only to such limitations as are determined by law solely for the purpose of securing due recognition and respect for the rights and freedoms of others and of meeting the just requirements of morality, public order and the general welfare in a democratic society.
(3) These rights and freedoms may in no case be exercised contrary to the purposes and principles of the United Nations.

Article 30

Nothing in this Declaration may be interpreted as implying for any State, group or person any right to engage in any activity or to perform any act aimed at the destruction of any of the rights and freedoms set forth herein.

Appendix 2

The European Convention for the Protection of Human Rights and Fundamental Freedoms

As amended by Protocol No. 11

The governments signatory hereto, being members of the Council of Europe,

Considering the Universal Declaration of Human Rights proclaimed by the General Assembly of the United Nations on 10th December 1948;

Considering that this Declaration aims at securing the universal and effective recognition and observance of the Rights therein declared;

Considering that the aim of the Council of Europe is the achievement of greater unity between its members and that one of the methods by which that aim is to be pursued is the maintenance and further realisation of human rights and fundamental freedoms;

Reaffirming their profound belief in those fundamental freedoms which are the foundation of justice and peace in the world and are best maintained on the one hand by an effective political democracy and on the other by a common understanding and observance of the human rights upon which they depend;

Being resolved, as the governments of European countries which are like-minded and have a common heritage of political traditions, ideals, freedom and the rule of law, to take the first steps for the collective enforcement of certain of the rights stated in the Universal Declaration,

Have agreed as follows:

Article 1: Obligation to respect human rights

The High Contracting Parties shall secure to everyone within their jurisdiction the rights and freedoms defined in Section I of this Convention.

Section I

Article 2: Right to life

1. Everyone's right to life shall be protected by law. No one shall be deprived of his life intentionally save in the execution of a sentence of a court following his conviction of a crime for which this penalty is provided by law.
2. Deprivation of life shall not be regarded as inflicted in contravention of this article when it results from the use of force which is no more than absolutely necessary:
   a. in defence of any person from unlawful violence;
   b. in order to effect a lawful arrest or to prevent the escape of a person lawfully detained;
   c. in action lawfully taken for the purpose of quelling a riot or insurrection.

Article 3: Prohibition of torture

No one shall be subjected to torture or to inhuman or degrading treatment or punishment.

Article 4: Prohibition of slavery and forced labour

1. No one shall be held in slavery or servitude.
2. No one shall be required to perform forced or compulsory labour.
3. For the purpose of this article the term "forced or compulsory labour" shall not include:
   a. any work required to be done in the ordinary course of detention imposed according to the provisions of Article 5 of this Convention or during conditional release from such detention;
   b. any service of a military character or, in case of conscientious objectors in countries where they are recognised, service exacted instead of compulsory military service;
   c. any service exacted in case of an emergency or calamity threatening the life or well-being of the community;
   d. any work or service which forms part of normal civic obligations.

Article 5: Right to liberty and security

1. Everyone has the right to liberty and security of person. No one shall be deprived of his liberty save in the following cases and in accordance with a procedure prescribed by law:
   a. the lawful detention of a person after conviction by a competent court;
   b. the lawful arrest or detention of a person for non-compliance with the lawful order of a court or in order to secure the fulfilment of any obligation prescribed by law;
   c. the lawful arrest or detention of a person effected for the purpose of bringing him before the competent legal authority on reasonable suspicion of having committed an offence or when it is reasonably considered necessary to prevent his committing an offence or fleeing after having done so;
   d. the detention of a minor by lawful order for the purpose of educational supervision or his lawful detention for the purpose of bringing him before the competent legal authority;
   e. the lawful detention of persons for the prevention of the spreading of infectious diseases, of persons of unsound mind, alcoholics or drug addicts or vagrants;
   f. the lawful arrest or detention of a person to prevent his effecting an unauthorised entry into the country or of a person against whom action is being taken with a view to deportation or extradition.
2. Everyone who is arrested shall be informed promptly, in a language which he understands, of the reasons for his arrest and of any charge against him.
3. Everyone arrested or detained in accordance with the provisions of paragraph 1.c of this article shall be brought promptly before a judge or other officer authorised by law to exercise judicial power and shall be entitled to trial within a reasonable time or to release pending trial. Release may be conditioned by guarantees to appear for trial.
4. Everyone who is deprived of his liberty by arrest or detention shall be entitled to take proceedings by which the lawfulness of his detention shall be decided speedily by a court and his release ordered if the detention is not lawful.
5. Everyone who has been the victim of arrest or detention in contravention of the provisions of this article shall have an enforceable right to compensation.

Article 6: Right to a fair trial

1. In the determination of his civil rights and obligations or of any criminal charge against him, everyone is entitled to a fair and public hearing within a reasonable time by an independent and impartial tribunal established by law. Judgment shall be pronounced publicly but the press and public may be excluded from all or part of the trial in the interests of morals, public order or national security in a democratic society, where the interests of juveniles or the protection of the private life of the parties so require, or to the extent strictly necessary in the opinion of the court in special circumstances where publicity would prejudice the interests of justice.

2. Everyone charged with a criminal offence shall be presumed innocent until proved guilty according to law.
3. Everyone charged with a criminal offence has the following minimum rights:
   a. to be informed promptly, in a language which he understands and in detail, of the nature and cause of the accusation against him;
   b. to have adequate time and facilities for the preparation of his defence;
   c. to defend himself in person or through legal assistance of his own choosing or, if he has not sufficient means to pay for legal assistance, to be given it free when the interests of justice so require;
   d. to examine or have examined witnesses against him and to obtain the attendance and examination of witnesses on his behalf under the same conditions as witnesses against him;
   e. to have the free assistance of an interpreter if he cannot understand or speak the language used in court.

Article 7: No punishment without law

1. No one shall be held guilty of any criminal offence on account of any act or omission which did not constitute a criminal offence under national or international law at the time when it was committed. Nor shall a heavier penalty be imposed than the one that was applicable at the time the criminal offence was committed.
2. This article shall not prejudice the trial and punishment of any person for any act or omission which, at the time when it was committed, was criminal according to the general principles of law recognised by civilised nations.

Article 8: Right to respect for private and family life

1. Everyone has the right to respect for his private and family life, his home and his correspondence.
2. There shall be no interference by a public authority with the exercise of this right except such as is in accordance with the law and is necessary in a democratic society in the interests of national security, public safety or the economic well-being of the country, for the prevention of disorder or crime, for the protection of health or morals, or for the protection of the rights and freedoms of others.

Article 9: Freedom of thought, conscience and religion

1. Everyone has the right to freedom of thought, conscience and religion; this right includes freedom to change his religion or belief and freedom, either alone or in community with others and in public or private, to manifest his religion or belief, in worship, teaching, practice and observance.

2. Freedom to manifest one's religion or beliefs shall be subject only to such limitations as are prescribed by law and are necessary in a democratic society in the interests of public safety, for the protection of public order, health or morals, or for the protection of the rights and freedoms of others.

Article 10: Freedom of expression

1. Everyone has the right to freedom of expression. This right shall include freedom to hold opinions and to receive and impart information and ideas without interference by public authority and regardless of frontiers. This article shall not prevent States from requiring the licensing of broadcasting, television or cinema enterprises.
2. The exercise of these freedoms, since it carries with it duties and responsibilities, may be subject to such formalities, conditions, restrictions or penalties as are prescribed by law and are necessary in a democratic society, in the interests of national security, territorial integrity or public safety, for the prevention of disorder or crime, for the protection of health or morals, for the protection of the reputation or rights of others, for preventing the disclosure of information received in confidence, or for maintaining the authority and impartiality of the judiciary.

Article 11: Freedom of assembly and association

1. Everyone has the right to freedom of peaceful assembly and to freedom of association with others, including the right to form and to join trade unions for the protection of his interests.
2. No restrictions shall be placed on the exercise of these rights other than such as are prescribed by law and are necessary in a democratic society in the interests of national security or public safety, for the prevention of disorder or crime, for the protection of health or morals or for the protection of the rights and freedoms of others. This article shall not prevent the imposition of lawful restrictions on the exercise of these rights by members of the armed forces, of the police or of the administration of the State.

Article 12: Right to marry

Men and women of marriageable age have the right to marry and to found a family, according to the national laws governing the exercise of this right.

Article 13: Right to an effective remedy

Everyone whose rights and freedoms as set forth in this Convention are violated shall have an effective remedy before a national authority notwithstanding that the violation has been committed by persons acting in an official capacity.

Article 14: Prohibition of discrimination

The enjoyment of the rights and freedoms set forth in this Convention shall be secured without discrimination on any ground such as sex, race, colour, language, religion, political or other opinion, national or social origin, association with a national minority, property, birth or other status.

Article 15: Derogation in time of emergency

1. In time of war or other public emergency threatening the life of the nation any High Contracting Party may take measures derogating from its obligations under this Convention to the extent strictly required by the exigencies of the situation, provided that such measures are not inconsistent with its other obligations under international law.
2. No derogation from Article 2, except in respect of deaths resulting from lawful acts of war, or from Articles 3, 4 (paragraph 1) and 7 shall be made under this provision.
3. Any High Contracting Party availing itself of this right of derogation shall keep the Secretary General of the Council of Europe fully informed of the measures which it has taken and the reasons therefore. It shall also inform the Secretary General of the Council of Europe when such measures have ceased to operate and the provisions of the Convention are again being fully executed.

Article 16: Restrictions on political activity of aliens

Nothing in Articles 10, 11 and 14 shall be regarded as preventing the High Contracting Parties from imposing restrictions on the political activity of aliens.

Article 17: Prohibition of abuse of rights

Nothing in this Convention may be interpreted as implying for any State, group or person any right to engage in any activity or perform any act aimed at the destruction of any of the rights and freedoms set forth herein or at their limitation to a greater extent than is provided for in the Convention.

Article 18: Limitation on use of restrictions on rights

The restrictions permitted under this Convention to the said rights and freedoms shall not be applied for any purpose other than those for which they have been prescribed.

Section II: European Court of Human Rights

Article 19: Establishment of the Court

To ensure the observance of the engagements undertaken by the High Contracting Parties in the Convention and the Protocols thereto, there shall be set up a European Court of Human Rights, hereinafter referred to as "the Court". It shall function on a permanent basis.

Article 20: Number of judges

The Court shall consist of a number of judges equal to that of the High Contracting Parties.

Article 21: Criteria for office

1. The judges shall be of high moral character and must either possess the qualifications required for appointment to high judicial office or be jurisconsults of recognised competence.
2. The judges shall sit on the Court in their individual capacity.
3. During their term of office the judges shall not engage in any activity which is incompatible with their independence, impartiality or with the demands of a full-time office; all questions arising from the application of this paragraph shall be decided by the Court.

Article 22: Election of judges

1. The judges shall be elected by the Parliamentary Assembly with respect to each High Contracting Party by a majority of votes cast from a list of three candidates nominated by the High Contracting Party.
2. The same procedure shall be followed to complete the Court in the event of the accession of new High Contracting Parties and in filling casual vacancies.

Article 23: Terms of office

1. The judges shall be elected for a period of six years. They may be re-elected. However, the terms of office of one-half of the judges elected at the first election shall expire at the end of three years.
2. The judges whose terms of office are to expire at the end of the initial period of three years shall be chosen by lot by the Secretary General of the Council of Europe immediately after their election.
3. In order to ensure that, as far as possible, the terms of office of one-half of the judges are renewed every three years, the Parliamentary Assembly may decide, before proceeding to any subsequent election, that the term or terms of office

of one or more judges to be elected shall be for a period other than six years but not more than nine and not less than three years.

4. In cases where more than one term of office is involved and where the Parliamentary Assembly applies the preceding paragraph, the allocation of the terms of office shall be effected by a drawing of lots by the Secretary General of the Council of Europe immediately after the election.

5. A judge elected to replace a judge whose term of office has not expired shall hold office for the remainder of his predecessor's term.

6. The terms of office of judges shall expire when they reach the age of 70.

7. The judges shall hold office until replaced. They shall, however, continue to deal with such cases as they already have under consideration.

Article 24: Dismissal

No judge may be dismissed from his office unless the other judges decide by a majority of two-thirds that he has ceased to fulfil the required conditions.

Article 25: Registry and legal secretaries

The Court shall have a registry, the functions and organisation of which shall be laid down in the rules of the Court. The Court shall be assisted by legal secretaries.

Article 26: Plenary Court

The plenary Court shall:

a. elect its President and one or two Vice-Presidents for a period of three years; they may be re-elected;
b. set up Chambers, constituted for a fixed period of time;
c. elect the Presidents of the Chambers of the Court; they may be re-elected;
d. adopt the rules of the Court; and
e. elect the Registrar and one or more Deputy Registrars.

Article 27: Committees, Chambers and Grand Chamber

1. To consider cases brought before it, the Court shall sit in committees of three judges, in Chambers of seven judges and in a Grand Chamber of seventeen judges. The Court's Chambers shall set up committees for a fixed period of time.

2. There shall sit as an *ex officio* member of the Chamber and the Grand Chamber the judge elected in respect of the State Party concerned or, if there is none or if he is unable to sit, a person of its choice who shall sit in the capacity of judge.

3. The Grand Chamber shall also include the President of the Court, the Vice-Presidents, the Presidents of the Chambers and other judges chosen in accordance with the rules of the Court. When a case is referred to the Grand Chamber under Article 43, no judge from the Chamber which rendered the judgment shall sit in the Grand Chamber, with the exception of the President of the Chamber and the judge who sat in respect of the State Party concerned.

Article 28: Declarations of inadmissibility by committees

A committee may, by a unanimous vote, declare inadmissible or strike out of its list of cases an application submitted under Article 34 where such a decision can be taken without further examination. The decision shall be final.

Article 29: Decisions by Chambers on admissibility and merits

1. If no decision is taken under Article 28, a Chamber shall decide on the admissibility and merits of individual applications submitted under Article 34.
2. A Chamber shall decide on the admissibility and merits of inter-State applications submitted under Article 33.
3. The decision on admissibility shall be taken separately unless the Court, in exceptional cases, decides otherwise.

Article 30: Relinquishment of jurisdiction to the Grand Chamber

Where a case pending before a Chamber raises a serious question affecting the interpretation of the Convention or the protocols thereto, or where the resolution of a question before the Chamber might have a result inconsistent with a judgment previously delivered by the Court, the Chamber may, at any time before it has rendered its judgment, relinquish jurisdiction in favour of the Grand Chamber, unless one of the parties to the case objects.

Article 31: Powers of the Grand Chamber

The Grand Chamber shall:

a. determine applications submitted either under Article 33 or Article 34 when a Chamber has relinquished jurisdiction under Article 30 or when the case has been referred to it under Article 43; and
b. consider requests for advisory opinions submitted under Article 47.

Article 32: Jurisdiction of the Court

1. The jurisdiction of the Court shall extend to all matters concerning the interpretation and application of the Convention and the protocols thereto which are referred to it as provided in Articles 33, 34 and 47.

2. In the event of dispute as to whether the Court has jurisdiction, the Court shall decide.

Article 33: Inter-State cases

Any High Contracting Party may refer to the Court any alleged breach of the provisions of the Convention and the protocols thereto by another High Contracting Party.

Article 34: Individual applications

The Court may receive applications from any person, non-governmental organisation or group of individuals claiming to be the victim of a violation by one of the High Contracting Parties of the rights set forth in the Convention or the protocols thereto. The High Contracting Parties undertake not to hinder in any way the effective exercise of this right.

Article 35: Admissibility criteria

1. The Court may only deal with the matter after all domestic remedies have been exhausted, according to the generally recognised rules of international law, and within a period of six months from the date on which the final decision was taken.
2. The Court shall not deal with any application submitted under Article 34 that:
   a. is anonymous; or
   b. is substantially the same as a matter that has already been examined by the Court or has already been submitted to another procedure of international investigation or settlement and contains no relevant new information.
3. The Court shall declare inadmissible any individual application submitted under Article 34 which it considers incompatible with the provisions of the Convention or the protocols thereto, manifestly ill-founded, or an abuse of the right of application.
4. The Court shall reject any application which it considers inadmissible under this Article. It may do so at any stage of the proceedings.

Article 36: Third party intervention

1. In all cases before a Chamber or the Grand Chamber, a High Contracting Party one of whose nationals is an applicant shall have the right to submit written comments and to take part in hearings.
2. The President of the Court may, in the interest of the proper administration of justice, invite any High Contracting Party which is not a party to the proceedings or any person concerned who is not the applicant to submit written comments or take part in hearings.

Article 37: Striking out applications

1. The Court may at any stage of the proceedings decide to strike an application out of its list of cases where the circumstances lead to the conclusion that:
    a. the applicant does not intend to pursue his application; or
    b. the matter has been resolved; or
    c. for any other reason established by the Court, it is no longer justified to continue the examination of the application.

However, the Court shall continue the examination of the application if respect for human rights as defined in the Convention and the protocols thereto so requires.

2. The Court may decide to restore an application to its list of cases if it considers that the circumstances justify such a course.

Article 38: Examination of the case and friendly settlement proceedings

1. If the Court declares the application admissible, it shall:
    a. pursue the examination of the case, together with the representatives of the parties, and if need be, undertake an investigation, for the effective conduct of which the States concerned shall furnish all necessary facilities;
    b. place itself at the disposal of the parties concerned with a view to securing a friendly settlement of the matter on the basis of respect for human rights as defined in the Convention and the protocols thereto.
2. Proceedings conducted under paragraph 1.b shall be confidential.

Article 39: Finding of a friendly settlement

If a friendly settlement is effected, the Court shall strike the case out of its list by means of a decision which shall be confined to a brief statement of the facts and of the solution reached.

Article 40: Public hearings and access to documents

1. Hearings shall be in public unless the Court in exceptional circumstances decides otherwise.
2. Documents deposited with the Registrar shall be accessible to the public unless the President of the Court decides otherwise.

Article 41: Just satisfaction

If the Court finds that there has been a violation of the Convention or the protocols thereto, and if the internal law of the High Contracting Party concerned allows only partial reparation to be made, the Court shall, if necessary, afford just satisfaction to the injured party.

Article 42: Judgments of Chambers

Judgments of Chambers shall become final in accordance with the provisions of Article 44, paragraph 2.

Article 43: Referral to the Grand Chamber

1. Within a period of three months from the date of the judgment of the Chamber, any party to the case may, in exceptional cases, request that the case be referred to the Grand Chamber.
2. A panel of five judges of the Grand Chamber shall accept the request if the case raises a serious question affecting the interpretation or application of the Convention or the protocols thereto, or a serious issue of general importance.
3. If the panel accepts the request, the Grand Chamber shall decide the case by means of a judgment.

Article 44: Final judgments

1. The judgment of the Grand Chamber shall be final.
2. The judgment of a Chamber shall become final:
   a. when the parties declare that they will not request that the case be referred to the Grand Chamber; or
   b. three months after the date of the judgment, if reference of the case to the Grand Chamber has not been requested; or
   c. when the panel of the Grand Chamber rejects the request to refer under Article 43.
3. The final judgment shall be published.

Article 45: Reasons for judgments and decisions

1. Reasons shall be given for judgments as well as for decisions declaring applications admissible or inadmissible.
2. If a judgment does not represent, in whole or in part, the unanimous opinion of the judges, any judge shall be entitled to deliver a separate opinion.

Article 46: Binding force and execution of judgments

1. The High Contracting Parties undertake to abide by the final judgment of the Court in any case to which they are parties.
2. The final judgment of the Court shall be transmitted to the Committee of Ministers, which shall supervise its execution.

Article 47: Advisory opinions

1. The Court may, at the request of the Committee of Ministers, give advisory opinions on legal questions concerning the interpretation of the Convention and the protocols thereto.
2. Such opinions shall not deal with any question relating to the content or scope of the rights or freedoms defined in Section I of the Convention and the protocols thereto, or with any other question which the Court or the Committee of Ministers might have to consider in consequence of any such proceedings as could be instituted in accordance with the Convention.
3. Decisions of the Committee of Ministers to request an advisory opinion of the Court shall require a majority vote of the representatives entitled to sit on the Committee.

Article 48: Advisory jurisdiction of the Court

The Court shall decide whether a request for an advisory opinion submitted by the Committee of Ministers is within its competence as defined in Article 47.

Article 49: Reasons for advisory opinions

1. Reasons shall be given for advisory opinions of the Court.
2. If the advisory opinion does not represent, in whole or in part, the unanimous opinion of the judges, any judge shall be entitled to deliver a separate opinion.
3. Advisory opinions of the Court shall be communicated to the Committee of Ministers.

Article 50: Expenditure on the Court

The expenditure on the Court shall be borne by the Council of Europe.

Article 51: Privileges and immunities of judges

The judges shall be entitled, during the exercise of their functions, to the privileges and immunities provided for in Article 40 of the Statute of the Council of Europe and in the agreements made thereunder.

Section III: Miscellaneous Provisions

Article 52: Inquiries by the Secretary General

On receipt of a request from the Secretary General of the Council of Europe any High Contracting Party shall furnish an explanation of the manner in which its internal law ensures the effective implementation of any of the provisions of the Convention.

Article 53: Safeguard for existing human rights

Nothing in this Convention shall be construed as limiting or derogating from any of the human rights and fundamental freedoms which may be ensured under the laws of any High Contracting Party or under any other agreement to which it is a Party.

Article 54: Powers of the Committee of Ministers

Nothing in this Convention shall prejudice the powers conferred on the Committee of Ministers by the Statute of the Council of Europe.

Article 55: Exclusion of other means of dispute settlement

The High Contracting Parties agree that, except by special agreement, they will not avail themselves of treaties, conventions or declarations in force between them for the purpose of submitting, by way of petition, a dispute arising out of the interpretation or application of this Convention to a means of settlement other than those provided for in this Convention.

Article 56: Territorial application

1. Any State may at the time of its ratification or at any time thereafter declare by notification addressed to the Secretary General of the Council of Europe that the present Convention shall, subject to paragraph 4 of this Article, extend to all or any of the territories for whose international relations it is responsible.
2. The Convention shall extend to the territory or territories named in the notification as from the thirtieth day after the receipt of this notification by the Secretary General of the Council of Europe.
3. The provisions of this Convention shall be applied in such territories with due regard, however, to local requirements.
4. Any State which has made a declaration in accordance with paragraph 1 of this article may at any time thereafter declare on behalf of one or more of the territories to which the declaration relates that it accepts the competence of the Court to receive applications from individuals, non-governmental organisations or groups of individuals as provided by Article 34 of the Convention.

Article 57: Reservations

1. Any State may, when signing this Convention or when depositing its instrument of ratification, make a reservation in respect of any particular provision

of the Convention to the extent that any law then in force in its territory is not in conformity with the provision. Reservations of a general character shall not be permitted under this article.

2. Any reservation made under this article shall contain a brief statement of the law concerned.

Article 58: Denunciation

1. A High Contracting Party may denounce the present Convention only after the expiry of five years from the date on which it became a party to it and after six months' notice contained in a notification addressed to the Secretary General of the Council of Europe, who shall inform the other High Contracting Parties.

2. Such a denunciation shall not have the effect of releasing the High Contracting Party concerned from its obligations under this Convention in respect of any act which, being capable of constituting a violation of such obligations, may have been performed by it before the date at which the denunciation became effective.

3. Any High Contracting Party which shall cease to be a member of the Council of Europe shall cease to be a Party to this Convention under the same conditions.

4. The Convention may be denounced in accordance with the provisions of the preceding paragraphs in respect of any territory to which it has been declared to extend under the terms of Article 56.

Article 59: Signature and ratification

1. This Convention shall be open to the signature of the members of the Council of Europe. It shall be ratified. Ratifications shall be deposited with the Secretary General of the Council of Europe.

2. The present Convention shall come into force after the deposit of ten instruments of ratification.

3. As regards any signatory ratifying subsequently, the Convention shall come into force at the date of the deposit of its instrument of ratification.

4. The Secretary General of the Council of Europe shall notify all the members of the Council of Europe of the entry into force of the Convention, the names of the High Contracting Parties who have ratified it, and the deposit of all instruments of ratification which may be effected subsequently.

The International Covenant on Civil and Political Rights

Adopted and opened for signature, ratification and accession by General Assembly resolution 2200A (XXI) of 16 December 1966

entry into force 23 March 1976, in accordance with Article 49

Preamble

The States Parties to the present Covenant,

Considering that, in accordance with the principles proclaimed in the Charter of the United Nations, recognition of the inherent dignity and of the equal and inalienable rights of all members of the human family is the foundation of freedom, justice and peace in the world,

Recognizing that these rights derive from the inherent dignity of the human person,

Recognizing that, in accordance with the Universal Declaration of Human Rights, the ideal of free human beings enjoying civil and political freedom and freedom from fear and want can only be achieved if conditions are created whereby everyone may enjoy his civil and political rights, as well as his economic, social and cultural rights,

Considering the obligation of States under the Charter of the United Nations to promote universal respect for, and observance of, human rights and freedoms,

Realizing that the individual, having duties to other individuals and to the community to which he belongs, is under a responsibility to strive for the promotion and observance of the rights recognized in the present Covenant,

Agree upon the following Articles:

Part I

Article 1

1. All peoples have the right of self-determination. By virtue of that right they freely determine their political status and freely pursue their economic, social and cultural development.
2. All peoples may, for their own ends, freely dispose of their natural wealth and resources without prejudice to any obligations arising out of international economic co-operation, based upon the principle of mutual benefit, and international law. In no case may a people be deprived of its own means of subsistence.
3. The States Parties to the present Covenant, including those having responsibility for the administration of Non-Self-Governing and Trust Territories, shall promote the realization of the right of self-determination, and shall respect that right, in conformity with the provisions of the Charter of the United Nations.

Part II

Article 2

1. Each State Party to the present Covenant undertakes to respect and to ensure to all individuals within its territory and subject to its jurisdiction the rights recognized in the present Covenant, without distinction of any kind, such as race, colour, sex, language, religion, political or other opinion, national or social origin, property, birth or other status.
2. Where not already provided for by existing legislative or other measures, each State Party to the present Covenant undertakes to take the necessary steps, in accordance with its constitutional processes and with the provisions of the present Covenant, to adopt such laws or other measures as may be necessary to give effect to the rights recognized in the present Covenant.
3. Each State Party to the present Covenant undertakes:
   (a) To ensure that any person whose rights or freedoms as herein recognized are violated shall have an effective remedy, notwithstanding that the violation has been committed by persons acting in an official capacity;

(b) To ensure that any person claiming such a remedy shall have his right thereto determined by competent judicial, administrative or legislative authorities, or by any other competent authority provided for by the legal system of the State, and to develop the possibilities of judicial remedy;

(c) To ensure that the competent authorities shall enforce such remedies when granted.

Article 3

The States Parties to the present Covenant undertake to ensure the equal right of men and women to the enjoyment of all civil and political rights set forth in the present Covenant.

Article 4

1. In time of public emergency which threatens the life of the nation and the existence of which is officially proclaimed, the States Parties to the present Covenant may take measures derogating from their obligations under the present Covenant to the extent strictly required by the exigencies of the situation, provided that such measures are not inconsistent with their other obligations under international law and do not involve discrimination solely on the ground of race, colour, sex, language, religion or social origin.

2. No derogation from Articles 6, 7, 8 (paragraphs 1 and 2), 11, 15, 16 and 18 may be made under this provision.

3. Any State Party to the present Covenant availing itself of the right of derogation shall immediately inform the other States Parties to the present Covenant, through the intermediary of the Secretary-General of the United Nations, of the provisions from which it has derogated and of the reasons by which it was actuated. A further communication shall be made, through the same intermediary, on the date on which it terminates such derogation.

Article 5

1. Nothing in the present Covenant may be interpreted as implying for any State, group or person any right to engage in any activity or perform any act aimed at the destruction of any of the rights and freedoms recognized herein or at their limitation to a greater extent than is provided for in the present Covenant.

2. There shall be no restriction upon or derogation from any of the fundamental human rights recognized or existing in any State Party to the present Covenant pursuant to law, conventions, regulations or custom on the pretext that the present Covenant does not recognize such rights or that it recognizes them to a lesser extent.

Part III

Article 6

1. Every human being has the inherent right to life. This right shall be protected by law. No one shall be arbitrarily deprived of his life.
2. In countries which have not abolished the death penalty, sentence of death may be imposed only for the most serious crimes in accordance with the law in force at the time of the commission of the crime and not contrary to the provisions of the present Covenant and to the Convention on the Prevention and Punishment of the Crime of Genocide. This penalty can only be carried out pursuant to a final judgement rendered by a competent court.
3. When deprivation of life constitutes the crime of genocide, it is understood that nothing in this Article shall authorize any State Party to the present Covenant to derogate in any way from any obligation assumed under the provisions of the Convention on the Prevention and Punishment of the Crime of Genocide.
4. Anyone sentenced to death shall have the right to seek pardon or commutation of the sentence. Amnesty, pardon or commutation of the sentence of death may be granted in all cases.
5. Sentence of death shall not be imposed for crimes committed by persons below eighteen years of age and shall not be carried out on pregnant women.
6. Nothing in this Article shall be invoked to delay or to prevent the abolition of capital punishment by any State Party to the present Covenant.

Article 7

No one shall be subjected to torture or to cruel, inhuman or degrading treatment or punishment. In particular, no one shall be subjected without his free consent to medical or scientific experimentation.

Article 8

1. No one shall be held in slavery; slavery and the slave-trade in all their forms shall be prohibited.
2. No one shall be held in servitude.
3.
    (a) No one shall be required to perform forced or compulsory labour;
    (b) Paragraph 3 (a) shall not be held to preclude, in countries where imprisonment with hard labour may be imposed as a punishment for a crime, the performance of hard labour in pursuance of a sentence to such punishment by a competent court;
    (c) For the purpose of this paragraph the term "forced or compulsory labour" shall not include:

(i) Any work or service, not referred to in subparagraph (b), normally required of a person who is under detention in consequence of a lawful order of a court, or of a person during conditional release from such detention;

(ii) Any service of a military character and, in countries where conscientious objection is recognized, any national service required by law of conscientious objectors;

(iii) Any service exacted in cases of emergency or calamity threatening the life or well-being of the community;

(iv) Any work or service which forms part of normal civil obligations.

Article 9

1. Everyone has the right to liberty and security of person. No one shall be subjected to arbitrary arrest or detention. No one shall be deprived of his liberty except on such grounds and in accordance with such procedure as are established by law.

2. Anyone who is arrested shall be informed, at the time of arrest, of the reasons for his arrest and shall be promptly informed of any charges against him.

3. Anyone arrested or detained on a criminal charge shall be brought promptly before a judge or other officer authorized by law to exercise judicial power and shall be entitled to trial within a reasonable time or to release. It shall not be the general rule that persons awaiting trial shall be detained in custody, but release may be subject to guarantees to appear for trial, at any other stage of the judicial proceedings, and, should occasion arise, for execution of the judgement.

4. Anyone who is deprived of his liberty by arrest or detention shall be entitled to take proceedings before a court, in order that that court may decide without delay on the lawfulness of his detention and order his release if the detention is not lawful.

5. Anyone who has been the victim of unlawful arrest or detention shall have an enforceable right to compensation.

Article 10

1. All persons deprived of their liberty shall be treated with humanity and with respect for the inherent dignity of the human person.

2.
   (a) Accused persons shall, save in exceptional circumstances, be segregated from convicted persons and shall be subject to separate treatment appropriate to their status as unconvicted persons;
   (b) Accused juvenile persons shall be separated from adults and brought as speedily as possible for adjudication.

3. The penitentiary system shall comprise treatment of prisoners the essential aim of which shall be their reformation and social rehabilitation. Juvenile

offenders shall be segregated from adults and be accorded treatment appropriate to their age and legal status.

Article 11

No one shall be imprisoned merely on the ground of inability to fulfil a contrac-
tual obligation.

Article 12

1. Everyone lawfully within the territory of a State shall, within that territory,
   have the right to liberty of movement and freedom to choose his residence.
2. Everyone shall be free to leave any country, including his own.
3. The above-mentioned rights shall not be subject to any restrictions except
   those which are provided by law, are necessary to protect national security,
   public order (ordre public), public health or morals or the rights and freedoms
   of others, and are consistent with the other rights recognized in the present
   Covenant.
4. No one shall be arbitrarily deprived of the right to enter his own country.

Article 13

An alien lawfully in the territory of a State Party to the present Covenant may be
expelled therefrom only in pursuance of a decision reached in accordance with law
and shall, except where compelling reasons of national security otherwise require,
be allowed to submit the reasons against his expulsion and to have his case
reviewed by, and be represented for the purpose before, the competent authority
or a person or persons especially designated by the competent authority.

Article 14

1. All persons shall be equal before the courts and tribunals. In the determination of any criminal charge against him, or of his rights and obligations in a
   suit at law, everyone shall be entitled to a fair and public hearing by a competent, independent and impartial tribunal established by law. The press and
   the public may be excluded from all or part of a trial for reasons of morals,
   public order (ordre public) or national security in a democratic society, or
   when the interest of the private lives of the parties so requires, or to the
   extent strictly necessary in the opinion of the court in special circumstances
   where publicity would prejudice the interests of justice; but any judgement
   rendered in a criminal case or in a suit at law shall be made public except
   where the interest of juvenile persons otherwise requires or the proceedings
   concern matrimonial disputes or the guardianship of children.
2. Everyone charged with a criminal offence shall have the right to be presumed
   innocent until proved guilty according to law.

3. In the determination of any criminal charge against him, everyone shall be entitled to the following minimum guarantees, in full equality:
   (a) To be informed promptly and in detail in a language which he understands of the nature and cause of the charge against him;
   (b) To have adequate time and facilities for the preparation of his defence and to communicate with counsel of his own choosing;
   (c) To be tried without undue delay;
   (d) To be tried in his presence, and to defend himself in person or through legal assistance of his own choosing; to be informed, if he does not have legal assistance, of this right; and to have legal assistance assigned to him, in any case where the interests of justice so require, and without payment by him in any such case if he does not have sufficient means to pay for it;
   (e) To examine, or have examined, the witnesses against him and to obtain the attendance and examination of witnesses on his behalf under the same conditions as witnesses against him;
   (f) To have the free assistance of an interpreter if he cannot understand or speak the language used in court;
   (g) Not to be compelled to testify against himself or to confess guilt.
4. In the case of juvenile persons, the procedure shall be such as will take account of their age and the desirability of promoting their rehabilitation.
5. Everyone convicted of a crime shall have the right to his conviction and sentence being reviewed by a higher tribunal according to law.
6. When a person has by a final decision been convicted of a criminal offence and when subsequently his conviction has been reversed or he has been pardoned on the ground that a new or newly discovered fact shows conclusively that there has been a miscarriage of justice, the person who has suffered punishment as a result of such conviction shall be compensated according to law, unless it is proved that the non-disclosure of the unknown fact in time is wholly or partly attributable to him.
7. No one shall be liable to be tried or punished again for an offence for which he has already been finally convicted or acquitted in accordance with the law and penal procedure of each country.

Article 15

1. No one shall be held guilty of any criminal offence on account of any act or omission which did not constitute a criminal offence, under national or international law, at the time when it was committed. Nor shall a heavier penalty be imposed than the one that was applicable at the time when the criminal offence was committed. If, subsequent to the commission of the offence, provision is made by law for the imposition of the lighter penalty, the offender shall benefit thereby.
2. Nothing in this Article shall prejudice the trial and punishment of any person for any act or omission which, at the time when it was committed, was criminal according to the general principles of law recognized by the community of nations.

Article 16

Everyone shall have the right to recognition everywhere as a person before the law.

Article 17

1. No one shall be subjected to arbitrary or unlawful interference with his privacy, family, home or correspondence, nor to unlawful attacks on his honour and reputation.
2. Everyone has the right to the protection of the law against such interference or attacks.

Article 18

1. Everyone shall have the right to freedom of thought, conscience and religion. This right shall include freedom to have or to adopt a religion or belief of his choice, and freedom, either individually or in community with others and in public or private, to manifest his religion or belief in worship, observance, practice and teaching.
2. No one shall be subject to coercion which would impair his freedom to have or to adopt a religion or belief of his choice.
3. Freedom to manifest one's religion or beliefs may be subject only to such limitations as are prescribed by law and are necessary to protect public safety, order, health, or morals or the fundamental rights and freedoms of others.
4. The States Parties to the present Covenant undertake to have respect for the liberty of parents and, when applicable, legal guardians to ensure the religious and moral education of their children in conformity with their own convictions.

Article 19

1. Everyone shall have the right to hold opinions without interference.
2. Everyone shall have the right to freedom of expression; this right shall include freedom to seek, receive and impart information and ideas of all kinds, regardless of frontiers, either orally, in writing or in print, in the form of art, or through any other media of his choice.
3. The exercise of the rights provided for in paragraph 2 of this Article carries with it special duties and responsibilities. It may therefore be subject to certain restrictions, but these shall only be such as are provided by law and are necessary:
   (a) For respect of the rights or reputations of others;
   (b) For the protection of national security or of public order (ordre public), or of public health or morals.

Article 20

1. Any propaganda for war shall be prohibited by law.
2. Any advocacy of national, racial or religious hatred that constitutes incitement to discrimination, hostility or violence shall be prohibited by law.

Article 21

The right of peaceful assembly shall be recognized. No restrictions may be placed on the exercise of this right other than those imposed in conformity with the law and which are necessary in a democratic society in the interests of national security or public safety, public order (ordre public), the protection of public health or morals or the protection of the rights and freedoms of others.

Article 22

1. Everyone shall have the right to freedom of association with others, including the right to form and join trade unions for the protection of his interests.
2. No restrictions may be placed on the exercise of this right other than those which are prescribed by law and which are necessary in a democratic society in the interests of national security or public safety, public order (ordre public), the protection of public health or morals or the protection of the rights and freedoms of others. This Article shall not prevent the imposition of lawful restrictions on members of the armed forces and of the police in their exercise of this right.
3. Nothing in this Article shall authorize States Parties to the International Labour Organisation Convention of 1948 concerning Freedom of Association and Protection of the Right to Organize to take legislative measures which would prejudice, or to apply the law in such a manner as to prejudice, the guarantees provided for in that Convention.

Article 23

1. The family is the natural and fundamental group unit of society and is entitled to protection by society and the State.
2. The right of men and women of marriageable age to marry and to found a family shall be recognized.
3. No marriage shall be entered into without the free and full consent of the intending spouses.
4. States Parties to the present Covenant shall take appropriate steps to ensure equality of rights and responsibilities of spouses as to marriage, during marriage and at its dissolution. In the case of dissolution, provision shall be made for the necessary protection of any children.

Article 24

1. Every child shall have, without any discrimination as to race, colour, sex, language, religion, national or social origin, property or birth, the right to such measures of protection as are required by his status as a minor, on the part of his family, society and the State.
2. Every child shall be registered immediately after birth and shall have a name.
3. Every child has the right to acquire a nationality.

Article 25

Every citizen shall have the right and the opportunity, without any of the distinctions mentioned in Article 2 and without unreasonable restrictions:

    (a) To take part in the conduct of public affairs, directly or through freely chosen representatives;

    (b) To vote and to be elected at genuine periodic elections which shall be by universal and equal suffrage and shall be held by secret ballot, guaranteeing the free expression of the will of the electors;

    (c) To have access, on general terms of equality, to public service in his country.

Article 26

All persons are equal before the law and are entitled without any discrimination to the equal protection of the law. In this respect, the law shall prohibit any discrimination and guarantee to all persons equal and effective protection against discrimination on any ground such as race, colour, sex, language, religion, political or other opinion, national or social origin, property, birth or other status.

Article 27

In those States in which ethnic, religious or linguistic minorities exist, persons belonging to such minorities shall not be denied the right, in community with the other members of their group, to enjoy their own culture, to profess and practise their own religion, or to use their own language.

Part IV

Article 28

1. There shall be established a Human Rights Committee (hereafter referred to in the present Covenant as the Committee). It shall consist of eighteen members and shall carry out the functions hereinafter provided.

2. The Committee shall be composed of nationals of the States Parties to the present Covenant who shall be persons of high moral character and recognized competence in the field of human rights, consideration being given to the usefulness of the participation of some persons having legal experience.
3. The members of the Committee shall be elected and shall serve in their personal capacity.

Article 29

1. The members of the Committee shall be elected by secret ballot from a list of persons possessing the qualifications prescribed in Article 28 and nominated for the purpose by the States Parties to the present Covenant.
2. Each State Party to the present Covenant may nominate not more than two persons. These persons shall be nationals of the nominating State.
3. A person shall be eligible for renomination.

Article 30

1. The initial election shall be held no later than six months after the date of the entry into force of the present Covenant.
2. At least four months before the date of each election to the Committee, other than an election to fill a vacancy declared in accordance with Article 34, the Secretary-General of the United Nations shall address a written invitation to the States Parties to the present Covenant to submit their nominations for membership of the Committee within three months.
3. The Secretary-General of the United Nations shall prepare a list in alphabetical order of all the persons thus nominated, with an indication of the States Parties which have nominated them, and shall submit it to the States Parties to the present Covenant no later than one month before the date of each election.
4. Elections of the members of the Committee shall be held at a meeting of the States Parties to the present Covenant convened by the Secretary-General of the United Nations at the Headquarters of the United Nations. At that meeting, for which two thirds of the States Parties to the present Covenant shall constitute a quorum, the persons elected to the Committee shall be those nominees who obtain the largest number of votes and an absolute majority of the votes of the representatives of States Parties present and voting.

Article 31

1. The Committee may not include more than one national of the same State.
2. In the election of the Committee, consideration shall be given to equitable geographical distribution of membership and to the representation of the different forms of civilization and of the principal legal systems.

Article 32

1. The members of the Committee shall be elected for a term of four years. They shall be eligible for re-election if renominated. However, the terms of nine of the members elected at the first election shall expire at the end of two years; immediately after the first election, the names of these nine members shall be chosen by lot by the Chairman of the meeting referred to in Article 30, paragraph 4.
2. Elections at the expiry of office shall be held in accordance with the preceding Articles of this part of the present Covenant.

Article 33

1. If, in the unanimous opinion of the other members, a member of the Committee has ceased to carry out his functions for any cause other than absence of a temporary character, the Chairman of the Committee shall notify the Secretary-General of the United Nations, who shall then declare the seat of that member to be vacant.
2. In the event of the death or the resignation of a member of the Committee, the Chairman shall immediately notify the Secretary-General of the United Nations, who shall declare the seat vacant from the date of death or the date on which the resignation takes effect.

Article 34

1. When a vacancy is declared in accordance with Article 33 and if the term of office of the member to be replaced does not expire within six months of the declaration of the vacancy, the Secretary-General of the United Nations shall notify each of the States Parties to the present Covenant, which may within two months submit nominations in accordance with Article 29 for the purpose of filling the vacancy.
2. The Secretary-General of the United Nations shall prepare a list in alphabetical order of the persons thus nominated and shall submit it to the States Parties to the present Covenant. The election to fill the vacancy shall then take place in accordance with the relevant provisions of this part of the present Covenant.
3. A member of the Committee elected to fill a vacancy declared in accordance with Article 33 shall hold office for the remainder of the term of the member who vacated the seat on the Committee under the provisions of that Article.

Article 35

The members of the Committee shall, with the approval of the General Assembly of the United Nations, receive emoluments from United Nations resources on such terms and conditions as the General Assembly may decide, having regard to the importance of the Committee's responsibilities.

Article 36

The Secretary-General of the United Nations shall provide the necessary staff and facilities for the effective performance of the functions of the Committee under the present Covenant.

Article 37

1. The Secretary-General of the United Nations shall convene the initial meeting of the Committee at the Headquarters of the United Nations.
2. After its initial meeting, the Committee shall meet at such times as shall be provided in its rules of procedure.
3. The Committee shall normally meet at the Headquarters of the United Nations or at the United Nations Office at Geneva.

Article 38

Every member of the Committee shall, before taking up his duties, make a solemn declaration in open committee that he will perform his functions impartially and conscientiously.

Article 39

1. The Committee shall elect its officers for a term of two years. They may be re-elected.
2. The Committee shall establish its own rules of procedure, but these rules shall provide, inter alia, that:
   (a) Twelve members shall constitute a quorum;
   (b) Decisions of the Committee shall be made by a majority vote of the members present.

Article 40

1. The States Parties to the present Covenant undertake to submit reports on the measures they have adopted which give effect to the rights recognized herein and on the progress made in the enjoyment of those rights:
   (a) Within one year of the entry into force of the present Covenant for the States Parties concerned;
   (b) Thereafter whenever the Committee so requests.
2. All reports shall be submitted to the Secretary-General of the United Nations, who shall transmit them to the Committee for consideration. Reports shall indicate the factors and difficulties, if any, affecting the implementation of the present Covenant.

3. The Secretary-General of the United Nations may, after consultation with the Committee, transmit to the specialized agencies concerned copies of such parts of the reports as may fall within their field of competence.
4. The Committee shall study the reports submitted by the States Parties to the present Covenant. It shall transmit its reports, and such general comments as it may consider appropriate, to the States Parties. The Committee may also transmit to the Economic and Social Council these comments along with the copies of the reports it has received from States Parties to the present Covenant.
5. The States Parties to the present Covenant may submit to the Committee observations on any comments that may be made in accordance with paragraph 4 of this Article.

Article 41

1. A State Party to the present Covenant may at any time declare under this Article that it recognizes the competence of the Committee to receive and consider communications to the effect that a State Party claims that another State Party is not fulfilling its obligations under the present Covenant. Communications under this Article may be received and considered only if submitted by a State Party which has made a declaration recognizing in regard to itself the competence of the Committee. No communication shall be received by the Committee if it concerns a State Party which has not made such a declaration. Communications received under this Article shall be dealt with in accordance with the following procedure:
   (a) If a State Party to the present Covenant considers that another State Party is not giving effect to the provisions of the present Covenant, it may, by written communication, bring the matter to the attention of that State Party. Within three months after the receipt of the communication the receiving State shall afford the State which sent the communication an explanation, or any other statement in writing clarifying the matter which should include, to the extent possible and pertinent, reference to domestic procedures and remedies taken, pending, or available in the matter;
   (b) If the matter is not adjusted to the satisfaction of both States Parties concerned within six months after the receipt by the receiving State of the initial communication, either State shall have the right to refer the matter to the Committee, by notice given to the Committee and to the other State;
   (c) The Committee shall deal with a matter referred to it only after it has ascertained that all available domestic remedies have been invoked and exhausted in the matter, in conformity with the generally recognized principles of international law. This shall not be the rule where the application of the remedies is unreasonably prolonged;
   (d) The Committee shall hold closed meetings when examining communications under this Article;

(e) Subject to the provisions of subparagraph (c), the Committee shall make available its good offices to the States Parties concerned with a view to a friendly solution of the matter on the basis of respect for human rights and fundamental freedoms as recognized in the present Covenant;

(f) In any matter referred to it, the Committee may call upon the States Parties concerned, referred to in subparagraph (b), to supply any relevant information;

(g) The States Parties concerned, referred to in subparagraph (b), shall have the right to be represented when the matter is being considered in the Committee and to make submissions orally and/or in writing;

(h) The Committee shall, within twelve months after the date of receipt of notice under subparagraph (b), submit a report:

    (i) If a solution within the terms of subparagraph (e) is reached, the Committee shall confine its report to a brief statement of the facts and of the solution reached;

    (ii) If a solution within the terms of subparagraph (e) is not reached, the Committee shall confine its report to a brief statement of the facts; the written submissions and record of the oral submissions made by the States Parties concerned shall be attached to the report. In every matter, the report shall be communicated to the States Parties concerned.

2. The provisions of this Article shall come into force when ten States Parties to the present Covenant have made declarations under paragraph 1 of this Article. Such declarations shall be deposited by the States Parties with the Secretary-General of the United Nations, who shall transmit copies thereof to the other States Parties. A declaration may be withdrawn at any time by notification to the Secretary-General. Such a withdrawal shall not prejudice the consideration of any matter which is the subject of a communication already transmitted under this Article; no further communication by any State Party shall be received after the notification of withdrawal of the declaration has been received by the Secretary-General, unless the State Party concerned has made a new declaration.

Article 42

1.

(a) If a matter referred to the Committee in accordance with Article 41 is not resolved to the satisfaction of the States Parties concerned, the Committee may, with the prior consent of the States Parties concerned, appoint an ad hoc Conciliation Commission (hereinafter referred to as the Commission). The good offices of the Commission shall be made available to the States Parties concerned with a view to an amicable solution of the matter on the basis of respect for the present Covenant;

(b) The Commission shall consist of five persons acceptable to the States Parties concerned. If the States Parties concerned fail to reach agreement within three months on all or part of the composition of the Commission, the members of the Commission concerning whom no agreement has been reached shall be elected by secret ballot by a two-thirds majority vote of the Committee from among its members.

2. The members of the Commission shall serve in their personal capacity. They shall not be nationals of the States Parties concerned, or of a State not Party to the present Covenant, or of a State Party which has not made a declaration under Article 41.

3. The Commission shall elect its own Chairman and adopt its own rules of procedure.

4. The meetings of the Commission shall normally be held at the Headquarters of the United Nations or at the United Nations Office at Geneva. However, they may be held at such other convenient places as the Commission may determine in consultation with the Secretary-General of the United Nations and the States Parties concerned.

5. The secretariat provided in accordance with Article 36 shall also service the commissions appointed under this Article.

6. The information received and collated by the Committee shall be made available to the Commission and the Commission may call upon the States Parties concerned to supply any other relevant information.

7. When the Commission has fully considered the matter, but in any event not later than twelve months after having been seized of the matter, it shall submit to the Chairman of the Committee a report for communication to the States Parties concerned:

   (a) If the Commission is unable to complete its consideration of the matter within twelve months, it shall confine its report to a brief statement of the status of its consideration of the matter;

   (b) If an amicable solution to the matter on the basis of respect for human rights as recognized in the present Covenant is reached, the Commission shall confine its report to a brief statement of the facts and of the solution reached;

   (c) If a solution within the terms of subparagraph (b) is not reached, the Commission's report shall embody its findings on all questions of fact relevant to the issues between the States Parties concerned, and its views on the possibilities of an amicable solution of the matter. This report shall also contain the written submissions and a record of the oral submissions made by the States Parties concerned;

   (d) If the Commission's report is submitted under subparagraph (c), the States Parties concerned shall, within three months of the receipt of the report, notify the Chairman of the Committee whether or not they accept the contents of the report of the Commission.

8. The provisions of this Article are without prejudice to the responsibilities of the Committee under Article 41.

9. The States Parties concerned shall share equally all the expenses of the members of the Commission in accordance with estimates to be provided by the Secretary-General of the United Nations.

10. The Secretary-General of the United Nations shall be empowered to pay the expenses of the members of the Commission, if necessary, before reimbursement by the States Parties concerned, in accordance with paragraph 9 of this Article.

Article 43

The members of the Committee, and of the ad hoc conciliation commissions which may be appointed under Article 42, shall be entitled to the facilities, privileges and immunities of experts on mission for the United Nations as laid down in the relevant sections of the Convention on the Privileges and Immunities of the United Nations.

Article 44

The provisions for the implementation of the present Covenant shall apply without prejudice to the procedures prescribed in the field of human rights by or under the constituent instruments and the conventions of the United Nations and of the specialized agencies and shall not prevent the States Parties to the present Covenant from having recourse to other procedures for settling a dispute in accordance with general or special international agreements in force between them.

Article 45

The Committee shall submit to the General Assembly of the United Nations, through the Economic and Social Council, an annual report on its activities.

Part V

Article 46

Nothing in the present Covenant shall be interpreted as impairing the provisions of the Charter of the United Nations and of the constitutions of the specialized agencies which define the respective responsibilities of the various organs of the United Nations and of the specialized agencies in regard to the matters dealt with in the present Covenant.

Article 47

Nothing in the present Covenant shall be interpreted as impairing the inherent right of all peoples to enjoy and utilize fully and freely their natural wealth and resources.

Part VI

Article 48

1. The present Covenant is open for signature by any State Member of the United Nations or member of any of its specialized agencies, by any State Party to the Statute of the International Court of Justice, and by any other State which has been invited by the General Assembly of the United Nations to become a Party to the present Covenant.
2. The present Covenant is subject to ratification. Instruments of ratification shall be deposited with the Secretary-General of the United Nations.
3. The present Covenant shall be open to accession by any State referred to in paragraph 1 of this Article.
4. Accession shall be effected by the deposit of an instrument of accession with the Secretary-General of the United Nations.
5. The Secretary-General of the United Nations shall inform all States which have signed this Covenant or acceded to it of the deposit of each instrument of ratification or accession.

Article 49

1. The present Covenant shall enter into force three months after the date of the deposit with the Secretary-General of the United Nations of the thirty-fifth instrument of ratification or instrument of accession.
2. For each State ratifying the present Covenant or acceding to it after the deposit of the thirty-fifth instrument of ratification or instrument of accession, the present Covenant shall enter into force three months after the date of the deposit of its own instrument of ratification or instrument of accession.

Article 50

The provisions of the present Covenant shall extend to all parts of federal States without any limitations or exceptions.

Article 51

1. Any State Party to the present Covenant may propose an amendment and file it with the Secretary-General of the United Nations. The Secretary-General of the United Nations shall thereupon communicate any proposed amendments to the States Parties to the present Covenant with a request that they notify him whether they favour a conference of States Parties for the purpose of considering and voting upon the proposals. In the event that at least one third of the States Parties favours such a conference, the Secretary-General shall convene the conference under the auspices of the United Nations. Any amendment adopted by a majority of the States Parties present and voting at the

conference shall be submitted to the General Assembly of the United Nations for approval.

2. Amendments shall come into force when they have been approved by the General Assembly of the United Nations and accepted by a two-thirds majority of the States Parties to the present Covenant in accordance with their respective constitutional processes.

3. When amendments come into force, they shall be binding on those States Parties which have accepted them, other States Parties still being bound by the provisions of the present Covenant and any earlier amendment which they have accepted.

Article 52

Irrespective of the notifications made under Article 48, paragraph 5, the Secretary-General of the United Nations shall inform all States referred to in paragraph 1 of the same Article of the following particulars:

(a) Signatures, ratifications and accessions under Article 48;
(b) The date of the entry into force of the present Covenant under Article 49 and the date of the entry into force of any amendments under Article 51.

Article 53

1. The present Covenant, of which the Chinese, English, French, Russian and Spanish texts are equally authentic, shall be deposited in the archives of the United Nations.

2. The Secretary-General of the United Nations shall transmit certified copies of the present Covenant to all States referred to in Article 48.

International Covenant on Economic, Social and Cultural Rights

Adopted and opened for signature, ratification and accession by General Assembly resolution 2200A (XXI) of 16 December 1966

entry into force 3 January 1976, in accordance with article 27

Preamble

The States Parties to the present Covenant,

Considering that, in accordance with the principles proclaimed in the Charter of the United Nations, recognition of the inherent dignity and of the equal and inalienable rights of all members of the human family is the foundation of freedom, justice and peace in the world,

Recognizing that these rights derive from the inherent dignity of the human person,

Recognizing that, in accordance with the Universal Declaration of Human Rights, the ideal of free human beings enjoying freedom from fear and want can only be achieved if conditions are created whereby everyone may enjoy his economic, social and cultural rights, as well as his civil and political rights,

Considering the obligation of States under the Charter of the United Nations to promote universal respect for, and observance of, human rights and freedoms,

Realizing that the individual, having duties to other individuals and to the community to which he belongs, is under a responsibility to strive for the promotion and observance of the rights recognized in the present Covenant,

Agree upon the following articles:

Part I

Article 1

1. All peoples have the right of self-determination. By virtue of that right they freely determine their political status and freely pursue their economic, social and cultural development.
2. All peoples may, for their own ends, freely dispose of their natural wealth and resources without prejudice to any obligations arising out of international economic co-operation, based upon the principle of mutual benefit, and international law. In no case may a people be deprived of its own means of subsistence.
3. The States Parties to the present Covenant, including those having responsibility for the administration of Non-Self-Governing and Trust Territories, shall promote the realization of the right of self-determination, and shall respect that right, in conformity with the provisions of the Charter of the United Nations.

Part II

Article 2

1. Each State Party to the present Covenant undertakes to take steps, individually and through international assistance and co-operation, especially economic and technical, to the maximum of its available resources, with a view to achieving progressively the full realization of the rights recognized in the present Covenant by all appropriate means, including particularly the adoption of legislative measures.
2. The States Parties to the present Covenant undertake to guarantee that the rights enunciated in the present Covenant will be exercised without discrimination of any kind as to race, colour, sex, language, religion, political or other opinion, national or social origin, property, birth or other status.
3. Developing countries, with due regard to human rights and their national economy, may determine to what extent they would guarantee the economic rights recognized in the present Covenant to non-nationals.

Article 3

The States Parties to the present Covenant undertake to ensure the equal right of men and women to the enjoyment of all economic, social and cultural rights set forth in the present Covenant.

Article 4

The States Parties to the present Covenant recognize that, in the enjoyment of those rights provided by the State in conformity with the present Covenant, the State may subject such rights only to such limitations as are determined by law only in so far as this may be compatible with the nature of these rights and solely for the purpose of promoting the general welfare in a democratic society.

Article 5

1. Nothing in the present Covenant may be interpreted as implying for any State, group or person any right to engage in any activity or to perform any act aimed at the destruction of any of the rights or freedoms recognized herein, or at their limitation to a greater extent than is provided for in the present Covenant.
2. No restriction upon or derogation from any of the fundamental human rights recognized or existing in any country in virtue of law, conventions, regulations or custom shall be admitted on the pretext that the present Covenant does not recognize such rights or that it recognizes them to a lesser extent.

Part III

Article 6

1. The States Parties to the present Covenant recognize the right to work, which includes the right of everyone to the opportunity to gain his living by work which he freely chooses or accepts, and will take appropriate steps to safeguard this right.
2. The steps to be taken by a State Party to the present Covenant to achieve the full realization of this right shall include technical and vocational guidance and training programmes, policies and techniques to achieve steady economic, social and cultural development and full and productive employment under conditions safeguarding fundamental political and economic freedoms to the individual.

Article 7

The States Parties to the present Covenant recognize the right of everyone to the enjoyment of just and favourable conditions of work which ensure, in particular:

(a) Remuneration which provides all workers, as a minimum, with:
   (i) Fair wages and equal remuneration for work of equal value without distinction of any kind, in particular women being guaranteed conditions of work not inferior to those enjoyed by men, with equal pay for equal work;
   (ii) A decent living for themselves and their families in accordance with the provisions of the present Covenant;
(b) Safe and healthy working conditions;
(c) Equal opportunity for everyone to be promoted in his employment to an appropriate higher level, subject to no considerations other than those of seniority and competence;
(d) Rest, leisure and reasonable limitation of working hours and periodic holidays with pay, as well as remuneration for public holidays.

Article 8

1. The States Parties to the present Covenant undertake to ensure:
   (a) The right of everyone to form trade unions and join the trade union of his choice, subject only to the rules of the organization concerned, for the promotion and protection of his economic and social interests. No restrictions may be placed on the exercise of this right other than those prescribed by law and which are necessary in a democratic society in the interests of national security or public order or for the protection of the rights and freedoms of others;
   (b) The right of trade unions to establish national federations or confederations and the right of the latter to form or join international trade-union organizations;
   (c) The right of trade unions to function freely subject to no limitations other than those prescribed by law and which are necessary in a democratic society in the interests of national security or public order or for the protection of the rights and freedoms of others;
   (d) The right to strike, provided that it is exercised in conformity with the laws of the particular country.
2. This article shall not prevent the imposition of lawful restrictions on the exercise of these rights by members of the armed forces or of the police or of the administration of the State.
3. Nothing in this article shall authorize States Parties to the International Labour Organization Convention of 1948 concerning Freedom of Association and Protection of the Right to Organize to take legislative measures which would prejudice, or apply the law in such a manner as would prejudice, the guarantees provided for in that Convention.

Article 9

The States Parties to the present Covenant recognize the right of everyone to social security, including social insurance.

Article 10

The States Parties to the present Covenant recognize that:

1. The widest possible protection and assistance should be accorded to the family, which is the natural and fundamental group unit of society, particularly for its establishment and while it is responsible for the care and education of dependent children. Marriage must be entered into with the free consent of the intending spouses.
2. Special protection should be accorded to mothers during a reasonable period before and after childbirth. During such period working mothers should be accorded paid leave or leave with adequate social security benefits.
3. Special measures of protection and assistance should be taken on behalf of all children and young persons without any discrimination for reasons of parentage or other conditions. Children and young persons should be protected from economic and social exploitation. Their employment in work harmful to their morals or health or dangerous to life or likely to hamper their normal development should be punishable by law. States should also set age limits below which the paid employment of child labour should be prohibited and punishable by law.

Article 11

1. The States Parties to the present Covenant recognize the right of everyone to an adequate standard of living for himself and his family, including adequate food, clothing and housing, and to the continuous improvement of living conditions. The States Parties will take appropriate steps to ensure the realization of this right, recognizing to this effect the essential importance of international co-operation based on free consent.
2. The States Parties to the present Covenant, recognizing the fundamental right of everyone to be free from hunger, shall take, individually and through international co-operation, the measures, including specific programmes, which are needed:
   (a) To improve methods of production, conservation and distribution of food by making full use of technical and scientific knowledge, by disseminating knowledge of the principles of nutrition and by developing or reforming agrarian systems in such a way as to achieve the most efficient development and utilization of natural resources;
   (b) Taking into account the problems of both food-importing and food-exporting countries, to ensure an equitable distribution of world food supplies in relation to need.

Article 12

1. The States Parties to the present Covenant recognize the right of everyone to the enjoyment of the highest attainable standard of physical and mental health.

2. The steps to be taken by the States Parties to the present Covenant to achieve the full realization of this right shall include those necessary for:

(a) The provision for the reduction of the stillbirth-rate and of infant mortality and for the healthy development of the child;

(b) The improvement of all aspects of environmental and industrial hygiene;

(c) The prevention, treatment and control of epidemic, endemic, occupational and other diseases;

(d) The creation of conditions which would assure to all medical service and medical attention in the event of sickness.

Article 13

1. The States Parties to the present Covenant recognize the right of everyone to education. They agree that education shall be directed to the full development of the human personality and the sense of its dignity, and shall strengthen the respect for human rights and fundamental freedoms. They further agree that education shall enable all persons to participate effectively in a free society, promote understanding, tolerance and friendship among all nations and all racial, ethnic or religious groups, and further the activities of the United Nations for the maintenance of peace.

2. The States Parties to the present Covenant recognize that, with a view to achieving the full realization of this right:

(a) Primary education shall be compulsory and available free to all;

(b) Secondary education in its different forms, including technical and vocational secondary education, shall be made generally available and accessible to all by every appropriate means, and in particular by the progressive introduction of free education;

(c) Higher education shall be made equally accessible to all, on the basis of capacity, by every appropriate means, and in particular by the progressive introduction of free education;

(d) Fundamental education shall be encouraged or intensified as far as possible for those persons who have not received or completed the whole period of their primary education;

(e) The development of a system of schools at all levels shall be actively pursued, an adequate fellowship system shall be established, and the material conditions of teaching staff shall be continuously improved.

3. The States Parties to the present Covenant undertake to have respect for the liberty of parents and, when applicable, legal guardians to choose for their children schools, other than those established by the public authorities, which conform to such minimum educational standards as may be laid down or approved by the State and to ensure the religious and moral education of their children in conformity with their own convictions.

4. No part of this article shall be construed so as to interfere with the liberty of individuals and bodies to establish and direct educational institutions, subject always to the observance of the principles set forth in paragraph 1 of

this article and to the requirement that the education given in such institutions shall conform to such minimum standards as may be laid down by the State.

Article 14

Each State Party to the present Covenant which, at the time of becoming a Party, has not been able to secure in its metropolitan territory or other territories under its jurisdiction compulsory primary education, free of charge, undertakes, within two years, to work out and adopt a detailed plan of action for the progressive implementation, within a reasonable number of years, to be fixed in the plan, of the principle of compulsory education free of charge for all.

Article 15

1. The States Parties to the present Covenant recognize the right of everyone:
   (a) To take part in cultural life;
   (b) To enjoy the benefits of scientific progress and its applications;
   (c) To benefit from the protection of the moral and material interests resulting from any scientific, literary or artistic production of which he is the author.
2. The steps to be taken by the States Parties to the present Covenant to achieve the full realization of this right shall include those necessary for the conservation, the development and the diffusion of science and culture.
3. The States Parties to the present Covenant undertake to respect the freedom indispensable for scientific research and creative activity.
4. The States Parties to the present Covenant recognize the benefits to be derived from the encouragement and development of international contacts and co-operation in the scientific and cultural fields.

Part IV

Article 16

1. The States Parties to the present Covenant undertake to submit in conformity with this part of the Covenant reports on the measures which they have adopted and the progress made in achieving the observance of the rights recognized herein.
2.
   (a) All reports shall be submitted to the Secretary-General of the United Nations, who shall transmit copies to the Economic and Social Council for consideration in accordance with the provisions of the present Covenant;
   (b) The Secretary-General of the United Nations shall also transmit to the specialized agencies copies of the reports, or any relevant parts therefrom,

from States Parties to the present Covenant which are also members of these specialized agencies in so far as these reports, or parts therefrom, relate to any matters which fall within the responsibilities of the said agencies in accordance with their constitutional instruments.

Article 17

1. The States Parties to the present Covenant shall furnish their reports in stages, in accordance with a programme to be established by the Economic and Social Council within one year of the entry into force of the present Covenant after consultation with the States Parties and the specialized agencies concerned.
2. Reports may indicate factors and difficulties affecting the degree of fulfilment of obligations under the present Covenant.
3. Where relevant information has previously been furnished to the United Nations or to any specialized agency by any State Party to the present Covenant, it will not be necessary to reproduce that information, but a precise reference to the information so furnished will suffice.

Article 18

Pursuant to its responsibilities under the Charter of the United Nations in the field of human rights and fundamental freedoms, the Economic and Social Council may make arrangements with the specialized agencies in respect of their reporting to it on the progress made in achieving the observance of the provisions of the present Covenant falling within the scope of their activities. These reports may include particulars of decisions and recommendations on such implementation adopted by their competent organs.

Article 19

The Economic and Social Council may transmit to the Commission on Human Rights for study and general recommendation or, as appropriate, for information the reports concerning human rights submitted by States in accordance with articles 16 and 17, and those concerning human rights submitted by the specialized agencies in accordance with article 18.

Article 20

The States Parties to the present Covenant and the specialized agencies concerned may submit comments to the Economic and Social Council on any general recommendation under article 19 or reference to such general recommendation in any report of the Commission on Human Rights or any documentation referred to therein.

Article 21

The Economic and Social Council may submit from time to time to the General Assembly reports with recommendations of a general nature and a summary of the information received from the States Parties to the present Covenant and the specialized agencies on the measures taken and the progress made in achieving general observance of the rights recognized in the present Covenant.

Article 22

The Economic and Social Council may bring to the attention of other organs of the United Nations, their subsidiary organs and specialized agencies concerned with furnishing technical assistance any matters arising out of the reports referred to in this part of the present Covenant which may assist such bodies in deciding, each within its field of competence, on the advisability of international measures likely to contribute to the effective progressive implementation of the present Covenant.

Article 23

The States Parties to the present Covenant agree that international action for the achievement of the rights recognized in the present Covenant includes such methods as the conclusion of conventions, the adoption of recommendations, the furnishing of technical assistance and the holding of regional meetings and technical meetings for the purpose of consultation and study organized in conjunction with the Governments concerned.

Article 24

Nothing in the present Covenant shall be interpreted as impairing the provisions of the Charter of the United Nations and of the constitutions of the specialized agencies which define the respective responsibilities of the various organs of the United Nations and of the specialized agencies in regard to the matters dealt with in the present Covenant.

Article 25

Nothing in the present Covenant shall be interpreted as impairing the inherent right of all peoples to enjoy and utilize fully and freely their natural wealth and resources.

Part V

Article 26

1. The present Covenant is open for signature by any State Member of the United Nations or member of any of its specialized agencies, by any State Party to the

Statute of the International Court of Justice, and by any other State which has been invited by the General Assembly of the United Nations to become a party to the present Covenant.

2. The present Covenant is subject to ratification. Instruments of ratification shall be deposited with the Secretary-General of the United Nations.
3. The present Covenant shall be open to accession by any State referred to in paragraph 1 of this article.
4. Accession shall be effected by the deposit of an instrument of accession with the Secretary-General of the United Nations.
5. The Secretary-General of the United Nations shall inform all States which have signed the present Covenant or acceded to it of the deposit of each instrument of ratification or accession.

Article 27

1. The present Covenant shall enter into force three months after the date of the deposit with the Secretary-General of the United Nations of the thirty-fifth instrument of ratification or instrument of accession.
2. For each State ratifying the present Covenant or acceding to it after the deposit of the thirty-fifth instrument of ratification or instrument of accession, the present Covenant shall enter into force three months after the date of the deposit of its own instrument of ratification or instrument of accession.

Article 28

The provisions of the present Covenant shall extend to all parts of federal States without any limitations or exceptions.

Article 29

1. Any State Party to the present Covenant may propose an amendment and file it with the Secretary-General of the United Nations. The Secretary-General shall thereupon communicate any proposed amendments to the States Parties to the present Covenant with a request that they notify him whether they favour a conference of States Parties for the purpose of considering and voting upon the proposals. In the event that at least one third of the States Parties favours such a conference, the Secretary-General shall convene the conference under the auspices of the United Nations. Any amendment adopted by a majority of the States Parties present and voting at the conference shall be submitted to the General Assembly of the United Nations for approval.
2. Amendments shall come into force when they have been approved by the General Assembly of the United Nations and accepted by a two-thirds majority of the States Parties to the present Covenant in accordance with their respective constitutional processes.

3. When amendments come into force they shall be binding on those States Parties which have accepted them, other States Parties still being bound by the provisions of the present Covenant and any earlier amendment which they have accepted.

Article 30

Irrespective of the notifications made under article 26, paragraph 5, the Secretary-General of the United Nations shall inform all States referred to in paragraph 1 of the same article of the following particulars:

(a) Signatures, ratifications and accessions under article 26;

(b) The date of the entry into force of the present Covenant under article 27 and the date of the entry into force of any amendments under article 29.

Article 31

1. The present Covenant, of which the Chinese, English, French, Russian and Spanish texts are equally authentic, shall be deposited in the archives of the United Nations.

2. The Secretary-General of the United Nations shall transmit certified copies of the present Covenant to all States referred to in article 26.

Bibliography and References

Most of the declarations, treaties, and historic rights documents listed below can be found online by using a search engine such as Google or Yahoo. Because web addresses often change, they are not provided in this bibliography except in cases where they provide the only citation available for an item.

Ackerman, B. 2004. "The Emergency Constitution." *Yale Law Journal* 113: 1029.

African Union. 1981. "African Charter on Human and Peoples' Rights." In I. Brownlie and G. Goodwin-Gill (eds.), *Basic Documents on Human Rights,* 5th edn. Oxford: Oxford University Press, 2006.

Aiken, W., and LaFolette, H. (eds.) 1996. *World Hunger and Morality.* Upper Saddle River, NJ: Prentice-Hall.

Alston, P. 1987. "Out of the Abyss: The Challenges Confronting the New UN Committee on Economic and Social Rights." *Human Rights Quarterly* 9: 332–81.

Alston, P., and Crawford, J. (eds.) 2002. *The Future of UN Human Rights Treaty Monitoring.* Cambridge: Cambridge University Press.

American Anthropological Association. 1947. "Statement on Human Rights." *American Anthropologist* 49: 539–43.

Anaya, S. 2004. *Indigenous Peoples in International Law.* Oxford: Oxford University Press.

Anaya, S., and Williams, R. 2001. "The Protection of Indigenous People's Rights over Lands and Natural Resources under the Inter-American Human Rights System." *Harvard Human Rights Journal* 14: 33.

Anderson, M., and Boyle, A. 1996. *Human Rights Approaches to Environmental Protection.* Oxford: Clarendon Press.

An-Na'im, A. (ed.) 1992. *Human Rights in Cross-Cultural Perspectives: A Quest for Consensus.* Philadelphia: University of Pennsylvania Press.

Arneson, R. 1990. "Is Work Special? Justice and the Distribution of Employment." *American Political Science Review* 84: 1127–47.

Ashworth, A. 1998. *The Criminal Process.* Oxford: Oxford University Press.

Baderin, M. 2005. "Human Rights and Islamic Law: The Myth of Discord." *European Human Rights Law Review* 2: 165–85.

Bailey, S. 1994. *The UN Security Council and Human Rights*. New York: St. Martin's Press.

Baker, J. 1994. *Group Rights*. Toronto: University of Toronto Press.

Banton, M. 1996. *International Action against Racial Discrimination*. Oxford: Clarendon Press.

Bauer, J., and Bell, D. (eds.) 1999. *The East Asian Challenge for Human Rights*. Cambridge: Cambridge University Press.

Bayefsky, A. 2001. *The UN Human Rights Treaty System: Universality at the Crossroads*. Ardsley, NY: Transnational Press.

Bayefsky, A., and Fitzpatrick, J. (eds.) 2000. *Human Rights and Forced Displacement*. The Hague: Martinus Nijhoff.

Beetham, D. 1995. "What Future for Economic and Social Rights?" *Political Studies* 43: 41–60.

Beitz, C. 1999. *Political Theory and International Relations*, rev. edn. Princeton, NJ: Princeton University Press.

Beitz, C. 2001. "Human Rights as Common Concern." *American Political Science Review* 95: 269–82.

Beitz, C. 2004. "Human Rights and the Law of Peoples." In Deen Chatterjee (ed.), *The Ethics of Assistance*, 193–214. Cambridge: Cambridge University Press.

Bell, D. 2000. *East Meets West: Human Rights and Democracy in East Asia*. Princeton, NJ: Princeton University Press.

Bentham, J. 1962. *Works*. New York: Russell & Russell.

Bentham, J. 1970. "Anarchical Fallacies." In A. Melden (ed.), *Human Rights*, 30–1. Belmont, CA: Wadsworth.

Binion, G. 1995. "Human Rights: A Feminist Perspective." *Human Rights Quarterly* 17: 509–26.

Boerefijn, I. 1999. *The Reporting Procedure under the Covenant on Civil and Political Rights: Practice and Procedures of the Human Rights Committee*. Antwerp: Intersea-Hart.

Bowen, J. 2000. "Should We Have a Universal Concept of 'Indigenous People's Rights'?" *Anthropology Today* 16: 12–16.

Brackney, W. (series editor) 2004. *Human Rights and the World's Major Religions*, vol. 1: *The Jewish Tradition*, ed. P. Hass; vol. 2: *The Christian Tradition*, ed. W. Brackney; vol. 3: *The Islamic Tradition*, ed. M. Abd al-Rahim; vol. 4: *The Hindu Tradition*, ed. H. Coward; vol. 5: *The Buddhist Tradition*, ed. R. Florida. Westport, CT: Praeger.

Bradley, A., Janis, M., and Kay, R. (eds.) 1995. *European Human Rights Law: Text and Materials*. Oxford: Oxford University Press.

Brandt, R. 1983. "The Concept of a Moral Right." *Journal of Philosophy* 80: 29–45.

Brandt, R. 1992. *Morality, Utilitarianism, and Rights*. Cambridge: Cambridge University Press.

Brownlie, I., and Goodwin-Gill, G. (eds.) 2006. *Basic Documents on Human Rights*, 5th edn. Oxford: Oxford University Press.

Buchanan, A. 1984. "What's So Special about Rights?" *Social Philosophy & Policy* 2: 61–83.

Buchanan, A. 1989. "Assessing the Communitarian Critique of Liberalism." *Ethics* 99: 852–82.

Buchanan, A. 1991. *Secession*. Boulder, CO: Westview Press.

Buchanan, A. 2004. *Justice, Legitimacy, and Self-Determination: Moral Foundations for International Law*. Oxford: Oxford University Press.

Buchanan, A. 2005. "Equality and Human Rights." *Politics, Philosophy & Economics* 4: 69–90.

Bunch, C. 1990. "Women's Rights as Human Rights." *Human Rights Quarterly* 12: 486–98.

Burgers, J. 1992. "The Road to San Francisco: The Revival of the Human Rights Idea in the Twentieth Century." *Human Rights Quarterly* 14: 447.

Cahn, S. (ed.) 2002. *The Affirmative Action Debate*, 2nd edn. London: Routledge.

Caney, S. 2002. *Justice Beyond Borders: A Global Political Theory*. Oxford: Oxford University Press.

Chapman, A. 2002. "Core Obligations Related to the Right to Health." In A. Chapman and S. Russell (eds.), *Core Obligations: Building a Framework for Economic, Social, and Cultural Rights*. Antwerp: Intersentia.

Chapman, A., and Russell, S. (eds.) 2002. *Core Obligations: Building a Framework for Economic, Social, and Cultural Rights*. Antwerp: Intersentia.

Christiano, T. 1996. *The Rule of the Many: Fundamental Issues in Democratic Theory*. Boulder, CO: Westview Press.

Cohen, J. 2004. "Minimalism about Human Rights: The Most We Can Hope For?" *Journal of Political Philosophy* 12: 190–213.

Cook, R. (ed.) 1994. *Human Rights of Women: National and International Perspectives*. Philadelphia: University of Pennsylvania Press.

Coomans, F. 2002. "In Search of the Core Content of the Right to Education." In A. Chapman and S. Russell (eds.), *Core Obligations: Building a Framework for Economic, Social, and Cultural Rights*. Antwerp: Intersentia.

Council of Europe. 1950. "European Convention for the Protection of Human Rights and Fundamental Freedoms." In I. Brownlie and G. Goodwin-Gill (eds.), *Basic Documents on Human Rights*, 5th edn. Oxford: Oxford University Press, 2006.

Council of Europe. 1961. "European Social Charter." In I. Brownlie and G. Goodwin-Gill (eds.), *Basic Documents on Human Rights*, 5th edn. Oxford: Oxford University Press, 2006.

Cowan, J., Dembour, M., and Wilson, R. (eds.) 2001. *Culture and Rights: Anthropological Perspectives*. Cambridge: Cambridge University Press.

Cranston, M. 1967. "Human Rights, Real and Supposed." In D. Raphael (ed.), *Political Theory and the Rights of Man*. London: Macmillan.

Cranston, M. 1973. *What Are Human Rights?* London: Bodley Head.

Crawford, J. 1992. *The Rights of Peoples*. Oxford: Clarendon Press.

Darwall, S. 1998. *Philosophical Ethics*. Boulder, CO: Westview Press.

Davidson, S. 1997. *The Inter-American Human Rights System*. Aldershot: Dartmouth.

Deigh, J. 1988. "On Rights and Responsibilities." *Law and Philosophy* 7: 147–78.

Dershowitz, A. M. 2004. *Rights from Wrongs: A Secular Theory of the Origins of Rights*. New York: Basic Books.

de Soto, H. 1989. *The Other Path*. New York: Harper & Row.

Donaldson, T. 1989. *The Ethics of International Business*. New York: Oxford University Press.

Donnelly, J. 1985. *The Concept of Human Rights*. New York: St. Martin's Press.

Donnelly, J. 2003. *Universal Human Rights in Theory and Practice*, 2nd edn. Ithaca, NY and London: Cornell University Press.

Duff, R. 1986. *Trials and Punishments*. Cambridge: Cambridge University Press.

Dworkin, A. 2005. "Military Necessity and Due Process: The Place of Human Rights in the War on Terror." In D. Wippman and M. Evangelista (eds.), *New Wars, New Laws? Applying the Laws of War in 21st Century Conflicts*. Ardsley, NY: Transnational.

Dworkin, R. 1977. *Taking Rights Seriously*. Cambridge, MA: Harvard University Press.

Dworkin, R. 2002. "Terror and the Attack on Civil Liberties." *New York Review of Books* (February 28): 50.

Dyck, A. 1994. *Rethinking Rights and Responsibilities*. Cleveland, OH: Pilgrim Press.

Edmundson, W. 2004. *An Introduction to Rights*. Cambridge: Cambridge University Press.

Eide, A. 1989. "The Realisation of Social and Economic Rights and the Minimum Threshold Approach." *Human Rights Law Journal* 10: 35–51.

European Court of Human Rights. 1959. *Lawless* v. *Ireland. Report of the European Commission*.

European Court of Human Rights. 1969. "The Greek Case." *Yearbook of the European Convention on Human Rights* 12: 1.

Evans, M., and Murray, R. (eds.) 2002. *The African Charter on Human and People's Rights: The System in Practice, 1986–2000*. Cambridge: Cambridge University Press.

Fabre, C. 2000. *Social Rights under the Constitution: Government and the Decent Life*. Oxford: Clarendon Press.

Farer, T. 1997. "The Rise of the Inter-American Human Rights Regime." *Human Rights Quarterly* 19: 510–46.

Feinberg, J. 1970. "The Nature and Value of Rights." *Journal of Value Inquiry* 4: 243–51.

Feinberg, J. 1973. *Social Philosophy*. Englewood Cliffs, NJ: Prentice-Hall.

Feinberg, J. 1980. *Rights, Justice and the Bounds of Liberty*. Princeton, NJ: Princeton University Press.

Finnis, J. 1980. *Natural Law and Natural Rights*. Oxford: Oxford University Press.

Fitzpatrick, J. 1994. *Human Rights in Crisis: The International System for Protecting Human Rights during States of Emergency*. Philadelphia: University of Pennsylvania Press.

Flathman, R. 1976. *The Practice of Rights*. Cambridge: Cambridge University Press.

Flathman, R. 1984. "Moderating Rights." *Social Philosophy & Policy* 1: 149–71.

Flinterman, C., and Ankumah, E. 2004. "The African Charter on Human and Peoples' Rights." In H. Hannum (ed.), *Guide to International Human Rights Practice*, 171–88, 4th edn. Ardsley, NY: Transnational.

Freeman, M. 2002. *Human Rights*. Cambridge: Polity.

Frey, R. (ed.) 1984. *Utility and Rights*. Minneapolis: University of Minnesota Press.

Gallup Organization. 2002. *Gallup Poll of the Islamic World*.

Gauthier, D. 1986. *Morals by Agreement*. Oxford: Oxford University Press.

Gewirth, A. 1978. *Reason and Morality*. Chicago: University of Chicago Press.

Gewirth, A. 1981. "The Basis and Content of Human Rights." In R. Pennock and J. Chapman (eds.), *Nomos XXIII: Human Rights*, 119–47. New York: New York University Press.

Gewirth, A. 1982. *Human Rights: Essays on Justification and Applications*. Chicago: University of Chicago Press.

Glazer, N. 1983. *Ethnic Dilemmas*. Cambridge, MA: Harvard University Press.

Glendon, M. 1991. *Rights Talk: The Impoverishment of Political Discourse*. New York: Free Press.

Glendon, M. 2001. *A World Made New: Eleanor Roosevelt and the Universal Declaration of Human Rights*. New York: Random House.

Goodman, R., and Jinks, D. 2004. "How to Influence States: Socialization and International Human Rights Law." *Duke Law Journal* 54: 621.

Gould, C. 2004. *Globalizing Democracy and Human Rights*. New York: Cambridge University Press.

Griffin, J. 1996. *Value Judgement: Improving our Ethical Beliefs*. Oxford: Oxford University Press.

Griffin, J. 2000. "Discrepancies between the Best Philosophical Account of Human Rights and the International Law of Human Rights." *Proceedings of the Aristotelian Society* 101: 1–28.

Griffin, J. 2001. "First Steps in an Account of Human Rights." *European Journal of Philosophy* 9 (3): 306–27.

Gross, O. 2003. "Providing for the Unexpected: Constitutional Emergency Provisions." *Israel Yearbook on Human Rights* 33: 13–43.

Gurr, T. 1993. *Minorities at Risk*. Washington, DC: United States Institute of Peace Press.

Halstead, P. 2002. "Human Property Rights." *Conveyancer and Property Lawyer* 66 (Mar.–Apr.): 153–73.

Hannum, H. 1990. *Autonomy, Sovereignty, and Self-Determination*. Philadelphia: University of Pennsylvania Press.

Hart, H. 1955. "Are there Any Natural Rights?" *Philosophical Review* 64: 175–91.

Hart, H. 1997. *The Concept of Law*, 2nd edn. Oxford: Clarendon Press.

Hartman, J. 1981. "Derogation from Human Rights Treaties in Public Emergencies." *Harvard International Law Journal* 22: 1–52.

Haworth, L. 1986. *Autonomy*. New Haven, CT: Yale University Press.

Hayden, P. (ed.) 2001. *The Philosophy of Human Rights*. St. Paul, MN: Paragon House.

Hayek, F. 1960. *The Constitution of Liberty*. Chicago: University of Chicago Press.

Held, V. 1989. *Rights and Goods*. Chicago: University of Chicago Press.

Henkin, L. 1978. *The Rights of Man Today*. Boulder, CO: Westview Press.

Henkin, L. 1994. "Economic Rights under the United States Constitution." *Columbia Journal of Transnational Law* 32: 97–132.

Henrard, K. 2000. *Devising an Adequate System of Minority Protection*. The Hague: Martinus Nijhoff.

Hobbes, T. 1981. *Leviathan*. In C. Macpherson (ed.), *Leviathan*. Harmondsworth: Penguin. Originally published 1651.

Hodgson, D. 1998. *The Human Right to Education*. Aldershot: Ashgate.

Hohfeld, W. 1964. *Fundamental Legal Conceptions*. New Haven, CT: Yale University Press.

Holmes, S., and Sunstein, C. 1999. *The Cost of Rights: Why Liberty Depends on Taxes*. New York: W. W. Norton.

House of Lords. 2005. *A. v. Secretary of State for the Home Department*. 3 WLR 1249.

Howard, R. 1987. "The Full-Belly Thesis: Should Economic Rights Take Priority over Civil and Political Rights?" *Human Rights Quarterly* 5: 467–90.

Howard, R. 1993. "Cultural Absolutism and the Nostalgia for Community." *Human Rights Quarterly* 15: 315–38.

Howard, R. 1995. *Human Rights and the Search for Community*. Boulder, CO: Westview Press.

Huemer, M. 2005. *Ethical Intuitionism*. New York: Palgrave Macmillan.

Hunt, P. 1996. *Reclaiming Social Rights: International and Comparative Perspectives*. Aldershot: Dartmouth.

Ignatieff, M. 2000. *Human Rights as Politics and Idolatry*. Princeton, NJ: Princeton University Press.

Ignatieff, M. 2004. *The Lesser Evil*. Princeton, NJ: Princeton University Press.

Ishay, M. (ed.) 1997. *The Human Rights Reader*. New York: Routledge.

Jacobs, F., and White, R. 1996. *The European Convention on Human Rights*, 2nd edn. Oxford: Clarendon Press.

Jaggar, A. 2005. "What is Terrorism, Why is it Wrong, and Could it Ever be Morally Permissible?" *Journal of Social Philosophy* 36: 202–17.

Janis, M., Kay, R., and Bradley, A. (eds.) 1995. *European Human Rights Law: Texts and Materials*. Oxford: Oxford University Press.

Jinks, D. 2001. "The Anatomy of an Institutionalized Emergency: Preventive Detention and Personal Liberty in India." *Michigan Journal of International Law* 22: 311–70.

Jones, Charles. 1999. *Global Justice*. Oxford: Oxford University Press.

Joseph, S., Schultz, J., and Castan, M. (eds.) 2000. *The International Covenant on Civil and Political Rights: Cases, Materials, and Commentary.* New York: Oxford University Press.

Katayanagi, M. 2002. *Human Rights Functions of United Nations Peacekeeping Operations.* The Hague: Kluwer.

Kelly, E. 2004. "Human Rights as Foreign Policy Imperatives." In D. Chatterjee (ed.), *Ethics of Assistance.* Cambridge: Cambridge University Press.

Korey, W. 1998. *NGOs and the Universal Declaration of Human Rights.* New York: St. Martin's Press.

Kuflik, A. 1986. "The Utilitarian Logic of Inalienable Rights." *Ethics* 97 (1) (Oct.): 75–87.

Kymlicka, W. 1989. *Liberalism, Community, and Culture.* Oxford: Clarendon Press.

Kymlicka, W. 1995a. *Multicultural Citizenship: A Liberal Theory of Minority Rights.* Oxford: Clarendon Press.

Kymlicka, W. 1995b. *The Rights of Minority Cultures.* Oxford: Oxford University Press.

Lauren, P. 1998. *The Evolution of International Human Rights.* Philadelphia: University of Pennsylvania Press.

Levinson, S. (ed.) 2004. *Torture: A Collection.* New York: Oxford University Press.

Liebenberg, S. 2005. "The Value of Human Dignity In Interpreting Socio-Economic Rights." *South African Journal on Human Rights* 21: 1–31.

Lijphart, A. 1995. "Self-Determination versus Pre-Determination of Ethnic Minorities in Power-Sharing Systems." In W. Kymlicka (ed.), *The Rights of Minority Cultures.* Oxford: Oxford University Press.

Locke, J. 1986. *The Second Treatise on Civil Government.* New York: Prometheus Books. Originally published 1689.

Lomasky, L. 1987. *Persons, Rights and the Moral Community.* New York: Oxford University Press.

Lukes, S. 1993. "Five Fables about Human Rights." In S. Hurley and S. Shute (eds.), *On Human Rights.* New York: Basic Books.

Lyons, D. 1970. "The Correlativity of Rights and Duties." *Nous* 4: 45–55.

Lyons, D. 1982. "Utility and Rights." In J. Pennock and J. Chapman (eds.), *Ethics, Economics, and the Law,* 107–38. New York: New York University Press.

Lyons, D. 1992. "Utilitarianism." In L. Becker (ed.), *The Encyclopedia of Ethics.* New York: Garland Publishing.

McCloskey, H. J. 1967. "Rights." *Philosophical Quarterly* 15: 118–19.

McCloskey, H. J. 1976. "Rights – Some Conceptual Issues." *Australasian Journal of Philosophy* 54: 99–115.

MacCormick, N. 1976. "Children's Rights: A Test-Case for Theories of Rights." *Archiv für Rechts und Sozialphilosophie* 62: 305–17.

McGoldrick, D. 1994. *The Human Rights Committee: Its Role in the Development of the International Covenant on Civil and Political Rights.* Oxford: Clarendon Press.

Machan, T. 1989. *Individuals and Their Rights.* LaSalle, IL: Open Court.

McKaskle, P. 2005. "The European Court of Human Rights: What it is, How it Works, and its Future." *University of San Francisco Law Review* 40: 1–84.

Mackie, J. 1978. "Can There be a Right-Based Moral Theory?" *Midwest Studies in Philosophy* 3: 350–9.

Martin, R. 1980. "Human Rights and Civil Rights." *Philosophical Studies* 37: 391–403.

Martin, R. 1993. *A System of Rights.* Oxford: Clarendon Press.

Martin, R., and Nickel, J. 1980. "Recent Work on the Concept of Rights." *American Philosophical Quarterly* 17: 165–80.

Martin, R. and Reidy, D. (eds.) 2006. *Rawls's Law of Peoples: A Realistic Utopia?* Oxford: Blackwell Publishing.

Merry, S. 2005. *Human Rights and Gender Violence: Translating International Law into Local Justice.* Chicago: University of Chicago Press.

Meyers, D. 1985. *Inalienable Rights: A Defense.* New York: Columbia University Press.

Meyers, D. 1991. *Self, Society, and Personal Choice.* New York: Columbia University Press.

Mill, J. 1848. *Principles of Political Economy.* London: Longmans, Green & Co.

Mill, J. 2002a. *On Liberty.* In J. Schneewind (ed.), *The Basic Writings of John Stuart Mill.* New York: Modern Library. Originally published 1859.

Mill, J. 2002b. *Utilitarianism.* In J. Schneewind (ed.), *The Basic Writings of John Stuart Mill.* New York: Modern Library. Originally published 1863.

Montague, P. 1988. "When Rights are Permissibly Infringed." *Philosophical Studies* 53: 347–66.

Morris, C. 1998. *An Essay on the Modern State.* Cambridge: Cambridge University Press.

Morsink, J. 1999. *Universal Declaration of Human Rights: Origins, Drafting, and Intent.* Philadelphia: University of Pennsylvania Press.

Mower, A. 1991. *Regional Human Rights: A Comparative Study of the West European and Inter-American Systems.* New York: Greenwood Press.

Nagel, T. 1995. "Personal Rights and Public Space." *Philosophy & Public Affairs* 24: 83–107.

Nagel, T. 2005. "The Problem of Global Justice." *Philosophy & Public Affairs* 33: 113–47.

Nelson, W. 1985. "Positive Rights, Negative Rights and Property Rights." *Tulane Studies in Philosophy* 33: 43–9.

Nickel, J. 1987. *Making Sense of Human Rights.* Berkeley and Los Angeles: University of California Press.

Nickel, J. 1993a. "How Human Rights Generate Duties to Protect and Provide." *Human Rights Quarterly* 14: 77–86.

Nickel, J. 1993b. "The Human Right to a Safe Environment." *Yale Journal of International Law* 18: 281–95.

Nickel, J. 1995. "A Human Rights Approach to World Hunger." In Will Aiken and Hugh Lafollette (eds.), *World Hunger and Morality*, 2nd edn. Englewood Cliffs, NJ: Prentice-Hall.

Nickel, J. 1997. "Group Agency and Group Rights." In I. Shapiro and W. Kymlicka (eds.), *Ethnicity and Group Rights*, 235–56. New York: New York University Press.

Nickel, J. 2000. "Economic Liberties." In V. Davion and C. Wolf (eds.), *The Idea of Political Liberalism*, 155–75. Lanham, MD: Rowman & Littlefield.

Nickel, J. 2005. "Poverty and Rights." *Philosophical Quarterly* 55: 385–402.

Nickel, J. 2006. "Are Human Rights Mainly Implemented by Intervention?" In R. Martin and D. Reidy (eds.), *Rawls's Law of Peoples: A Realistic Utopia?* Oxford: Blackwell Publishing.

Nozick, R. 1974. *Anarchy, State, and Utopia*. New York: Basic Books.

Nussbaum, M. 2001. *Women and Human Development: The Capabilities Approach*. Cambridge: Cambridge University Press.

Okin, S. 1998. "Feminism, Women's Human Rights, and Cultural Differences." *Hypatia* 13: 32–52.

O'Neill, O. 1988. "Hunger, Needs, and Rights." In S. Luper-Foy (ed.), *Problems of International Justice*. Boulder, CO: Westview Press.

Oraa, J. 1992. *Human Rights in States of Emergency in International Law*. Oxford: Oxford University Press.

Orend, B. 2001. *Human Rights: Concept and Context*. Peterborough, Ont.: Broadview Press.

Organization of American States. 1948. "American Declaration of the Rights and Duties of Man." In I. Brownlie and G. Goodwin-Gill (eds.), *Basic Documents on Human Rights*, 5th edn. Oxford: Oxford University Press, 2006.

Organization of American States. 1969. "American Convention on Human Rights." In I. Brownlie and G. Goodwin-Gill (eds.), *Basic Documents on Human Rights*, 5th edn. Oxford: Oxford University Press, 2006.

Peffer, R. 1978. "A Defense of Rights to Well-Being." *Philosophy & Public Affairs* 8 (1): 65–87.

Perry, M. 1998. *The Idea of Human Rights*. New York: Oxford University Press.

Pettit, P. 1988. "The Consequentialist can Recognise Rights." *Philosophical Quarterly* 38: 42–55.

Pew Research Center. 2003. "Pew Global Attitudes Project: Views of a Changing World." Available at <http://people-press.org/reports/pdf/185.pdf> (accessed May 2006).

Phillips, A. 1995. "Democracy and Difference: Some Problems for Feminist Theory." In W. Kymlicka (ed.), *The Rights of Minority Cultures*. Oxford: Oxford University Press.

Philpott, D. 1995. "In Defense of Self-Determination." *Ethics* 105: 352–85.

Pogge, T. 2000. "The International Significance of Human Rights." *Journal of Ethics* 4: 45–69.

Pogge, T. 2001a. "How should Human Rights be Conceived?" In P. Hayden (ed.), *The Philosophy of Human Rights*, 187–210. St. Paul, MN: Paragon House.

Pogge, T. 2001b. "Rawls on International Justice." *Philosophical Quarterly* 51: 246.

Pogge, T. 2002. *World Poverty and Human Rights.* Cambridge: Polity.

Power, S. 2002. *A Problem from Hell: America and the Age of Genocide.* New York: Basic Books.

Preis, A. 1996. "Human Rights as Cultural Practice: An Anthropological Critique." *Human Rights Quarterly* 18: 286–315.

Ramcharan, B. 2002. *The Security Council and the Protection of Human Rights.* The Hague: Martinus Nijhoff.

Rawls, J. 1971. *A Theory of Justice.* Cambridge, MA: Harvard University Press.

Rawls, J. 1993. *Political Liberalism.* New York: Columbia University Press.

Rawls, J. 1999. *The Law of Peoples.* Cambridge, MA: Harvard University Press.

Raz, J. 1984. "On the Nature of Rights." *Mind* 93: 194–214.

Raz, J. 1987. *The Morality of Freedom.* Oxford: Oxford University Press.

Raz, J. 1994. *Ethics in the Public Domain.* Oxford: Oxford University Press.

Reidy, D. 2005. "An Internationalist Conception of Human Rights." *Philosophical Forum* 36: 367–97.

Reidy, D., and Sellers, M. (eds.) 2005. *Universal Human Rights.* Blue Ridge Summit, PA: Rowman & Littlefield.

Renteln, A. 1988. "Relativism and the Search for Human Rights." *American Anthropologist* 90: 56–72.

Rodley, N. 1999. "United Nations Non-Treaty Procedures for Dealing with Human Rights Violations." In H. Hannum (ed.), *Guide to International Human Rights Practice,* 3rd edn. Ardsley, NY: Transnational Press.

Rorty, R. 1993. "Human Rights, Rationality, and Sentimentality." In S. Shute and S. Hurley (eds.), *On Human Rights: The Oxford Amnesty Lectures.* New York: Basic Books.

Ross, D. 1930. *The Right and the Good.* Oxford: Clarendon Press.

Schabas, W. 2000. *Genocide in International Law.* Cambridge: Cambridge University Press.

Schabas, W. 2001. *An Introduction to the International Criminal Court.* Cambridge: Cambridge University Press.

Schachter, O. 1983. "Human Dignity as a Normative Concept." *American Journal of International Law* 77: 848–54.

Schulz, W. 2001. *In Our Own Best Interest: How Defending Human Rights Benefits Us All.* Boston, MA: Beacon Press.

Seiderman, I. 2001. *Hierarchy in International Law: The Human Rights Dimension.* Antwerp: Intersentia-Hart.

Sen, A. 1981. *Poverty and Famines.* Oxford: Oxford University Press.

Sen, A. 1982. "Rights and Agency." *Philosophy & Public Affairs* 11: 3–39.

Sen, A. 1984. "Rights and Capabilities." In *Resources, Values and Development.* Cambridge: Cambridge University Press.

Sen, A. 1985. "Well-being, Agency, and Freedom." *Journal of Philosophy* 85: 477–502.

Sen, A. 1999a. *Commodities and Capabilities.* Oxford: Oxford University Press.

Sen, A. 1999b. *Development as Freedom.* Oxford: Oxford University Press.

Sen, A. 2004. "Elements of a Theory of Human Rights." *Philosophy & Public Affairs* 32: 315–56.

Shue, H. 1996. *Basic Rights*, 2nd edn. Princeton, NJ: Princeton University Press.

Silverstein, H. 1996. *Unleashing Rights: Law, Meaning, and the Animal Rights Movement*. Ann Arbor: University of Michigan Press.

Simmons, J. 1992. *The Lockean Theory of Rights*. Princeton, NJ: Princeton University Press.

Smith, M. 1979. "Ethical Intuitionism and Naturalism: A Reconciliation." *Canadian Journal of Philosophy* 9: 609–29.

Steiner, H., and Alston, P. (eds.) 2000. *International Human Rights in Context*. Oxford: Oxford University Press.

Stone, J. 1932. *International Guarantees of Minority Rights*. Oxford: Oxford University Press.

Subrata, R. 1989. *The Rule of Law in a State of Emergency: The Paris Minimum Standards of Human Rights Norms in a State of Emergency*. New York: St. Martin's Press.

Sumner, L. W. 1987. *The Moral Foundation of Rights*. Oxford: Clarendon Press.

Sunstein, C. 2004. *The Second Bill of Rights: FDR's Unfinished Revolution and Why We Need it More than Ever*. New York: Basic Books.

Sweet, W. 1998. "Human Rights and Cultural Diversity." *International Journal of Applied Philosophy* 12: 117–32.

Talbott, W. 2005. *Which Rights Should be Universal?* Oxford: Oxford University Press.

Tan, K. 1998. "Liberal Toleration in Rawls's Law of Peoples." *Ethics* 108: 276.

Tasioulas, J. 2002a. "From Utopia to Kazanistan: John Rawls and The Law of Peoples." *Oxford Journal of Legal Studies* 22: 367.

Tasioulas, J. 2002b. "Human Rights, Universality and the Values of Personhood: Retracing Griffin's Steps." *European Journal of Philosophy* 10: 79–100.

Teson, F. 1995. "The Rawlsian Theory of International Law." *Ethics and International Affairs* 9: 79–99.

Teson, F. 2005. *Humanitarian Intervention: An Inquiry into Law and Morality*, 3rd edn. Ardsley, NY: Transnational Press.

Thomson, J. 1986. *Rights, Restitution, and Risk: Essays in Moral Theory*. Cambridge, MA: Harvard University Press.

Thomson, J. 1990. *The Realm of Rights*. Cambridge, MA: Harvard University Press.

Toebes, B. 1999. "Towards an Improved Understanding of the International Right to Health Care." *Human Rights Quarterly* 21: 661.

Tolley, H. 1987. *The U.N. Commission on Human Rights*. Boulder, CO: Westview Press.

United Nations. 1945. "Charter of the United Nations." In I. Brownlie and G. Goodwin-Gill (eds.), *Basic Documents on Human Rights*, 5th edn. Oxford: Oxford University Press, 2006.

United Nations. 1948a. "Convention on the Prevention and Punishment of the Crime of Genocide." In I. Brownlie and G. Goodwin-Gill (eds.), *Basic Documents on Human Rights*, 5th edn. Oxford: Oxford University Press, 2006.

United Nations. 1948b. "Universal Declaration of Human Rights." In I. Brownlie and G. Goodwin-Gill (eds.), *Basic Documents on Human Rights*, 5th edn. Oxford: Oxford University Press, 2006.

United Nations. 1965. "International Convention on the Elimination of All Forms of Racial Discrimination." In I. Brownlie and G. Goodwin-Gill (eds.), *Basic Documents on Human Rights*, 5th edn. Oxford: Oxford University Press, 2006.

United Nations. 1966a. "International Covenant on Civil and Political Rights." In I. Brownlie and G. Goodwin-Gill (eds.), *Basic Documents on Human Rights*, 5th edn. Oxford: Oxford University Press, 2006.

United Nations. 1966b. "International Covenant on Economic, Social and Cultural Rights." In I. Brownlie and G. Goodwin-Gill (eds.), *Basic Documents on Human Rights*, 5th edn. Oxford: Oxford University Press, 2006.

United Nations. 1977. "General Assembly Resolution on the Indivisibility of Human Rights." General Assembly Resolution 32/130.

United Nations. 1979. "Convention on the Elimination of All Forms of Discrimination against Women." In I. Brownlie and G. Goodwin-Gill (eds.), *Basic Documents on Human Rights*, 5th edn. Oxford: Oxford University Press, 2006.

United Nations. 1984. "Convention against Torture and Other Cruel, Inhuman or Degrading Treatment or Punishment." In I. Brownlie and G. Goodwin-Gill (eds.), *Basic Documents on Human Rights*, 5th edn. Oxford: Oxford University Press, 2006.

United Nations. 1985. "United Nations Economic and Social Council, Siracusa Principles on the Limitation and Derogation Provisions in the International Covenant on Civil and Political Rights." UN Doc. E/CN 4/1985/4, Annex.

United Nations. 1989. "Convention on the Rights of the Child." In I. Brownlie and G. Goodwin-Gill (eds.), *Basic Documents on Human Rights*, 5th edn. Oxford: Oxford University Press, 2006.

United Nations. 1991. "Committee on Economic, Social, and Cultural Rights, General Comment No. 3." UN Doc. E/1991/23, Annex III.

United Nations. 1992. "Declaration on the Rights of Persons belonging to National or Ethnic, Religious and Linguistic Minorities." General Assembly Resolution 47/135.

United Nations. 1994. "Draft Declaration on the Rights of Indigenous Peoples." In I. Brownlie and G. Goodwin-Gill (eds.), *Basic Documents on Human Rights*, 5th edn. Oxford: Oxford University Press, 2006.

United Nations. 1995. "Declaration on the Elimination of All Forms of Religious Intolerance." General Assembly Resolution 50/183.

United Nations. 1998. "Rome Statute of the International Criminal Court." In I. Brownlie and G. Goodwin-Gill (eds.), *Basic Documents on Human Rights*, 5th edn. Oxford: Oxford University Press, 2006.

United States Supreme Court. 2004. *Hamdi v. Rumsfeld*. 542 US 507.

United States Supreme Court. 2006. *Hamdan v. Rumsfeld*. 542 US.

Urofsky, M., and Finkelman, P. (eds.) 2002. *Documents of American Constitutional and Legal History*, vol. 1. Oxford: Oxford University Press.

Vance, C. 1977. "Human Rights and Foreign Policy." *Georgia Journal of International & Comparative Law* 7: 223.

van Parijs, P. 1998. *Real Freedom for All.* Oxford: Oxford University Press.

Vasek, K. 1977. "A 30-Year Struggle: The Sustained Efforts to Give Force of Law to the Universal Declaration of Human Rights." *Unesco Courier* 10: 29–30.

Veach, H. 1985. *Human Rights: Fact or Fancy.* Baton Rouge: Lousiana State University Press.

Waldron, J. (ed.) 1984. *Theories of Rights.* New York: Oxford University Press.

Waldron, J. (ed.) 1987. *Nonsense on Stilts: Bentham, Burke and Marx on the Rights of Man.* London: Methuen.

Walzer, M. 1977. *Just and Unjust Wars.* New York: Basic Books.

Weissbrodt, D. 2005. "Business and Human Rights." *University of Cincinnati Law Review* 74: 55–73.

Wellman, Carl. 1968. "A New Conception of Human Rights." In E. Kamenka and S. Tay (eds.), *Human Rights.* New York: St. Martin's Press.

Wellman, Carl. 1975. "Upholding Legal Rights." *Ethics* 86: 49–60.

Wellman, Carl. 1995. *Real Rights.* New York: Oxford University Press.

Wellman, Carl. 1999. *The Proliferation of Rights: Moral Progress or Empty Rhetoric?* Boulder, CO: Westview Press.

Wellman, Christopher. 1995. "A Defense of Secession and Political Self-Determination." *Philosophy & Public Affairs* 24: 142–71.

Wenar, L. 2005. "The Nature of Rights." *Philosophy & Public Affairs* 33: 223–52.

Werhane, P., Gini, A., and Ozar, D. (eds.) 1986. *Philosophical Issues in Human Rights.* New York: Random House.

Wilson, R. (ed.) 1997. *Human Rights, Culture and Context: Anthropological Perspectives.* London: Pluto Press.

Wilson, W. 1987. *The Truly Disadvantaged.* Chicago: University of Chicago Press.

World Bank. 2006. "Data and Statistics." Available at <http://web.worldbank.org/WBSITE/EXTERNAL/DATASTATISTICS/0,contentMDK:20535285~menuPK:1192694~pagePK:64133150~piPK:64133175~theSitePK:239419,00.html> (accessed May 2006).

Young, I. 1989. "Polity and Group Difference: A Critique of the Ideal of Universal Citizenship." *Ethics* 99: 261.

Zogby International. 2002. *What Arabs Think: Values, Beliefs, and Concerns.* Utica, NY: Zogby International.

Index